I0123490

THE WORLD IS JUST LIKE A VILLAGE

GLOBALIZATION AND TRANSNATIONALISM OF ITALIAN MIGRANTS FROM TUSCANY IN WESTERN AUSTRALIA

by

Adriano Boncompagni, PhD

EUROPEAN PRESS ACADEMIC PUBLISHING

2001

To my father Giordano Bruno, who has so greatly enriched my life

On the cover
Group of Migrants from San Romano Garfagnana (Tuscany), taken in Bassandean (Western Australia), early 1950s, courtesy of Mr Ferdinando Grassi, Perth (Western Australia)

All rights reserved. No part of this book shall be reproduced, stored in a retrieval system, or transmitted by any means, electronic, mechanical, photocopying, recording, or otherwise, without written permission from the publisher.

ISBN 88-8398-009-3

©2001 by European Press Academic Publishing
Via Valle Bantini,4 - Fucecchio (FI) Italy
www.e-p-a-p.com
Proprietà letteraria riservata - *Printed in Italy*

TABLE OF CONTENTS

GLOSSARY/DEFINITIONS XI

ACKNOWLEDGMENTS XIII

AUTHOR'S DECLARATION XIV

PREFACE XV

INTRODUCTION 17
Purpose of this Work 17
Migration Studies and Geography 18
Theories of Migration and Research Methods 19
Italian Migration Studies 24
Migration Studies and Geography in Australia 27
Value of the Present Research 30
Book Outline 33

CHAPTER 1 - ITALIAN MIGRATION TO OVERSEAS DESTINATIONS 37
Introduction 37
History of Italian Migration 41
i. From century-long Traditions to the Unification of Italy 41
ii. From the Unification to Fascism 43
iii. From Fascism to present 46
Historical Trends of Italian Migration 49
Destination of Italian Migration 54
i. France 54
ii.Great Britain 55
iii.Argentina 56
iv. Brazil 58
v. United States 59
vi. Canada 61
vii. Australia 62

CHAPTER 2 - THE AREA OF ORIGIN OF TUSCAN MIGRANTS IN WESTERN AUSTRALIA - HISTORICAL AND SOCIO-ECONOMIC CONTEXT 65
Introduction 65
The Geographical Setting of Lunigiana and Garfagnana 69
The historical Setting of the Province of Lucca 71
i. From the Roman Colony to the Counter-Reform 71
ii. From the Sixteenth Century to the Unification of Italy 76
The historical Setting of the Province of Massa-Carrara 80
The Economic Conditions of the Province of Lucca 81
The Economic Context 84
i. Agriculture 84
ii. Pastures 86
iii. Mining 88
iv. Industries 89
The Economy of the Rural Society 91
i. Peasants 91
ii. Mezzadria 93
iii. Small land Ownership 95
Aspects of the Economy of Lucca from Unification to Present 100
Conclusions 105

CHAPTER 3 - THE LUCCHESE 'DIASPORA' - DISTRIBUTION OF MIGRANTS FROM LUCCA ABROAD 109
Signs of Lucchese Mass Migration 109
Figurinai (Plaster makers) from Lucca 113
Destinations of Tuscan Migrants 118
i. Corsica 118
ii. From Corsica, France and Great Britain to 'America' 124
iii. Argentina and Brazil 128
iv. United States and Canada 132

CHAPTER 4 - ITALIANS AND TUSCANS IN AUSTRALIA 141
Italians in Australia 141
i. The Early Stage 141
ii. Italians in Anglo-Australian Working Society, 1890-1920 144
iii. The Growth of the Italian-Australian Community,

1921-1945 149
iv. The Italian post-war mass migration to Australia, 1946-197 155
Geographical Distribution of Italians in Australia 157
'Lucchesi' and Tuscans in Australia 161

CHAPTER 5 - TUSCAN MIGRANTS IN WESTERN AUSTRALIA - SOURCES AND METHODS 169
Sources of Information 169
Methodological Problems 176
Preliminary Considerations on first Settlements of Tuscan Migrants in Western Australia 182
Chain Migration 185
Migratory Chains from Tuscany to Western Australia 190

CHAPTER 6 - THE SPATIAL DISTRIBUTION OF TUSCAN MIGRANTS IN WESTERN AUSTRALIA 195
Introduction 195
The pioneering Period of Tuscans to Perth, 1890-1918 196
The inter-war Period, 1920-1939 198
Lucchesi in rural Western Australia, 1890-1939 210
Lucchesi in the Goldfields of Western Australia, 1920-1939 213
Post-war mass Migration of Lucchesi in Western Australia, 1946-1970s 221
Migrants' occupational and residential interaction between Perth and the rest of the State, 1946-1970s 228
"*Tutto il mondo è paese*" (The World is just like a Village) 230
Conclusions 235

CHAPTER 7 - THE SOCIAL LIFE OF TUSCANS IN WESTERN AUSTRALIA 239
Introduction 239
Italian and Tuscan (and Lucchese…?) Identity 240
'*Campanilismo*' in Australia 242
The Social Aggregation of Lucchesi 245
Reasons for Social Aggregation 248
The Toscany Club of Western Australia 252
The Club's Membership 256
Direct Observation of the Club's Activity and Conclusions 258
'*Campanilismo*' again 261

CHAPTER 8 - A SURVEY OF FIRST-GENERATION MIGRANTS FROM TUSCANY IN WESTERN AUSTRALIA 265
Selection of Sample 265
The Interview Schedule and Situation 269
About Tuscan Migrants before migrating 272
Reasons to Migrate and Expectations about Australia 275
Life Conditions and Accommodation at Arrival 278
Occupational and Settlement Patterns 280
Accommodation and English Language Skills 282
Inter-Marriage 286
Second Generation and Language Interaction with First-Generation Tuscans 288
'Transnationalism' versus Italian Identity 290
Perception of Quality of Life in Australia and Conclusions 295

CONCLUSIONS 299
Main Findings 300

NOTES 303

BIBLIOGRAPHY 329
Archival Sources 329
General Texts, Articles, Newspapers and Circulars 330
Official Publications and Other Documents 355
Unpublished Material - Manuscript Sources 356
Personal Communications and Interviews 357

INDEX 359
Index of Names 359
Index of Places 366

List of Tables and Figures

Table 1-1 - Italian Migrants to selected destinations, 1876-1975 39
Table 1-2 - Italian Migration to Australia 53
Table 2-1 - Distribution of land-use (in sq. kms.) within the two major areas of the rural territory of Lucca 87
Table 2-2 - Farms of Lucca and Tuscany run in Mezzadria (sharecropping system) per sq. Kms, 1936-1970 93
Table 2-3 - Small landowners and sharecroppers in Garfagnana in the 1870s, per single municipality 96
Table 2-4 - Family composition in Garfagnana in 1871 per single Commune 98
Table 2-5 - Population of the Communes of the Province of Lucca, according to various Italian Census data (1861-1971) 104
Table 3-1 - Migratory rates (for 1,000 inhabitants) of the Province of Lucca and Italy, 1876-1915 111
Table 3-2 - Number of foreign passports issued to *Figurinai* in single Communes of Lucca, 1809 and 1812 115
Table 3-3 - Occupation of Migrants from Tuscan provinces, 1870 118
Table 3-4 - Total number of passports issued for foreign destinations and for Corsica, 1805-1809 120
Table 3-5 - Total number of foreign passports and for Corsica, 1805-1809 in the Commune of Pescaglia 120
Table 3-6 - Number of Migrants from single Tuscan provinces, split per urban/rural origin and gender, 1870 122
Table 3-7 - Total number of passports issued for foreign destinations in the Commune of Pescaglia, 1873 124
Table 3-8 - Migrants from Tuscany to Canada and the United States, 1876-1915 136
Table 3-9 - Number of Migrants from selected communes of

the Province of Lucca to foreign destinations, 1950-1998 140
Table 4-1 - Italian-born Migrants in Australia according to Australian Census 158
Table 4-2 - Number of Migrants from Tuscany to Australia, 1876-1925 165
Table 5-1 - Number of Migrants from Tuscany to Western Australia and to Australia, 1920-1969 172
Table 5-2 - Number of Migrants from the high and mid-valley of River Serchio to Australia and to Western Australia, 1921-1991 174
Table 5-3 - Number of Migrants from the high valley of River Serchio to Australia, compared to the number to Western Australia, 1950s 175
Table 6-1 - Occupational distribution of Migrants from Tuscany in Western Australia (Perth, rural W.A. and mining areas), 1921-1939 207
Table 6-2 - Occupational distribution of Migrants from Tuscany in Western Australia, 1921-1939 208
Table 6-3 - Sex Ratio amongst Tuscan and Italian Migrants in some mining areas of Western Australia, 1921-1939 214
Table 6-4 - Number and Percentage of Migrants from Garfagnana to Australia and Western Australia, 1951-60, split by Occupation 228
Table 7-1 - Geographical Origin of the Members of the Toscany Club of Balcatta, Perth 257
Table 8-1 - Communes of origin of the Interviewees 272
Table 8-2 - Activity performed by the Interviewees'fathers in Italy 273
Table 8-3 - Occupation performed by Interviewees in Italy before Migration 274
Table 8-4 - Reasons for migrating to Australia 275
Table 8-5 - Expectations about Australia before migrating 276
Table 8-6 - Relatives of Migrants living in Australia at time of their Arrival 279

Table 8-7 - Occupations performed since arrival in Australia 281
Table 8-8 - Colleagues in the working environment 282
Table 8-9 - Self-perception of the level of English known 285
Table 8-10 - Geographical origin of Interviewees' Partners 287
Table 8-11 - Frequency of trips to Italy 293

Figure 2-1 - The Regions of Italy, Tuscany and the Location of the province of Lucca 67
Figure 2-2 - The Communes of Garfagnana and Mid-Valley of the Serchio 68
Figure 2-3 - The Dominions of Lucca in 1328 73
Figure 2-4 - Historical Factors that have affected Migration of People from Lucca (Drawn by the Author) 107
Figure 3-1 - Migrants from the Province of Lucca, Garfagnana and Tuscany, 1876-1915 123
Figure 4-1 - Italian Migrants to Australia, 1924-1972 150
Figure 4-2 - Number of Italian Males and Females arriving in Australia, 1917-1940 152
Figure 6-1 - Distribution of Farmers from Tuscany in Perth Metropolitan Area, 1920-1940 205
Figure 6-2 - Distribution of Miners from Tuscany in Western Australia 213
Figure 6-3 - Distribution of Migrants from Tuscany in Perth Metropolitan Area, 1946-1965 223
Figure 6-4 - Distribution of Migrants from Tuscany in rural Western Australia, 1890s-1970s 234
Figure 7-1 - The shift of *Campanilismo* from within Italy to overseas Italian communities 245

Glossary/Definitions

For the present study, the major problem was to collate the maze of terminology used both in the political administration of Italian local councils and the various regions of Italy over the past two centuries. What follows is a glossary of relevant terms encountered in the primary governmental sources and in the daily Italian rural life, and a classification scheme indicating the English phrases used to convey these terms.

Comune — literally 'Commune' or 'Municipality', it is the local government unit, irrespective of size or population, therefore corresponding to any one of shire, town or city in Australia.[1] There are over 8,000 *Comuni* in Italy.

Provincia — literally 'Province', is formed by a group of *Comuni* of a physical or historical area, which has no counterpart in Australia, and "...is administered by an elected body and by a *Prefetto*, appointed by the national government, with functions partly similar to those of a governor".[2] There are over 90 *Province* in Italy.

Regione — literally 'Region', it is the upper tier of government, and is formed by a group of Province of a physical or historical area, with its own Council, whose members are elected by the voters residing within its territory. Since 1970, it has functions partly similar to those of an Australian state, although more limited and for specific sectors only (tourism, transportation, health, etc.).

Unita' — it refers to the national unification of the several states of Italy into the Kingdom of Italy in 1860.

Paese — in Italian language, the word has the two meanings of 'village or small country town' and of 'country' (mostly 'country of birth or birthplace, as recorded in the census).

Proprietario — it refers to the 'landowner' as substantial land owner who does not do manual labour on his/her holdings.

Coltivatore — it refers to the 'smallholder', who does manual labour on his/her holding to generate the primary source of family income.

Mezzadro — it refers to a 'small sharecropper', who does manual labour within the agrarian contract of *Mezzadria*, in which the land if offered for free to the *Mezzadro's* family, with the condition to return fifty per cent of the crops to the landowner.

Bracciante — it is a generic term for 'agricultural wage labourer' on a daily, weekly or monthly contract basis.

Contadino — it is the Italian generic term for 'peasant', meaning either *Coltivatore*, *Mezzadro* or *Bracciante.*

ACKNOWLEDGMENTS

Dr Joe Gentilli (UWA), and Professor Leonardo Rombai (Universita' di Firenze) for starting the ball rolling.

Professor Dennis Haskell (UWA), Dr Patrick Bertola (Curtin University of Technology), Dr Bob Hay (UWA and Edith Cowan University), Dr Emilio Leoni (Edith Cowan University), Professor Carlo C. Corsini (Universita' di Firenze), Professor Rudy Vecoli (University of Minnesota) and Dr Gloria Nardini (University of Illinois at Chicago), who gave freely of their time in providing inspiration and information, are thanked for showing interest throughout the course of the research.

Associate Professor Dennis Rumley (UWA), gentleman and scholar.

The staff of the Australian Archives of W.A. of East Victoria Park (Australia) is particularly thanked for the comfortable environment they provided me during my archival research in 1997, while Professor Zeffiro Ciuffoletti (Universita' di Firenze) eased my access to archival documents and references on migration otherwise hardly retrievable. Mr Matthew Aylward (UWA) is also thanked for his assistance in drawing the GIS maps that illustrate Chapter 6.

Finally, Dottoressa Patrizia Gremigni is warmly thanked for providing criticism and support, and for living with ships' passenger lists, old photos and new graphs for the past three years.

AUTHOR'S DECLARATION

Aspects of this research have been orally presented at:

· the International Conference on European and Scandinavian Migration to Australia and New Zealand, in Stockholm (Sweden) and Turku (Finland) (June 1998);

· the Institute of Australian Geographers Conference, in Fremantle (Western Australia) (July 1998);

· the International Conference of Tuscan Migrants Around the World, in Lucca (Italy) (September 1998);

· the International Conference on Italian identity Abroad, in Rome (Italy) (November 1998);

· the Lectures on Italian Migration organised by the Italian-Australian Welfare and Cultural Centre, in Perth (Western Australia) (August 1999);

· the Biennial Conference on Australian Labour History, in Wollongong (New South Wales) (October 1999);

· the American Italian Historical Conference, in San Francisco (U.S.A.) (November 1999);

· the Conference of the Italian Communities in English-Speaking Countries, in Perth (Western Australia) (April 2000);

· the First Conference of the Italian-Australian Institute, in Melbourne (Victoria) (May 2000).

The research presented in this book was carried out by the Author and remains original, unless otherwise acknowledged. All tables, diagrams and maps, except those produced using Geographic Information Service (GIS) programs, were prepared by the author, unless otherwise acknowledged.

Adriano Boncompagni

PREFACE

by Roland Sarti

The title of this book, and its bringing together in one place subjects seemingly so diverse as history, anthropological fieldwork, population geography and sociology, mark a new departure in work on Italian migration studies.

The world is just like a village is in fact an exceedingly well-documented study of a particular migratory current from area of origin to area of settlement. It is worth emphasizing from the start that the transcontinental dimension is central since it enables the writer to make what strikes me as being the fundamental message of the book, namely that the culture of departure determines the patterns of settlement and adjustment in the receiving country. The transcontinental, cross-cultural approach is also very much in evidence in the more recent writings on migration by such scholars as Samuel Baily, John Briggs, Dino Cinel, Donna Gabaccia and others. In this respect, Boncompagni's book reflects the most recent and most promising approach to the study of migration.

Cross-cultural study requires familiarity with an unusual large body of literature as both the areas of departure and of reception need to be studied in depth. Boncompagni's book shows this required depth in this regard as well. I have been particularly impressed by how well he knows the provinces of Lucca and Massa Carrara in the Tuscan region, from where most of the migrants derive. This happens to be an area that I am also very familiar with, and I have looked at Boncompagni's coverage of it with extra care. I have not found a single statement of fact or interpretation that I would seriously challenge.

The work definitely makes a substantial and original contribution to the subject of Italian emigration to Australia. The fact that the population involved in this migratory process is relatively small does not in my opinion detract from the value of the study. Boncompagni does such a fine job of contextualizing it that one can easily see how this particular current fits into the larger picture. The book does not claim that emigration from western Tuscany is typical of Italian migration as a whole. It is precisely because the study shows the unique characteristics of this current (and that Boncompagni calls it the "Lucca model") that we get a sense of the complexity and diversity of national emigration. He is able to put this particular current in a larger perspective thanks to his thorough command of the literature on Italian emigration.

I would also like to briefly comment on another admirable trait of the work, namely its interdisciplinary scope. While geography is clearly the central discipline, as a historian I am particularly pleased to see how well the book incorporates historical insights. Without the historical dimension showing the gradual development of migratory patterns (seasonal, temporary, long term, permanent) in the course of several centuries, it would be impossible to explain the vitality of this migratory current. Awareness of the historical context enables Boncompagni to refine the 'push-pull' model of migration by showing the power of attraction of the communities of origin. The high rate of return evident among first generation migrants suggests to Boncompagni that the mechanism at work should be rather described as 'push-pull-pull(back). In this instance, Boncompagni uses historical evidence to reformulate a social science model.

Finally, I find the organization of the book logical and the findings clearly set out and summed up. There are inevitably some minor omissions in a book such as this, pioneering in new interdisciplinary areas related to migration studies. However, if this book succeeds both in being informative about the Tuscan migratory current within the Italian national context, and in indicating the several forms of its settlement in Australia, and the many different ways into studying it, then it will have successfully achieved its main aims.

Professor Roland Sarti

University of Massachussets at Amherst

INTRODUCTION

PURPOSE OF THIS WORK

The central aim of this study is to show how the historical and past socio-economic factors of Tuscany (Italy) have been conducive to overseas migration over a long period, with particular regard to Australia as a destination. Furthermore, the work analyses, as a case study, the patterns of geographical and occupational distribution of Tuscan migrants in Western Australia, as well as their social adjustment to the host country.

Although the historical and economic background of the area of origin and the features of Italian settlements in Australia have been studied and described, the relationship between these two research fields has never been fully explored. Therefore, in order to explain that relationship and how migrants from a geographically circumscribed area of Italy are linked to the society in which they settle, a fully integrated analysis of this migratory process is carried out.

The study weaves together seemingly disparate strands of thought from history, geography, population studies and other social sciences, in order to explain the relationship between past and present, different (and distant) geographical areas, within the migratory flow of people from Tuscany in Western Australia. This process is intended to show the influence of particular historical, social and cultural legacies in the settlement of a specific migratory group within Australia, and in the residential, occupational and social patterns by the same people.

The approach is multidisciplinary because it brings together and relates different aspects - economic, social, spatial and cultural - of the studied group. Three main aims are to be fulfilled through this work:

· The first aim is to determine the factors influencing the century-long process of internal and overseas emigration from Tuscany within the wider Italian migratory flow. An integrated multidisciplinary approach is taken.

· The second aim is to make a contribution to Australian migration studies, through the analysis of residential, occupational and social patterns of migrants from Tuscany in Western Australia.

· In doing so, the third aim is to identify the factors influencing the patterning of an ethnic group, in this case Tuscans in Western Australia, within its social and cultural legacies. From the identification and the lessons provided by the case study, in future studies it will be possible to re-use this method in order to analyse the settlement, occupational and social patterns of other migratory groups in Australia.

MIGRATION STUDIES AND GEOGRAPHY

The dictionary definition of the verb 'to migrate' is to 'move from one place (country, town, house) to another'. The geographer's simple definition of migration is not very different from this general view: a migration is a change in the place of residence.

Geographers, with their concern for spatially-expressed processes, are attracted by the study of relocation of people or the movement of individuals and groups from one location to another. They search to understand the spatial consequences of migration, while, for example, economists view migration as a normal opportunistic response to market forces. Similarly, anthropologists and sociologists look at migration for indications of change to cultural and social functioning, while psychologists delve into the issues surrounding the migrant's experience, and historians look at migratory processes in a diachronic perspective, so that they all provide additional meanings to the migratory process. Nevertheless, the interest of so many disciplines in the migration process is not immune from problems and misunderstandings. In this regard, Jan and Luc Lucassen write:

> *"The migration landscape is full of canyons and fast running rivers. The deepest canyon separates social scientists from historians, and swift rivers divide scholars within disciplines. Intellectuals are often unaware (or only vaguely aware) of each other's progress. Focusing mainly on historical or historicizing studies manifests this flaw in the form of a great number of typologies intended to grasp the huge and intricate migration phenomenon. Intrinsically, these shortcomings are of course useful and even necessary. The problem, however, is that the rapid reduction of many of these typologies to fixed dichotomies often causes the dividing and isolating capacity of an analytical framework to overshadow its clarifying and explanatory potential".*[1]

The background of the geographic study of human mobility is always a global concept of inhabited space. Consequently, the study of the geographical and socio-economic differentiation of the spaces of origin and destination of the population flows is a priority for the geographer.[2] In the light of the concern expressed by the French scholars, the present study aims to utilise the outcomes and the results of research on migration theories, drawn from different disciplines, in order to develop a research framework with a multidisciplinary scope.

THEORIES OF MIGRATION AND RESEARCH METHODS

Migration occurs because "...migrants believe that they will be more satisfied in their needs and desires in the place that they move to than in the place from which they come".[3] An important emphasis must be placed on the word 'believe', as the migration process occurs as a result of decisions made by individuals in the light of what they perceive the objective world to be like. In other words, the migration process permits matching human resources, located in a specific place, to move towards perceived opportunities located elsewhere.

During the recent years, it has become more than clear to geographers and historians working in the field of migration that this phenomenon has to be regarded as a normal and structural element of human societies throughout history. Generally, migration is no longer viewed as a sign of crisis, as a phenomenon exclusive to the industrial period, or as a typically Western occurrence.[4] Migration is part of the general human pattern, essential for the functioning of families and society. Most basic decisions by human beings often entail leaving the place of birth or residence. While they may not go far, nevertheless their moves lead them to other social and geographical environments.

At present, there is no single, coherent theory of migration, only a fragmented set of theories that have developed largely in isolation from one another, sometimes but now always segmented by disciplinary boundaries. "Current patterns and trends in immigration, however, suggest that a full understanding of contemporary migratory processes will not be achieved by relying on the tools of one discipline alone".[5]

Nevertheless, it is important to distinguish between two methodologies that may be adopted in the analysis of migration flows. The inductive approach seeks to identify and describe process and pattern as a preliminary to inquiries of a more explanatory nature, taking as its starting point information on actual migrations. In the deductive approach, it is usual to begin the sequence of analysis by formulating logical and internally consistent theories which may then be tested empirically against data drawn from actual observations. Clearly, these two approaches are not mutually exclusive; neither is the "correct" one to use, since both make important contributions to social scientific inquiries.

Many theories on internal and international migration have been elaborated since the first general "laws of migration", published by the geographer and demographer Ravenstein in 1871 in the *Geographical Magazine*, began to form the basis for most modern research on migration.[6] Probably the oldest and most solid modern theory of migration was originally developed to explain labour migration in the process of economic development. According to this theory, internal and international migrations are caused by purely geographic differences in the supply of and demand for labour. People from countries with a large labour force endowment will flow towards labour-scarce countries. It is the classical view in which "...migration exists to restore equilibrium between locations",[7] as a self-regulating process through which locational differences in labour demand and labour supply adjust themselves.

Corresponding to this economic model is another model of individual choice.[8] In this scheme, individual actors decide to migrate because a cost-benefit calculation leads them to expect a positive net return, usually monetary, so that migration is conceptualised as a form of investment in human capital. People choose to move to where they can be most productive, "...where the expected net returns are greatest over some time".[9] A variation of this theory, involving a wider analysis of the several factors affecting the perception of lifestyle in the countries of origin and destination, is known as the "push-pull" theory. This approach sees labour flows as an outcome of poverty and backwardness in the source areas.[10] Perspective migrants examine lists of "push factors", such as economic, social and political hardships in the country of origin, and "pull factors", under the form of comparative advantages in the country of destination, as casual variables determining the size and direction of immigrant flows. Within the migratory process, one objection to this theory is that the list of push and pull factors can be invariably elaborated and drawn after the migration has already been initiated, whereas, before migration, the pull factors can only be perceived and not personally assessed. A second difficulty with standard push-pull theories is their inability to account for individual differences in patterns of migration. As Portes and Borocz wrote: "Given the same set of expelling forces and external inducements, why is it that some individuals leave while others stay?".[11]

Lee's general framework for analysing migration, based on Ravenstein's earlier analysis, provides the basis for considering social and economic causes of migration with an implicit push-pull perspective.[12] Each origin and destination is hypothesised to have a set of positive and negative factors which attract and repel migrants. The greater the differences among these push and pull factors, the higher the probability of migration, with effects varying with the potential migrant's personal characteristics, such as education, skill level, gender, personality and aspirations.

A problem for migration research has been that people are assumed to make their migratory decisions as a reaction to the economic and social structure of the region of origin. Even though it cannot be denied that people decide within economic parameters, what seems to be missing is the knowledge of the cultural experiences used by migrants in their decision-making motivation. If economic advantage were the only major determinant, then in some economically depressed areas there would be mass out-migration, which does not take place. A key insight of this objection is that migration decisions are not made by isolated individual actors, but by larger units of related people, typically families or households, in which people act collectively "...not only to maximise expected incomes, but also to minimise risks and loose constraints".[13] The Australian geographer Bruce Moon has conceptualised the variables in migration decision-making in the notion of moorings, as those social expressions "...which not only allow a person to materialise his or her physical, psychological and emotional well-being but also serve to bind a person to a particular place. Thus a person's perception of his or her relative stability in a place will hinge on how well he or she values his or her moorings".[14] As a result, unlike push-pull factors, people can express some degree of personal control over each mooring issue that impacts their life.

Lastly, with respect to the methodologies implied in migration research, quantitative approaches, drawn from primary and secondary sources, have certainly dominated in the economic, historical and demographic modelling of migration, and in the analysis of migratory flows, the socio-demographic characteristics of migrants, their destinations, occupational and settlement patterns. Conversely, much contemporary work involves qualitative approaches, such as archival research, for example, investigating social and family practices, and following biographical paths and family genealogies, thus highlighting personal and social factors affecting the migration-decision process. Nevertheless, a thorough review of migration research over the last several decades reveals that diverse methods have continually been employed to understand migration processes. In particular, the American geographers Rachel Silvey and Victoria Lawson have argued that "...the diversity of methods employed in migration studies are a key element of continuity in this field".[15] Further in their contribution, they write:

> *"Migration studies are beginning to draw on these insights in order to explore new sites and scales of analysis. Specifically, interpreting the voices of migrants themselves as theoretically meaningful allows researchers to open up 'development' and critique categorizations of place as undeveloped, backward, and traditional".*[16]

While more theories on migration will be taken into account when the chain migration process will be discussed, here it is necessary to explain that one aim of the present research is to frame the object of the study within a methodological multidisciplinary approach that incorporates previous theories on migration within a new perspective. In other words, the goal is to demonstrate that, while most modern theories on migration are able to interpret the migratory dynamics object of this study, an additional, multidisciplinary interpretation of the several reasons affecting emigration from the country of origin and immigration to the host country takes place in our case study.

The approach that we intend to present in this study aims to fill the gap in migration studies so vividly represented by the cited "canyons" depicted by Jan and Luc Lucassen, and offers a new interpretation of the complex process of migration. In order to reach this objective, it is necessary to briefly examine the state of migration studies both in Italy and in Australia, the two countries between which the migratory flow takes place.

ITALIAN MIGRATION STUDIES

Academic and research interest for the history of Italian emigration, since the unification of Italy in 1860, has slowly grown from the 1970s onwards, torn apart by different perspectives, such as the history of the workers' movement[17]and the studies on migrants' spatial distribution in the host countries. For quite a long time, a social history of Italian migration has been identified with a "...timeless sociology of the uprooted Italian migrant abroad", as the scholar of Italian migration Ercole Sori described the state of migration studies until the late 1970s.[18]

Some good works have been written on Italian socio-historical processes that have generated migration towards overseas countries, regardless of the settlement processes in the host countries. The Italian scholars Ciuffoletti and Degl'Innocenti have written a monumental study about Italian governmental policy on emigration from the mid-nineteenth century to the Second World War,[19] while Ercole Sori has looked at the socio-economic aspects of Italy during the highest peaks of emigration.[20] Furthermore, Gianfausto Rosoli has written a comprehensive analysis of the overall destinations of Italian migrants during the last one hundred years,[21] and the historian Emilio Franzina has recollected the Italian socio-cultural environments of the early twentieth century at time of departure for overseas destinations.[22] More recently, exhaustive historiographical reports on Italian national and regional migration have been written.[23]

However, the global view of such a complex phenomenon as Italian migration history raises a series of theoretical and practical issues with respect to both the areas of origin of migrants and the host countries. These questions include, for example, the definition of theories and methods to adopt, and a systematic approach to a century-long social movement, as well as the adoption of a comparative approach in order to delineate similarities and differences in Italy and in the countries of destination of Italian migrants.[24] Few scholars have raised the issue of a global approach or, alternatively, a compared analysis of Italian migration. And, in these few cases, the comparative studies are without pre-defined criteria, as in the classical work on Italian migration abroad by the American Robert Foerster.[25]

In order to go beyond the limits of national boundaries, during the 1960s and 1970s some historians, such as Barton,[26] Briggs[27] and Baily,[28] have examined aspects of Italian migration overseas in a comparative perspective, both at the macro and micro levels. In this latter case, some scholars have studied both two or more groups of migrants (Italians included) in American cities, in order to delineate differences in the processes of assimilation and interaction, and the Italian ethnic group in the host country originating from different regional areas of Italy.[29] Conversely, other historians have looked at the same ethnic group, namely the Italians, in two or more areas of destination, mainly urban, in order to highlight similarities and differences between social environments.[30] Yet other scholars have highlighted Italian migration as a "transnational" process of the Italian diaspora, in which Italy and its culture remain a central part of a world-wide network, with the aim to "internationalise" the history of Italy through the comparative study of its national and regional communities abroad.[31]

One of most "creative" approaches within the study of Italian migration[32] has possibly come from the study area of Italian communities across the two sides of the Atlantic Ocean. Some scholars have chosen geographically circumscribed Italian regional areas with high migration rates and one specific American destination, and have studied in detail the socio-economic characteristics of the regions of origin and the process of adaptation to American society.[33]

However, the Italian contribution to the growth of societies in many overseas countries was certainly differentiated and vitally important. This contribution represents one of the most substantial forms of the international presence of modern Italy.[34] Consequently, the growing interest for the Italian migration has opened a large debate both in the Italian historiography[35] and among the social sciences that share an interest in Italian migration issues.

During recent years, historiographic research on Italian migration has been enriched by new methodological approaches, and, in particular, by studies now based on an Italian regional or sub-regional perspective.[36] The studies by the Italian historian Emilio Franzina on the migratory flow from the geographically circumscribed area of Veneto,[37] in Northern Italy, have opened the road to an important series of other contributions based and filtered through an Italian regional or local perspective of research. These works represent a sort of theorisation of the need to highlight the several Italian "migratory regions"[38] in which the migration flows were born, autonomously, in the early nineteenth century, thus stressing the different migratory patterns towards different destinations.

These migratory areas or regions within Italy hold such ethnic, cultural and social peculiarities in comparison to the overall Italian migration flow, to induce the researcher to carefully evaluate the relationship between some of these areas of origin and the countries of destination.[39] There have been a few studies on the different processes of integration within the host countries, with a focus on the family and social strategies of mutual help abroad[40] as well as in the case of the Italian regional or smaller community-based associations overseas.[41] The close relation linking a geographically circumscribed Italian area of origin with a specific destination abroad has also been studied.[42]

Some Italian migration scholars describe the state of these studies in Italy as a "new season", in which two new trends have come to light. These trends are the gradual abandonment of discussions on the "causal knots" of the push-pull factor theory,[43] and the opening up to contributions focussing on the "transnational perspective" of migrants across different cultural worlds, in which the general issues of migration integrate with the particular aspects of the personal experience of the migrants themselves, in order to stimulate a more articulated knowledge of the migration process.[44]

Developments of research focused on a specific, circumscribed area of origin of migration will allow an interdisciplinary project between history of migration, social and economic history, anthropology, population geography and demography. This new trend of Italian migration studies can be accepted and put forward only on condition of being interdisciplinary. "In some periods of the transformation of Italian economy and society, migration played such an incisive role to be indicated as one of the main factors affecting the Italian model of industrialisation",[45] and to cast light on the many issues related to Italian-born population in many countries of destination.

MIGRATION STUDIES AND GEOGRAPHY IN AUSTRALIA

Immigration has played an important role in the growth and development of Australia, although its significance has varied greatly since European settlers first arrived over 200 years ago. Until the late nineteenth century, net migration was clearly the dominant component of population growth in Australia, but with the onset of major economic depressions during the 1890s and 1930s and two world wars, the proportion of Australia's population growth due to net migration declined substantially.

Since 1945, however, a vigorous immigration program has contributed about 40 per cent of population growth.[46] Postwar immigration transformed Australia from a culturally homogeneous country to one of diversity, as it represented a total break with past immigration, in its scale and for the arrival of large numbers of migrants of other than British origin. "Between 1947 and 1991, the national population increased from 7.6 to 16.9 million and the 5.2 million new settlers arriving in Australia over that period accounted directly or indirectly (via their childbearing) for around half of that growth".[47]

The subject of immigration and ethnic composition of the society within Australia has been therefore the stimulus for considerable academic inquiry in the post-war period. There is a considerable amount of literature on Italian immigration to Australia, reflecting the historically long migratory flow from Italy to Australia. Many researchers have been involved, including historians, anthropologists, political scientists, demographers, social psychologists, and, to a lesser extent, geographers. Fundamental works by Australian demographers and population study scholars are those by Borrie[48] and Price.[49] They both examined the demographic aspects related to Italian migration and settlement at the early stage of these two processes during the 1950s. Drawing conclusions from widespread quantitative research, Charles Price was the first scholar in Australia to highlight the different patterns of Italian settlement and occupational mobility in urban Australia according to the Italian regional composition of migrants' arrivals in Australia. Finally, Helen Ware has brought more recent figures than those supplied by Borrie and Price, to the demographic issues related to the Italian presence in Australia.[50]

Many other studies have been conducted on different aspects of Italian migrants in Australia. Overall historical analyses of Italian settlements in Australia have been conducted by Hempel[51] and Douglass[52] in Queensland, Martinuzzi O'Brien,[53] Robert Pascoe[54] and Charles D'Aprano[55] in Victoria, Joseph Gentilli in Western Australia,[56] Giorgio Cheda, who embarked in a very detailed archival research on Italians of Swiss nationality across Australia,[57] Richard Bosworth, who studied the Italian presence in fishing city of Fremantle in Western Australia,[58] and Desmond O'Connor in South Australia.[59]

Specific historical issues related to the presence of Italians in Australia have been analysed by Gianfranco Cresciani, who studied the Italian fascist and anti-fascist movements during the period 1921-45,[60] and later addressed the wider issue of the Italian identity in the country of destination in an edited book,[61] as did Gaetano Rando.[62] In addition, Stephanie Lindsay Thompson has addressed aspects related to return migration of Italians,[63] while Ellie Vasta has approached the socio-cultural issues related to Italian women in Australia.[64]

An anthropological approach has been carried out over thirty years ago by Constance Cronin, who looked at the social and cultural adaptation of Italian migrants from Sicily in the host country.[65] She showed the processes of cultural change by explaining how the particular economic conditions, expectations, and opportunities in Italy and in Australia affected the migrants. This work was followed by the deeper insight of the research by Rina Huber on the presence of Italians from the north-eastern part of Veneto in Sydney.[66] More recently, Loretta Baldassar has offered an interpretation of the cultural dynamics of Italian Australians returning to visit Italy[67] and the behaviour of second-generation young women in urban Australia.[68]

With respect to Western Australia, a more limited number of studies have been conducted. These comprise the cited major works by the geographer Joseph Gentilli, on the Italian regional composition of migrants in the State, and that of the historian Richard Bosworth, on the formation process of the Italian identity of the city of Fremantle. Other studies, both published and unpublished, are those by Charles Gamba,[69] Dino Gava,[70] and Charles Iraci,[71] which all deal with the economics and sociology of Italian migrants, as well as with the residential decision-making processes of Italians within Perth, as in the case of the thesis by Wigley.[72] Finally, Patrick Bertola and Adelma Longton have briefly looked at some historical aspects of the presence of Italian migrants in the Western Australian goldfields.[73]

These studies are directed at different aspects of the phenomenon, and thus a study into the causes of migration - and their effect on spatial, occupational and social adjustment of migrants to the host environment - can prove fruitful, especially since motives for migration change with time. The cited works are either framed within specific Australia geographical contexts or try to respond to issues related to settlement and occupational mobility, as well as of cultural adaptation. No attempt has been recently made to examine the historical causes of migration that pushed so many Italians to move to Australia, and how these causes have influenced the occupational, social and cultural adjustment of Italians in Australia.

To date, published geographical studies have been mainly preoccupied with the analysis of the spatial distribution of immigrants and associated ethnic groupings, together with issues of residential and occupational disadvantage within the major cities.[74]

The basic objective has often been to establish the pattern of recent immigration and to indicate some of the processes of adjustment and absorption as revealed through statistical data, documentary material, and field surveys. Since the early 1960s, these studies have moved towards the sociological from a quantitative, statistical basis.[75] Some of the matters which this migration research has been designed to examine aim to respond to where immigrants have come from; where have they settled; what has been the extent of group settlement; what have been their employment patterns; and, what changes have they affected in the demographic and spatial pattern of the population.

However, it is the spatial impact of these groups, through developing and modifying urban and rural structures, which must be the focus of work by geographers involved in migration studies. That is, the processes and the implications of these processes must be studied to fully elucidate the dynamic nature of the spatial differentiation within cities and rural areas, which are the resultants from these ethnic concentrations.

Within the research area of this work, the grouping, mobility and ramification of spatial and social patterns of migrants are being studied to provide an insight into the overall geographical context of settlement, occupational and social patterns. The social and spatial perspectives must be combined to develop a complete background, against which spatial, occupational and social patterns of the migrants, who are the object of this study, can be understood. A sociological and a spatial consciousness must be evolved to obtain a complete understanding of the formation of space occupied by foreign-born people in Australia, whether in rural or urban contexts.

VALUE OF THE PRESENT RESEARCH

The decision to deepen a study on Tuscan migration to Western Australia was related to a long-standing desire to synthetise a dual interest in the social sciences on the one hand, and in history on the other. Exploration of works on Italian emigration and Australian immigration convinced me that investigation of the phenomenon was important in its own right, since international migrations touched the lives of vast masses of various peoples after the nineteenth century. To follow a migrant from the mountain communities of Central Italy to Perth, Western Australia, from one point to another, is to compare past to present, a before to an after, and ultimately the experience in the country of arrival with that in the country of departure. By examining group and individual choices of settlement, spatial distribution, social and occupational patterns, within geographical and historical frameworks, we can move towards the examination and reinterpretation of the structures surrounding the migration process in light of individual choices and vice versa. The analysis of a specific migration process is fundamental to the understanding of many aspects of the societies of departure (the inner valleys of central Italy) and arrival (Western Australia and the urban context of Perth). One of the tasks of all social sciences is, in fact, to explain diversity, whether it is in economic well-being, in social or cultural structures, in patterns of social evolution or in the spatial distribution of people over the territory.

As previously reported, migration studies in Italy tend now to focus on local communities of departure of the migratory flow, because it is through this more capillary analysis that it is possible to trace new research paths and highlight new elements of knowledge of the whole process.[76] Within the investigation of the social and historical factors affecting emigration, this study intends to follow this new Italian methodological approach, examining the flow of migrants from Tuscany towards their overseas destinations and in particular towards Australia. This examination will be pivotal to frame the interpretation of the process of migrants' settlement in Western Australia, and their spatial, occupational and social patterns in the light of their social, historical and economic background.

In Australia, despite a policy of multiculturalism, immigration of people of non-English-speaking background is still of marginal interest to most social scientists and historians. As the Australian anthropologist Bottomley states:

> *"The crucial element of Australian industrialisation, labour migration, is completely absent from most economics courses, and the emphasis in historical studies is on Britain, Australia and their interconnections. 'Australian Studies' rarely include the reality of mass immigrant settlement, and popular representations reinforce stereotypes, such as the Italian greengrocer and the Chinese cook".*[77]

With respect to geographical and population studies, there has been a similar concern, expressed by very few Australian scholars, who study migration and its interaction with space. Australian geographer Ian Burnley wrote in 1993 that there is insufficient information on how newly-arrived migrants in Australia enter migration streams, the role of residential preferences, and the cultural or economic factors affecting the residential mobility of migrants, suggesting the need to further analyse the specific role of international migration in labour force growth and changes in urban regions of Australia.[78]

Others have emphasised that research has tended to be concentrated in particular areas and has been hindered by the limited nature of available data sources, thus lacking studies that focus more on elucidating the process of migration, especially within the growing global immigration "industry".[79] In particular, Australian geographer, Graeme Hugo, states that little attention has been devoted to the causes of migration at the micro level of the individual, family and small group. He writes: "Perhaps because the bulk of studies of immigration to Australia have been undertaken at the destination end of the migration process, study of the decision whether or not to immigrate to Australia has been neglected".[80] Further, he states: "Virtually all of the research into Australian immigration is undertaken from the perspective of Australia. It looks at immigrants resident in Australia and not prior to their arrival".[81]

In the light of the new Italian tendencies in migration studies and the need to fill the research gaps in the study of migrants' spatial and occupational patterns in Australia, this work will show, first of all, the significance of historical, social and economic factors in the development of patterns of settlement of Tuscan migrants in Western

Australia. Stress will be placed on the historical background of migrants in the country of departure, as pivotal in creating a 'model' of migration, which is exclusive to Central Italian people, although framed within the Italian national context.

Secondly, beyond the analysis of the geographical and occupational distribution of migrants from Tuscany in Western Australia throughout the whole period of their settlement in the host country, the study will suggest that people find it easier to settle in a new country if supported by an extended network of relatives and friends, helping migrants to ease the process of adaptation to the host environment, and if customs and institutions can be adapted or reconstructed to dovetail the new ones.

Through quantitative (archives in Australia and in Italy, statistical data, secondary and additional sources) and qualitative analyses (a survey among Tuscan migrants), the study attempts to present a picture of the growth of the Tuscan community in Western Australia from its very early beginning to the present. Extensive use of archival material has made it possible to pinpoint the lack of extensive and reliable material on the many aspects of the spatial and occupational patterns of migrants, while the in-depth interviews have confirmed the trends in settlement, occupations and social life already highlighted by the quantitative research.

The outcomes of the research confirm the correctness of the mixed methods used - quantitative and qualitative - across the two worlds of departure and arrival. Furthermore, these outcomes hopefully address the need to study, as Hugo wrote, the micro level of individuals and families prior their arrival to Australia, as this should offer an additional key of interpretation of their settlement process in the host country.

BOOK OUTLINE

The material has been divided into eight chapters. The first part of the thesis sets out the 'what, where, when and why' of the study in four chapters.

This chapter introduced the aims of the study within its multidisciplinary context, along with the literature review, highlighting the value and the originality of the study. In Chapter 1 (Italian Migration to Overseas Destinations) the main destinations of the Italian migratory flow are discussed and linked to the national and international historical and economic contexts, which have been conducive to overseas migration. Following that discussion, a focus on the historical, economic and social background of Tuscany is presented in Chapter 2 (The Area of Origin of Tuscan Migrants in Western Australia. Historical and Socio-Economic Background). Diverse material from history, anthropology, economics and geography illustrate the reasons for the century-long migratory movement from the Tuscany Region and, in particular, from the areas around the Tuscan city of Lucca, towards different destinations. Chapter 3 (The Lucchese 'Diaspora'. Distribution of Migrants from Lucca Abroad) emphasises the main migratory destinations of Tuscans, both internal and international, during the nineteenth and twentieth centuries. The analysis is framed within the economic, social and cultural background of the studied area of origin, and highlights patterns of residential and occupational choices, which are distinctive of Lucchese overseas migration. In Chapter 4 (Italians and Tuscans in Australia), the settlement process of Italian and Tuscan migrants in Australia is analysed since its early beginning in the 1880s and 1890s. The study of residential and occupational patterns of Italian migrants highlights general similarities and differences with the first concentrations of Tuscans in Australia, in order to lead to a more focused examination of the latter group.

An in-depth analysis of the migratory patterns of Tuscans in Western Australia is presented in Chapters 5, 6, and 7. In Chapter 5 (Tuscan Migrants in Western Australia. Sources and Methods), sources of the quantitative study are explained, and material discussed. The emphasis in this chapter is on the use of different methods, which are not confined to any one discipline, and are therefore multidisciplinary in character. Nevertheless, the selection and use of approaches and methods from different disciplines are based upon their compatibility and their analytical value. Chapter 6 (The Spatial Distribution of Tuscan Migrants in Western Australia) describes the patterning of Tuscans within the rural and urban areas of the State as a century-long process, which draws its geographical and occupational aspects from the unique history of social and cultural events of which these migrants are carriers. The residential aspects that are particular to each Tuscan settlement in Western Australia, and the aspects in common are presented for contrast and comparison, and always filtered in the light of the specific culture of origin of its members. Chapter 7 is focused on the social life of Tuscans in Western Australia, while Chapter 8 (A Survey of First-Generation Migrants from Tuscany in Western Australia) identifies and confirms, through a qualitative survey among first-generation migrants from Tuscany, the spatial, occupational and social patterns already analysed on the large-scale study of Chapter 6. This identification is a final step towards confirming the hypothesis that the way Tuscan migrants settled in Western Australia is indeed a product of their culture, although within the frame of the wider Italian migratory process.

CHAPTER 1

ITALIAN MIGRATION TO OVERSEAS DESTINATIONS

"Dopo la formazione di una borghesia nazionale e dopo l'avvento del capitalismo, si e' iniziata l'emigrazione del popolo lavoratore...[...]... Questi elementi (gli emigranti italiani) sono andati perduti in grandissima parte, incorporandosi nelle nazionalita' straniere in funzione subalterna".
Antonio Gramsci, Quaderni del Carcere[1]

(After the formation of a national bourgeois, and the birth of capitalism, we have the emigration of the working class...[...]... These elements (Italian migrants) are mainly lost, as they embodied into foreign countries in a subaltern function).

INTRODUCTION

Italian migration has been one of the most extraordinary migratory movements in human history. In the number of people it has involved, in the range of activities that Italian migrants have performed across the world and in the long continuance of the flow, it has no equal in modern history. Italian mass migration began after the political unification of Italy in 1860 and lasted until the mid-1970s. Small-scale until the mid-nineteenth century, the exodus steadily increased in number through the second half of the past century and reached its peak, 2,743,053 migrants, during the years 1911-1915.[2] The American scholar Robert Foerster stated: "The Italians are not a population: they are a stream, which surges forward and subsides, acknowledging no law but that of change".[3]

Although it began in the nineteenth century, its origin is more ancient. For many centuries, colonies of Italian merchants were to be found all across Europe, in London and Antwerp, Seville and Paris. "Italian immigrants were not just merchants. In the course of the time, they were painters and musicians, ice cream vendors and coal miners, tumblers and masons".[4]

Between 1876 and 1975, more than 25 million Italians left their country.[5] By the mid 1970s the migratory flow had ceased, mainly due to improved economic conditions in Italy. On the contrary, since the early 1980s, Italy has become a country of immigration. It has been noted that the number of Italians who left the country was the same as the total Italian population at the time of political unification in 1861.[6] Italian migration developed on a massive scale in the late nineteenth century, rose to dramatic levels in the 1910s and, except for a temporary increase after the First World War, it dwindled between the wars and rose again after the Second World War. Originally it was mainly directed towards European destinations (France and Switzerland in particular), the United States and Latin America countries such as Argentina and Brazil. However, since 1945, there has been a marked decrease in overseas emigration with respect to European destinations. The three main overseas countries of destination for Italian migrants in the 1950s and 1960s were the United States, Australia and Canada.

Before the First World War, some 450,000 Italians resided in France[7] and 135,000 in Switzerland with a total of more than 5 million Italians living abroad.[8] The Great War halted the stream, but in 1920 almost 615,000 Italians had already migrated. Again, the movement of people was rising when it met obstacles presented by the restrictive Italian emigration law and the immigration policies of various countries, especially of the United States.

In the meantime, huge numbers had already reached the Latin American countries: between 1870 and 1930 nearly one and a half million Italians were admitted to Brazil,[9] and between 1857 and 1926 nearly three million went to Argentina.[10] By the outbreak of the Second World War, about 20 million Italians had gone through the emigration process since the unification of Italy. Again, after 1945, almost seven more million left.[11]

It is possible to estimate that people of Italian origin and/or ancestry around the world are about 50 million, with more than 30 million in the Americas[12] (Table1-1). The Italian contribution to the growth of societies of both Italy and the host countries was certainly a differentiated contribution, but a vitally important one.

Table 1-1 - Italian Migrants to selected destinations, 1876-1975

Country of destination	*Migrants*
France	4,320,662
Switzerland	3,961,196
Germany	2,421,425
Great Britain	261,637
USA	5,684,332
Canada	633,531
Argentina	2,967,362
Brazil	1,454,118
Australia	454,840

Source: Rosoli, 1978

A study of the Italian migration process presents complex dynamics mainly due to the long period during which Italian migration took place and the fact that the wide spatial context (regions of origin and areas of destination) presents a heterogeneity of sources to be studied.[13] As mentioned earlier, well before the unification of Italy, some Italian regional and sub-regional groups had already established a pattern of overseas migration,[14] such as the Venetian estuary population settling major trading posts in Eastern Europe, while the Ligurians favoured the close French estuarine area of the Rhone river or the rich and virgin regions of the Americas, with a preference for the South American continent.[15]

In the mid-nineteenth century, Italian migration followed from the Provinces of northern Piedmont, especially from the poorest areas of the Alpine basin. Later, it was the itinerant workers, labourers owning no property that might tie them to the land, who left Liguria, northern Apennine Tuscany and the coastal areas of southern Italy.[16] Conversely, emigration from the Southern Italian regions became increasingly popular from the 1890s.

To discern the larger causes of Italian migration is no simple matter. Current trends in migration studies suggest that a full understanding of migratory processes passes through theories that incorporate a variety of perspectives, levels and assumptions. Probably the oldest and best-known theory of international migration was developed to explain labour migration in the process of economic development and within the context of geographical differences in the supply of and demand for labour.[17] All migrations take place within an economic, social or political context, which, in some way, links the areas of origin of the migrants with the areas of destination. In the particular case of the Italy, the mentioned 'push and pull' factors have been pivotal in the expansion and contraction of migration from Italy toward selected overseas destinations.

The most conspicuous difference of level between the regions of Italy from which emigration proceeded and the countries of immigration is economic, as the American scholar on Italian migration Robert Foerster indicated in his pioneering study of the early 1920s.[18] The causes, which have sustained an emigration of millions of persons for about one century, constitute an inadequacy in the Italian economic system, as well as being the effect of the expulsive force of overpopulation. Corresponding to an economic model of interpretation of migratory processes is a micro-economic model of 'individual choice'.[19] Individual migrants decide to migrate because a cost-benefit calculation leads them to expect a positive return, so that international migration is conceptualised as a form of investment in human capital.

These factors indicate that the answer to the question concerning the importance of forces 'pushing' persons from their homeland, and forces 'pulling' them toward the host countries[20] was pivotal, from the unification of Italy to the mid-1970s, in the decision-making process of Italian migrants from most of the regions of Italy going abroad.

HISTORY OF ITALIAN MIGRATION

i. From century-long Traditions to the Unification of Italy

Chi non s'attenta, stenta

("Dare nothing, get little")

Great significance has been attributed to Italian peasant proverbs. As the Italian-American historian Roland Sarti stressed, "peasant behaviour is explicable in terms of rational choice and that what peasants ultimately choose depends on their estimate of what different alternatives promise to yield ". Actually, this proverb could be used as the paradigm of the history of Italian migration. The search for bread was common among Italians and took them almost everywhere in the world. Massive mobility in time helped create an "Italian culture of migration", which rendered long journeys to work normal.[22]

As mentioned earlier, the beginning of Italian mass emigration can be located in the second half of the nineteenth century, but the movement of labouring people, both within the Italian peninsula and abroad, had been a traditional mode of life for many Italians from time immemorial. Seasonal migration, particularly to neighbouring European countries, was a habit of the rural society during the eighteenth and nineteenth centuries.[23] Men emigrated in small groups formed on the basis of trade. Family links provided information on the labour market, and a network of social relations controlled the possible places to visit and opportunities to exploit.[24]

Even prior to the eighteenth century, and especially since the Renaissance, skilled artisans and people of high status made significant contributions to the social and economic life of most northern European countries. Migration from Italy emerged from Italians' early importance as craftsmen, traders and skilled labourers.

It was a century-long alternative to restricted opportunities in traditional agrarian and newly urban societies, and largely towards economic goals.

Overall Europe, the agricultural transformation inherited from the previous centuries, and the slow process of industrialisation during the mid-nineteenth century produced an extensive surplus of population. The Italian migration scholar Ercole Sori[25] identifies the early nineteenth century as the historical phase in which the capacity of adaptability of the Italian economy to the growing English industrialisation was set, and during which the newly-born European capitalistic dynamics of production imposed processes of modernisation. This Italian capacity was extremely weak, especially within the agricultural sector: Italian agriculture was mainly extensive, based on the expansion of the lands to cultivate rather than on an increase of productivity. Such a rural system created a substantial immobility of the structures and the 'expulsion' of considerable masses of peasants from a permanent productive role in agriculture.

In addition, the European increase in population was the abiding element that accompanied changing economic and social patterns, and fuelled emigration. Between 1800 and 1900, the population of Europe rose from 180 to 400 million and, as a direct consequence, over the period from 1815 to 1914, some 65 million left Europe for overseas destinations, with the peak being between 1870 and 1914, when 35 million emigrated.[26]

The American historian Donna Gabaccia writes:

> *"Italian emigration was a by-product of complex and interacting economic forces unleashed by the political changes of unification. These included the new demands of the nation state for peasant taxes, the formation of a national market and the opening of that market to foreign imports, and - finally - falling world prices for important Italian exports, from wheat, wine and oil, to sulphur".*[27]

In 1871, when the first overseas census of Italians was held, 238,000 subjects were identified as living abroad, but, by 1881, they had already become over one million.

Italian emigration began in the northern and central provinces of the Alpine and Apennine valleys, where rural subsistence within extremely parcelised properties had always created harsh conditions. By 1870, international emigration increased dramatically because Italian unification had generated a wide range of problems, such as social turmoil in the countryside due to the establishment of new taxes. It was still economically useful for northerners to supplement their meagre earnings with temporary employment abroad. It is the mountain people of Piedmont and Lombardy, Liguria and Tuscany, who headed towards the close port of Genoa and spread mainly in the direction of American destinations.[28]

The passage from transportation by sail-ships to steamships in the early 1870s eased relevant changes in the world sea transportation business and contributed to dramatically reduced sea fares and, as a direct consequence, to increased overseas migration.[29]

The first migrants to leave were the northern and central Italian peasants,[30] already supported by a century-long 'apprenticeship' of temporary migration to neighbouring countries,[31] although from the 1900s, the largest component of Italian migrants would have been made by Southern Italians. While the average number of migrants per thousand inhabitants in Italy shows that for the period 1891-1900 the highest component of emigrants is still supplied by those coming from the north-eastern and central regions (12.94), while those from Southern Italy and Sicily are less (7.64), during the next decade (1901-1910), the situation is overturned: 21.65 migrants per thousand inhabitants in Southern Italy migrated against 17.98 from the north-eastern and central regions,[32] according to a trend which will remain unsurpassed.

ii. From the Unification to Fascism

It is extremely difficult to identify the wide range of factors effecting

Italian emigration since unification, even if we can contribute to outline the most important ones. The first factor was rural stagnation in most of the productive agricultural areas of Italy, together with a relatively slow and unsteady industrial development, generally confined within the northern regions of Italy. Secondly, and as a direct consequence, there was a generally spread distrust for the real capacity of the newly-unified Kingdom of Italy to spread social welfare so openly promised to Italians during the struggle period for independence. Thirdly, another cause of discontent - which prompted the masses to seek relief elsewhere - was probably taxes. In fact, in 1868, the national government provided for graduated taxes on the grinding of grains. It was called the *tassa sul macinato* (grist tax) which was especially opposed by southern Italians[33] who claimed it discriminated against them since it provided for higher taxes on the grinding of wheat, the staple food in the southern Italian diet. The work strikes of the 1880s prove how the situation had already reached socially dangerous levels, inducing many Italians to emigrate mainly overseas.

The emigration policy of the new Italian national state was born within the aristocracy lobbies, standing for a drastic opposition to mass emigration, and the unconditional support, offering a wide range of intermediate positions. Discussions on emigration offered different standpoints, swinging between the politicians who considered it a problem related to the social conditions of rural Italy - thus promoting its repression - and others - intellectuals and sociologists - who saw it as the best antidote to mend rural discontent. In this latter case, migration was therefore perceived as a kind of social 'safety valve'.[34] While Cavour, first Prime Minister of the Kingdom of Italy, had declared his favourable stand for emigration, after the first alarming census results of the early 1870s, the Italian government invited local Italian councils to monitor the flow and to rather discourage overseas emigration.[35]

Two main national economic debates arose during the same years from the migration process: the so-called *questione agraria* (the agrarian situation) and *questione meridionale* (the Southern Italian problem), which imposed a nationally-spread inquiry on overall

Italian rural conditions, with a particular emphasis on the southern Italian regions.[36]

Within the migration process, the Italian *Parlamento* (the legislative council) issued a *Legge sull'emigrazione* (Migration Act) in 1888, which still did not consider emigration as the effect of an unsolved 'social question'.[37] The law simply reflected the strong pressure of the lobbies interested in an ample de-regulation of the migration flow and of its wide process involved (migration agents, ship agents, and foreign governments interested in supplying low cost labour force).

It is only with the additional Migration Act of 1901 that Italy looked at its migratory flow and created a kind of 'safety net' for Italian migrants abroad. The law established stricter forms of control on the migrants' choice, protecting them from the illegal action of agents and intermediaries, both in Italy (from the villages to the ports of embarkation) and abroad, through the institution of committees of migrants abroad and the creation of a more capillary network of Italian consular offices. Rather than establishing a free migratory flow, as it was previously, the Act aimed to consider emigration as an element of national economic progress, thus requiring the action of the state against free economic market fluctuations. The Act of 1901, along with the dramatic increase of migrants, highlighted the 'question of the migrants' also within the Church. Thus, Pope Pius X established in 1912 a special Vatican office, superintending the international emigration of catholic people, and also the Pontifical College of Emigration in 1914,[38] although the migration problem had already been raised by the Bishop of Piacenza, Giovan Battista Scalabrini, who founded the Institute of Protection of the Migrants before the turn of the century.[39] As a direct effect of all of these concurrent interests of the State and the Church, even the International Socialist League adopted a strategy of 'conquest of emigration', resulting in an information and trade union education policy through the socialist newspapers and party activities across the major European migrants' concentration areas of Zurich, Vienna and Paris.[40]

As previously stated, between 1910 and 1914, Italian emigration reached a peak of almost 3,250,000 people, with an annual average of about 650,000 emigrants. After the migratory flow was interrupted due to the First World War, there was a period of economic and political adjustment to the new world system, which was redefining relations among nations, as well as a considerable debate on the concept of society itself. Among the European nations, Italy reacted to the new order by embarking on a strong nation-building programme and developing a regime that started depending on national exclusiveness. In a few years from the rise of Fascism, Italy proscribed emigration on the grounds that population was an important national resource.

iii. From Fascism to present

In 1922, the Italian Parlamento expressed its concern about the high post-war unemployment of one and a half million Italians, suggesting emigration as the only 'really practical solution'.[41] Actually, the Italian foreign affairs policy kept the same direction of the pre-war Liberal government. Until 1926, overpopulation was still considered a negative factor, a source for possibly dangerous social tensions and, consequently, emigration was considered a "physiological necessity".[42]

Only in the following years, emigration was perceived to be correlated with the demographic question in nationalistic terms, and as an excuse for the development of an Italian African neo-colonialism: the demographic "exuberance" of the Italian population became a reason to conquer new "vital spaces".[43] By 1927, the Fascist government virtually prohibited emigration, with stricter control concerning the issue of passports, permitted only in cases of existing contracts abroad or for specific call requests by close relatives abroad.[44] Freedom of movement was hardly compatible with a regime based on an orderly compliance, with a network of demands promoted in the interests of the national well being. In the mid-late 1920s, the decline of overseas migration was not the only outcome of a policy pursued in Italy. Migration had been caught up in the destabilising effect that had come to mark international relations. After the First

World War, there were also the first economic world crisis and the Great Depression of the 1930s.

The restrictions introduced by the United States in the early 1920s greatly reduced the number of Italians arriving there. Since the United States was the paradigm of Italian mass migration venues up to that time,[45] the halt was significant.[46] Furthermore, during the following years, Canada, Brazil and Australia - all other popular destinations of Italian migrants - restricted their intake of Italians. Thus, permanent emigration was perceived with a negative connotation, whereas temporary migration was still considered to be a source of supply of unquestionable economic advantages.[47]

As noted by Bosworth, "another Fascist preoccupation was to attach to the regime the 9 million or more Italians who lived outside Italy",[48] through the setting up of a widespread network of *Fasci all'estero* (representative offices of the Italian Fascist Party). The Fascist regime also increased the number of diplomatic missions abroad. Between 1928 and 1929, it opened about seventy new consular offices and sent more than 120 new Fascist consuls to missions around the world.[49] As a consequence of the Fascist policy, Italian emigration virtually ceased by the mid-late 1930s, leaving family reunion as the only option for migration. It was only after the Second World War that Italy saw a steady migratory flow starting again. For the majority of Italians, the end of the conflict raised the hope for a quick return to better conditions of life. During the late 1940s governments tried to repair the most pressing damage and to attain a standard of living that would guarantee a minimum livelihood to everyone.

The most serious and widespread destruction was caused by the movement of the war front and the retaliations imposed by the retreating German army. More than 2,000,000 rooms of civilian dwellings were destroyed in Italy, corresponding approximately to ten per cent of the housing space before the war. After-war production in agriculture showed a decrease of 60 per cent compared to that of 1938 and, in industry, the total losses corresponded to 20 per cent of all installations existing in 1939. In addition to this, a shortage of raw materials and foreign currency reserves made the Italian economic situation critical. Finally, as a result of the return of war prisoners and reduced economic activity, unemployment increased alarmingly, with over two million unemployed registered.[50] There was a large rural segment, parts of which were unproductive, and limited resources to absorb this workforce. The new direction thus left a surplus of population which, as in the earlier times, turned to emigration as an alternative to poverty. Emigration was manipulated by the Italian government as a "safety valve", in order to diminish pressure on the social structure, and thus avoid social conflict. It is not surprising, therefore, that, by early 1949, the Italian government had already planned the emigration of approximately four million Italians, resulting from the number of unemployed present after WWII.[51]

Since the early 1940s, leaders of the future moderate Italian Christian Democrat Party, which, after WWII, ran the government for the ensuing four decades, wrote that emigration was the best "vehicle" to eliminate economic conflict between countries, through a more equal "distribution of men on earth".[52] This view affected the post-war migration policy, easing a trend to endow the reasons of economic privatism, since the only criteria to establish the migratory flow lay in the "natural ways of spontaneous encounter between offer and demand", in the century-long combination of demand for labour and abundant supply of needy workers.[53]

It has to be said that transoceanic migration in the period after the Second World War became a more controlled operation, both in exit and entry, than its counterpart in the late nineteenth century, "In that it came to reflect the overall functioning of the world system and in particular the international economic system".[54] The Italian government estimated that an average of between 90,000 and 100,000 workers left the country from the late 1940s to 1962. "Learn a language and go abroad" was the slogan that the Italian Prime Minister, Alcide De Gasperi, kept on repeating in the early 1950s.[55] The surplus of population that had to emigrate came mainly from the rural background of southern Italy, because it was within this category that the highest rates of unemployment existed. Figures show that, between 1951 and 1971, Southern Italy lost more than four million inhabitants, in internal and international emigration.[56] Since 1945 to the early 1970s, emigration represented therefore the only economic safety valve of most southern Italian peasants.

Great Britain, France and Switzerland had recruited the Italian workforce since the nineteenth century and Federal Germany was added to them from the late 1950s. The traditional Latin American destinations remained popular, whereas quota limits restricted entry to the United States. Such restrictions pushed Italian migrants to search for other countries where to migrate. Hence, Australia and Canada became the major overseas destinations. Often, emigration was financed and strengthened by the migration chains of the communities established in the Americas, as examined in the Introduction. During the Italian post-war 'reconstruction', emigration facilitated the taking off of the national economy, through the absorption of millions of unemployed and the money remittances from abroad.

Since the mid 1970s, after a century-long emigration process, Italy has gained better economic conditions and is now a country of immigration, although there are still more than five million Italian-born migrants abroad.[57] In addition, there are now over fifty million people of Italian ancestry all around the world, giving to the Italian 'diaspora' a pivotal role in the understanding of world history.

HISTORICAL TRENDS OF ITALIAN MIGRATION

Mamma mia, dammi cento lire Che in America voglio andar[58]

("Mother, give me one hundred lira because I want to go to America")

As stated earlier, between 1861 and 1940 the total number of Italian migrants going abroad was about 20 millions, in a country which, in 1901, numbered about 33 million inhabitants. The first to leave were the peasants of the mountain communities of Northern Italy who went across the Alps to France - where in 1861 there were already 16,000 Italians residing[59] - and Switzerland. Well before the flow opened to overseas destinations, these first migratory currents represented an accepted means of subsidising the family economy as an in-built safety valve that was turned on and off and adjusted to the needs of each individual extended family,[60] employing migrants in a wide range of activities which contributed to the formation of the total family income.

Transoceanic emigration obviously required high costs and risks, hence becoming a real venture, involving tight family links that could supply the necessary financial reserves. The immediate effects of overseas emigration were therefore the strengthening of kinship links in the areas of origin, and of neighbouring proximity in the areas of destination.[61] Each village of overseas migration origin developed its own migration tradition. The Canadian historian John Zucchi states: "Steamships and labour agents and subagents, specific migration occupations and destinations, the fellow townsman who kept a boarding house in the target city, they were all part of the town's migration lore".[62]

The most relevant difference between overseas and European migration is that the first was characterised by a settlement, which tended to become permanent, whereas the latter often had a provisional character. In broad terms, and with the many exceptions to be explained further in details, it is said that nineteenth century Italian migration often involved a pattern of return migration, whereas, from the turn of the century, overseas migratory flows started losing this temporary component.[63] During the past century, the major aim of Italian migrants was to subsidise the family economy. Hence, the departure was pushed by economic necessities. From the turn of the century, migrants were stimulated by the intention to enhance their own economic situation, passing from the uncertainty and irregularity of unpleasant jobs to the comfort of higher stability.[64]

Seasonal migration was rooted in ancient tradition. Agricultural resources in the northern Italian mountain communities were never entirely sufficient to support the population: the soil was poor, and agricultural holdings were extremely fragmented. Some people migrated in winter - when agricultural work was slow - and returned to the village of residence in summer to work their own fields.

Having decided to migrate, the question is about the choice of destination. Migration was a way to exploit resources outside the community of origin. "In order to emigrate, people needed information on existing opportunities and access to these opportunities".[65] Both information and possibilities of employment depended on family and social relationships, standing between the individual and the wider society. In the north-western Italian communities at the turn of the century, these social relationships were generated by family, kin or social groups based on common interests. The ties between those who emigrated and those who remained "...provided channels through which a continuous flow of information reached a geographical area extending far beyond the borders of any given region".[66]

As previously discussed, this was the first pattern of departures and destinations of the 1870s. Emigration from Italy soon became a mass movement, almost a "flood".[67] While in the 1860s and early 1870s overseas migration was still an uncommon event, after 1875 it gained momentum. From the mid-late 1870s, an average of more than 100,000 Italians left the country every year. By 1887 the annual departures were over 200,000, in the 1890s they reached 300,000, and in the 1900s, over 350,000.[68]

Until the mid 1880s, most Italians left for South America (in particular Argentina, Uruguay and Brazil), but in the late 1880s an increasing number went to the United States. The main reason of this new choice was the changing geographical component of the origin of the flow: while the number of northern Italian migrants remained high, the one of southerners, who mainly chose northern American destinations (the United States and its eastern coast in particular), grew dramatically.[69] Also the occupational composition changed before the turn of the century. Italian migrants with agricultural skills slightly prevailed over all other occupations (including those classified as unskilled migrants) in the late 1880s: 115,147 coming from agriculture against 71,302 from all other occupational areas in

1887, passing respectively to 147,193 against 85,881 in 1888. Their percentage began to decline during the mid-1890s (112,447 against 135,248 in 1897 and, one year later, 102,735 against 140,760),[70] according to a trend which will show, from these years onwards, a larger prevalence of unskilled labourers going abroad, over the previously contingent of peasants.

From the turn of the century to the outbreak of the First World War, migration from Italy became almost an exodus, such that more than one third of all the expatriations during the period 1876-1975 took place during these fifteen years: about 9 million migrants, more than half a million per year, figures that doubled in the period 1875-1900. Destinations were mainly towards overseas, with 59% of the whole flow,[71] and the United States become the major host country of Italian migrants. Again, the choice of the United States as main destination was due to the growing importance of migration from southern Italy. Switzerland and France remained the first European destinations, demonstrating once again how the neighbouring countries of Italy were the favourite ones for seasonal migration, because of the proximity to the country of origin, thus making easy a periodical return home. After the First World War, the Italian migration flow was characterised by a renewal of departures towards Argentina and the United States, even if the latter country established stricter migration entry quotas, which were even more drastically reduced in 1924. Along with the mentioned restrictions adopted by the Fascist government, these two factors were conducive to a drastic decrease of migrants until the outbreak of the Second World War, although more than 3.7 million Italians were still able to migrate between 1921 and 1945.[72]

After WWII, migration from Italy took off again, even if the only overseas destinations were now represented by Australia (Table 1-2) and Canada, whose governments had embarked on mass immigration programs which were to change not only the countries' demographic and economic structures, but also their ethnic, social and, to some extent, religious composition and national economic structures. Latin American countries and the United States declined as preferred destinations.

Table 1-2 - Italian Migration to Australia

Years	*Migrants*
1876-1880	456
1881-1885	534
1886-1890	1,057
1891-1895	1,204
1896-1900	2,236
1901-1905	3,512
1906-1910	4,026
1911-1915	6,248
1916-1920	1,229
1921-1925	16,337
1926-1930	17,201
1931-1935	5,853
1936-1940	8,524
1941-1945	0
1946-1950	19,462
1951-1955	93,510
1956-1960	99,314
1961-1965	77,476
1966-1970	70,631
1971-1975	26,030

Source: Dept. Immigration, 1982

Other countries of heavy post-WWII absorption of Italian workers were those of the newly-born European Community, such as West Germany and Belgium. It was a sort of temporary migration flow of young males, who brought back to Italy a notable amount of money remittance. The new European host countries required a high turnover of workers,[73] since it was hard to migrate with the family or live in an environment, which was often socially hostile.

Between 1946 and 1970, more than eight million migrants, mainly from the central and southern areas of Italy, left the country. European destinations became so prevalent as to represent 74 per cent of the whole migratory flow between 1966 and 1970.[74] Still, a sort of equal distribution of the Italian migratory flow between overseas and European destination gained a hold upon the whole period, spanning from the first phase of gestation of Italian migration (mid-1870s) until its general decline (mid-1970s).[75]

DESTINATIONS OF ITALIAN MIGRATION

i. France

> *E fu lavoro e sangue, e fu fatica uguale mattina e sera, Per anni di prigione, di birra e di puttane, di giorni duri. Di negri e di irlandesi, polacchi ed italiani nella miniera, Sudore ed antracite in Pennsylvania, Arkansas, "Tex", Missouri.*
>
> ***Francesco Guccini, "Amerigo"***[76]

> *(It was labour and blood, hard work day and night, long years of prison, beer, prostitutes and hard days. Blacks and Irish, Polish and Italians in the mine, Sweat and coal in Pennsylvania, Arkansas, "Tex", Missouri).*

France welcomed more than four million Italian immigrants during the one hundred years of the great Italian diaspora, so that they have come to be the most numerous foreigners in the country. Italians represented, in 1851, 16.7% of all the foreigners residing in France, and the proportion passed to 27.7% in 1896 and to 31.8% in 1901.[77] Italian migrants living in France increase from 292,000 in the same year to 419,234 in 1911 and 992,061 in 1924.[78] Down from the mountains into the plains the current of Italian migrants proceeded towards France for a long time.[79] From the Italian Alps into the lowland has lain the way of the Piedmontese and their neighbours from Lombardy, Liguria and Northern Tuscany.[80] "Generally the lowland has been Italy, but more and more, for a long time past, it has been France".[81]

Later on the mountain peoples have continued their migration paths, but their numbers have increased and they have drawn from most of the regions of Italy. The migratory flow towards France had a twofold aspect. While the majority of Italian migrants was employed as labour force by the newly-born industry, on the other hand, a small component found its outlet into dozens of minor activities flowering outside the capitalistic production, such as travelling organ grinders, plaster-makers and sellers of alabaster statuettes from Lucca areas,[82] chimney-sweepers, shoe-blacks, etc. This latter component was undoubtedly pivotal for the creation of Italian stereotypes abroad, but also made the French authorities and public opinion realise the abundance of a low-cost labour force coming from Italy,[83] and useful to be employed for the economic take-off of the country. From the mid-nineteenth century, these itinerant activities declined and remained the last fringes of what has been called the "proto-history" of Italian migration to France.[84]

Between 1870 and the turn of the century, France received an average of 35,000 migrants from Italy per year, and the figures grew to 70,000 before the outbreak of the First World War. With respect to the occupations, the French census of 1926 states that 85.5% of Italians in France worked in factories, mines, commerce and in the building industry, while only the remaining 14.5 per cent was employed in rural activities.[85] As stated earlier, from the end of WWII, the flow towards France declined and other European destinations were preferred.[86]

ii. Great Britain

"Italian immigration into Great Britain has had a long and peculiar, if never a broad, development".[87] Since the thirteenth century, Lucchese, Lombard and Florentine bankers and wool merchants settled in England but - with particular respect to a labouring force - it is only in the early nineteenth century that the first Italians began to arrive, and were employed mainly in itinerant activities, as street musicians, pedlars and ice-cream vendors, reinforcing - as we stated for similar activities held by Italians in France - the stereotyped perception of helpless individuals to the limit of folklore. With respect to Great Britain, Foerster states:

> *"In no other country, be it said, for so long a stretch of time, have the Italians so generally been circum-ambulant in their trades. By 1750 certainly, the organ grinders had begun to come. Before 1800 monkeys had become the street musicians' adjuncts, and soon birds and bears were exhibited.*

Contrasting with the old barrel organ were, presently, the concertina, accordion, harp and violin".[88]

The number of Italians remained low for a long time when, in 1861, the first census with comprehensive information about foreigners was taken. In England and Wales there were almost 73,500 other-than-British European-born people, and Italians ranked fourth after Germans, French and Dutch.[89] In 1891, 19,196 Italians residing in Great Britain were recorded.[90] Italians were never regarded as a threat in any sense, because they did not compete with the labour market and they never reached the massive levels of other ethnic groups in Great Britain. Their presence, therefore, both in qualitative and quantitative terms, was sometimes regarded as "an odd curiosity, sometimes as a superficial nuisance; normally, however, it was ignored".[91]

Figures show that there was an increase in the number of Italian migrants during the 1910s, and a downturn from the 1920s until the outbreak of WWII. Italian migration to Great Britain reached its peak in the late 1950s, although figures show, once again, how the intake was considerably lower than those who chose Switzerland or Germany (46,057 migrants for the period 1956-1960, against, respectively, 422,756 and 158,009). Nevertheless, in the early 1970s, the number of people of Italian ancestry residing in Great Britain was calculated to be about 200,000.[92]

Until the mid-1880s, the bulk of Italian migration had headed towards European and other Mediterranean countries.[93] Since 1887 the flow started following a different path. During the early 1880s the main destinations became Argentina and Uruguay, whilst in the 1890s Brazil became more popular.

iii. Argentina

Undoubtedly, Argentina has been the first South American country to receive Italian immigrants, and the one that absorbed more. The first Italian migrants arrived in Buenos Aires in 1854 and, within ten years, Argentina had become the new homeland for more than

23,000 Italians,[94] who formed the most important foreign colony of the host country. While Italians calling into Argentine ports in 1882 numbered 29,587, three years later they were already more than twice this number.[95] The massive Italian presence was reflected in the 1895 census, where 1.7 million foreign residents were counted and 49 per cent of them were of Italian origin. Still, Italian migration to Argentina reached its peak after the turn of the century: 2.2 million migrants arrived from Italy between 1880 and 1922 and, in 1925, the Argentine census recorded the presence in the country of more than 1.8 million Italians.[96]

Italian immigration in Argentina in the late-nineteenth century underwent periods of highs and lows, but, nevertheless, after the weak flows of Italians until the 1880s, the arrivals from Italy became steady and grew unceasingly until the outbreak of the First World War. This enormous flow took place on the eve of a long phase of continuous economic worsening of production trade between the 'new territories' and the industrialised countries. These factors can explain the economic difficulties that many Italian migrants to Latin America faced despite their expectations, thus changing the attitude of the Italian 'migratory culture'.[97] As a result and through a tight network based on kinship, since the turn of the century, Italian migrants put more attention to the changes of the economic situation of the host countries as a factor affecting the choice of the destination.

Some scholars[98] stressed that the Italian labour force was induced by South American countries, such as Argentina, Uruguay and Brazil, to prop up - within an environment of heavy exploitation - the "...tired energies of a world growth model and development of international trade which had characterised the late nineteenth century". Such a pattern of Italian migration to Latin America is evidence of the role that Italian migrants played within the labour international market. Italian migration to Argentina saw more highs and lows between the two world wars. After the peak of 1923, with 103,845 Italian migrants arriving in Argentina, the 1930s registered a decrease,[99] due to the restrictions on emigration operated by the Italian fascist regime.

Immediately after WWII, the migration flow resumed so considerably that more than 274,000 Italian migrants are recorded arriving in Argentina between 1946 and 1950. From these year onwards, figures show a slow but incessant decline of the number of migrants until the end of the Italian flow in the late 1960s.

iv. Brazil

During the early 1890s, Italian migration, which had headed mainly towards Argentina, changed its route and chose Brazil. The number of Italians entering Brazil increased from about nine thousand in 1875 to more than 123,000 in 1891, and even more during the following years. They represented 57.4 per cent of all the migrants who reached South American countries between 1880 and 1904.[100] In 1910, the number of Italians residing in Brazil was over 1.5 million, passing to 1,837,887 in 1924,[101] with a bulk of 50 per cent living in the province of Sao Paulo.[102] Italian migration to Brazil is characterised by a strong compactness of the arrival time and, consequently, by a higher stability of the family and group links in comparison to other Italian communities abroad. The shorter migratory cycle, combined with the prevalence of male migrants from rural areas of northern Italy, soon joined by their families, is the main reason of the presence of such solidity of identity within the Italian-Brazilian community.[103]

The Italian migration presence consists of a flow calculated to be 1.5 million Italians who entered Brazil during the period 1876-1975. In 1902, the Italian government took drastic action to markedly reduce departures towards Brazil.[104] Departure to Brazil during the late 1890s had in fact assumed the form of a real mass migration, which preoccupied the Italian authorities and whose fear is reflected also in a popular song of 1899, which states:

Italia bella mostrati gentile
E i tuoi figli non li abbandonare,
Senno' ne vanno tutti ni' Brasile.[105]
(Beautiful Italy, just be fair,
and do not abandon your children,
otherwise they will all go to Brazil).

The biggest bulk of migrants arrived from 1888 onwards, after slavery abolition in Brazil, which required the owners of large coffee plantations of the region of Sao Paulo to attract their agricultural labour force from Europe with pre-paid transoceanic fares for north-eastern Italian peasants. The Veneto region and other rural areas of northern Italy were in fact the tanks which offered the main labour force for Brazil, as the name of many southern Brazilian cities still explains quite clearly: Nova Venezia, Nova Milano, Nova Padova.[106] Within the global economy, Brazil absorbed what the Argentine economic crisis of the early 1890s and the insufficient European labour demand had rejected, even if the Brazilian economic cycle turned down from the First World War onwards. Consequently, Italian migration to Brazil declined between the two world wars and had only a weak resumption after WWII, when a peak of 62,000 Italian migrants was recorded between 1951 and 1955.

v. United States

Italian migration to the United States dates almost back to the arrival of Christopher Columbus in late fifteenth century. "Between 1535 and 1538, we find six (Italians) from the Kingdom of Naples, two from Milan, three from the Kingdom of Sicily, one from Lucca, one Florentine, fourteen Genoans, one from Piedmont, and one from Cremona",[107] with no further details on their activities, presumably within trade and commerce. Though the number is low, it is worth remembering that foreign emigration to America was prohibited, and that these Italians represented exceptions. The first Italian workers to migrate to the United States were artisans (within the silk and glass industry), found among the early settlers in the English colony of Virginia in mid-seventeenth century.[108]

It is only after the end of the Napoleonic wars that the number of Italians departing for the United States slowly increased. The development of transportation by steamships, together with growth of the cities in the 'new country', and the colonisation of the Western States eased the crossing of the Atlantic Ocean, and attracted more and more migrants. Until 1850 Italian immigration had none of the marks of a mass movement. In fact, less than 4,500 were counted as residing.[109] From the unification of Italy, the number of Italians arriving in the United States kept on increasing,[110] starting consistent migratory flows characterised by the peculiarity of well identified 'skills' that Italians took abroad.[111] "Chiefly the arrivals were North Italians, and they included, besides traders, many Lucchese vendors of plaster statuettes and street musicians with monkeys - fantastic vanguard of the brawny army to follow".[112]

Prior to the 1880s, fewer than 100,000 migrated to the United States, coming from all parts of Italy, with a prevalence of northerners. Migration from Italy grew rapidly during the 1880s. The number who left the country increased, and so did the percentage of migrants who chose the United States as a destination: while 135,000 Italians went abroad in 1881, only 11,000 (less than 10 per cent of the total intake) left for the United States the same year. In 1901, on the contrary, 25 per cent of the bulk of Italian migrants opted for the United States.[113]

The majority of Italian migrants arrived between 1900 and 1914, with a peak of more than 285,000 being recorded in 1907.[114] While the first arrivals were mainly from Northern Italy and followed specialised occupations such as fruit merchants, barbers and plaster workers,[115] from the mid-1880s the southerners took over in most of the American urban areas where they tended to concentrate. The unification of Italy had brought no prosperity to the Italian South. Brigandage, poor land, tiny holdings and large families had made life harder and harder and pushed many to leave for a better life abroad.

Italian migrants in the United States did not follow the agricultural work patterns of many other Italians in different countries of destinations. Most of the southern Italians were engaged in gang labour in the excavating and building industry, and on the railroads,[116] such that they became best known as human steam shovels on railroad construction sites.[117] While the previous migratory flow had followed agricultural pursuits, the new wave of migrants was attracted by the large markets of unskilled labour tasks of the American cities of the Eastern States.[118]

They lived concentrated in peripheral urban areas, and the censuses of 1910, 1920, and 1930 showed that Italians in the major American cities had indices of segregation higher than any other immigrant group.[119]

The peak of the late 1900s remained unsurpassed. Because of the entry restrictions adopted in the early 1920s by the American immigration authorities, Italian mass migration searched for other destinations overseas. Notwithstanding, the intake of Italians remained significant for the whole period considered, with about 66,000 Italians entering the United States between 1931 and 1935, and a similar number between 1946 and 1950. According to the figures, a relatively higher peak of over 100,000 Italians was registered during the periods 1956-1960 and 1966-1970, even if the flow towards the United States finished shortly after the late 1960s. As a result of this massive migration, Italians residing in the United States were calculated to be about 3.5 millions already in 1924.[120] More recently, the 1980 US Census records the presence of 12,183,692 persons of Italian ancestry in the United States, rising to 14.7 million with the 1990 Census,[121] gathering under this classification the Italy-born residents and the Italian-American of second, third and fourth generations now living in the country.[122]

vi. Canada

The choice of Canada as a main destination of Italian migration began immediately after the Second World War. From the figures recording the intake of Italians during the period 1876-1975, it is evident that Canada was considered a land of good working opportunities only from the turn of the century. Still, during the highest peak of Italian migration (1900-1913), less than 100,000 Italians migrated to Canada. In addition, Canadian authorities tried by all means in the same period to discourage the entrance of migrants from Southern European countries, and in particular from Italy.[123] In the early-1920s, following similar dispositions adopted by the immigration authorities of the United States, Canada restricted entry to Italians. Furthermore, the economic depression of the early 1930s and stricter emigration rules by the Italian government sensibly reduced the Canadian intake of migrants. Since 1951, and until the early 1970s, a continuing high Italian migratory flow began again towards Canada, at an annual average of about 20,000, reaching the highest peaks in 1958 with 28,502 migrants, and in 1966 with 28,541.[124]

Italians, mainly coming from the southern regions of Italy, settled in Canadian urban centres and were employed in steel and food processing factories, excavating and building industries. Within two decades (1950 and 1960), the newly-arrived migrants from Italy outnumbered the older Italo-Canadians by four to one:[125] while there were 150,000 people of Italian descent in Canada in 1951, there were more than half a million by the early-1960s. Ontario has the highest number of Italians, with 63 per cent of the whole Italian-Canadian community.[126] In particular, Toronto has seen the presence of Italians raising from the 2,000 of 1900 to almost 20,000 at the outbreak of WWII.[127] Furthermore, in the late 1970s they number almost 600,000 within the larger metropolitan area.

vii. Australia

The most recent censuses showed that more than 250,000 Italian-born people were resident in Australia, and that the Italian language is used at home by half a million people in the country. These figures give some idea of the significant economic, social and cultural impact of Italian migrants on Australian society. Australia was not a popular destination for Italians during the nineteenth century. There were only about 7,000 Italian-born people in Australia in 1911.[128] Italians began to arrive in Australia in somewhat larger numbers in the 1920's, mainly because entry to the United States was virtually barred. Still, in 1933 there were only 27,000 Italians in Australia. As stated with respect to Canada, after WWII, Australia embarked on a mass migration program that was to change the ethnic composition of the country. During the 1950s, Italian migrants began to arrive in Australia at an average of about 20,000 per year, a flow that continued for the whole 1960s with an annual intake of more than 15,000 Italians. Finally, it decreased in the early 1970s, within the wider general phenomenon of the end of Italian emigration. Over

360,000 Italians came to Australia between 1947 and 1975, although about 90,000 departed making a net migration of about 270,000 for the whole period.[129] Italian emigration to Australia was heaviest and earliest from the northern areas of Italy,[130] such as the Alpine and Apennines areas of Lombardy, Piedmont and Tuscany. On the contrary, after WWII, Italian mass migration to Australia recruited labour force amongst migrants originally from the southern regions of Calabria, Sicily, Abruzzo and Campania, although there were still large contingents from Central and Northern Italy, particularly the Veneto, Friuli and Tuscany regions.[131]

The majority of the Italian migrants were from rural areas. Nevertheless, they soon concentrated in Australia's growing industrial cities.[132] During the 1950s and the 1960s, many of the Italian workers were directed into hard manual jobs in the industrial sector or on large-scale construction projects. Others were sent to economically strategic areas of Australia, such as the mining districts of Western Australia and the sugar cane industry of Queensland. While nearly five million people migrated to Australia and settled permanently between 1945 and the mid-1980s, Italians still represent the second-largest group after the British, a presence of more than 8 per cent of the Australia's overseas-born population.[133]

These general aspects of Italian migration to Australia - which can be seen as part of the more general flow of Italians to a number of major destinations during the period 1876-1975 - will be the focus of this work. In particular, the figures offer plenty of opportunities to investigate the historical background, the geographical distribution, the work patterns and, more generally, the social role of the Italian sub-regional group of migrants coming from Tuscany and settling in Western Australia, as will be examined further.

CHAPTER 2

THE AREA OF ORIGIN OF TUSCAN MIGRANTS IN WESTERN AUSTRALIA- HISTORICAL AND SOCIO-ECONOMIC CONTEXT

Alla fine di tanti guai,Un lucchese non manca mai.[1]

(On top of so many troubles,there is always a Lucchese).

INTRODUCTION

One of the main areas from which Italians migrated during the nineteenth century was, together with the Alpine mountain districts, the Apennines mountain area of north-western Tuscany, south of the Po Valley. This chapter will examine the historical and socio-economic background of the Tuscan areas that have seen a large migratory flow to overseas destinations. The goal is to analyse the factors that have affected such a high migratory movement of people, in order to see whether some of these historical and social reasons can be interpreted as causes for the specific spatial and occupational patterns that migrants followed in Western Australia. In order to do so, this chapter will first introduce the geographical setting of the area, together with its historical and economic conditions throughout these recent centuries.

The Tuscany region may be represented as a triangle, whose northern side follows the natural border of the Apennines mountain ridge, from the neighbouring Liguria region in the north-western sector, along the Emilia region border and down to the eastern side which divides Tuscany from the Umbria region. From here, the regional boundary follows the hills that mark the Lazio region to the coast. The third side of the imaginary triangle of Tuscany is represented by the 200 Kilometre coastline (Figure 2-1). While the hilly areas of the Arno River basin (which crosses the whole region from east to west) are the ones most renowned among tourists, several other territories and landscapes are represented, such as the coastal areas and the Apennine valleys. The latter represent a consistent portion of the whole administrative territory of Tuscany, running crosswise to the Apennine ridges.

Geographically, the point of origin of this study is the area at the juncture of the administrative Provinces (*Provincia*, in Italian) of Lucca and Massa-Carrara, both located in the north-western part of the region (*Regione*, in Italian) of Tuscany, and from where a large majority of Tuscan migrants to Australia originate (Figure 2-2). The two different administrative provinces (Lucca and Massa-Carrara) largely correspond to the basin of the rivers Serchio (whose area is called Garfagnana) and Magra (called Lunigiana), flowing from the Apennine ridges to the Tyrrhenean Sea. The two basins are mainly constitued - in their upper areas - by mountains rising up to 2,000 meters,[2] covered by chestnut trees and beeches and identified by cold, snowy winters and cool summers. The two valleys are, in many respects, 'mountainous', with uncultivable land, often rising straight up from the valley roads, with narrow side-valleys running through gorges up to high pastures; places which are fairly different from the well-known stereotype that many have of the Tuscan landscape. These areas follow a historical path similar to the Tuscan one, although they are distinguishable from it in some respects, like their economy and society and, consequently, the migratory patterns that developed.

Figure 2-1 - The Regions of Italy, Tuscany and the Location of the province of Lucca

Figure 2-2 - The Communes of Garfagnana and Mid-Valley of the Serchio

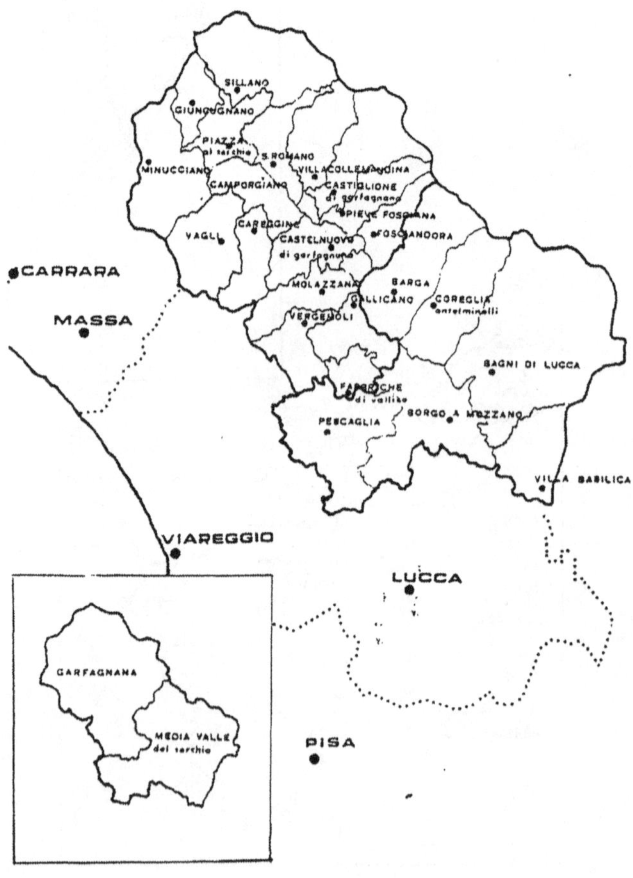

THE GEOGRAPHICAL SETTING OF LUNIGIANA AND GARFAGNANA

"La vita pastorale ed agreste degli abitanti di cotesta provincia, e fors'anche la geografica posizione, influirono sul carattere e sull'indole del popolo, ardito, fiero...".
Emanuele Repetti, Garfagnana[3]

(Pastoral and rural life of inhabitants of this province, and its geographical position, influenced the temper of the people, who are brave, proud...).

The Province of Massa-Carrara covers, almost precisely, the territory represented by the basin of the River Magra (1,662 kmsq),[4] better known as Lunigiana. The Lunigiana landscape is typically mountainous and variable. The complex geological and tectonic history has produced a heterogeneous landscape. The structural element is represented, on the northern part, by the ridgeline of the Apennine, which separates Tuscany from the Northern Italian Po Valley. On the south-eastern part of the Province there are the Apuan Alps, world renowned for the quarries of Carrara marble and called 'Alps', rather than Apennines, because of their geomorphologic aspect. They are a series of steep marble and limestone peaks, a smaller version of the Dolomites and nearly as popular with alpinists. The mountain slopes are steep on the Lunigiana's valley sides[5] of both the Apennines and the Apuan Alps, thus rendering agriculture impossible to practice over 500-600 meters of altitude. The valley develops for about 40-50 kilometres in the province of Massa-Carrara, whilst the lowest part of the river Magra flows into the Tyrrhenean Sea, crossing an area which no longer belongs administratively to the province of Massa-Carrara, but to the Province of La Spezia, in the Region of Liguria. The capital of the Province of Massa-Carrara, holding the same name (since Italian practice denotes the Provincial units by the same name as their main city and capital), is instead situated further south of the river mouth and near the coastline, adjacent to the Province of Lucca.

As stated earlier, some specific areas of the Province of Massa-Carrara have registered consistent migratory flows. Whilst the whole territory has been affected by the migratory process,[6] only a few *Comune* - corresponding to the minimal administrative territory in Italy, equivalent to a rural or urban municipality, (which, together with others, forms a *Provincia*) - record a notable presence of migrants in Western Australia, such as Casola Lunigiana, Fivizzano and Tresana. These communes are located in the highest and most eastern part of the basin of the River Magra, and in the vicinity of the Province of Lucca, thus confirming how the migratory flow from the Provinces of both Massa-Carrara and Lucca to Australia has common patterns. Consequently, the two areas will be further examined as if they were a single area, although they belong to two different valleys and administrative territories.

The Province of Lucca has an extension similar to that of Massa-Carrara (1,772 kmsq),[7] from the northern Apennines ridges to the Tyrrhenean Sea coastline. It corresponds to the hydrographic basin of the River Serchio, and this area, in its higher mountain section, is called Garfagnana. The basin occurs between the Apennines in the north and the Apuan Alps on the south-western side, with the River Serchio flowing crosswise, from north to south, into the open valley where Lucca - the capital of the Province - is located. As it is for Lunigiana, the River Serchio flows for about 40 kilometers in the highest and mountainous part of Garfagnana,[8] whose slopes are characterized by steepness,[9] roughness[10] and consistent chestnut tree forests.[11] South of Garfagnana, the river runs through a mid-valley and then through Lucca, before flowing into the Tyrrhenean Sea. Except for a few coastline communes -where sea activities have always absorbed most of the labour force[12] - all others have been marked by a century-long migratory flow.[13] The communes of the Province of Lucca with such a peculiar migratory process are the sixteen belonging to the Garfagnana area (Camporgiano, Careggine, Castelnuovo Garfagnana, Castiglione, Fabbriche Vallico, Fosciandora, Gallicano, Giuncugnano, Minucciano, Molazzana, Piazza Serchio, Pieve Fosciana, San Romano, Sillano, Vagli Sotto and Vergemoli), the six of the mid-valley (Bagni Lucca, Barga, Borgo Mozzano, Coreglia Antelminelli, Pescaglia and Villa Basilica)

(Figure 2-2) and five on the inland plain of Lucca (Altopascio, Capannori, Lucca, Montecarlo and Porcari). While each of these communes have some specific historical and economic aspects which could be worth outlining, for the purposes of the present work it has been preferred to consider all the communities as a whole territory, thus stressing the homogeneity within the migratory flow, rather than the differences.

These communes, along with a few from the adjacent Province of Massa-Carrara, constitute a homogeneous trans-provincial mountain area of Central Italy, characterised by age-long migration to many overseas destinations. This territory has experienced a common history since the Middle Ages, as well as common economy and society. Hence, for decades and even centuries, the word 'Lucchesi' (which, in Italian, literally means 'people from Lucca' and from its Provincial territory) has always had, abroad, the wider meaning of Central Italian migrants[14] and, sometimes, has even identified Italians *tout-court*.[15] These circumstances do not have an equal in any other Italian district, and thus deserve more careful examination.

THE HISTORICAL SETTING OF THE PROVINCE OF LUCCA

i. From Roman Colony to the Counter-Reform period

The history of the Province of Lucca is inseparable from both the history of its capital, Lucca, and its mountainous area of Garfagnana. As Wickham has shown, the real strength of Lucca was the city itself as the focal point for intra-urban social relationships.[16]

Lucca was founded by the Ligurians, a pre-Roman people, more than 3,000 years ago and its name comes from the Celtic-Ligurian root *luk*, which meant swamp, probably identifying the humid areas of the mouth of the River Serchio, where Lucca is located. It belonged to the Etruscan people and later (89 B.C.) became a Roman colony.[17] Part of the fortunc of Lucca is ascribed to its location, being at the crossroad of the Roman roads Aurelia (the road that led from Rome, via Florence, to France) and Cassia (the road that led from Rome to the north-western Alps). For a while, in the late sixth and early seventh century,[18] the road through Lucca was the only link between Northern Italy and Tuscany. Its importance grew under the Goths, and later on became the capital of the Longobard Region of Tuscia (the equivalent of present Tuscany). In 1186, its autonomy was declared by the Emperor, Henry the Sixth,[19] and Lucca and its territory then increased in political, economic and military power until the sixteenth century.

Lucchese interest and involvement in the valley was certainly linked to its roads, not only because of their intrinsic importance, but because the early importance of Lucca itself was very closely tied to its control of the Northern Tuscan road system. The northern and north-western European peoples found themselves forced to pass through Lucca in their trading routes towards Rome and Central Italy, thus coming into contact with Lucca and purchasing the products of the silk textile industry, which was flowering in the city since the thirteenth century,[20] such that it was called the "golden century"[21] of Lucca. The possibility to trade silk products resulted in the establishment of more than 3,000 looms in the whole territory: virtually every farmhouse in the countryside had some sort of silk-worm production and related looms. By the end of the conquests of the military leader Castruccio Castracani in 1328, the state of Lucca had extended its dominion to most of the territory of present Western Tuscany (Figure 2-3). It included a vast part of the Tuscan Apennines in the north, the middle and lower valley of the Arno River to the east, the inland areas of southern Tuscany in the south, and the majority of Lunigiana to the west.[22]

During this period, the first manifestations of the propensity of many Lucchese to look for new business opportunities abroad became evident. By the end of the thirteenth century, many businessmen were stimulated by the opportunities offered through the development of new markets in Northern Europe - France, England and the Low Countries - and expanded their trading organizations abroad through the establishment of little colonies of merchants from Lucca.[23]

Figure 2-3 - The Dominions of Lucca in 1328

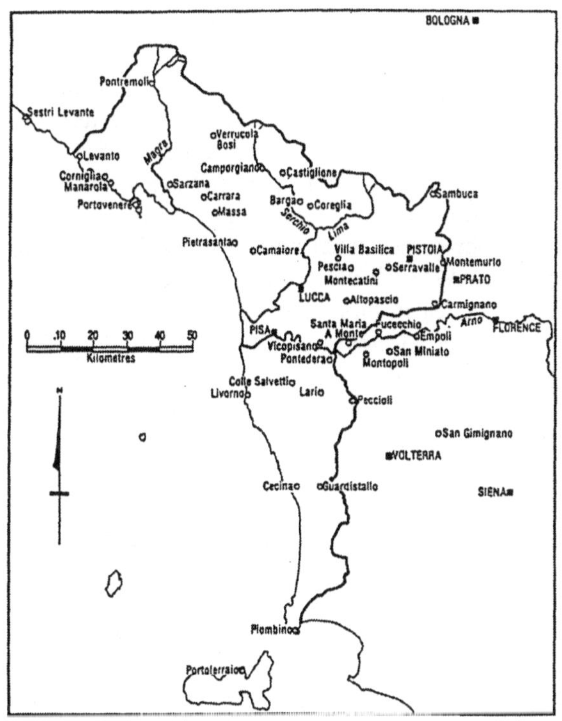

"The main point of contact between Lucca and the North, in the thirteenth century, was the fairs of Champagne. Merchants of Lucca had been visiting the fairs at least since the middle of the twelfth century, and some Lucchese appear to have settled in Champagne by the latter half of the century".[24]

The initiative and cleverness of the Lucchese merchants were renowned in most of the Italian peninsula and in Northern Europe. Citizens from Lucca are traceable not only in Sicily, Genoa and Venice,[25] but also in Antwerp, Paris[26] and England.[27] Their trade always involved some kind of temporary migration of merchants belonging to the most well-known Lucchese families. These traders, operating throughout Northern Europe, were at the cutting edge of Italian economic penetration, and their role was critical to the economic development of some European countries, such as England, in the thirteenth century.[28]

With respect to the geographical distribution of Lucchese merchants into foreign cities during the thirteenth and fourteenth centuries, some[29] have noted how they tended to concentrate in a few areas, whilst immigrants and merchants from other countries tended to disperse to all parts of host urban areas. Although an immediate explanation can be found in the professional homogeneity that characterized the Lucchese community, such clustered settlements were also adopted by people from Lucca in cities like Paris, where the range of their activities had a wider spectrum than mere silk trading. Such a trend may have played a pivotal role in the ensuing centuries, when a large number of migrants from Lucca moved abroad and kept, as will be discussed further in this study, their strong identity not simply as Italians, but rather as Lucchesi.

As reported by Pascal about the Lucchese merchants:

> *"Le grandi distanze, i pericoli dei viaggi e dei trasporti, sembrano quasi non esistere per questi intrepidi mercanti, che girano instancabili di citta' in citta', di fiera in fiera, cercando sempre nuovi smerci ai loro prodotti, nuovi campi alla loro inesauribile attivita', nuova gloria e ricchezza per se' e per la patria".*[30]
>
> *(Great distances and the danger of travel and transportation seem not to exist for these brave merchants, who travel restlessly from city to city, from fair to fair, always in search of new markets for their products, new fields for their inexhaustible activity, new glory and wealth for themselves and their homeland).*

This migratory flow did not appear yet as an exodus of craftsmen and labourers, as it became manifest in the eighteenth and nineteenth century. Nevertheless, within the establishment of small communities of Lucchese merchants abroad, it is possible to delineate some sort of a "paradigm of adaptability" to travel abroad, in search of better economic opportunities, which has characterized Lucchese people for generations.

The strong political and economic position of Lucca did not last, due to a number of factors. Local and international wars plagued Italy during the fifteenth and sixteenth centuries; new trade routes were opened up by the geographical discoveries of the late fifteenth and early sixteenth centuries; and the silk industry expanded in Northern Europe. These circumstances were conducive to the decline of the silk production, so that many merchants became bankrupt. At the beginning of the eighteenth century, the 3,000 looms, which were operating within Lucca territory, were reduced to 700 and, at the end of the same century, there were only 300.[31] According to the government of Lucca, the rural territory outside the urban area had always represented a natural "appendix" of the city, a sort of military and economic "belt" around its urban walls.[32] The countryside, and the wealth coming from its crops, became the best warden of the economic strength of the city.

It is said that mercantile activity in Lucca had been so busy and frantic during the fourteenth and fifteenth centuries that it had "absorbed" the most live and creative energies of the city and its territory.[33] When producers became unable to sell silk, which was a luxury product, and so found a crisis of overproduction, it became a natural consequence for Lucca to limit it. This limitation sent many producers and merchants bankrupt, but the biggest effect was felt in the territory external to the city, whose economy was dramatically impoverished by the drastic decrease in incomes once created by silk production. While the ensuing discussion will delineate the economic situation of Lucca on the eve of the large migratory flow of the nineteenth century, it is worth repeating that, at the turn of the sixteenth century, the rural areas outside the city of Lucca bore the biggest repercussions of the economic crisis of the city. During the same years, Lucca experienced a political crisis consequent upon the wider European scenario of a clash between France, from one side, and Spain and the Empire on the other; a clash which saw Italy as the main military battlefield because of the political division of the country into a large number of states. For the state of Lucca, the priority - and the 'nightmare' [34] - was to keep foreign troops away, and defend its boundaries.

In addition, there were also "enemies" within the boundaries of the city. The century-long presence of merchants from Lucca in the Northern European markets had exposed them to Protestant Reform, which flourished in most of Europe. As Le Roy Ladurie states with respect to the French merchants and artisans,[35] also in Lucca the diffusion of the reformed faith affected the merchants' families,[36] although there were also followers within the lower classes.[37] They had brought back Protestantism from their established colonies in Northern Europe into Lucca, which became one of the very few Italian geographical areas affected by the Reform movement. Although Lucca was within the political sphere of influence of the Emperor, and fiercely banned the Reform as heresy,[38] the diffusion of Protestantism into Lucca certainly contributed to the formation of a new ethic for the accumulation of money and savings' appreciation, which played a role in the character and life perception of Lucchese people.

ii. From the Sixteenth century to the Unification of Italy

In the late sixteenth century, thanks to the wealth of the State Treasury, Lucca literally bought its peace from the Emperor, Carl the Fifth,[39] with a decree that guaranteed the freedom of its Republic and remained virtually undamaged by the wars that plagued most of Italy. By the mid-seventeenth century, a new, powerful wall system around the city was completed: while the military defence of the city was deputed to the new wall system, the external boundaries of the territory were guaranteed by the Emperor's protection and by the strong loyalty of the country people. Such faithfulness of the country and mountain people of Lucca territory had been built during past centuries, with the establishment in the countryside of the silk-worm industry, thus giving some relief to the meagre incomes there - a fidelity which, in the ensuing centuries, would manifest in a strong Lucchese identity for its migrants (of city and countryside) abroad.

Because of the Emperor's protection and the walls' fortification, the Republic of Lucca always maintained its prudent policy of avoiding clashes and conflicts with neighbouring states, in particular with the strong Grand Duchy of Tuscany, to whom, in the meantime, it had surrendered part of its territories in the lower valley of the River Arno.[40] Nevertheless, Lucca emphasized the oligarchic and narrow-minded character of its ruling class. During the seventeenth and eighteenth centuries, the Republic was ruled by conservative politics, under the political influence of Spain and the Emperor.[41] Paradoxically, while Lucca was consolidating its political autonomy, by the end of the seventeenth century, it lost its economic prosperity, previously based on the silk industry. In this regard, while the economic conditions were tolerable in the countryside immediately around the city and the plain, they were unbearable in the mountain areas of Garfagnana. Although most of the upper valley did not belong to the Republic of Lucca,[42] there are records of a plague in 1632 that decimated the district,[43] and of poverty,[44] often conducive to incidents of crime. Hence, in the past, Garfagnana has often been nicknamed *Terra di lupi e di briganti* (land of wolves and bandits),[45] although, until the nineteenth century, these events were frequent all along the Tuscan Apennines ridges.[46] However, the absence of large feuds, and the discrete political autonomy within the area of Garfagnana, have always avoided the rising of social revolts in these mountain areas.[47]

In 1799, Lucca was occupied by Napoleon's troops and the Republic, including the whole territory of Garfagnana, was transformed into a Principality, held by the Emperor's sister Elisa and her husband Felice Baciocchi. The new dynasty tried to improve the economic state of Lucca, facilitating the exportation of olive oil,[48] which was one of the main agricultural productions of the Lucchese countryside, and to revive the silk industry, which had reached its lowest point. The city finally experienced some sort of rebirth. Its external territory gained some advantages via the increase in oil production, but the new wind did not last, due to Napoleon's misfortunes. During the Congress of Vienna, a political delegation from Lucca made every possible attempt with the European powers to save the autonomy of the city and restore the Republic.[49] Unfortunately, autonomy and Republic were incompatible to the eyes of the new great powers of Europe, which looked with suspicion on a Republican regime, sounding revolutionary after the post-Napoleon Restoration. As a consequence, participants to the Congress assigned Lucca as a Duchy to Marie Louise Bourbon.[50]

In a certain way, this decision relieved people from Lucca, who could still count on some degree of autonomy for a few decades. Until 1847, Lucca resisted being politically 'absorbed' by the dominating Grand Duchy of Tuscany, keeping alive its own political and administrative institutions, under whose patronage it grew for centuries as a peculiarly united society.[51] The economic and social order created by the Lucchese ruling class of merchants since the thirteenth century had sedimented in the century-long survival of the political autonomy of the State of Lucca. The political establishment was able to impose on the social classes, especially[52] in the countryside, a conservative model of lifestyle (represented by love for order, defense of property and pleasure for money earning and saving) as a perennial guarantee against social disorders. This lifestyle generated a sense of social stability and creating political consensus. With respect to the Lucca society of the 1830s and 1840s, the local historian Sardi commented:

> *"I malcontenti non mancavano [...] ma mancavano quelle cause per le quali il malcontento produce le reazioni che, alla loro volta, eccitando il risentimento e la volonta', costituiscono il programma di molti"* .[53]
>
> *(Discontent spread through the people [...] but there were not present the causes for which discontent produces the reactions that, raising the consequent resentment, are in the plans of many trouble-makers).*

The main concern of Lucchese politicians in their relationship with the rural territory outside the city walls became *la concordia*[54] (harmony), to preserve the general welfare (and the social order). Camaiani[55] observes how the nobility and the clergy of Lucca could still count on the strong and deep support of the rural masses, even on the eve of the unification of Italy. While the properties or rural masses were marginal in the mid-nineteenth century, due to the Napoleonic confiscation and the rise of the middle class, nevertheless peasants regarded the middle class as the *signori* (the lords), the trustees of the most respected (and conservative) values of moderation, such as the subjection to the authorities and social harmony.

This sense of moderation must have been present even in the twentieth century amongst Central Italian migrants in Australia, as the Australian economist McDonald states: "There was no sign of extreme, 'typically' Southern style, anti-social individualism in these areas. Yet, nor was there much evidence of economic behaviour in concert, outside the nuclear family".[56] As will be discussed extensively in the following chapters, these circumstances also have repercussions in the sense of identity of many of the Lucchese who started migrating abroad from the turn of the nineteenth century, possibly leaving 'traces' of them within the present communities of Lucchese abroad.

In 1847, the Duchy of Lucca was passed by the Bourbons to the Grand Duchy of Tuscany and, finally, in 1859-1860, together with the rest of Tuscany, it joined the newly formed Kingdom of Italy. From this date onwards, the history of Lucca becomes part of the history of unified Italy. Administratively, the Province of Lucca was formed in 1859 with 21 communes, which became 26 in 1865, including the mid-valley of the River Serchio, the inland plain and the coastline. In 1923 the Province of Lucca included also the communes of Garfagnana, the higher basin of Serchio, which had belonged to the province of Massa-Carrara since 1859.[57] The administrative composition of the Province of Lucca was completed in 1928 (as it is at present) when, due to the constitution of the province of Pistoia - located between Florence and Lucca - 10 communes, previously belonging to the province of Lucca, passed under the new administration (Figure 2-2).

These changes, which occurred from the unification of Italy in 1860, are relevant in order to understand which communes of the Province of Lucca were affected by the migratory flow. In particular, between 1859 and 1923, the 16 communes of Garfagnana, all affected by relevant forms of migration overseas, belonged to the neighbouring Province of Massa-Carrara. Garfagnana had been part of the Republic of Lucca until the mid-fifteenth century and since then it passed under the Este family of Ferrara (1452).[58] Later, this territory was assigned to the Duchy of Modena, in Northern Italy, which extended its dominion from the Po valley across the Apennines. Although Garfagnana has not always been under the political and administrative influence of Lucca, the upper-valley area of the River Serchio has constantly been under its cultural influence and, as such, it has followed the economic and social events of the Tuscan republic, migration included.

As stated earlier, other areas showing a high degree of emigration are the mid-valley of the River Serchio, which always belonged to the territory of Lucca, and its plain valley communes. There are also some neighbouring communes of the province of Massa-Carrara (Casola Lunigiana and Fivizzano), belonging to the valley of Lunigiana, where the migration rate was high. Due to their proximity to the higher Garfagnana, with which they share the same forms of rural society and traditions, they are considered here as part of the whole district, which is the object of the study.

THE HISTORICAL SETTING OF THE PROVINCE OF MASSA-CARRARA

The history of the territory now covered by the Province of Massa-Carrara has a path similar to that of Lucca until the twelfth century. From this period onwards, it differs. As the location of Lucca had a decisive role in its economic development, the location of Lunigiana, wedged between the north-western Italian coastline and the Apennines, made the territory sought after by the political powers of the Middle Ages. Such powers saw in the military possession of the district the chance to dominate the major part of the land communications between Northern and Southern Italy. While the low valley of the River Magra became a territory of conquest for the Republic of Florence in the late fourteenth century, the higher valley was submitted to the dominion of the Viscounts of Milano.[59]

By the early fifteenth century, the southern and north-eastern parts of Lunigiana (the mountain area neighbouring Garfagnana and corresponding to the present municipalities with marked number of migrants) passed under the possession of the Grand Duchy of Tuscany, while the western areas went under the control of the local feudal Malaspina family, and the north-western parts were owned by the Milano family of the Sforzas.[60] The Medici grand dukes of Tuscany slowly increased their presence in Lunigiana, purchasing the feud from the Sforzas with the aim of creating a contiguous territory within Tuscany totally under their control, a dream that never came true because of the political autonomy of the Republic of Lucca, squeezed and almost surrounded by the Grand Duchy of Tuscany.

After Napoleon and the Restoration, Lunigiana was handed to the Este Duchy of Ferrara,[61] until the unification of Italy in 1860. From this date onwards, Lunigiana has always belonged to the Province of Massa-Carrara.

THE ECONOMIC CONDITIONS OF THE PROVINCE OF LUCCA

D'indole tradizionalista, calma, fredda, Il lucchese bada ai suoi affari E cerca di far parte per se stesso. Il gusto dell'indipendenza si collega All'inclinazione al commercio; E i lucchesi hanno il genio del commercio.[62]

(Conservative, quiet, cold, Lucchese people mind their own businesses, And take care only of themselves. Pleasure for independence is linked To the inclination for trading; And Lucchesi are very smart in trading).

The historical outline of this area confirms how even the most secluded and distant mountain areas of Tuscany, away from Florence and the major urban centres of the region, witnessed the passage of military leaders and troops and were involved in events linked to the history of Europe. Many would be inclined to consider such districts destined to political isolation but, because of their strategic military position, Garfagnana and Lunigiana often became key geographical areas of conquest to many different political powers.[63]

Unfortunately, the same importance cannot be said with respect to the economy of the area. As stated earlier, since the thirteenth century, the fortunate geographical location of Lucca made the city renowned as a prestigious silk production centre. The ability of Lucchese merchants to sell their products all over Northern Europe facilitated the establishment of a network of looms for the silk industry within the rural areas of the countryside. The system produced a good socio-economic effect. The organization of structuring a wide circuitry of looms in the countryside,[64] in fact, permitted the Republic of Lucca to create a strong allegiance of rural population to the city, thus avoiding the risk of social turmoil and conflicts for many centuries to come. In addition, such a network relieved the modest economic and social conditions of the Lucchese rural territory.[65] The mountain areas of Garfagnana remained excluded from these forms of economic 'relief' offered by the city of Lucca, although the silk worm industry is recorded also in the upper valley.[66]

The geographic shape of the territory of the Province (once Republic) of Lucca, with a large extension of forests,[67] and tracks crossing the Apennine ridges, favoured since the Middle Ages the activities linked to such conformation. For centuries, it was possible to obtain firewood and charcoal[68] from the upper valley forests, from where the products were carried to Lucca and across the Apennine ridges into the Po valley[69] by the charcoal burners of Garfagnana. It is not a coincidence that such activity can also be seen as one of the first tasks performed by Lucchese lower-class people, particularly those from the mountain territories of Garfagnana (and from the nearby communes of Lunigiana with similar poor economic conditions),[70] in search of new markets beyond the boundaries of the Republic of Lucca. This process established a pattern of temporary migration and resembled, on a smaller scale, the search for new businesses operated by the wealthy silk traders of the city of Lucca.

It was also possible to gain the necessary energy from rivers and creeks to transform primary sources. Mills to grind cereals and chestnuts were, until a few years ago, the main forms of exploitation of the rivers' flow, up in the highest areas of Garfagnana. In particular, chestnut trees have been cultivated for centuries on the highest slopes of Garfagnana.[71] Until a few decades ago, chestnuts still represented the staple food of the populations of the higher areas of the Province of Lucca, as well of the whole Central Apennines district. For centuries, local historians and reporters to the city of Lucca have noted the hard conditions of the mountain people of Garfagnana, only partially relieved by the large supply of chestnut tree forests. In 1785 it is stated:

> *"E a quei generi di prodotti nostrali, che non bastano al bisogno della popolazione, viene abbondevolmente supplito col frutto de' castagneti, che vi sono frequenti, ma opportunamente distribuiti".*[72]
>
> *(Chestnuts, which grow everywhere and are suitably distributed on the territory, abundantly supply the other natural food products that are not enough for the need of the people).*

A century later, the social conditions of the most mountainous areas of Garfagnana were no better since in 1879, another chronicler wrote a report on the municipality of Fosciandora in Garfagnana and stated:

> *"Le campagne, fino a una certa altezza, sono fertili e producono, proporzionalmente, buoni e copiosi cereali, che non bastano pero' al consumo degli abitanti, i quali solo dalle vastissime selve di castagni, che ricuoprono due terzi del suolo di questo Comune, raccolgono il loro principale nutrimento".*[73]
>
> *(The soil is fertile up to a certain altitude and, accordingly, produces a large amount of cereals, which are not sufficient to the local sustenance of the inhabitants. It is only from*

the chestnut trees - cultivated on two thirds of the whole commune's territory - that locals obtain their staple commodity).

Such harsh conditions of the upper Garfagnana, which still have not always belonged to the Republic of Lucca, can partly explain the century-long search of its inhabitants for a better life through the long established pattern of temporary migration.

THE ECONOMIC CONTEXT

i. Agriculture

"...Lucchesia dai prati troppo umani".[74]
Pier Paolo Pasolini, L'Appennino
(Lucchesia, with your too 'human' countryside).

Since the foundation of the Republic of Lucca in the mid-fourteenth century, agriculture became more important than any other economic activity, especially in the mid-valley of the River Serchio and the valley around the city of Lucca. In the plain areas, agriculture was not very successful, because of the presence of marshes and swamps, due to the proximity of the two major rivers of Tuscany, Arno and Serchio. Nevertheless, agriculture was the only sector of the Lucchese economy that did not suffer any strong agitation or fall for centuries,[75] as occurred with the silk industry. This circumstance ensured an income, and even became a rural model to other areas of Italy, due to the continuous and passionate application of the "subjects" to this secure resource.[76]

While agriculture within the Province of Lucca created some sort of welfare, the same cannot be said with respect to the nearby valley of Lunigiana, now belonging to the Province of Massa-Carrara, where, until a few decades ago, the economic conditions of the rural society were harsher. The political and military history of Lunigiana was different from the nearby united Republic of Lucca, such to suggest that this factor was fundamental in its different economic background. However, Caciagli[77] notes how the presence of marble quarries, with a century-long tradition of unionised workers, and the closeness of Lunigiana to the large industrial port of La Spezia (belonging to the Region Liguria), along with its consequent capacity to absorb considerable contingents of workforce, have formed a different labouring class, less bound to rural activities. By the late nineteenth century, these activities, which were, and still are, present within the whole extension of Lunigiana, had already lost their primacy in the valley, in favour of a more diversified economy, unlike Garfagnana.[78] This partially explains how it is only in a few areas, specifically the mountain communes of Fivizzano and Casola Lunigiana, that we have evidence of agriculture and, consequently, migration patterns similar to the Lucchese. Such districts, located in the most eastern part of Lunigiana and near the communes of Garfagnana, have the same historical background as the Lucchese and as such follow the same trend of mountain-based social and economic path outlined with respect to the Lucca area.

In Lucca and its territory, the main agricultural productions were grains, olive oil and wine. While wheat and other grains showed some variations, due to episodes of famine during the sixteenth and seventeenth centuries, and have seldom been sufficient for local needs,[79] the olive oil production was steady and regular from the early fourteenth century, thus becoming the first and major product of the Republic of Lucca.[80] Olive tree orchards had been planted since time immemorial on the gentle slopes of the mid-valley of Serchio and the lower parts of the Garfagnana valley.[81] As such, the olive oil of Lucca was renowned worldwide, as it still is today.

The wine production of the Lucca district also offered good quality outcomes for centuries,[82] and vineyards were established even on the upper areas of Garfagnana,[83] thus reaching one of the highest points of its natural climatic distribution. At the end of the nineteenth century a minor production of hemp is recorded along the banks of the River Serchio,[84] and as a supplementary income for rural households. There are also records of its cultivation on the highest parts of Garfagnana.[85]

After the variable crop results of the late eighteenth century, due to climatic factors, the presence of an olive tree parasite, episodes of epidemics and the Napoleonic wars, agriculture finally experienced a period of prosperity. There are records of good, stable harvests from 1818 to 1850,[86] both in the countryside and in the mountain areas, where chestnuts had been the main crops. As an apparent contradiction, with the increase in the number of migrants who were leaving Lucca, with respect to the rural society in the 1820s and 1830s, the local historian Sardi states:

> *'Il lavoro era intenso e produttivo. La famiglia colonica era numerosa; moderata nelle voglie, non correva dietro al superfluo ma non mancava mai del necessario ed anzi viveva in una relativa agiatezza'.*[87]
>
> *(Work was intense and productive. The farm's family was numerous; moderate in its wishes, it did not run after the superfluous and had what was necessary; on the contrary, it had some economic comfort).*

The contradiction between such an idyllic representation of the rural society of Lucca and the growing number of emigrants from these areas is apparent. In fact, as will be stressed later in this study, other factors have affected emigration from these areas: factors which are not exclusively and directly linked to the economic conditions of the Lucchese area, as other authors have argued.[88]

ii. Pastures

For centuries the highest slopes of the Apennine ridges (called *Alpi* in Italian) have been used for pasture and mixed cultivation (Table 2-1).

Within the upper Garfagnana and the neighbouring highest slopes of Lunigiana, cattle, and particularly sheep, breeding have been established for several centuries, as a typical Apennine pattern that has lasted until the 1960s.

"Villages increasingly became communities of small cultivators, and shepherds were pushed into adopting the pattern of transhumance, whereby they moved with their flocks to the high grazing grounds of the alpi in the summer and to those of the Maremma (Southern Tuscany plains) lowlands in winter".[89]

Table 2-1 - Distribution of land-use (in sq. kms.) within the two major areas of the rural territory of Lucca

Type of Cultivation	Mid and Upper Valley of River Serchio	%	Plain areas	%
'Seminativo' (Ready to be sown)	1,156.79	18.42%	5,087.47	64.29
Wood	460.25	7.33%	1,160.11	14.66
Chestnut trees	2,888.15	45.98%	697.53	8.81
Meadows/Pastures	1,776.54	28.28%	968.45	12.24
TOTAL	6,281.73	100.00%	7,913.56	100.00

Source: Biagioli, 1975:207

Even in an agrarian report on the two areas written in 1883, it is stated that there were more than 50,000 sheep,[90] annually sold to northern Italian traders, and such to an "extraordinary" income.[91] The seasonal arrival of buyers from Northern Italy since the eighteenth century, generically nicknamed *lombardi* by the Garfagnana people[92] (presumably because they come from the northern region of Lombardy), suggests another opportunity of contact between the rural populations of the secluded areas of Garfagnana and people from other regions of Italy. This circumstance can be interpreted as an additional factor conducive to the migration of many from such areas. In fact, it must be stressed that until unification in 1860, Italy was divided into many different states and there were several political and social boundaries, language barriers and strict forms of customs within the country, certainly not facilitating the exchange of news among its inhabitants. Consequently, such contacts were pivotal to Lucchese migration decision-making.

In particular, the first Italian migrants who came in noticeable numbers to Australia, following the Victorian gold rush and, later on, moving to the Western Australian goldfields, were from the Northern Italy Region of Lombardy,[93] the same region that had established trading contacts with the Garfagnana mountain people. This circumstance suggests possible links and exchange of information between the pioneering stage of Lombard migration to Australia and the perspective migrants from the Tuscan area, which might have been conducive to increase the interest of Garfagnana people towards Australia as a migratory destination.

iii. Mining

The main products of the subsoil were, and still are, represented by the large deposits of marble of the Apuan Alps, located between the provinces of Lucca and Massa Carrara. Marble from Carrara has been extracted from the local quarries since Roman times, and has always represented the main economic resource of the area. Improved economic conditions of the area can be singled out in the increasing value of marble within the world market since the eighteenth century, as analysed by the Italian economist Gestri.[94] Marble production decreased during the late nineteenth century, mainly due to international customs wars that worsened work conditions, creating unemployment and consequently generating strong labour unions of left and anarchist orientation. The political background of Lunigiana can be defined totally different from that of the ‘peaceful’ Republic (and later Province) of Lucca, and such to generate a different attitude towards economy, society and emigration.

Notwithstanding the ups-and-downs of the marble industry, the unemployment rate since the unification of Italy has been considerably lower than in the residual mountain territories, thus presenting a related lower migration rate. For the period between 1898 and 1913 (the highest peak of Italian migration), Gestri states that there were substantial investments in the marble quarries located in the commune of Fivizzano, one of the few of upper Lunigiana from where a number of migrants moved to Western

Australia, such to almost double the work-force[95] and, consequently, to reduce the number of migrants.

These are the few districts where for centuries there have been enough employment to absorb the local workforce. Since the late eighteenth century, the dynamic process of industrialization linked to marble extraction involved Lunigiana and the coastal area of the Province of Lucca, generating a process of abandonment of rural activities.[96] This partly explains why the few communes of the Province of Massa-Carrara, which are located on the edge of the expansion of the marble industry, are those with marked migration rates, similar to those of neighbouring Garfagnana.

Other subsoil products were represented by deposits of iron and copper in Garfagnana,[97] that geologists and entrepreneurs tried to exploit from the mid-eighteenth century, although with marginal results, due to the harshness of the upper valley and the lack of durable roads to carry the products to the major centres. In addition, there are also records of minor deposits of gypsum[98] in the commune of S.Romano Garfagnana, of lead[99] (exported to England, by the end of the eighteenth century[100]) and silver[101] in the commune of Vagli of Garfagnana and, finally, of asbestos[102] within the commune of Villa Comandina, still in Garfagnana. As will be later discussed, the presence of asbestos in Garfagnana coincidentally (and tragically) matches the blue asbestos mines of Wittenoom (Western Australia) which, in the 1950s and 1960s, employed several Lucchese migrants.

iv. Industries

While it is common in Italian migration studies to deal with the agricultural background of the country of origin, little mention is made of its industrial activity. More accurately, we should speak here of a 'rural industrial' past. As a general type, rural industry was not, of course, 'modern industry'. Where the former existed side by side with agricultural production, was small scale and dominated by merchant capital, the latter is urbanised and based on economy of scale. While these differences existed, rural industry was the necessary precursor of the factory system and the urban industrialization, which in the Lucca area took place only from the 1960s.

Until the mid-nineteenth century, together with the silk industry, the production of chestnuts beams, tables and furniture was notable,[103] reaching its peak during the seventeenth century when many saw mills operated along the banks of the River Serchio. This was one of the typical activities of the Apennines people, as an integrating economic resource of the mountain areas, and partially reflecting the skills and the work patterns of many Tuscan migrants coming to Australia - as woodcutters - since the turn of the twentieth century. However, the saw mill industry of Garfagnana never went beyond the boundaries of the Republic, and remained confined to local trade and utilization.

A remunerative industrial sector was represented by the several iron factories that flourished from the fifteenth century. Iron was extracted in the mines of the Tuscan Island of Elba (Figure 2-1), carried to the Republic of Lucca and worked in a large number of small factories located in the mid-valley of the River Serchio, where it was possible to exploit the large supply of wood from the local forest and the powerful water streams. The iron factories supplied most of the arms for the troops of the Republic of Lucca and of other European powers. By the turn of the seventeenth century, as a consequence of the discovery of gunpowder, this sector declined, reconverting into a smaller-scale artisan production.

From the sixteenth century, an additional way to exploit the river's flow was the establishment of numerous paper-mills along the banks of the River Serchio, which permitted the growth of the typographic activities that flourished in Lucca.[104] This was such a profitable industrial activity that many paper-mills are still present in the Province of Lucca, although located now in the plain rather than in the mid-valley areas.

These were the strongholds of the industrial economy of Lucca at the turn of the nineteenth century, and at the eve of mass migration, although agriculture always remained the main resource of most of the population of the territory of the Republic.

THE ECONOMY OF THE RURAL SOCIETY

i. Peasants

Un campettino da vangare, un nido Da riposare: riposare, e ancora Gettare in sogno quel lontano grido: Will you buy...per Chicago e Baltimora, Buy images...per Troy, Memphis, Atlanta.[105]

Giovanni Pascoli, Poesie

(A small plot to dig, a nest to rest: to rest, and still dreaming and yelling: "Will you buy"...in Chicago and Baltimore, "Buy images"...in Troy, Memphis and Atlanta).

Unlike peasant life, there was a more uncomfortable economic situation amongst the *operai*, the labouring class of Lucca, its territory and also the nearby Lunigiana, as well as within the rural work-force situated on the edge of the agricultural production, the *braccianti*. They were farm-hands paid daily for their labour (the word *braccia* means in fact 'arms', the only tool most of these peasants had in order to generate an income), without holding or claiming any possession on the land. Camaiani states that the daily income of *operai* and *braccianti* in 1861, when Italy was unified, was hardly enough to meet their daily need of bread.[106]

As Moch states with respect to overall Western Europe, this brought a trend to proletarianization, accompanied by a population increase at the expense of the peasantry.[107] Many public works were not completed and many factories had to close, due to their incapacity to be competitive with those of Northern Italy, which had invested capital in modern systems of production. Hence, many labourers were made redundant, such as miners, stonecutters and bricklayers, who were already living on a day-to-day basis.[108] In addition, the building of a railway line connecting Lucca to Pisa and to the harbour of Livorno in the mid 1850s put in crisis commerce between the two centres, leaving a large number of labourers unemployed, such as those who relied on road activities, like carters, stable-men, sand-diggers and kilnmen.[109] While such a rural crisis initially affected more dramatically the mountain areas, Douki asserts that by the mid-1860s it involved the rural areas of the plains around Lucca, where the economic conditions were not so harsh as in

Garfagnana, but the birth rate had increased.[110] This explains why the migration rate from some communes of the plain has been markedly high since then. A necessary consequence was to search for remunerative working opportunities somewhere else, going *a opre* (a Tuscan dialectal form to mean 'to work') outside the boundaries of the Republic of Lucca and towards neighbouring countries, wherever and whenever there were seasonal job opportunities.[111] The Po Valley became a popular destination for centuries, absorbing each year at least 50,000 seasonal migrant workers from the surrounding Alpine and Apennine areas.[112]

There were specific times and destinations, as well as occupations, as has been first stated by Foerster:[113] woodcutters and charcoal burners used to set off for the nearby islands of Corsica and Sardinia, while herdsmen used to take their summer charges to the Southern Tuscany plains. There were also colourful migrants engaged as tinsmiths, masons, vendors of vegetables, and *figurinai* (statuette makers), as will be discussed extensively in the next chapters.

> *"These migrations differed in point of origin, destination, and profitability, but they had enough in common to be considered a distinct genre. They all required non-agricultural skills, were more remunerative than the seasonal migrations of shepherds, woodcutters and charcoal makers, and were temporary, itinerant and seldom purely individual ventures".*[114]

In addition, in winter there were peasants travelling outside the boundaries of the Republic of Lucca to undertake rural activities in Southern Italy, Corsica or the French Riviera,[115] where the climate was milder and they could be employed, while the first snows in Garfagnana interrupted any other rural activity. Furthermore, once migrants began to cross the oceans, whether they were *braccianti* (peasants) or *operai* (labourer), many of them, especially those from Lunigiana,[116] ended up working in the American factories or on railway lines. It is such a complex scenario of different forms of seasonal and temporary migration of Lucchese people of rural and mountain areas of Central and Northern Italy, to deserve more extensively studied in the next chapter.

The prosperity of agriculture during this period did not match with other sectors, such as commerce. The dynasties of merchants - enriched during the 'golden' centuries of the silk industry - had slowly reconverted their investments into large estates, in the rural plain areas around Lucca and in the most fertile slopes, along the banks of the mid and lower Serchio, with the confidence that the land would always produce a stable income. When, by the turn of the nineteenth century, Napoleon suppressed the religious orders and confiscated most of their land possessions, many of the estates, owned by the formerly rich merchants of Lucca, ended under the same measures. Consequently, by the 1810s, several estates were dissolved, divided in smaller parcels of land and later purchased by the emerging urban middle class[117] and by single, small savers.

ii. Mezzadria

Urban bourgeois invested in such properties and allocated a family farm under the agrarian contract called *mezzadria* (sharecropping). Under the classical *mezzadria*, the peasant cultivated land for a landlord - often living in the city of Lucca and using the estate as an investment[118] - on condition of receiving a share (usually half, *mezzo* in Italian, thus the word *mezzadria*) of its produce, the owner furnishing the whole or part of the capital required. The farmer and his family worked the mixed farm (cereals, wine and oil production) as a unit, and the size of the holding was adjusted and decided by the entrepreneur to the size of the family labour force,[119] according to parameters of land fertility, location and established plants.

Table 2-2 - Farms of Lucca and Tuscany run in Mezzadria (sharecropping system) per sq. Kms, 1936-1970

	1936	%	1961	%	1970	%
Province of Lucca	8,080	8.51	6,454	8.54	2,715	9.53
Rest of Tuscany	94,908		75,530		28,481	

Source: Cianferoni et al., 1991: 208

From the late Middle Ages until WWII, *mezzadria* was the main form of agriculture in a sizeable portion of the Italian peninsula. Its stronghold was in Central Italy - Tuscany, Umbria and the Marches - and the adjoining Region of Emilia, extending along the Po Valley

The sharecropping system has often been portrayed as an economy of subsistence, with sharecroppers growing the crops necessary to feed and clothe their families without resorting to the market. Paradoxically, Cianferoni et al.[120] observe that it was the peasant head of the family who had to adjust to the property's resource and not the opposite, a "...compromise between the former feudal relationship that tied the peasantry to the nobles, and the developing capitalistic relationship between a rural work force and an expanding urban-based bourgeoisie".[121] The larger the work-force the family could offer, the larger the property they were given to sharecrop. Accordingly, the harder the peasants worked, the more they were rewarded by the crop sharing. Hence, the relative convenience and welfare of *mezzadria* for the rural family, which led to a proportionately low number of migrants, as it created a social class that was less affected by the socio-economic conditions of the area than other farming and labouring categories.

In 1912, at the peak of Italian migration, the Italian agronomist Sanminiatelli states:

> *"Quando mi faccio a considerare il tenore di vita raggiunto dalle famiglie coloniche nelle zone toscane di mezzadria perfetta, quando lo paragono a quello, pur tanto migliorato in questi ultimi anni, delle classi rurali di altre regioni d'Italia e della stessa fertilissima valle padana [...] non mi so capacitare che, scontento d'un vivere materiale in genere soddisfacente e che sempre va migliorando, il guardingo mezzadro nostro voglia, arrisicando il bene, correr dietro ad un meglio ipotetico. E difatti, come le agitazioni agrarie sono state in Toscana episodi isolati, cosi' pure è lieve il contingente che la classe colonica da' all'emigrazione".*[122]
>
> *(When I think of the welfare reached by the sharecroppers' families in the Tuscan areas run under the mezzadria system, and I compare it to the one - although improved in these recent years - of the rural classes of other regions of Italy and of the fertile Po Valley [...], I cannot understand why, dissatisfied by a generally decent standard of living, our*

> *cautious Tuscan sharecropper should risk his welfare to run after an unlikely improvement. As a consequence, as much as rural riots have been very few in Tuscany, so it is low the number of sharecroppers who migrate).*

Although it is true that few peasants working under the *mezzadria* system in Central Italy migrated, more recent studies outline how migration might have played a pivotal role within such a land tenure system.[123] Migration became a 'safety' valve against the demographic increase: the departure of one of two members of the farmer's family could have guaranteed the subsistence of the rest of the family.

While many became sharecroppers after the land confiscation of the Napoleon period, other estates were purchased by single farmers. The size of such properties was notably smaller,[124] thus creating problems of insufficient economic sustenance.[125] In this latter case, in fact, some peasants, small traders or former craftsmen had sufficient cash to purchase a fraction of larger estates, to have them run by their families.[126] In his study on the Lucchese and Italian community in San Francisco, Cinel suggests that this process of buying land by a new class of owner-farmers may have been a result of the pre-unification seasonal migration of Lucchese to the Po plains, and also to some European countries.[127] Some migrants might have accumulated enough money during their seasonal migration to return to their community of origin and settle more permanently through the purchase of a land property. It is such a fascinating hypothesis of 'migration to return' that finds some confirmation in the migratory patterns of first-generation Tuscan migrants in Western Australia.

iii. Small land Ownership

This was the second system of land tenure used within the Lucchese area. The *coltivatori diretti* (landed peasants) owned and worked their own family plots. Because of their limited purchasing capability, the properties were often located in the less fertile areas or on the steep slopes of the Serchio Valley, thus limiting the crop production, rendering the land insufficient for the needs of a family.[128] Camaiani states that by 1835 more than 80 per cent of the rural households within the Duchy of Lucca (25,000 out of 30,000) were owned by this class of farmers.[129] Sarti[130] reports that in Garfagnana, with a population of about 40,000 souls, divided into 8,000 family units, there were in 1871 more than 6,000 landowners (Table 2-3).

Table 2-3 - Small landowners and sharecroppers in Garfagnana in the 1870s, per single municipality

	Small landowners	Sharecroppers
Camporgiano	133	386
Careggine	692	175
Castelnuovo	112	194
Castiglione	245	720
Fosciandora	374	8
Gallicano	350	87
Giuncugnano	42	33
Minucciano	290	55
Molazzana	82	152
Piazza Serchio	256	253
Pievefosciana	59	260
S.Romano	175	310
Sillano	1,000	21
Trassilico	216	322
Vagli	1,750	22
Vergemoli	130	25
Villa Comandina	237	114
TOTAL	6,143	3,137

Source: Distretto Scolastico Garfagnana, 1984: 137

This offers an idea of the very modest extent of most of the properties, and possibly of the poor quality of soil on the highest slopes, thus producing only subsistence yields, since the line of cultivation reached the uppermost line of growth.[131] Two consequences must be pointed out. Firstly, from an economic point of view, the picture is one of mere subsistence in a self-contained economy. Each peasant would draw from the small plot worked on a variety of agricultural products, so as to meet basic needs and those of the family. Secondly, in social terms, the result of cultural diversification combined with mere subsistence living conditions was an integrated and interdependent social structure characterized by stability and conservatism. This is not to say that there were no claims, no confrontations; but any antagonism would generally come down to conflicts among individuals and families, rather than classes.

As reported by Cinel with respect to an Italian national agrarian survey of the 1880s, one expert wrote to the Director of the agricultural committee in Lucca: "After trying to organize meetings in the evenings and visiting peasants in the fields during the day, I came to the conclusion that resistance to any kind of change is the very nature of these people".[132] As a brief consideration on the social attitude of the contado (the countryside) of Lucca, this diffused ownership certainly contributed to the conservatism of the Lucchese peasantry, already outlined in the previous sections, stressing the isolation and self-sufficiency of farmers' families. The lack of capital prevented small plot owners from investing and, consequently, improving the production systems, thus restricting the expansion of the market economy.[133] In spite of the strong social links of the Lucchese rural society, social isolation and sense of self-sufficiency are additional elements conducive to a general positive attitude towards migration in order to ameliorate the household's financial situation.

As previously stated, after the dissolution of the state of Lucca and the unification of Italy, most of these small land owners had to face the newly-imposed Italian tax system. In addition, the birth rate of Garfagnana and Lucchesia, which had been below the national average until the 1840s,[134] increased dramatically after the unification of Italy[135] (Table 2-4).

The Italian demographer Livi-Bacci, in his study of Italian fertility during the last two centuries, has shown how high was the marital fertility of the Province of Lucca in 1861. Lucca ranks as the sixth highest province (out of 73) of the newly unified Kingdom of Italy, with a marital fertility of 0.738, whereas the maximum value is represented by 0.763 of the Province of Sondrio (Region of Lombardy)[136] from where the first migrants to Australia are documented since the 1870s and 1880s. Hence the confirmation of high fertility rates are often in direct relation to migration.

Table 2-4 - Family composition in Garfagnana in 1871 per single Commune

Communes	Families	Inhabitants	Members per Family (average)
Camporgiano	452	2,603	5.8
Careggine	353	1,458	4.1
Castelnuovo Garfagnana	950	4,841	5.1
Castiglione Garfagnana	637	3,526	5.5
Fosciandora	264	1,503	5.7
Gallicano	625	3,211	5.1
Giuncugnano	175	1,086	6.2
Minucciano	545	2,500	4.6
Molazzana	436	2,378	5.5
Piazza Serchio	359	2,055	5.7
Pieve Fosciana	510	2,779	5.4
San Romano Garfagnana	355	1,787	5.0
Sillano	371	1,676	4.5
Trassilico	512	2,269	4.4
Vagli Sotto	498	1,772	3.6
Vergemoli	388	1,744	4.5
Villa Collemandina	572	2,171	3.8
TOTAL	8,002	39,359	4.9

Source: Distretto Scolastico Garfagnana, 1984: 33

The consequent need for greater food supply worsened the economic conditions of many *coltivatori diretti*, who were already exploiting their land to the highest degree.[137] Such land exploitation on the steepest slopes was evident through intensive cultivation[138] and the terracement of the parcels, as they are still visible in the upper Garfagnana[139] and in many other areas of the Apennines. As an obvious consequence, these lands were the first to be abandoned once migration to the bottom of the valley and abroad arose dramatically. The Italian agronomist Pasquali reported in 1922 about the migratory flow of small plot owners of the Province of Lucca:

> *"L'espatrio assai rilevante non dipende pero' di regola da cattive condizioni economico-sociali della classe e nemmeno, come pel mezzogiorno, da depressione dell'agricoltura locale, ma ha invece la principale ragione di essere in cause demografiche".*[140]
>
> *(The marked emigration is not caused by their bad socio-economic conditions and not even by the depression of local agriculture, as it happens in Southern Italy, but rather by demographic factors).*

As Sturino has shown in his case study of Italian migration to the United States,[141] the prevalence of land fragmentation was closely related to population pressure, but migration also reflected the inadequacies in the new Italian state's agrarian policy which, made the peasantry's life more onerous with the introduction of the hated *macinato* or grist tax.

Altogether, *mezzadria* (sharecropping) and *coltivazione diretta* (land ownership) were the two main land systems operating in Lucca[142] and Lunigiana,[143] although there were additional, but minor, forms of land lease.[144] The first system was prevalent in the fertile areas around the city of Lucca and in the mid-valley of the River Serchio,[145] whilst the higher slopes of Garfagnana were never reached by the century-long process of 'urban colonization' (as *mezzadria* was called),[146] and where direct ownership prevailed. In the late 1930s, land ownership was over 90 per cent of the productive surface in most of the communes of Garfagnana.[147] The Italian geographer Telleschi has pointed out that the high fragmentation of plots was conducive to the migration decision-process.[148] As a confirmation, in other areas of Tuscany where *mezzadria* was markedly prevalent, the migratory flow has always been very limited. Paradoxically, both land tenures were going to create economic instability within the rural class. While Cianferoni et al.[149] remark as *mezzadria* was a static land system, incapable of impressing modern dynamism into agriculture (although remunerative for the landowner), on the other hand, direct ownership had brought such a land property fragmentation to become inadequate to satisfy the farmers' needs, and to push many of them to migrate temporarily.

Rural populations chose emigration as an alternative to the old order in the area. As reported by Pugi, in a relation written by the *Prefetto* of Lucca (equivalent to a central state representative for such province) in 1881, it is stated:

> *"Coloro che partono non sono i piu' poveri fra i contadini. Si tratta generalmente di adulti che possono lasciare le loro famiglie in Italia, nella certezza che le famiglie possono tirare avanti da se' per alcuni mesi, senza di loro".*[150]
>
> *(Those who leave are the poorest peasants. Usually they are male adults who can leave their families behind with the certainty that their families can cope for a few months without them).*

Again, in 1922 Pasquali commented on the migratory push of Lucchese peasants:

> *"I contadini si muovono spesso anche quando le loro condizioni sono buone o discrete, con l'intenzione di migliorarle ancora"*[151]
>
> *(Peasants migrate even when their conditions are good, with the intention to improve them more).*

ASPECTS OF THE ECONOMY OF LUCCA FROM UNIFICATION TO PRESENT

> *Giovanottino, diamoci la mano Oggi e domani me ne vado via; E vado in un paese tanto strano. Chi sa se non mi moro per la via!*[152]
>
> ***Lucchese migrant song***
>
> *(Young boy, shake my hand; Today or tomorrow I will leave; I will go to such a strange country. That I might die on the way!)*

The mercantile "genius"[153] of Lucchesi had already been swept away at the turn of the eighteenth century. The decline of silk trade first, along with the Napoleonic land reforms and the political events later, which will cause the state of Lucca to merge into the newly-born Kingdom of Italy in 1860, were going to ordain the end of the century-long Republic of Lucca. A political decline, which was also, undoubtedly, economic. As reported by Cinel, Lucca was "isolated from the surrounding regions".[154]

One first component was the rise of custom fares operated by some countries, such as France,[155] where many agricultural and industrial products of Lucca were directed, since the rural and semi-industrial Lucchese production (olive oil, silk threads, marble) was directed overseas. French customs barriers were put in place during the first half of the nineteenth century and generated their effects shortly after. These barriers created an overproduction of crops and manufactured articles not otherwise saleable, thus affecting the rural world. In particular, after 1860, the demand for olive oil decreased as did the price, falling more than 36 per cent.[156] Many farming families had to cope with the difficulties of their small parcels of land,[157] due to their extreme division into smaller parcels amongst the numerous offspring,[158] and to fight in order to keep an income that, until a few years earlier, had been considered sufficient. Due to subsequent land divisions, in the late 1880s there was already excessive "pulverization"[159] of the properties such that, during the late 1930s there is a record of a parcel of land of one hectare in the commune of Minucciano in Garfagnana owned by 40 different proprietors![160]

As an established pattern of the century-long attitude of Lucchese and of many Apennines populations[161] of searching for new economic opportunities beyond the boundaries of the Republic of Lucca, migration became a viable option, and the number of peasants and mountain people migrating grew dramatically.[162] While the population rose and the properties became more and more fragmented, the traditional manufacturing activities used as economic relief, such as charcoal making, suffered from growing industrial competition.[163] Hence emigration abroad became more and more popular.

As reported by Dada',[164] scholars have already identified more than seven different steady migratory systems in Europe from the turn of the nineteenth century according to geographically different areas, one of which concerns the Central Apennines area of this present study. In spite of considerable differences of latitude among the European migratory flows, the drift of migrants is constant: from the mountains to the plains, following the natural boundaries of ridges and valleys.[165] As will be examined in the next chapter, the migratory movement of Lucchese had already begun on a small seasonal scale since the eighteenth century,[166] with a fluctuant seasonal population moving from the upper valleys of Garfagnana and Lunigiana towards the mid-valley in search of some employment in agriculture,[167] or to the plain and the city of Lucca.[168] After the unification of Italy, the customs war with France pushed the migratory flow to acquire higher proportions, becoming a mass migration[169] directed towards overseas destinations and, although temporary, for longer periods of time.[170]

With the unification of Italy, Lucca merged administratively into Tuscany and within the national economy. As outlined in the previous chapter, unification required severe forms of adjustment to the less economically developed areas of the country, and to the law and tax impositions of the central authority. This was an additional circumstance conducive to mass migration. As stated, the economy of Lucchesia (indicating with this term the plain and mid-valley areas of the present Province of Lucca) and Garfagnana was strongly based on agriculture, and, as such, it remained until a few decades ago. From the turn of the twentieth century, the whole area was only marginally involved in the process of modernization that took place in most of the economically advanced areas of Italy. The 'safety valve' of any economic instability was still migration and, as such, the Lucca area ranked, from the 1910s to 1930s, as one of the top ten Italian Provinces affected by the migratory flow.[171] Such a high mobility of peasants and mountain people raised serious concerns about social order within the government.[172]

The process of industrialization has slowly taken place since the end of WWII, first involving the city of Lucca, the plain area around the city and, finally, the mid-valley, which had been involved in forms of proto-industrialization since the early nineteenth century through the outlined presence of saw and paper mills. In 1951, the population employed in agriculture in Garfagnana was still 44.61 per cent, against the fall to 17.87 per cent in 1971.[173] By the early 1960s, the sharecropping system of *mezzadria* collapsed within the whole Central Italian areas.[174]

The 1950s and 1960s are the two decades that witnessed the highest number of Lucchese migrants going to Australia. As the local Lucchese reporter Rovai cites from the historian Manselli, "I Lucchesi sono pronti a partire oggi per l'Australia, con la stessa serena rassegnazione con la quale andarono a Bruges, Londra, Lione"[175] (Lucchese are ready to leave for Australia nowadays with the same serene endurance as once they headed to Brugges, London and Lyon). From the early 1950s to the 1970s, while many migrated, a large proportion of the active population of Garfagnana and the mid-valley of Serchio shifted towards the bottom of the valley of Serchio, towards the growing industrial sector (which recorded an increase from 43.98 per cent in 1951 to 56.54 per cent in 1971) and the tertiary activities of the city of Lucca and the adjacent areas (from 15.18 per cent to 27.10 per cent for the same period)[176] (Table 2-5).

While the mid-valley, and in particular the communes of Barga and Bagni di Lucca, have some forms of industrial presence and they still retain it with a large metal factory and a few paper mills, Garfagnana has developed a small-scale manufacturing industry only in recent years. Nevertheless, all the communes of both the upper and the mid valley of Serchio have been large sources of migrants for a long time and until the late 1960s, together with a few rural communes of the plain around Lucca (Capannori and Porcari in particular[177]).

The industrialization of the Province of Lucca, especially during the 1960s and 1970s, has been the vehicle of vital changes affecting the economy, society and culture of the whole area. The most immediate result of this deep change in the lifestyle of the many involved in the process has certainly been the end of the century-long migration process of Lucchese, according to a chronologically similar pattern that has affected the rest of Italy. The social and economic circumstances stated in the previous chapter with respect to Italian migration in general are similar to the conclusions that can be drawn for the Lucca area. Although the aim here is to demonstrate the specific factors affecting the growth of the migratory process which involved the territory of Lucca, the reasons for the end of the migratory flow lie with the process of industrialization affecting Italy since the early 1960s.

Table 2-5 - Population of the Communes of the Province of Lucca, according to various Italian Census data (1861-1971)

	1861	**1881**	**1901**	**1921**	**1936**	**1951**	**1971**
Altopascio	5,395	6,237	8,177	8,546	7,647	7,254	8,688
Bagni Lucca	11,394	12,518	13,685	13,926	12,064	11,567	8,153
Barga	7,830	8,560	8,100	10,158	11,708	11,770	10,959
Borgo Mozzano	8,467	9,284	10,352	9,315	8,037	8,406	7,785
Camporgiano	2,384	2,799	2,841	3,185	3,250	3,300	2,758
Capannori	38,352	43,673	48,217	41,828	41,033	41,874	41,403
Minucciano	2,354	2,790	2,816	3,620	4,432	4,334	3,227
Careggine	1,563	1,808	1,507	1,730	1,705	1,688	984
Castelnuovo Garfagnana	4,847	5,094	5,198	5,789	5,915	6,309	6,316
Castiglione Garfagnana	3,087	3,644	3,359	3,715	3,318	3,271	2,206
Coregli Antelminelli	4,668	5,197	4,871	5,434	5,716	5,564	4,940
Fabbriche Vallico	1,792	1,679	1,400	1,382	1,249	1,213	821
Fosciandora	1,496	1,554	1,502	1,452	1,370	1,296	862
Gallicano	3,879	4,361	4,027	4,649	4,801	5,145	4,398
Giuncugnano	1,102	1,229	1,162	1,254	1,174	1,112	697
Lucca	66,061	70,404	73,465	77,880	82,300	88,302	90,995
Molazzana	2,230	2,600	2,214	2,311	2,412	2,306	1,534
Montecarlo	3,309	3,787	4,478	4,658	4,298	3,834	3,300
Pescaglia	7,033	7,655	8,023	7,079	6,241	5,725	3,859
Piazza Serchio	1,953	2,309	2,393	2,915	2,938	2,984	2,673
Pieve Fosciana	2,566	2,941	2,591	2,861	2,911	2,999	2,492
Porcari	4,246	5,110	5,796	6,001	5,482	5,403	6,044
S.Romano Garfagnana	1,787	1,890	2,002	2,127	2,187	2,010	1,535
Sillano	1,951	2,132	2,379	2,228	1,902	1,598	1,032
Vagli Sotto	1,881	1,688	1,772	2,489	2,434	2,294	1,537
Vergemoli	1,909	2,071	2,213	1,844	1,448	1,282	736
Villa Collemandina	2,229	2,268	2,141	2,206	1,970	1,969	1,532

CONCLUSIONS

This chapter has highlighted the socio-economic background of the Province of Lucca and of the neighbouring communes of Lunigiana, which have witnessed large migratory flows to overseas destinations. The aim was to delineate historical factors which have affected Lucchese migration. There is a stress on these factors as possible causes of the spatial and occupational patterns of migrants from Lucca in Western Australia, as will be outlined in the next chapters.

As shown in Figure 2-4, a historical diagram outlines these factors in chronological order, and according to their classification as economic, political, religious and social. While the presence of Lucchese silk-traders from the fourteenth century has generated amongst Lucchesi an attitude to leave in search of better economic opportunities, and to become the 'paradigm of adaptability' to foreign environments, the economy of the Apennines mountains favoured the seasonal migration of woodcutters and peasants beyond the boundaries of the Republic. These temporary migrations allowed many of them to have contacts with other Northern Italian populations, and with earlier patterns of overseas migration, and to integrate the meagre incomes of mountain people.

The chapter has also stressed how it was not only a response to the ductility of the silk production economy, but also a strategy to generate the century-lasting faithfulness of the rural community to the central authority of the city of Lucca. Together with the conservative politics of the Republic and the presence of Protestantism in Lucca, these circumstances have certainly contributed to become interrelated factors of love for order, sense of stability and savings' appreciation. Factors that are intrinsically linked to a wider attitude which can be recognized in the migration's decision making process, as will be outlined more extensively in the next chapters.

Besides the historical episodes that generated such attitudes, the previous discussion stressed other more recent economic and demographic factors, which can be identified as conducive to the Lucchese mass migration from the mid-nineteenth century. They are the fragmentation of the agricultural plots of the upper and mid valley of the River Serchio from the early nineteenth century, the high fertility rate that was present in most rural areas of Lucca territory since 1840s, and more specific economic factors within the national (the introduction of the grist tax in the 1870s) and the international context (the establishment of higher customs barriers by France to limit the import of Italian agricultural products).

The next chapter will examine the main destinations of the temporary and permanent migratory flow of people from the Lucca area, and how these trends have been influenced by the specific Lucchese pattern of migration.

Figure 2-4 - Historical Factors that have affected Migration of People from Lucca (Drawn by the Author)

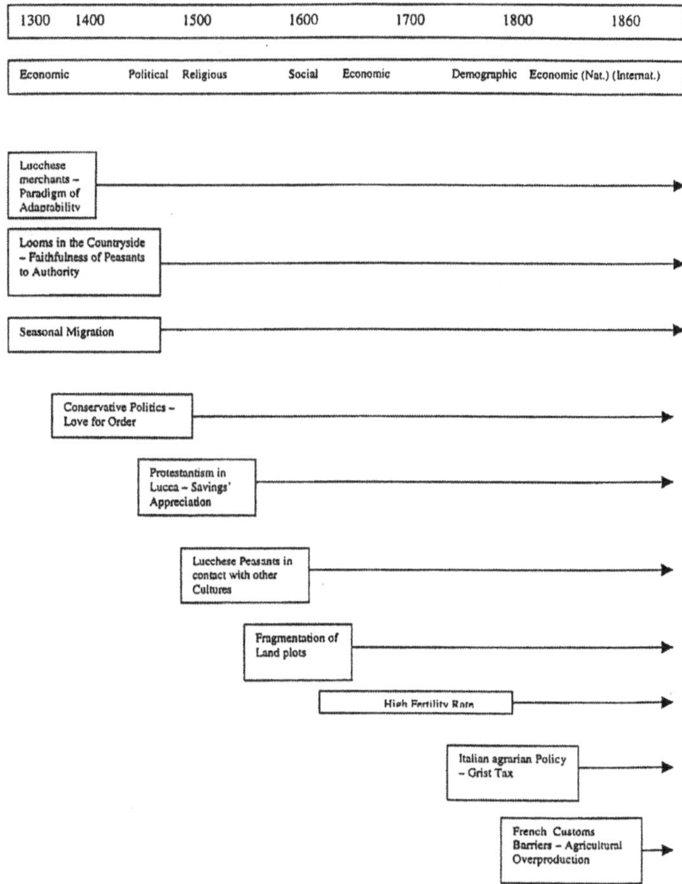

CHAPTER 3

THE LUCCHESE 'DIASPORA' - DISTRIBUTION OF MIGRANTS FROM LUCCA ABROAD

La Porti un bacione a Firenze, Io vivo sol per rivederla un di'. Son figlia d'emigrante,per questo son distante, lavoro perche' un giorno a casa tornero.'[1]

Popular Tuscan song of the 1920s and 1930s

(Bring a kiss to Florence, I live just to see her again one day. My parents are migrants, thus I am away; I work because one day I will come home).

SIGNS OF LUCCHESE MASS MIGRATION

In her analysis of the phenomenon of migration from Garfagnana and the Lucca areas in general, the Italian geographer Farnocchia states that, from the beginning of the nineteenth century, the area represents a "territory in crisis", the result of a long series of negative economic processes, amongst which the missed structural transformation of agriculture and the isolated position of the upper valley of Garfagnana appear the main ones.[2] Such isolation of Garfagnana has certainly contributed to its small-scale integration with the economy of the plain of Lucca and generated the migratory "bleeding" - although temporary at first - in search of better opportunities in other areas. Already in 1910, the Italian geographer Mori showed how Tuscan migration was in direct relation to altitude: altimetrical curves ran parallel to the curves representing the intensity of the migratory flow from these areas.[3] While the mountain communities of Lunigiana, Garfagnana and the Tuscan Apennines in general contributed to migration with a high number of workers since the unification of Italy, the hilly and plain areas of central and southern Tuscany presented minor contingents of migrants.

During the seventeenth and eighteenth centuries, which preceded mass migration from the Lucca area, many different social and economic factors affected the migratory flow, which reached its peak between 1870 and the outbreak of the First World War (Table 3-1).

As stated in the previous chapter, the unemployment rate, caused by the decline of silk production, the recurrent agricultural crises and famines within the Lucchese territory and the excessive splitting of rural properties were the main factors conducive to temporary and permanent migration from Garfagnana and the Lucchese countryside. The migratory experience of many Central Italian migrants, and Lucchese, began from remote and isolated areas and involved many members of the community. For example, in 1908:

> *"Molti di questi lavoratori, bisognosi di pane e lavoro, cominciarono da molto tempo indietro ad allontanarsi dalla casa natia portandosi ovunque."* [4]
>
> *(Many of these workers, in search of bread and working opportunities, began a long time ago to leave their home and go everywhere).*

The habit for temporary migration became, from the elitist experience of the wealthy Lucchese families of merchants of the Middle Ages, common practice among peasant communities. Prospective migrants did not leave at random: they received information from relatives and friends who had already expatriated and returned.

Table 3-1 - Migratory rates (for 1,000 inhabitants) of the Province of Lucca and Italy, 1876-1915

1876	11,80	4,02
1877	11,29	3,67
1878	11,61	3,27
1879	16,00	4,35
1880	15,68	4,36
1881	20,00	4,85
1882	17,20	5,69
1883	20,24	5,87
1884	17,74	5,06
1885	23,92	5,38
1886	25,04	5,71
1887	26,83	7,28
1888	24,23	9,79
1889	21,07	7,28
1890	22,00	7,19
1891	22,84	9,55
1892	20,77	7,30
1893	20,41	8,01
1894	16,58	7,26
1895	17,32	9,39
1896	17,90	9,79
1897	20,20	9,48
1898	23,50	8,92
1899	24,97	9,54
1900	25,94	10,95
1901	28,24	16,46
1902	30,74	16,30
1903	25,79	15,48
1904	24,04	14,27
1905	27,20	21,87
1906	31,50	23,58
1907	30,62	20,85
1908	21,57	14,39
1909	27,57	18,43
1910	28,13	19,04
1911	27,43	15,45
1912	29,44	20,31
1913	30,22	24,63
1914	17,11	13,36
1915	4,33	4,02

Source: Pasquali, 1922

They left with means sufficient to pay the fare, through some personal savings or the outcome of good harvests.[5] Most of them travelled with kin or compatriots, heading toward a destination where they knew someone who would help them, because "most migrants were neither rootless nor friendless".[6] Hence, these families and communities have maintained for centuries an economic and social structure almost untouched, due to the possibility of integrating the scarce income generated locally with the earnings gained outside of Lucchese boundaries. As the Italian economist Ottolenghi reported:

> *"Nella zona montana (l'emigrazione) e' quasi un'istituzione integrale dell'organismo agrario"*[7]
>
> *(In the mountain areas, migration is almost an integrated institution of the agrarian system).*

Migration became a stable pattern of the social and economic fabric of the area, generating the capacity of progressive uprooting from the community, due to the physical and interior habit of 'leaving' family and community links. Paradoxically, Dada' stresses the pattern of 'migration in order to stay', in order to consolidate the migrants' economic position within their community.[8] This pattern, peculiar to the mountain communities of Central and northern Italy, could be interpreted as a specific application of the 'push and pull' theory,[9] and labelled 'push-double-pull'. Within the Lucchese context, the generic elements of the economic 'push' from a rural area (such as poor agricultural outcomes, poverty, famine) and 'pull' towards another of better opportunities, play in favour of an additional 'pull' factor towards the community of origin when the financial situation has been consolidated with the work abroad. In fact, the constant aspiration of many temporary migrants was to extend their rural ownership or to finally become owners of at least a small plot in the country of origin.[10] Coming from an archaic society, in which economic relations were perceived as interdependent, rather than juxtaposed, and social values were a unifying rather than a divisive element, Lucchese migrants preserved a strong link with their valleys and the old way of life. As Camaiani has quite concisely stated, "the congenial outlet of a rural population demographically growing and loving the quiet living was but migration".[11]

Migration was partly facilitated by a cultural attitude, reinforced by the continuous presence of relatives and fellow-villagers abroad, and the relative ease with which itinerant people could envisage the journey. Furthermore, at the early stage of their settlement abroad, the link with land and communities of origin was to some extent functional to the very purpose of their emigration, and instrumental in the determination they consistently showed in maintaining an independent character and remaining aloof from the host society and its institutions.

Although many Lucchese migrants lacked any geographic knowledge of the places they were going to, the same cannot be said about their capacity to gain the maximum from the foreign environment they settled into, skills they had learned in a century-long habit of moving across boundaries. Hence, the proverbial astuteness of mountain people in contrast with a less acute city living life-style. As the saying goes:

> *Per gabbare un Garfagnino ci vuole tre Lucchesi e un Fiorentino.*[12]
>
> *(In order to cheat someone from Garfagnana, it is necessary to have three people from Lucca and one from Florence).*

FIGURINAI (PLASTER MAKERS) FROM LUCCA

Passeri e fiorentini sono per tutto il mondo[13]
Fifteenth century Florentine proverb

(Sparrows and Florentines are all over the world).

Braccianti and peasants, as well as particularly skilled craftsmen or simply vagrants, were the vanguards of the Italian migratory flow. In chronological terms, the first traces of a migratory flow of workers from the Lucca area are recorded in the sixteenth century. During the sixteenth century, "several dozens" of young men of Barga (in the mid-valley of the River Serchio), pushed by economic needs, enrolled as soldiers of fortune with the Florentine troops and participated in several battles in northern Italy.[14] Other forms of migrating workers from Lucca were represented by a marked number of families of vinedressers from the mid-valley of Serchio, who settled in the Island of Elba (belonging to the Grand Duchy of Tuscany) to plant vineyards in the early seventeenth century.[15] Since the seventeenth century, also woodcutters, charcoal makers and farmers began to leave Garfagnana in winter to go to Corsica (France), while *figurinai* (plaster makers) headed to France, England and Spain[16] for of up to 2-3 years,[17] called periods *campagne* (equivalent to 'campaigns').

As Sarti stressed in his work on a mid-valley community of the Province of Lucca, "whenever a community developed an occupational specialization, its practitioners would be forced to adopt an itinerant lifestyle because no single village could provide gainful employment for more than a few specialized workers".[18] This statement applies to the stonecutters from the Alpine villages of northern Italy, who were already well known in many parts of Italy since the sixteenth century,[19] as well as to the street musicians of the inner valleys of the Region of Liguria[20] and the Province of Parma,[21] and the itinerant booksellers from Lunigiana, who reached out to distant overseas destinations. From the fourteenth century, there are records of Lucca inbound migration from mountain areas. In particular, skilled blacksmiths from the sub-Alpine Province of Bergamo in the Lombardy region are recorded in Garfagnana, within the communal boundaries of Fabbriche Vallico[22] (where '*Fabbriche*' means factories), where they settled permanently and established a few flourishing iron factories, supplying lances and swords to most of the Central Italian states during the sixteenth century. These examples demonstrate how skilled groups or itinerant workers have been part of the northern and central Italian mountain communities for centuries.[23] Within the populations of the Alpine arc and the Italian Apennines, some have defined such itinerant activities as "national and regional professions"[24] because they characterized the origin of migrants as Italians, although coming from specific mountain areas. In the following centuries, at the time of street musicians and itinerant booksellers, the Lucchese *figurinai* (plaster makers) and their common regional origin were first noticed in the years following the end of the Napoleonic Wars. Sponza reports in his work on Italian migrants in Great Britain:

> *"London has been infested with ten or twelve lads (with dancing dolls), natives of Lucca...Lucca is also the birth place of most of those people who visit England to play the street organ, carry images, or attend dancing bears".*[25]

All of these activities required non-agricultural skills, were more remunerative than the seasonal migrations of shepherds, woodcutters and charcoal makers, and were temporary and itinerant. From the mid-valley of Lucca territory, and later from a few inland communities of Pisa and Massa Carrara, many young migrants moved abroad and overseas to work as makers of plaster statuettes. *Figurinai* were usually young males between 15 and 25,[26] who used to move in small groups of five to ten across northern Europe and, from the early decades of the nineteenth century, to overseas destinations (Table 3-1), bringing with them specific skills, and therefore less subject to the exploitation of intermediaries.

Table 3-2. Number of foreign passports issued to* Figurinai *in single Communes of Lucca, 1809 and 1812

	1809	%	1812	%
Bagni Lucca	40	11.43	92	22.44
Borgo Mozzano	54	15.43	52	12.68
Camaiore	0	0.00	26	6.34
Capannori	25	7.14	23	5.61
Coreglia Antelminelli	167	47.71	151	36.83
Fabbriche Vallico	12	3.43	0	0.00
Gallicano	10	2.86	0	0.00
Lucca	19	5.43	15	3.66
Pescaglia	23	6.57	51	12.44
TOTAL	350	100.00	410	100.00

Source: Lera 1986: 52

The art of making religious statuettes with plaster had been introduced in the rural areas of the Province of Lucca during the sixteenth century. These products created by local craftsmen became appreciated by the Lucchese authorities. Many of these plaster products, representing religious or political figures, were given by the state of Lucca to foreign sovereigns and were also sold by the Lucchese traders across northern Europe, generating the fame of Lucchese plaster makers abroad. Already in the mid-seventeenth century, a few *figurinai* from Coreglia Antelminelli (a commune in the mid-valley of the River Serchio) are registered in Rome working at the Papal court.[27] By the late eighteenth century, the plaster-making industry expanded in Germany, France and England. In the early nineteenth century, there are records of plaster-making companies formed by Lucchesi in several European capitals, especially in Paris and London (but also in Sweden and Russia), constituted not only by sellers but also by statuette makers. They were coming from the communes of the mid-valley of the Serchio River, and were still itinerant plaster-makers grouped in small numbers, heading for northern Europe in *campagne* (big 'tours' or 'journeys', taking up to 36 months). From the mid-eighteenth century, *figurinai* had become a familiar sight in the streets of London, Paris and Berlin. The journey on foot to Paris could take about one month, depending on the number of stops along the way, in accordance with the opportunities they had to sell their plaster statuettes at the local fairs. Other *compagnie* (literally companies) headed for more distant European destinations, such as Russia. In particular, in the early nineteenth century, a considerable number of plaster makers from Lucca were employed as interior plaster decorators in the wealthy mansions of Moscow and St.Petersburg.[28]

In their works on Lucchese plaster makers, the local historians Lera and Rovai state that the more adventurous groups of itinerant and more stable *figurinai* were in the vanguard of 'modern' Lucchese migration of the early nineteenth century[29] towards distant destinations such as northern Europe and America. The distinctive element of this peculiar form of Lucchese migration was by being organized in *compagnie*, in which the principal was at the same time owner and master of a group of four to six young men trained as plaster makers and street sellers.[30]

By the 1820s, there were already quite a few *compagnie* of plaster makers operating in Dusseldorf (Germany), Montreal (Canada),

New York and Chicago, Caracas (Venezuela), Pernambuco (Brazil) and New Zealand.[31]

The presence of economically established migrants from circumscribed communities of the inland areas of Lucca certainly played a pivotal role in attracting more migrants in search for fortune. As a primitive form of chain migration, many Lucchesi were called by their relatives and friends already settled in the host countries. By the mid-nineteenth century, and more rapidly after the unification of Italy in 1860, this peculiar form of skilled migration opened up new working opportunities to many inhabitants of the mid-valley of the River Serchio.

The unification of Italy and, consequently, the creation of a national market, broke the balances on which the mountain economy of the Apennines was based. In many areas of the middle and upper valley of the River Serchio, the revolution in the transportation system caused one more crisis to add to the economic turmoil outlined in the previous chapter. The role of the construction of infrastructure is pivotal to the changes that took place in these areas, both as attracting labour and as a means to facilitate the mobility of people. At the same time, the process of industrial and urban transformation widened the market of international labour, attracting a workforce for new building needs, rather than for artisan activities, which were slowly marginalised.

It is within this changing economic context that the tradition of Lucchese temporary migration continued, re-adjusting old skills and consolidating migratory routes and settlement patterns in the wider scenario of the host countries where Tuscan migrants were used to move. Since the turn of the twentieth century, some *figurinai* had already moved and settled in northern Europe and Scotland.

As previously stated, since the unification of Italy, new semi-skilled or unskilled migrants, such as tailors, shoemakers and bricklayers, joined peasants, *braccianti* and *figurinai* in their search for fortune abroad. This large number of migrants was often classified either as 'entrepreneurs' or 'labourers' by the Italian statistical and census authorities, thus showing their presence in the figures on occupations related to the Provinces of Lucca and Massa Carrara.

Table 3-3 - Occupation of Migrants from Tuscan provinces, 1870

	Traders	Profess.	Entrep.	Labourers	Farmers	Other	TOTAL
Arezzo	2	3	5	10	0	0	20
Firenze	116	67	82	207	521	98	1,091
Grosseto	0	2	2	2	3	1	10
Livorno	74	38	68	127	35	101	443
Lucca	25	20	998	192	1,166	178	2,579
Massa Carrara	20	25	101	671	628	21	1,466
Pisa	23	29	30	65	65	83	295
Siena	0	0	1	1	0	1	3
Tot. Tuscany	260	184	1,287	1,275	2,418	483	5,907
TOT. Italy	4,217	3,811	7,942	60,023	55,141	9,546	140,680

Source: Carpi, 1874

Even during the period 1921-1991, the number of activities performed by migrants of the Provinces of Lucca and Massa-Carrara reflected an occupational pattern similar to the earlier period, with a discrete presence of *figurinai* and semi-skilled workers ('traders/craftsmen') from the mid-valley, and a larger intake of generic labourers and farmers/peasants (including woodcutters) from Garfagnana.[32]

From this period onwards, the Lucchese habit of moving abroad in order to return with some savings to the community of origin opened the way to quite a migratory flow, which, within a few decades, will record such a high number of Lucchese migrants, equal to the total amount of the population of the Province of Lucca, going to Corsica and France, northern Europe, the United States, Argentina and Brazil.[33]

DESTINATIONS OF TUSCAN MIGRANTS

i. Corsica

Poveri, i lucchesi, piu' poveri dei corsi piu poveri, campavano con meno di quello col quale gli animali campano.[34]
(Poor Lucchesi, poorer than the poorest Corsicans, they survived with less food than animals need).

Since the mid-seventeenth century,[35] after the chestnut harvest in the local mountain communities in early Autumn, many men used to move down to Lucca and, after the necessary bureaucratic formalities, would embark for the Corsican port of Bastia. They worked in Corsica as soil-tillers, woodcutters and vinedressers from the beginning of winter until late springtime, when they moved back to Lucca. There are documents from 1642, drawn by officials of the Republic of Genoa (which owned Corsica at that time), asking the Republic of Lucca to inform its "mountain subjects" that in Corsica there were good work opportunities in deforesting and preparing the soil for cultivation,[36] according to the Genoese policy of increasing the agricultural colonization of the island.

Itinerant labour migration from naturally less productive regions to fertile valleys or easily tillable plains had been part of the Apennines rural life for centuries,[37] and, as such, the Corsican hilly territory became one of the most common destinations of people from Lucca and the mountain territory now belonging to the Province of Pistoia.[38] This occupational mobility involved an economic integration between the mountain areas and the most fertile valleys, drawing a complex network of geographical shifting labour force, and widely confirming the 'push and pull' factor theory.[39]

The opportunities were so good that by the late seventeenth century there were already more than 700 seasonal migrants from the Republic of Lucca working temporarily in Corsica.[40] The number increased during the eighteenth century, from 2,500 in 1760 and to more than 10,000 Lucchese workers by the 1870s.[41] As for the archive-based research by Dada', passports issued by the authorities in Lucca for overseas and, specifically, for Corsica, between 1805 and 1809 were as follows (Table 3-4).

There was a contraction in the number of temporary migrants in the early 1800s, probably due to the Napoleonic wars. Nevertheless, it was a steady seasonal migratory flow from the poorest areas of northern Tuscany to Corsica, which Dada' labelled as "an integrated labour-force market".[42] In fact, it was during the Napoleonic period, which brought an expansion in public works and a higher demand of labour force, that there was a consistent increase in temporary migration from the north-western Apennine mountains to Corsica.[43] Within specific archival research[44] for the same period, there are also the following records on one single commune of the Lucca territory, Pescaglia, in the mid-valley of the River Serchio (Table 3-5).

Table 3-4. Total number of passports issued for foreign destinations and for Corsica, 1805-1809

Years	Total	Corsica	% going to Corsica
1805	455	159	34.95
1806	1.636	242	14.79
1807	1.808	646	35.73
1808	2.186	661	30.24
1809	5.332	1.359	25.49
Total	11.417	3.067	26.86

Source: Dadà 1994

Table 3-5. Total number of foreign passports and for Corsica, 1805-1809 in the Commune of Pescaglia

Years	Men	Women	Total	Corsica	%
1805	95	2	97	84	86.60
1806	90	1	91	36	39.56
1807	61	0	61	32	52.46
1808	116	0	116	79	68.10
1809	168	3	171	99	57.89

Source: Tognetti 1993: 223

The first striking aspect of the above data is the very low number of women involved in migration, thus confirming how the migratory process from the Lucca area has been for centuries an almost exclusive male experience, aimed at quick earnings to bring back to the community of origin, where the rest of the families (women and children) were engaged in rural activities.

Comparing Tables 3-4 and 3-5, figures show that the local mid-valley community of Pescaglia had supplied a proportionately higher number of migrants to Corsica than the state of Lucca in general. This is probably due to the scarce options of foreign destinations available within the most internal areas of the territory of Lucca, suggesting how the migratory experience and related destinations were linked to the availability of local information within the rural communities. People of the rural plain surrounding the city of Lucca and those belonging to the upper-valley mountainous communities were more frequently in contact with other populations. The former were closer to the sea and to the bigger urban centres of Pisa and Florence (and consequently more in contact with foreigners and merchants), while the latter had established for centuries a wide range of contacts with traders of the northern Italian plains.

As a direct consequence of the spatial location of the single communes of the Lucca area, it can be argued that rural populations of the geographical 'edges' of the Lucchese territory (the plain and the mountain areas, where information was more widespread) were more accustomed to cross state boundaries and search for bread abroad. On the other hand, people of the 'intermediate' areas, such as those of the mid-valley of the River Serchio, initially stepped out of their own communities towards the valley and the city of Lucca, and only at a second stage would they set out for some selected foreign destinations.[45]

As reported by Foerster:

> *"Since the native population has no love for toiling in the fields, the sad truth emerges that the cultivation of Corsica is almost entirely the work of foreigners. If the help of the Lucchese and Tuscans were to fail, the position of this department would become truly critical".*[46]

The presence of migrants from Tuscany in Corsica is so marked that, for the entire nineteenth century, they represent more than 70 per cent of all the Italians working temporarily in the French island.[47] As reported by Carpi and calculated by Telleschi, in 1869 there were 8,373 migrants from Tuscany recorded in Corsica, and 4,571 (54 per cent) are registered as migrating to both Corsica and France. In this latter figure, 2,090 came from the Province of Massa Carrara and 1,235 from Lucca.[48] At that time Garfagnana belonged to the Province of Massa Carrara. It is evident that the real number of migrants from the Lucca areas is the sum of the two figures (3,325), thus representing almost 40 per cent of the total number of migrants from Tuscany in 1870 (Table 3-6). This high number of migrants, in comparison to the extension and the population of the province of Lucca (Figure 3-1), continued during the inter-war period,[49] thus confirming once again the necessity to study this migratory process.

Table 3-6 - Number of Migrants from single Tuscan provinces, split per urban/rural origin and gender, 1870

	Urban-M	Urban-F	% F	Rural-M	Rural-F	% F	TOTAL
Arezzo	11	1	9.09%	8	0	0.00	20
Firenze	200	73	36.50%	796	22	2.76	1,091
Grosseto	0	0	0.00%	8	2	25.00	10
Livorno	313	128	40.89%	1	1	100.00	443
Lucca	150	15	10.00%	2,329	85	3.65	2,579
Massa Carrara	131	6	4.58%	1,236	93	7.52	1,466
Pisa	93	31	33.33%	155	16	10.32	295
Siena	3	0	0.00%	0	0	0.00	3
Tot. Tuscany	901	254	28.19%	4,533	219	4.83	5,907
TOT. Italy	23,199	4,607	19.86%	103,632	9.242	8.92	140,680

Source: Carpi, 1874

Lucchese migrants in Corsica struggled and worked at the extreme of their stamina, always with the aim of returning to their communities of origin with the money earned. They worked long hours and lived in shacks on the fringes of Corsican towns and villages, with little or no interest in their dwellings, as the aspiration of money making and saving was stronger than any improvement in their temporary lifestyle.

> *"Svernavano nelle capanne e negli antri, dando la diuturna fatica alle opere di muratura e di legname, di abbattimento di selve e di bonifica di terre, di coltivazione della vite e dell'ulivo".*[50]
>
> *(They - the Lucchesi - spent winters in shacks and caves, working hard as bricklayers and woodcutters, clearing forests and reclaiming lands, cultivating vines and olive trees).*

Figure 3-1 - Migrants from the Province of Lucca, Garfagnana and Tuscany, 1876-1915

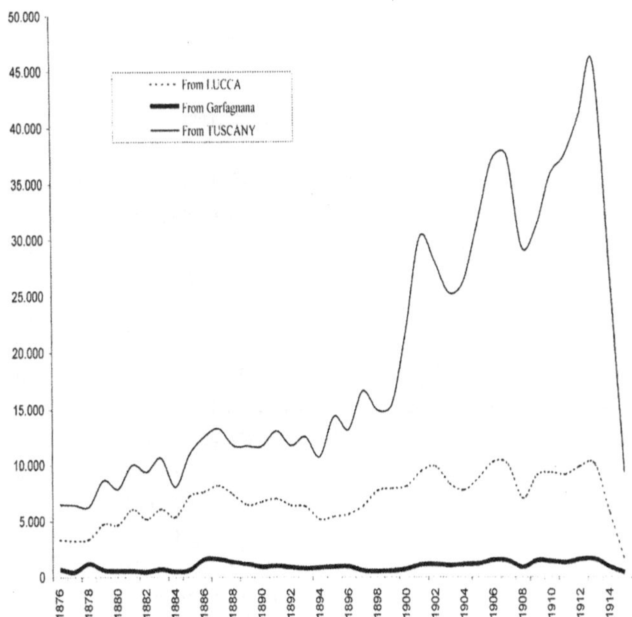

Source: Pasquali, 1922; Dadà, 1993

As reported by Pugi, Corsica owed to the Lucchese temporary workers the olive trees' pruning and manuring, and their harvesting and pressing.[51] While a few Lucchese settled permanently in Corsica, marrying locals and opening small businesses such as fruit or deli shops, the majority returned every year to Italy in late springtime, in order to attend to usual farming activities. Within the study on the Commune of Pescaglia,[52] these are the following figures on migration to foreign destinations in 1873 (Table 3-7): Although the number of temporary migrants going to Corsica is still high after the unification of Italy, America (namely United States, Argentina and Brazil), as a 'transoceanic' destination, appears as a new destination of Tuscan migrants, likewise the overall Italian trend.[53] With respect to the Commune of Pescaglia, it is only in 1893 that transoceanic destinations began to outnumber the European ones.[54]

Table 3-7. Total number of passports issued for foreign destinations in the Commune of Pescaglia, 1873

Total	Corsica	%	France	%	America	%	Europe	%
167	93	55.69	38	22.75	23	13.77	13	7.78

Source: Tognetti, 1993: 233

ii. From Corsica, France and Great Britain to 'America'

Ai nostri monti ritorneremo, l'antica pace ivi godremo.[55]
Azucena, "Il Trovatore"
(Back to our mountains, our steps retracing There, peace and quiet once more embracing)

By the early nineteenth century, other immediate destinations of Lucchese temporary migrants were the countries of the Mediterranean Sea basin, such as Tunisia and Algeria, where Lucchese planted the first vineyards and olive tree orchards.[56] Lucchesi also moved to the Provencal coast of southern France and the urban areas of Marseille, where they started arriving from Corsica, because of higher wages, increasing in number until the outbreak of the First World War.[57] As Lopez and Temime have outlined, few Tuscan migrants arrived in Marseille overland, through the Liguria region: the majority arrived by embarking in the Corsican port of Bastia,[58] following the word of mouth that characterized Lucchesi migrants in search of earning money. It must be stated that the higher intake of Italian migrants in France was also due to the abolition of the passport requirement between the two countries in 1874.[59]

Migration towards France not only involved single young men, as had been established in the pattern of temporary migration since the early nineteenth century. Many young women were required in the French urban centres as housemaids and especially as wet-nurses.[60] The healthy and strong Tuscan peasant women were particularly suited to breast-feeding, which was considered a debilitating experience for the young ladies of the French middle-class. The survey, conducted amongst first-generation Lucchese migrants in Western Australia, and whose outcomes will be amply discussed further in this thesis, collected memories of grandmothers or other older relatives who had gone to both France and Tunisia as wet-nurses, confirming that such information was not confined to isolated cases but rather widespread, as the Italian historian Adriana Dada' has pointed out.[61] This is an additional occupational pattern involving women which would deserve further research.

As noted with respect to the *figurinai*, there are also records of Lucchese migration to Scotland since the 1870s, when Glasgow had a flourishing shipyard industry.[62] This sector attracted a consistent number of Italian workers, with the prevalence of Tuscans from Lucca, in particular from the Garfagnana commune of Castelnuovo and the mid-valley commune of Barga.[63] With respect to this destination, immigration to Great Britain had been favoured since the last decades of the nineteenth century and, in particular, since the liberal policy in the 1910s, until the Work Permit Act (1919), which noticeably reduced the intake of migrants in order to restrict the massive migratory flow towards Great Britain.[64]

Until the 1880s, none of the common destinations of Tuscan migrants were considered especially alluring. None became myths similar to that surrounding 'America' that emerged in the last decades of the nineteenth century.[65] As Cinel reports from a relation of the *Prefetto* of Lucca, "most emigrants still go to France and Sardinia; but these places do not attract as many as before. Yet these people need outside income to survive. Lately, emigration to South America has increased, and I believe it is a consequence of the declining opportunities in Europe".[66]

By the first decades of the twentieth century, the steady and century-long migration flow towards Corsica had involved the whole basin of the River Serchio and, in some cases, had transformed from temporary to permanent. As Rovai reports:

> *"Talune delle vie che i nostri campagnoli, e specialmente i nostri montanari, seguirono erano gia' tracciate da secoli, ma altre essi ne tentarono fino oltre oceano".*[67]

> *(Some of the tracks that our peasants and mountain people followed had already been beaten for centuries, but others overseas were all new to them).*

Migrants from Tuscany who moved from Garfagnana or upper Lunigiana to Corsica and, later on, to Brazil and the United States, lacked the minds of geographers or the instruments of land surveyors- they did not measure distance. Nor, as Hoerder stresses,[68] did they consciously move between nations. They did not travel from the newly unified Italy to the United States, but from a community town of Garfagnana either to 'America' or, for example, to another urban community of Lucchese fruit sellers in Chicago, following mental maps of life-course development across space. As a confirmation, some Tuscan-Australian interviewees stated that their parents or grandparents were talking of Australia as *America lunga* (literally 'long America', but more precisely, 'a distant America'), with little or absolutely no knowledge of its geographic location. As there was an *America lunga*, so there was also an *America bona* (a 'good' America), to distinguish the United States from the *America non bona* (the 'not-good' America), the Latin American countries, because of the sad experiences of non-return, little luck and sometimes poverty of many migrants to Argentina and Brazil in particular.[69]

They also reported that until the late 1930s it was common that those who remained in the community villages labelled the community fellows, who migrated to either the United States or Australia, as gli *Americani* (the Americans). As Sturino reports with respect to a Southern Italian community in the United States, "The American dream was a dream of success".[70]

In 1908, when Italian and Tuscan migration to transatlantic countries outnumbered the European destinations, the *Prefettura* (the body of the Italian central administration located in each *Provincia* of the country) sent out a questionnaire to all the communes of the Province of Lucca in order to collect information and figures on migration. Among the many outcomes of the survey, Tognetti[71] stated that the average stay of migrants in the United

States was between five and ten years, and that about 90 per cent of the returnees migrate again within one year from their return to the communities. Hence, this is an additional confirmation of the temporary character of Tuscan overseas migration, and of its push-double-pull characteristic, that has played such an important role in establishing the Tuscan community in Australia. In another report on migration from Garfagnana in 1938, the following is stated with respect to the character of migrants:

> *"Raramente gli emigranti hanno dimenticato il loro paese. Gente di grande parsimonia e con uno spiccatissimo senso di risparmio, dopo aver raccolto talvolta con gravi stenti e privazioni un piccolo capitale preferirono ritornarsene alla loro terra".*[72]
>
> *(Migrants seldom forget their land. They are thrifty and have a great saving-power; after having collected a small capital abroad, often with efforts and privations, they prefer to come back to their homeland).*

Observers often noted that migrants returning from abroad had "enough money to buy some land and a house and get married", as Sarti also stated in his study of a Lucchese mountain community.[73] These impressions played a central role in the increasing "migrant fever" which sometimes became a frantic push, although related to problems of economic subsistence, as in the following report on Tuscan migration:

> *"Non senza ragione ho distinto, dandogli una egual quota d'influenza su l'emigrazione, il desiderio di far fortuna da quello della avventura e della intraprendenza, assai meno calcolatori, piu' geniali e piu' incerti. Non alla spinta della miseria, ma piu' spesso all'avidita' o ad una ferma volonta' di migliorare le proprie condizioni si deve questa forma dell'emigrazione"*[74]
>
> *(As migration factors, I enumerate with equal value the longing for money, the spirit of adventure and of enterprise; migrants are less careful and rather more clever and uncertain. They are not pushed by poverty, but often by either greediness or a firm will to improve their conditions).*

This "greediness" recalls the century-long tradition of conservatism and appreciation for money accumulation, which has played such an important role within *Lucchese* society.

iii. Argentina and Brazil

> *Weeping you watch the wretched emigrants They believe in God they pray The women suckle their infants They fill with their smell the station of Saint-Lazare Like the wise men from the east They have faith in their star They hope to prosper in the Argentine And to come home having made their fortune.*[75]

The number of migrants who left Italy for foreign destinations is over 16 million for the period 1876-1925. A large part of those who migrated overseas chose Argentina as their final destination, so that by 1840 a notable number of Italian workers are already recorded as being settled in Buenos Aires.[76] Unlike this general Italian migration trend, Tuscans and Lucchesi preferred Brazil as their main destination instead of Argentina.

Argentinean agricultural development took place in the 1870s, requiring a large intake of migrants to cultivate the land. As a consequence, Argentina witnessed the arrival of almost two million Italians[77] who, within a few decades, changed the Argentinean economy and society. Although considerable, the number of Tuscans and Lucchesi who participated in this major change of the country was lower than those who had moved to neighbouring Brazil.

Within the territory of Lucca and Garfagnana, the first sporadic moves towards Brazil began around the mid-nineteenth century, with itinerant workers in search of temporary opportunities to make some money. These migrants, often as *figurinai*, were the first vanguard of the many who followed in the ensuing decades.[78] As previously outlined, pushed by a spirit of adventure and search for new markets, some *figurinai* anticipated the transoceanic flow of Italian migrants, which characterized the last decades of the nineteenth century. Due to the migratory habit of groups of itinerant craftsmen and labourers, they undoubtedly represented the facilitators of Italian migration towards transatlantic destinations.

As Briganti has outlined in her work on migrants from a mid-valley community to Brazil, the transoceanic migration experience did not impact on *Lucchesia* as a socially deranging event, but was rather slowly introduced into the life cycle of these populations as a "normal" episode.[79] It was an event well framed within a society and a culture accustomed for centuries to experience new possibilities to make a living by going outside its boundaries. Consequently, these *figurinai*, who crossed the ocean towards Brazil, were the forerunners of the Italian overseas mass migration of the 1880s and 1890s. They arrived in Rio de Janeiro and the northern Brazilian states of Bahia and Pernambuco between 1850 and 1870, sailing on steamships from the French ports of Le Havre and Marseille.[80] The *figurinai* were employed as itinerant makers and sellers of statuettes, travelling inland and reaching most cities and towns. After a few years, most of them either returned to Lucca with a few savings or moved to Brazilian coastal cities, where they opened deli, fruit or clothes shops. The migratory flow consisted in itinerant and temporary migration of farmers and woodcutters. It was only from the 1870s that Lucchese migration to Latin American countries, and Brazil in particular, increased markedly, with the departure of peasants and generic labourers, who decided to settle more permanently due to favourable economic conditions.

While *figurinai* certainly acted as precursors of Italian mass migration and facilitated the departure of large numbers of *Lucchesi*, the opportunities to find employment and make money easier than in Corsica and France were also facilitated by migration agents, who had the specific task of attracting peasants and labourers to Latin American countries. To this aim, agents and appointed sub-agents travelled through the provinces of Lucca and Massa Carrara in order to convince prospective migrants to embark for Argentina or Brazil.[81]

By the 1870s, coffee had become the main Brazilian export, overcoming the production of sugar and cotton. As a consequence, the production and economic centre moved towards the northern areas of the country, thus creating the necessity to build new roads and railway lines to link the agricultural centres to the main cities and ports. It was within this new stage of economic development that the Brazilian government recognised the need for a larger labour force, which had to replace the use of African slaves after the abolition of slavery in 1888.[82] A solution was found with the lure of migration of European workforce, offering the cost of the journey, free transportation to the coffee plantation and an assignment of land. Agents and sub-agents created an effective and capillary network within Lucca and Garfagnana in order to spread information on the travelling facilities to migrate to Brazil and Argentina, thus confirming the internationalization of the migratory process, which would change the character of Lucchese and Italian mass migration in the ensuing decades. The activity of the agents and their contribution to the Italian migration process, in fact, which has been studied little,[83] created some concern for the Italian authorities. They perceived this intermediary occupation as a dangerous "external force" in generating a demographic exodus from many Italian rural areas. Briganti refers to a ministerial report of the period :

> *"Appariva incredibile che perfino nei villaggi piu' isolati potesse attuarsi, in apparente spontaneita' senza soccorsi esterni, un fatto complesso come quello emigratorio, e si cerco' di individuare quali forze estranee ordinassero l'esodo delle folle".*[84]
>
> *(It seemed improbable that even in the most isolated villages, such a complex phenomenon as migration could develop spontaneously, and apparently without the concourse of external forces. Consequently, an investigation was ordered to study which external activities generated the exodus of the populations).*

From the 1870s, the flow of migrants from the Province of Lucca and Garfagnana began to have such notable dimensions that the number of Tuscans represented 9 per cent of the total intake of Italians to the host country.[85] Between 1876 and 1900, Brazil absorbed an average of 14.7 per cent of all migrants from the Lucca area, both on temporary and permanent basis, which culminated in 68.6 per cent in 1896.[86] The flow of migrants towards Brazil was so steady that a new vice-consulate of Brazil was opened in Lucca in 1887, as requested by the *Prefetto* of Lucca (the head of *Prefettura*, as previously explained, was responsible for the public and social order of the Italian province of Lucca). The establishment of the consulate finally met the needs of prospective migrants to prepare their papers for expatriation to Brazil.[87]

Research by Briganti on the specific town of Borgo a Mozzano shows that departures for the Latin American countries steadily increased during the 1890s, reaching its peak in the late 1890s. Splitting the figures by gender, it is evident that the low number of migrant women of the 1880s rose for the following two decades.[88]

The higher number of women suggests that Lucchesi shifted from a pattern of temporary migration, in which the males left in search of job opportunities, to a more stable settlement in Brazil, once the economic conditions were good enough for them to be joined by wives and relatives.

Migrants from Tuscany to Brazil represented one of the largest Italian regional components,[89] and certainly the oldest one. Tuscans, and Lucchesi as their main element, were employed extensively in the coffee industry, as well as within urban marginal activities, as a consequence of the many labourers and craftsmen who had joined *figurinai* and peasants in Brazil since the early 1880s.

From 1898, Brazil was hit by a stern economic crisis, due to a fall in the price of coffee on international markets and, as a consequence, of the overproduction caused by the large intake of migrant labour in the previous years. This crisis generated a slow process of Brazilian city-bound movement of workers, and the return of many Italian and Lucchesi migrants to their communities of origin.[90]

Migration to these Latin American countries reached its peak between 1876 and 1925, with a prevalence of Lucchesi going to Brazil. While the migratory flow continued during the 1930s, and more vigorously in the 1950s, the number of Tuscan migrants slowly decreased, without ever reaching the peak of the immediate post-unification.[91] Since the end of WWII, the main Latin American destinations of Italian and Tuscan migrants became Argentina rather than Brazil,[92] due to better economic conditions and work opportunities in Argentina. Consequently, the Lucchese community was already well settled both in urban Argentina and rural Brazil,[93] thus consolidating its position and generating, in these recent decades, only minor patterns of chain migration.

iv. United States and Canada

> *In queste mura non ci si sta che di passaggio. Qui la meta e' partire. Mi sono seduto al fresco sulla porta dell'osteria Con della gente che mi parla di California Come d'un suo podere.*
>
> ***Giuseppe Ungaretti, Poesie***[94]
>
> *(Within Lucca's walls, people are just passers-by. Here the goal is to leave. I sat outside the tavern With people talking about California As if it were their own backyard).*

As reported by Rovai, in a note addressed to the State Secretary in 1880, the American Consul in Florence wrote that the first migrants from Tuscany to the United States were craftsmen who had left with the intention to settle there. Those who followed the 'pioneers' were small plot owners or peasants, who had planned to remain only for the time necessary to make enough money to buy some land once they returned to Italy.[95] From the late 1890s, the United States became one of the preferred destinations of migrants from the mid-valley of the River Serchio and Garfagnana.[96] In 1907, the highest peak of departures from the Province of Lucca[97] to the United States is recorded. The flow from the Province of Lucca and Garfagnana was impressive in the early 1910s. As a curiosity, it is worth stating that there are records of two Lucchesi who died aboard the Titanic when it sank in 1911, one of them leaving his wife as a survivor on the ocean liner.[98]

Migration from Tuscany to Northern America was mainly directed towards the United States, with a minor component to Canada. The flow of Tuscans and Lucchesi to the United States followed that of Italians, with a peak shortly before the outbreak of the Great War

(Table 3-7, p.136), a brief resumption after the war (until the entry restriction acts were introduced in 1924), and a smaller number of migrants after WWII, when Australia,[99] South Africa[100] and other European destinations were preferred by Tuscan migrants.

As previously stated, departures from Lucca areas ceased almost completely by the late 1960s.[101] The habit of temporary migration, soundly established for centuries and transferred to overseas destinations since the 1880s, remained a constant pattern for the ensuing decades, as the following report confirms.

> *"Siccome i Garfagnini hanno rare doti di sobrieta', di laboriosita', di resistenza e di adattabilita' alle piu' svariate specie di lavoro, ne segue che, dopo 8 o 15 anni di residenza all'estero, quando non preferiscono piu' rimanere cola', tornano in Italia provvisti di un buon gruzzolo, col quale non hanno altra ambizione che di fabbricarsi una casetta, acquistare un appezzamento di terra, fare insomma un po' di vita comoda e tranquilla...[...]... Nell'autunno del 1927, trovandomi nel comune di Fosciandora, ebbi occasione di intrattenermi con un vecchio e robusto montanaro che, dopo aver fatto ben 14 viaggi in America, si preparava a farne un altro".*[102]

> *(Since people from Garfagnana are quite sober, hard-working, resistant and adjust themselves to any sort of activity, after eight or fifteen years abroad, once they want to return home, they get back to Italy with considerable money. They do not have other ambition than to build a house, buy a plot of land to cultivate and finally live comfortably...[...]... In the Autumn of 1927, while I was in Fosciandora, I had the chance to meet an old but sturdy mountaineer who had already migrated to America fourteen times, and planned to go there once again).*

A report on migration from Tuscan mountains of 1908 states different possible outcomes:

> *"Le montagne hanno anch'esse perduto gran numero di lavoratori e specialmente carbonai e tagliatori di boschi,*

> *questi abituati a vita rozza considerano l'emigrazione una dolce villeggiatura, e ben difficilmente riprenderanno il vecchio mestiere".*[103]
>
> *(Mountains have lost a large number of workers, particularly charcoal burners and woodcutters, who - accustomed as they are to hard work - consider migration as a sweet holiday season, and will very seldom get back to their former activities).*

During the period from the unification of Italy to the outbreak of the Great War, the temporariness of Italian and Tuscan migrants is witnessed by the label 'birds of passage', which was given in the United States to southern European workers who stayed in the country for a few months. This pattern was facilitated by the increasing rapidity of travel by steamship. As Vecoli states, "the steamship had eliminated many of the perils and discomforts of oceanic migration, but the voyage in steerage was still a nightmare, with hundreds of immigrants crammed into narrow, stifling quarters".[104] In Latin America, especially Argentina, Italian temporary migrants were called *golondrinas* (swallows), because they used to travel to these countries from October to March, attending rural works, and returned home after a period of six or seven months. This time was sufficient to earn the return fare and bring back some savings to the community of origin.[105]

As indicated for other destinations, migrants from the Province of Lucca and Garfagnana travelled across the United States, finding employment in every geographical area and any occupational sector that could offer quick money earnings. The construction works of the Panama Canal, the large road system of the eastern states, the forests of Montana and Colorado were their first stops.[106] Following the trade route and crossing the American Mid-West, the first itinerant statuette makers and merchants from Lucca had arrived in San Francisco in the mid 1850s. As Cinel reports in his comprehensive work on Italians in San Francisco, "statuette merchants did not settle abroad. Now, even those who have never left the province of Lucca want to join the merchants who have founded several communities of Lucchesi in Europe and the Americas".[107]

The first immigrants from Lucca had already settled in San Francisco by the mid-nineteenth century, a few years after the Genoese. Many migrants from the nearby region of Liguria had become employed within the fruit and vegetable business, which, by the early 1860s, was strictly under their monopoly in the San Francisco area. Fruit and vegetables were carried from the rural outskirts to San Francisco on horse-drawn carts by the same market-gardeners, unloaded and sold in Sansome Street, which was the market centre of San Francisco. In 1874, they even founded an association to regulate their monopoly of market-gardeners and distributors.[108] Following a business pattern that will become more and more common, Lucchesi migrants in San Francisco tried to replace Genoese within the fruit and vegetable business. As stated in 1875 by the Italian Consul in San Francisco and reported by Cinel:

> *"Gli immigrati di Lucca hanno cercato piu' volte di diventare agricoltori, scontrandosi pero' con la dura opposizione dei Genovesi. Dopo la fondazione dell'associazione lo scorso anno, i Lucchesi fungono da distributori per il consumo, lavorando al mercato Colombo oppure come venditori ambulanti lungo le strade di San Francisco".*[109]
>
> *(Migrants from Lucca repeatedly tried to become market gardeners, but clashed with the fierce opposition of Genoese. After the foundation of the association last year, Lucchesi now work at the Colombo market or act as street sellers along the streets of San Francisco).*

The area around Sansome Street (in the centre of San Francisco) was in fact soon labelled the 'Colombo market', because of the large presence of Genoese and Lucchese migrants.[110] In the 1880s, more fruit and distribution companies founded by Lucchesi appeared in San Francisco. These distribution and commission houses not only sold farm produce, but also acted as loan companies advancing money to other Lucchesi farmers of the San Francisco Bay area, in view of the following year's crops for new irrigation systems, more plants or equipment.[111]

Table 3-8 - Migrants from Tuscany to Canada and the United States, 1876-1915

	Canada	UnitedStates
1876	0	123
1877	0	124
1878	0	140
1879	6	94
1880	0	180
1881	6	241
1882	0	338
1883	0	554
1884	4	227
1885	25	264
1886	19	358
1887	7	628
1888	1	764
1889	8	447
1890	2	359
1891	72	1,110
1892	9	1,170
1893	0	1,723
1894	2	1,048
1895	5	787
1896	10	1,153
1897	9	744
1898	15	1,469
1899	120	2,159
1900	77	2,242
1901	14	3,441
1902	23	5,281
1903	40	5,857
1904	53	6,746
1905	62	6,752
1906	68	10,031
1907	82	10,159
1908	24	4,457
1909	44	8,005
1910	58	8,794
1911	84	8,112
1912	132	9,676
1913	1,269	13,049
1914	69	6,240
1915	24	1,767

Source: Commissariato, 1926: 111

While the increasing presence of Lucchesi within the market gardening area is an indicator of their like for activities linked to the rural conditions of their communities of origin, the entrepreneural skills of many others is a reflection of their century-long tradition of trade and commerce. As previously outlined, both the rural origin of migrants and the pursuit of business opportunities are the two main factors which have affected the geographical distribution and occupational patterns of Lucchesi in most of the foreign destinations where they settled.

Migrants from Tuscany were present not only in San Francisco. They scattered all across the United States, with major concentrations in the inner city districts and the immediate countryside of Philadelphia, Chicago,[112] San Francisco and Toronto.[113] Within the urban areas, Lucchesi tended to concentrate in a limited range of activities. Apart from the establishment of a pattern of temporary migration, which had characterized for centuries the migratory flow from the mountain areas of northern Tuscany, the reason for the gravitation of Lucchesi into a restricted range of activities is linked to the traditional peasant desire for independence and to establish themselves in positions of security and proprietorship.[114] To achieve this sense of security, market gardening and small family-run businesses, as selling and catering, were ideally suited.[115] The explanation lay in the nature of their economic activities, which made it unnecessary for the majority of them to ever fully participate in American society. They followed occupations that generally did not bring them in competition with organised labour, as Price as noted with respect to Italian migrants in general to Australia.[116]

In her study of a small Lucchese community settled in the northern outskirts of San Francisco, the American anthropologist Sensi-Isolani outlines two factors that may have pushed the newly arrived migrants out of the urban area and into the surrounding countryside. The first was the network nature of Italian and Tuscan migration, and its pull factors in areas where other Lucchesi had already settled, as others have confirmed.[117] In this regard, she states that some migrants were responsible for the arrival of over 30 family members by the early 1900s.[118] Another factor affecting the settlement of Tuscans in the countryside was the feeling of both the San Francisco Italian community and the Italian emigration authorities that encouraging migrants to seek employment outside the city would avoid conflicts with established unions in San Francisco.[119] This circumstance, beyond the socio-historical background conducive to migration from the Lucca areas, certainly played a primary role in most of the Lucchese settlements in the United States. Lucchesi settled in several rural areas of California, especially northern and central, and were mostly employed in market gardening, for the fruit and vegetable supply of San Francisco, and in the lumber industry. By the 1880s, the first charcoal burners from Garfagnana - who had settled as woodcutters in the redwood forests of northern California[120] were joined by a large number of mountaineers, peasants and labourers from the upper valley of the River Serchio.

The preferred destinations of migrants from the middle valley of the River Serchio were the United States, Brazil and, after the mid-1920s, Australia. From Garfagnana, the most popular destination remained the United States, even if the number of migrants to Brazil and Australia was higher.[121] However, figures on migrants referred to those who, at present, reside in foreign countries, show different trends. Data taken from the Commune of Bagni di Lucca (mid-valley) show a large prevalence of migrants who settled in European countries and the United States (Table 3-9).

The number of migrants who moved from a low-valley Commune (Capannori) is higher towards most American destinations (United States, Canada, Argentina and Brazil), whereas from a Commune of Garfagnana (San Romano Garfagnana) a very large component of them moved to Australia. The apparent difference probably lies in the choice of sample for the additional archival research done in order to confirm figures drawn from different sources. The Commune of San Romano Garfagnana, which is situated in the upper valley of the River Serchio, is a small commune characterized by strong patterns of chain migration towards Australia. On the other hand, figures on migrants gathered at the local archive of Bagni di Lucca, representing a Commune of the mid-valley, confirm their similarity with those gathered by other sources, where, in fact, the United States is registered as the most common overseas European destination.

It is worth adding that, although migrants from Garfagnana were mainly peasants and mountaineers, once in California or in other rural areas of the United States, they were not employed exclusively in agriculture. While they raised pigs, chickens, planted fruit orchards, vegetable gardens and vineyards, many of them made money also through a combination of ranching, free enterprise in the lumber business and occasional wage labour, while women were often involved in the catering business.[122] This ability of Lucchesi to adjust their own skills and experiences, acquired within mountain and rural socio-economic contexts, to new and often urban environments has at least two explanations. Firstly, it is due to the capacity of peasants and farmers to become flexible in production and adjust to changing economic factors, as the Lucchese rural society had demonstrated for centuries with the fluctuation of its silk industry, famines and different tax impositions. Secondly, the creation of a century-long culture of entrepreneurship of Lucchese traders had forged within the whole Lucchese urban and rural society what could be called a paradigm of business hunting, which has often been expressed by the enterprising capacity of many Lucchesi migrants abroad.

Within the context of many foreign destinations and occupational patterns chosen by Lucchesi, this chapter has examined how it is possible to delineate a 'Lucca model' of migration. Its main components include migration as a 'community culture', a way to depart 'in order to stay', with males departing first, and going to work abroad within integrated niches of labour market, followed by the departure of women, if and when the economic position was sufficiently consolidated in the host country. These are all patterns of spatial distribution, of Lucchesi migrants that, although with some differences, due to social contexts in different host countries, are replicated in Western Australia, as will be outlined in the next chapters.

Table 3-9 - Number of Migrants from selected communes of the Province of Lucca to foreign destinations, 1950-1998

	BAGNI LUCCA			**CAPANNORI**			**S.ROMANO GARF.**		
	Male	**Female**	**TOT.**	**Male**	**Female**	**TOT.**	**Male**	**Female**	**TOT.**
Belgium	100	78	178	20	10	30	1	0	1
France	170	122	292	59	56	115	19	0	19
Germany	64	33	97	36	22	58	3	0	3
Holland	37	28	65	9	9	18	0	0	0
Switzerland	21	20	41	20	18	38	7	0	7
United Kingdom	35	17	52	22	16	38	9	0	9
Other Eur.Countries	48	38	86	10	10	20	3	0	3
United States	94	92	186	213	202	415	3	0	3
Canada	26	22	48	112	74	186	0	0	0
Argentina	9	7	16	155	141	296	0	0	0
Brazil	17	15	32	135	97	232	0	0	0
Colombia	20	13	33	2	2	4	0	0	0
Other Lat.Countries	18	22	40	21	21	42	3	0	3
Australia	12	1	13	38	26	64	79	38	117
TOTAL	671	508	1,179	852	704	1,556	127	38	165

CHAPTER 4

ITALIANS AND TUSCANS IN AUSTRALIA

ITALIANS IN AUSTRALIA

i. The Early Stage

"Addio miei cari tutti, addio patria diletta, Animato da un'idea forse un po' troppo ambiziosa, Vi lascio tutti ma vi lascio di fisico non di morale, Giacche' vi ho e vi avro' sempre nel mio cuore..."[1]

Hamburg, on board of the steamship Reichstag to Australia, June 1876

(So long my dear, so long my loved country, moved by an idea perhaps too ambitious, I am leaving you with my body but not with my heart, As I will always keep you in my heart...).

Italians have arrived in Australia in a very limited number since the last decades of the eighteenth century. Nevertheless, it is only from the 1840s that the country witnessed the arrival of a number of educated individuals who had left Italy for non-economic reasons, such as missionaries, political exiles, musicians, artists, professionals and businesspeople.[2] These northern and central Italian middle class professionals and entrepreneurs to Australia probably escaped the persecutions by Austrian authorities - under whose control were most of the northern regions of Italy until 1860 - especially after the failure of the revolts in many European cities in the 1840s and 1850s.

Through the 1840s and 1850s, the number of Italian migrants who came for economic reasons increased. Nevertheless, they did not come from the landless, poverty-stricken agricultural working class but from northern Italian rural families with at least sufficient means to pay their fare to overseas destinations.[3] Rando reports that a group of artisans skilled in terrazzo work settled in Melbourne, and stonemasons from Lombardy arrived to build a French-style village at Hunters Hill near Sydney. Furthermore, in the late 1850s, some 2,000 Swiss Italians migrated to the Victorian goldfields.[4]

As discussed in the previous chapters, the alpine areas of Piedmont, Lombardy and the Apennines areas of Liguria, Emilia and Tuscany had socio-economic conditions similar to those of the Swiss Italian Canton of Ticino. It is not difficult to assume, as D'Aprano does, that a similar number came also from these Italian areas, because such regions were also the targets of the shipping companies' drive to fill their Australia-bound ships.[5]

The number of Italians who arrived in Australia remained small during the last decades of the nineteenth century. The voyage was costly and complex, as no direct shipping link existed between the two countries until the late 1890s. The length of the voyage was over two months before the opening of the Suez Canal.[6] Italian migrants who intended to leave for Australia had to use German shipping lines that called at the ports of Genoa and Naples no more than once a month.[7] Therefore, other overseas destinations, such as the United States and the Latin American countries, proved to be much more attractive, thus allowing more quickly the establishment of migration patterns and drawing far greater numbers.

Nevertheless, the Victorian gold rush of the 1850s had attracted thousands of Italians and Swiss Italians to Australia. The drain on the labour supply occasioned by the gold rush caused Australia to seek workmen from Europe for land use and the development of cultivation, both in New South Wales and Queensland.[8] Unfortunately, the number of Italians who joined the Victorian gold mines is obscure and, until 1871, Italians did not receive a special place in any Australian Census figures. By 1881, the first year of Census figures on Italian migrants in all States, there were 521 Italians (representing 0.066% of the total population) in New South Wales, and 947 (0.10%) in Victoria, of whom one-third were in Melbourne and the rest in the goldfields. Queensland had 250

Italians, South Australia 141, Tasmania 11 and Western Australia only 10.[9] These Australian data correspond to similar figures from Italian sources.[10]

While Italians in Australia were less than 2,000, their number slowly tended to increase, because many migrants were attracted by the possibility of settling in areas capable of intense agricultural exploitation.[11] In this regard, it must be borne in mind again that, in the early 1880s, the newly-unified Italy was facing a strong economic crisis, which was going to push a hundred thousand Italians to seek a better life abroad. In addition, even Australian wealthy travellers, like Randolph Bedford, who visited Italy in the 1870s and 1880s, admitted the convenience of having a larger intake of Italian workers into Australia. As reported by Pesman in her study on Australian visitors to Italy, Bedford stated that Italians would adjust to the Australian climate better than the "pale" English migrant. As the job opportunities attracted so many British people to the colonies in order to be employed in agriculture, certainly the Italian peasant, accustomed to be a hard-worker, "frugal and sober", would be a very good immigrant for the Australia soil.[12]

Since the early 1880s, due to the socio-economic situation in Italy and the opportunities of settling in Australia as farmers, skilled or semi-skilled artisans and labourers, the number of Italians who left for Australia began to increase. In 1881, over 200 foreign immigrants, mainly from northern Italy, arrived in Sydney. They were the survivors from Marquis de Ray's ill-fated attempt at founding a colony, Nouvelle France, in New Ireland,[13] which later became part of Germany's New Guinea Protectorate. Many of them took up a conditional purchase farm of 40 acres near Woodburn, in the Northern Rivers District at what was subsequently known as 'New Italy'. By the mid-1880s, about 50 holdings of an aggregate area of more than 3,000 acres were under occupation, and the Italian population of New Italy had increased to 250.[14] Lyng reports:

> *"The land was very poor and heavily timbered and had been passed over by local settlers. However, the Italians set to*

> *work and by great industry and thrift succeeded in clearing some of the land and making it productive...[...]...Besides working on their own properties the settlers were engaged in the sugar industry, in timber squaring, grass seed gathering, and other miscellaneous work".*[15]

In 1883, a commercial treaty between United Kingdom and Italy was signed, allowing Italian subjects freedom of entry, travel and residence, and the rights to acquire and own property and to carry on business activities in Australia.[16] This agreement certainly favoured the arrival in Australia of many more Italians.

ii. Italians in Anglo-Australian working society, 1890-1920

> *"To be, notwithstanding anything, on the side of the losers, if not for anything for the haughty arrogance of the winners".*
> **Albert Camus**

Although Italian settlers and Australians had fairly harmonious relations through most of the nineteenth century, "matters began to change once Italian workers and *contadini* (peasants) began arriving in greater numbers", as Rando observed.[17] 1891 was the year in Queensland during which over 300 peasants from Northern Italy were scheduled to arrive, as the first contingent to replace 60,000 Kanakas brought to north Queensland since the mid-nineteenth century as exploitable labour for the sugarcane plantations. Until the early 1890s, Italians had been practically an unknown, or modest, quantity in Queensland.[18] As a result of the new White Australia policy, the Kanakas were now being deported.[19] While employment was guaranteed, wages were low and fixed.[20] The deciding factor in the whole matter was the plight of the sugar industry: docile gang labour was essential, and the 'frugal' Italian peasants were perfectly suited for such employment. The Australian Workers' Union (AWU) claimed that Italians would work harder than the Kanakas for lower pay, and take away work from Australians. Over 8,000 Queenslanders signed a petition requesting the project to be cancelled. Nonetheless, more Italian migrants arrived and nominated friends and relatives still in Italy. They slowly acquired a large number of sugar-cane plantations and gradually set up thriving Italian communities in north Queensland.[21]

A few years later, Italians were again the subject of public discussion in Western Australia. The Western Australian gold rush of the early 1890s and the subsequent labour disputes at the mines had belatedly attracted Italians in large number. Most of them were unskilled, and therefore usually employed on the surface of the mines, or cutting, loading and carting wood nearby. Pyke so described the situation:

> *"Popular agitation was prompted mainly by growing unemployment; even Italians had begun to write home about it. Italians, however, could still be readily employed, often in preference to other workmen, because of the contract system of employment. They had the virtue of comparative docility and temperance and the ability to work in the hottest of weather; consequently, they were sought after by contractors, a few of whom were themselves Italians".*[22]

The Italian general consul in Melbourne, Mr Corte reported about the behaviour of Italian migrants in Australia in 1898:

> *"Gli Italiani godono, a ben giusto titolo, in Australia ed altrove, fama di instancabili lavoratori, di sobrii, tranquilli ed intelligenti operai, e di contadini instancabili".*[23]
>
> *(Italians are highly regarded, in Australia and elsewhere, as tireless workers, sober, tranquil and intelligent labourers, as well as incomparable farmers).*

As previously stated with respect to the temporary migration of Tuscan migrants, Italians worked hard, and most of them saved steadily, by a simple and primitive mode of life, in order to buy land either in hospitable Australian urban areas or back in the Italian community of origin. They were clearly "the better men for the worse job",[24] as a pattern which was repeated itself also for Tuscans during the 1930s and the 1950s, as will be outlined further in this study. The early 1890s is a turning point in the Australian attitude toward Italian immigration. Pyke states:

"The Labour Movement was against Italian immigration to all areas, and particularly to these industries, inasmuch as it swelled the labour market and increased competition, thereby putting employers in the enviable position of being able to pick and choose and giving employees who wanted to labour and needed work, the opportunity of paying for employment and accepting low wages".[25]

Sugarcane activities in Queensland and mining in Western Australia, where most of the Italians were employed, became the targets of the Labour movement. As O'Connor reports in his work on the first Italian settlements of Australia, when Italians began to compete with Britishers for work on the Kalgoorlie goldfields, the Parliament was warned that they, along with Greeks and Hungarians, "had already become a greater pest in the United States than the coloured races".[26] In other words, during the 1890s, a political and social alliance was formed between the Australian Labour Party and the Anglo-Australian working class in order to react to Italian immigrants, with particular reference to northern and central Italian workers who lowered the level of wages.

Even in the Italian literature of the 1890s and early 1900s in travel reports and descriptions of Australia, there are notes about these frictions. The Italian Geographical Society (*Societa' Geografica Italiana*) reported as follows about the few Italian settlements in Australia:

"Nella maggior parte dei casi l'operaio (italiano) vive sotto la tenda, cosi' chiunque non sia dedito all'ubriachezza (cosa troppo comune in questi paesi, ma non fra i nostri connazionali) puo' facilmente risparmiare la meta' del suo salario. I nostri italiani, economi per eccellenza, risparmiano talvolta anche di piu'".[27]

(In the large majority of the cases, Italian labourers live in tents, so, whoever does not get drunk - which is such a common habit in this country, except amongst Italians - can easily save up to half his wage. Our Italians, extremely thrifty, save even more than that).

Among the many observations about his journey to Australia, the Italian priest and writer, Giuseppe Capra, notes in 1909:

> *"In questi ultimi cinquantacinque anni, in cui l'Italiano emigro' piu' numeroso in Australia, la sua condotta morale e' superiore a quella delle altre nazionalita' che qui sono rappresentate, l'inglese compreso. Amante del lavoro, del risparmio, intelligente, sobrio, e' sempre ricercatissimo: l'unico contrasto che talvolta incontra e' quello dell'operaio inglese che, forte della sua origine, si fa preferire e guarda al suo concorrente con viso arcigno, temendo, senza alcun fondamento, che l'Italiano si presti a lavori per salari inferiori ai proprii".*[28]
>
> *(During these recent 55 years, when Italians migrated more to Australia, their moral conduct had been superior to that of the many other nationals here represented, British included. Italians are work and savings-oriented, intelligent, sober and very much sought after. The only hostility comes from the British labourers who, confident of their origin, look at their Italian competitors with a surly mood, because they are afraid - without any evidence - that Italians could work for lower wages than theirs).*

Frictions between the established Australian working class and the newcomers suggest that, during periods of economic crisis and unemployment, immigration acted as a "tool of division and attack" by international capitalism to the working class organization.[29] A pattern that will recur again during the 1930s within the Italian and Tuscan mining community of Western Australia, as will be examined in the subsequent chapters.

There were also Italians in occupations other than in the sugarcane industry and mining. In Western Australia, fishing was next in popularity, followed by the usual urban pursuits associated with Italians and Tuscans of peasant origin, such as market gardening, restaurant ownership and fruit and vegetable trading. As Cresciani explained in his comprehensive study of Italian-Australian settlements in the early decades of the twentieth century, it was the small size and the type of the Italian settlement that also worked against a wider involvement of Italian migrants with organised labour.

> *"Most Italians were scattered in the countryside, on the goldfields, in the mines. As agricultural workers, fruit pickers, farmers, tobacco growers, canecutters. The distance and the lack of communication prevented them from organising themselves. Those in the cities, mainly greengrocers, market gardeners and labourers, because of the sheer lack of interest and capacity to understand the advantages that a political organisation would bring, kept themselves aloof from any active role in politics and from the people who were advocating it. Also, many migrants were seasonal workers, never stopping for long at any one place, thus making it difficult for them to take part in social or political activities".*[30]

By the early 1900s, there were over 5,000 Italians in Australia involved in a remarkable variety of occupations. In 1911, the Census claimed that there were 6,719 residents who had been born in Italy. Of these, 5,543 were males, whilst 2,683 had become naturalised. No less than 2,600 were in Western Australia.[31]

One of the most significant policy matters that the new Commonwealth Australian Parliament had to consider, after it was inaugurated in 1901, was immigration. Later that year, the Attorney-General Alfred Deakin introduced and passed into legislation the *Immigration Restriction Bill* and the allied *Pacific Island Labourers Act.* The goal was to ensure the White Australia policy by controlling entry into Australia and repatriating coloured labour from the Pacific Islands.[32] The concept was meant to safeguard the social 'white' purity and protect wage standards against cheap coloured labour. As the Restriction Act passed into legislation, there was some confusion as to whether Italians should be let into the country, or kept out by means of the 'Dictation test' provisions, as stated into the Act.[33] The Act did not specify a translation, but rather a dictation in a European language, the purpose of the test being to keep out of Australia non-Europeans, as a deterrent to unwanted immigrants. Although the test was initially to be administered in English, it was then tightened to any European language, "mainly through Labour insistence".[34] Such a firmly sustained system to select entries into Australia remained on the statute books until 1958, when it was replaced by a system of entry permits.

Fuelled both by the British-European feeling of loss of supremacy and the fears of the Labour Party in working sectors, where labourers were not exclusively Anglo-Celtics, anti-Italian sentiments gathered momentum in the United States in the early 1900s, in the wake of Italian mass migration. Such attitudes flourished also in Australia, as has been reported in the Queensland sugar-cane industry and the Western Australian mines. Nevertheless, a new attempt to found an Italian colony in Western Australia took place in 1906, when the western State offered to host about 100 Italian peasant families to settle in the south-western rural corner of Western Australia. A delegation of some northern Italian farmers, led by Leopoldo Zunini, an Italian career diplomat, visited most of these rural areas.[35] Although his report on soil fertility, quality of cattle to graze, transportation and accommodation for the Italian farmers was extremely positive and enthusiastic, the settlement scheme was not carried out. Again, Western Australian public opinion opposed the creation of an exclusively Italian settlement,[36] possibly caused by anti-Italian sentiment fuelled by these episodes of confrontation between the Labour movement and the cheap labour cost offered by Italian migrants.

iii. The Growth of the Italian-Australian Community, 1921-1945

Italian migration to Australia increased markedly only after heavy restrictions were placed on Italians' entry into the United States. More than two million Italian migrants entered the United States from the turn of the century to the outbreak of the First World War, whereas only about twelve thousand Italians had entered Australia in same period.[37] In 1917, while the war was still on, the United States introduced a *Literacy Act* to curtail its immigration flow, which had reached a high number before the war, and Canada enacted similar legislation two years later. In 1921, United States policy became even stricter, with the establishment of a quota system that limited the total intake of Italian immigrants in any one year to about 41,000 (calculated as 3 per cent of the number of Italians residing in the United States in 1910). Furthermore, in 1924, the figures related to the entry of Italians were cut almost to zero, as they meant to represent the 2 per cent of the Italian component in the United States in 1890.[38] Such severe restrictions meant that part of the great post-war stream of migrants from Italy was progressively diverted to Australia (Figure 4-1).

Figure 4-1 - Italian Migrants to Australia, 1924-1972

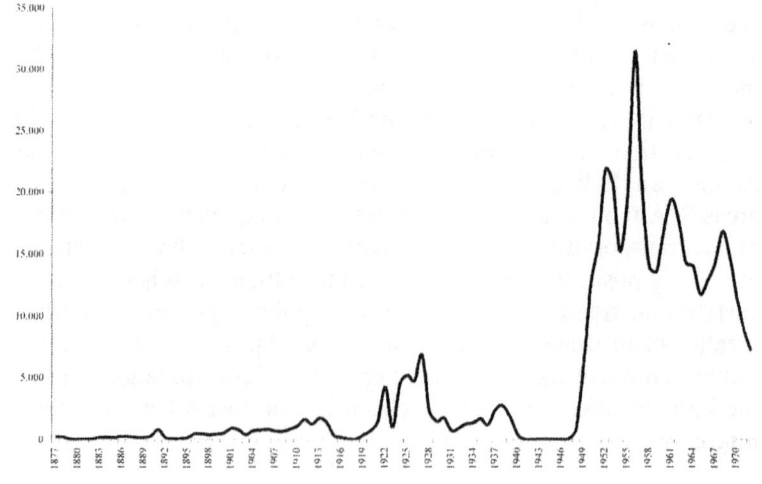

Source: Australian Immigration Statistics

Nevertheless, the way Italian migrants were conceived by Anglo-Australian society was not going to change after its perception had formed in the early 1900s. With respect to this attitude, MacDonald wrote:

> *"Italian immigration became the largest non-British movement after the entry of Melanesians and Asians was stopped by the new federal government in 1902. This put Italians at the bottom of the Australian 'racial totem pole', just above the Aborigines. The volume of arrivals, the proportion*

of settlers in the total population of Australia, and the size of Italian agglomerated settlements were trivial by international standards. Yet the establishment of fifty Italian households within a radius of five miles or the employment of twenty Italians on a job were cause for alarm in Australian eyes, The 'inferiority' of Italians was generally seen in racist terms as well as specifically in terms of their threatening to compete with labor of British stock because of their 'primitive' way of life".

This was the attitude present also in other English speaking countries, as Porter reported for Canada.[39] In his classical study of Italians in North Queensland, Douglass suggests other factors affecting this racist attitude, and reports a summary of the Commonwealth Parliamentary debate of 1927:

"The image of the Italian was nourished by the stereotype of the southerner, and particularly the Sicilian. Regardless of its veracity, it could be applied to only a minority of the new arrivals since, by Italian Government estimates, fully two-fifths of its emigrants to Australia were from the Veneto and another two-fifths were drawn from the Piedmont, Lombardy and Tuscany regions. Only one-fifth were from Sicily and Calabria".[40]

This disposition was hard to change if, as O'Connor reports by citing a previous work by Bromley, "darkness, smallness, noisiness, fatness and smelliness formed the Australian stereotype of the Italians".[41] Although the Australian attitude towards Italians was not friendly, from the early 1920s Italian migrants began to arrive in Australia in notable number. While the Australian Census of 1921 recorded 8,135 Italians residing in the country, during the years 1922-1925 a further 15,000 migrants arrived and, again, a similar number of Italians reached Australia during the period 1926-1930[42] (Figure 4-2).

Figure 4-2 - Number of Italian Males and Females arriving in Australia, 1917-1940

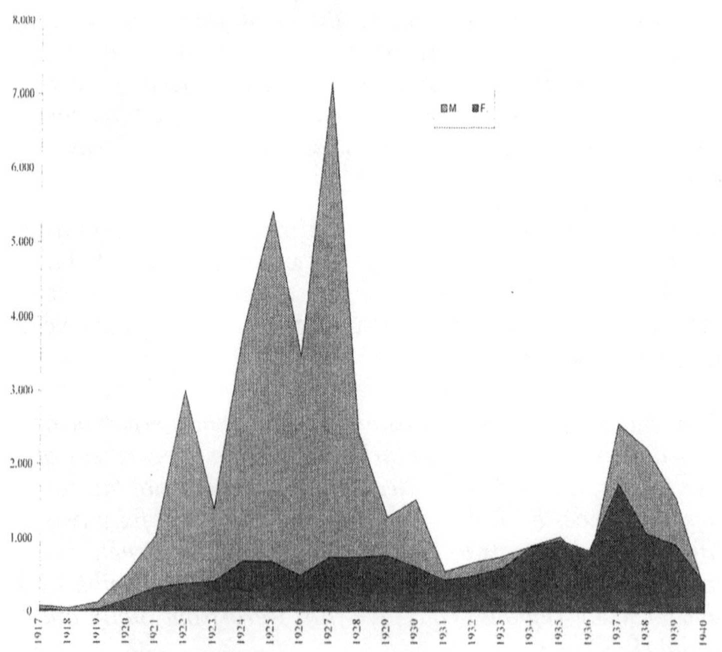

Source: Australian Demography Bulletins

Together with the entry restrictions adopted by the United States, another factor affecting Italian emigration during the early 1920s was the rise of Fascism in Italy in 1922. The concern of Mussolini about the high Italian emigration figures of the mid-1920s pushed the Fascist government's decision in 1927 to stop all migration to overseas countries, with few exceptions, apart from female and minor close relatives (under-age sons, unmarried daughters of any age, parents and unmarried sisters without family in Italy) dependent on residents abroad.[43]

In the early 1920s Italians had found that it was not difficult to enter Australia, as there were no visa requirements. The Amending Immigration Act of 1924 prohibited the entry of migrants unless they had a written guarantee completed by a sponsor, an *Atto di richiamo* ('Call notice').[44] In this case, any migrant could come to Australia free of charge. Without a sponsor, the required landing money was ten pounds until 1924 and forty since 1925.

Gradually, the array of migrants became formed also by a minor component of political opponents to Fascism, generally peasants of the northern Italian regions, who chose Australia as their destination.[45] Marchi notes the presence in Australia of a marked group of anarchists.[46] Furthermore, in his study on Italian migration to South Australia, O'Connor even reports on the presence, in 1926, in Adelaide of a dangerous anarchist 'subversive' from the village of Capoliveri, in the Tuscan Island of Elba, one Giacomo Argenti.[47]

Although there were certainly a number of opponents to Fascism amongst Italians in Australia,[48] the Fascist movement was generally accepted by a great majority of the thousand Italian-born migrants residing in Australia. Italian nationalism acted as an element of reaction and defence to the Australian environment. By the early 1930s, Italian diplomatic activity in Australia, as a direct expression of the Fascist government, became more incisive and oriented to make more and more Fascist proselytes among Italians. Migrants were invited to become members of the fascist political organisations of Australia, to come to fascist meetings and eventually to return to Italy, to consent to serve in the Italian armed forces, both in view of the Italian war campaign of Ethiopia (1936) and, later, at the outbreak of WWII.[49]

Australia, as the United States and most western countries, was hit by the economic Depression of 1929, which caused a serious recession during the following years. Even Australian legislation was changed consequently. Amendments to the Immigration Act in 1932 were more drastic and aimed at more effectively controlling the entry of 'white aliens' into Australia. The amendment extended the landing permit system to all categories of immigrants, while before it was applicable only to immigrants with a maintenance guarantee. The goal was to limit immigrants from competing in the local labour market to the detriment of the local unemployed.[50]

At the same time, the power to apply the dictation test was still available in order to restrict the landing of an immigrant whose admission was not desired.

The economic depression ignited another social tension, which fanned into racial hared again in 1934. In the gold-mining city of Kalgoorlie, Western Australia, an Australian who had expressed defamatory remarks about Italians in an Italian-owned hotel was knocked dead by the barman. This accident sparked the resentment of many Anglo-Australian miners against Italians residing in Kalgoorlie, which culminated in two days of riots. A raging crowd of miners devastated and burnt many shops and private adobes of Italians and other southern Europeans in Boulder and Kalgoorlie and pushed hundreds of Italian migrants to shelter in the surrounding countryside.[51] Notwithstanding the condemnation of the fact on media, the riots did not modify the attitude of public opinion toward Italians in general, as will be examined in detail in the next chapter.

Within Australian society there was an opposition to Italian immigration that stemmed from the fact that Italian migrants were often seen as "Mediterranean scum", or as a "grave industrial and political danger", as reported by Lampugnani.[52] This was the umpteenth episode that without doubt pushed the notable number of Italians now working and residing in Australia to sympathize with Fascism and devoted to the narrow circle of the Italian associations and the close relations of the family.

The Australia Census of 1933 claimed that 26,756 (against the 8,000 of 1921) were born in Italy.[53] Since that year, Italy-born residents in Australia began to represent the first non-English speaking ethnic group of the country,[54] replacing Germans and Chinese.[55] Notwithstanding, a very high proportion of them (20,064) was male.[56] Many Italian male migrants, who had in fact left Italy for Australia during the late 1920s and early 1930s, were joined by wives, working-age sons, daughters, brothers and sisters in the late 1930s. This pattern can be interpreted as a 'defence' from both the perceived hostile Australia environment and the political turmoil of pre-war Italy.

Until the outbreak of WWII, there was a considerable degree of segregation between Italians and Australians. As an additional reaction, a large proportion of Italians in Australia tended to defer naturalization (which could be granted after a period of five years of residence) until they had finally established their homes in Australia.[57] Consequently, it is not surprising that, with the outbreak of World War II, the Anglo-Australian opinion of Italian migrants naturally hardened. The entry of Italy into the war was followed by the internment of many Italians, especially in camps in Queensland, South Australia and Western Australia. Between 1940 and 1945, most of those who had not been naturalised before the war's outbreak were considered 'enemy aliens', and therefore either interned or subjected to close watch, with respect to personal movements and area of employment.[58]

iv. The Italian post-war mass migration to Australia, 1946-1970s

During WWII, more than 18,000 Italian prisoners of war were sent to internment camps throughout Australia.[59] Together with the interned 'enemy aliens', a large number of them were employed in inland farms without much surveillance. Many prisoners of war and Italian-Australian interned worked hard in farms and cattle stations, thus gaining a favourable opinion as hard and committed workers by their Australian employers.[60] This circumstance contributed to generate an environment more agreeable, than that before the war, for the Italian post-war migration to Australia.

After World War II, the attitude of Anglo-Australians towards Italians gradually began to change. At the same time, the Italian war experience helped to destroy many of the political and sentimental attachments that Italians had previously felt towards their country. As a consequence, the end of the war encouraged the naturalisation of many Italian migrants, who had been caught up as enemy aliens at the outbreak of the world conflict. At the end of 1947, only 21 per cent of the Italians residing in Australia were not yet naturalized.[61] Many of those becoming naturalized in the late 1940s so to allay the suspicion caused by the war. In his fundamental work on the assimilation of Italians and German in Australia, Borrie wrote:

"Naturalization was the obvious first step towards their rehabilitation. The war had also broken many of the links with Italy, and in addition it was still difficult to secure a shipping passage to return there. But while the act of naturalization may have been an irrevocable step which in turn provided an incentive to become socially and culturally assimilated, field investigations show clearly that Italians retained many traits, particularly within the circle of the home, which were not 'Australian'. And naturalized or not, they were still not fully accepted by Australians".[62]

Conversely, after the war experience, the Australian government embarked on the 'Populate or Perish' program, aimed to increase the population of the country for strategically important economic and military reasons. The immigration debate in postwar Australia assumed new dimensions as official policy sought a significant increase in the number and the diversity of immigrants, and to find a place for those coming from a tired and torn Europe. The war had occasioned a shift in migration patterns, pressing the need to place a large number of people who could not return to their own countries for a wide range of reasons. This was the case for over ten million people from central and north-eastern Europe, such as Poles, Germans, Greeks, Czechs and Slovaks.[63]

An important stage in this immigration program began with the Displaced Persons Scheme in 1947, which attracted over 170,000 displaced persons to Australia.[64] MacDonald writes in this regard:

"The reservoir of displaced persons who could be recruited for Australia was practically exhausted by 1950. So Italy was the only catchment area which offered more eager candidates than Australia was willing to accommodate and who could then be screened selectively. Italians were still considerably less desirable than central and northern Europeans, yet they were preferred to Cypriots, Greeks, and Maltese not only because there were more Italians to choose from but also because it was hoped that a large proportion could be drawn from the 'superior' peoples of Northern Italy. So they were admitted in greater numbers than had previously seemed conceivable, as a 'third-best' type".[65]

Italy's postwar migration certainly grew out of the country's policy of industrial development. Although there had been a significant industrial growth in Italy before the war, the devastation wrought by the conflict left the structure in ruins. This factor and the return of Italian soldiers from the war fronts generated a surplus of population, which turned to emigration as an alternative to poverty. By the early 1950s, Australian authorities negotiated formal migration agreements with Holland (1951) and West Germany (1952).[66] They also introduced a system of personal nominations and guarantees, opened to Italians, in order to permit families separated by the war to come together again. In addition, the Australian and Italian governments negotiated a scheme of recruitment and assisted passages, which became fully effective in 1952. As extensively outlined by MacDonald, the migration process, eased by the personal nomination scheme, seemed to be more flexible than the administrative machinery of the bilateral program. Personal nominees had a guarantee of assistance and contacts at their arrival in Australia, in order to help migrants to evaluate all employment possibilities.[67] From the mid-1950s, the Italian flow of migrants to Australia assumed a sort of mass migration. Either nominated by relatives in Australia as a major component, or as assisted migrants, a notable number of migrants left Italy for Australia.[68] Unlike the pre-war movement, most of the migrants of the 1950s and 1960s had planned to settle permanently in Australia.

Within these two decades, the number of Italians who came to the host country was so high, that their number in Australia increased ten times.[69] Although there are not precise figures, due to the fact that Australian Census refers only to Italian-born, some scholars have suggested that, with their Australian-born children, the Italian ethnic group in Australia could be approaching 500,000, thus still ranking it as the first non-English speaking ethnic community of Australia.[70]

GEOGRAPHICAL DISTRIBUTION OF ITALIANS IN AUSTRALIA

From the late 1960s, the Italian migratory flow towards Australia ceased. At present, the Italian Australian community is numerically stable and settled. The Australian Census of 1971 indicated over 289,000 people born in Italy, gradually decreasing to about 254,000 in the 1991 Census (Table 4-1).

Table 4-1 - Italian-born Migrants in Australia according to Australian Census

	VIC	NSW	SA	WA	QLD	ACT	TAS	NT	TOT
1891	1,717	1,477	185	36	438		36		**3,889**
1901	1,525	1,577	327	1,354	845		50		**5,678**
1911	1,499	1,723	184	2,361	929		21	2	**6,719**
1921	1,850	2,080	344	1,975	1,838		37	11	**8,135**
1933	5,860	6,319	1,489	4,588	8,355	16	92	37	**26,756**
1947	8,305	8,721	2,428	5,422	8,541	26	64	125	**33,632**
1954	42,429	29,940	11,833	17,295	16,795	328	975	302	**119,897**
1961	91,075	62,365	26,230	25,249	20,000	1,276	1,536	565	**228,296**
1966	111,219	72,875	30,848	28,141	20,272	1,876	1,448	646	**267,325**
1971	121,758	80,416	32,428	30,541	19,280	2,470	1,485	1,098	**289,476**
1976	116,712	78,396	31,943	29,317	18,875	2,697	1,423	790	**280,153**
1981	115,432	77,089	31,325	29,213	17,958	2,773	1,344	763	**275,897**
1986	109,204	73,185	29,616	27,747	17,410	2,716	1,262	752	**261,892**
1991	105,699	70,552	28,962	26,871	17,844	2,735	1,334	783	**254,780**

Hence, the progressive ageing process of its population is an indicator of the lack of turnover with the limited arrays of migrants from Italy. Nevertheless, Italians still represent over 2 per cent of the Australian population, more than 10 per cent of the total intake of overseas-born residents, and some scholars count them as over 630,000 including second and third generation Italians with at least one Italian parent or grandparent respectively.[71] Notwithstanding, their percentage in the total Australian population is slowly decreasing in favour of other ethnic groups, and in particular Asians.[72]

Italy-born migrants are mainly concentrated in urban areas, and within specific suburbs. In his study on ethnic diversity in Sydney and Melbourne, Hugo outlines patterns by referring to previous works by Price:

> *"The spatial distribution of ethnic groups in Sydney and Melbourne is of particular interest because, as Price demonstrates in his classic study of Southern Europeans in Australia, patterns of settlement are inextricably bound up with a whole range of social and economic elements that impinge upon the well-being of those groups".*[73]

It is not the aim of this work to investigate these elements. It is only necessary to outline how these factors have certainly contributed to the residential choice of Italian migrants.

Most of the Italian-born are now concentrated in Melbourne (over 100,000), Sydney (60,000), Adelaide (30,000) and Perth (28,000).[74] Unlike this trend, the number of Italians residing in Brisbane is negligible in comparison to a more notable distribution of Italians in rural Queensland, as Hempel has described in her research on post-war settlement of Italian immigrants in this state.[75] Data and circumstances have been confirmed by other studies.[76] This circumstance is a consequence of the migration patterns followed by Italians in the earlier stage of their settlement in Queensland, during the 1910s, 1920s and 1930s, when the sugarcane industry and the possibility of quick earnings attracted more 'temporary' migrants in the countryside. Conversely, in Australian cities, the Italian village or the region of origin have been significant in the formation of separate communities or neighbourhood groupings of Italians. The way in which a population subgroup is distributed across an area is of importance not only because it can tell us a great deal about the pattern of life of that group.[77] The Italian community has very distinctive patterns of distribution that differentiate it from the total population. Once again, the present study aims to demonstrate an even more distinctive pattern of spatial dispersion of Tuscan migrants, within the wider Italian community, as will be extensively outlined in the next chapter.

As Burnley reports in his study on Italian absorption in urban Australia, some Italian concentrations in the inner suburbs of Carlton, the traditional 'Little Italy' of Melbourne, and Leichhardt, its equivalent in Sydney, were made up of several groups from geographically circumscribed areas of Italy. Migrants from the Lipari Islands of Sicily, and from a few communities of the Province of Vicenza have formed the main Italian community core of Leichhardt, as well as Sicilians from the Province of Ragusa and the Commune of Vizzini have formed a large contingent in Brunswick, a local government authority of Melbourne containing over 10,000 Italians in the 1970s.[78]

Since the first notable arrival of Italians of the 1920s and 1930s, on a smaller scale but through similar patterns, other large communities of Italians were formed, in Adelaide, Perth and in minor cities of Victoria, New South Wales and Queensland. Most first-generation Italian migrants came to Australia due to the nomination of a close relative or a friend, as forms of chain migration, which will be investigated further with respect to the Lucchese community of Western Australia as a whole. With particular reference to Western Australia, Italians began to arrive in more notable number in the early 1890s, after the discovery of gold in the eastern goldfields. The Australian Census of 1911 records the presence of over 2,000 Italians in Western Australia. Only two years before, the Italian writer Capra had visited the state and reported:

> *"L'attuale emigrazione italiana in Australia e' poca cosa, e consta quasi esclusivamente di operai per le miniere e pel taglio della legna nella parte occidentale, e di lavoratori della canna da zucchero nel Queensland".*[79]
>
> *(Present Italian migration to Australia is negligible, almost exclusively limited to miners and woodcutters in the western state, and sugarcane cutters in Queensland).*

Capra details the professional distribution of Italians. Over two-thirds of all Italians were employed either in mines or in the mine-related woodcutting industry (respectively about 400 and 800), both in the gold mining districts of Gwalia, Day Down, Coolgardie and Cue, and the forests of Karrawong and Lakeside. The remaining Italian workers were involved in farming (250) and fishing (150).[80] As has been examined above, the occupational pattern of Italians in Western Australia did not change much with the more consistent migration flow of the late 1920s and early 1930s. During these two decades, Italian migrants to Australia continued to come from the north and central mountain areas of Italy, thus following a pattern of temporary migration that pushed them to look for jobs with potential for quick remuneration, as mining and woodcutting could offer. Changes in these patterns, together with the Italian mass-migration program of the 1950s and 1960s, have already been examined. Hence, the different component of regional origin of Italians in Western Australia and, subsequently, since the late 1950s, a more composite geographical distribution of Italian migrants in both urban and rural areas of the state.

'LUCCHESI' AND TUSCANS IN AUSTRALIA

As has been outlined, during the first half of the nineteenth century, Italians spread geographically across Australia, and were employed in a wide range of occupations. While many were peasants and skilled labourers, the first distinguished intellectuals, scientists, artists and traders, as the 'epitome' of the sophisticated cultured Italian, settled in Australia.[81] Nevertheless, there are records of two convicts from Tuscany (Giorgetti and Marselli) arriving in Fremantle respectively in 1866[82] and 1867[83]: they appear to be the first Tuscans to set foot in Western Australia.

Among the distinguished Italian personalities, those from Tuscany represented a notable majority.[84] The Grand Duchy of Tuscany and the Republic of Lucca, together with other few minor states of pre-unification Italy, had enjoyed for the last two centuries major freedom of expression in commerce, trade and liberal arts than the other Italian states of northern or southern Italy. These states were ruled under the stricter political dominion of either the Church (the Papal state) or the dynastic Augsburg or Bourbon families. Hence, a wider autonomy and enterprise capacity of many intellectuals, artists and businesspeople from Tuscany and Central Italy in general,[85] which was reflected in their search for new places in order to express their artistic skills or business capacities at the time of the political turmoil before Italian unification.

One of the best known in Australia was the Tuscan political intellectual Count Girolamo Carandini, who implanted Italian opera as a popular form of entertainment in the Australia colonies in the 1840s and 1850s.[86] Later, Dr Tommaso Fiaschi became one of the greatest Australian surgeons and, as Cecilia reported, "without a shadow of doubt, the finest figure and the most outstanding of all Italian migration".[87] Born in Florence in 1853 from an old Florentine family, he disembarked in 1875 in North Queensland, at the time of the gold seekers, and worked as a doctor. In 1879 he moved to Sydney and gradually became the most renowned surgeon of his time. He also played an important part in the spreading of the wine industry in Australia, as the owner of famous vineyards in New South Wales, which he called Tizzana from the Italian town in the territory of Lucca (now within the nearby Province of Pistoia) from where he came.[88] As a vigneron representing Australia, he also participated in the World Exposition, held in the Italian city of Turin in 1884.[89]

In Melbourne, Pietro Baracchi, Carlo Catani and Ettore Cecchi, also from Tuscany, each achieved prominence. Baracchi as Government Astronomer of Victoria in the late 1890s for his study of meteorological phenomena,[90] and Catani for numerous engineering projects, including the St.Kilda foreshore in Melbourne during the same period.[91] Cecchi, an engineer from Pisa, played an important role at the turn of the century in the development of irrigation on Victoria's drylands, and was appointed Chief Assistant Engineer for the Victoria water supply for many years.[92] Carlo Spadaccini and Andrea Stombuco, architects from Florence, arrived in Victoria in 1861, and there they designed the construction of important public buildings, churches and private houses during the 1870s and 1880s.[93] Finally, good artists were the Marquis Girolamo Nerli, from the Tuscan city of Siena, who emigrated to Sydney in 1886, and later in New Zealand, and Ugo Catani, a painter from Florence, who came to Australia the same year of Nerli.[94]

In his journalistic report on eminent Tuscans in Australia, Bosi states that there were 39 people from Tuscany present during the first Australia Census of 1871.[95] By the last decades of the nineteenth century, the flow of notable figures from Italy and from Tuscany in particular, ceased. In her interesting outline of early Italian migration to Australia, Alcorso writes:

> *"These early middle-class Italians in the colonies were able to have an important cultural impact, out of proportion to their numbers, and directly linked to their image as transmitters of European 'high' culture. As more Italian peasants migrated to Australia, becoming incorporated into the lowest ranks of the working class, the gap between the Italy of the bourgeois imagination and actual Italians in Australia became more obvious".*[96]

As stated in the previous chapter, Tuscan tradesmen, such as plaster statuette makers from Lucca and stonemasons from Massa Carrara, had begun to arrive in Australia between 1860 and 1870.[97] Certainly, they were not many, as the Italian authorities stated the arrival in Oceania (thus including New Zealand in the count) of only two people from Tuscany in 1872, two again in 1873 and fifteen in 1874.[98] As happened in other of their overseas destinations, they were the vanguard of the more considerable number of temporary and permanent migrants from the same communities of origin, who were going to follow within a few decades. In addition, agents to promote emigration to Australia and New Zealand had established their offices in Europe, and, by the mid 1870s, one also in the Tuscan city and port of Leghorn.[99] As a consequence, the flow of prospective migrants from Tuscany, and in particular from the area of Lucca and the Tuscan coast, was generated also by these additional factors.

While many historical and economic factors have been previously examined, here it is worth adding the circumstance of the establishment of an office in Tuscany to promote and facilitate migration to Australia. During the late 1870s, the migration agent in Leghorn, John Glyn, organized an efficient advertisement campaign within his area, and was able to organize the shipping of several loads of prospective migrants from Tuscany to both Australia and New Zealand. In many cases, the expectations of migrants were not fulfilled by the reality. Once the several loads of migrants arrived to final destinations, the prospective migrants and pioneers discovered that the promised land of settlement was inhospitable and not suitable for the cultivation they had hoped to set. With respect to the New Zealand Special Settlement Scheme of Jacksons Bay, the arrival in 1876 of about 60-70 Tuscan peasants, within a larger contingent of about 300 Italians, resulted in a total failure and abandonment of the area of destination.[100] During the same year, another migration agent in the German port of Hamburg, one William Kirchner, planned the shipping of 25 Tuscan peasant families in Queensland. They would pay their own passages, be granted suitable land and then cultivate vines, olives and mulberries in a colony-community to be called 'Toscano'.[101] Unfortunately, the project did not succeed. The departure of about 90 Tuscans, mainly from the Province of Pisa and the Island of Elba, was organised one year later in Leghorn, and the group arrived in Northern Queensland in 1877.[102] Soon they realized that the quality of the land where they were asked to settle was qualitatively below their expectations, and many of them were moved at government expense to Brisbane and Southern Queensland,[103] where, still now, a considerable number of Tuscans from the Island of Elba is recorded.[104]

The failure of these settlement schemes, as well as the adjustment of a few others involving Italian migrants to Australia, can be interpreted as an indicator of the impossibility, by the last decades of the nineteenth century, to direct Italian migration flow from the top. Italian migrants, whether temporary or permanent, were more often accustomed to follow the overseas paths of their pioneering predecessors on their way in search of work. Tuscan migrants followed the same patterns. Since the 1880s, the majority of them had arrived in Australia as single men to join friends and relatives, usually with the intention of returning home after a few years with their fortunes made.[105] For a few more years, Tuscan migration to Australia was insignificant in numerical terms, if compared with the corresponding transoceanic emigration as a whole (Table 4-2).

Apart from the number of *figurinai* from Lucca, it was hard to discern a marked relationship between occupations in Australia and places of origin in Tuscany, as from a miscellany of different areas within Tuscany had come a small number of farmers, shopkeepers, bootmakers, carpenters and professional people.[106]

Table 4-2 - Number of Migrants from Tuscany to Australia, 1876-1925

1876-80	66
1881-86	28
1886-90	31
1891-95	28
1896-1900	134
1901-05	110
1906-10	196
1911-15	249
1916-20	17
1921-25	601

Source: Commissariato Generale Emigrazione, 1926: 18

The established community of the few Lucchesi peasants and *figurinai* in Australia, together with their frequent return to the communities of origin, pushed more migrants in search of fortune in the *America lunga.* By the early 1910s, Australia was ceasing to be an alien land for many Lucchesi. The country was acquiring popularity in a few towns and villages of Garfagnana and "this familiarity was the most powerful influence on the direction of future migrations", as Templeton analysed with respect to migrants from Valtellina (Lombardy) to Australia.[107] It was the familiarity of a century-long culture of emigration to nearby territories that ensured that, in the following decades, most Tuscan emigrants would set their course along the same beaten tracks.

After a pioneering stage, the period between 1890 and 1940 represents the intermediate time in which the number of Tuscans increased dramatically. Although some destinations, such as France, Brazil and the United States, were already popular among Lucchesi during the 1880s and 1890s, from the turn of the century Tuscans migrated abroad some 10,000 per year.[108] Due to the entry restrictions adopted by the United States in 1924, Australia became increasingly popular as an overseas destination of Tuscan labour. According to MacDonald's estimations, re-elaborated on a previous work by Price, the number of Italian male settlers for the period 1919-1927, split by Province, ranked Lucca as seventh (on a total number of about 95 Italian provinces), which shifts to ninth for the wider period 1919-1940.[109] The shifting of the Province of Lucca from seventh to ninth position is certainly due to a major component of women and children who arrived during the 1930s. Nevertheless, the distribution of migrants from Tuscany to Australia is the highest of central Italy for the period 1899-1939.[110]

In his work on southern Europeans in Australia, Price records a presence of about 1,500 migrants from Tuscany who arrived in Australia during the period 1890 and 1940, thus confirming the figures of the Italian source (Table 4-2). If figures are disaggregated by areas of origin, we can observe an overwhelming number of people (about 1,000) from the two Provinces of Lucca and Massa Carrara (which included the upper valley of Garfagnana), while the bulk of remainder came from the coastal areas and the Island of Elba (about 200 persons).[111]

As previously stated, it is only with the early 1950s that Italian migration to Australia increased markedly, so that, during those years, the highest number of Lucchesi entering Australia is recorded.[112] Still, the figures show a higher intake of adult male settlers arriving to Western Australia, whereas women and children have higher numbers of arrivals in the late 1950s, when their husbands and partners had already settled and could afford to be joined by their families.[113] As a result, the Tuscan migration pattern of the 1950s has a stronger component of definitive migration.

Bosi empirically limits the number of arrivals from Tuscany in the 1950s to about 1,000[114] and Hempel indicates as about 2,800 the number of migrants from Tuscany arrived in Australia by ship between 1952 and 1956.[115] Furthermore, Bertelli, an Australian scholar of Italian migration, singles out a net intake of about 4,000 arriving during the period 1920-1976[116] and 1,500 exclusively during 1959-79.[117] Research, conducted in the local archives of three selected communes of the studied area, shows that the number of migrants now residing in Australia is considerable (over 200 people).

In particular, it is interesting to note that over 100 migrants from the Commune of San Romano Garfagnana are recorded as residing in Western Australia. The three communes where the archival research was conducted belong to different geographical areas of the Province of Lucca. Bagni di Lucca is a mid-valley commune of medium demographic characteristics, Capannori is a low valley Commune with a large population, whereas San Romano Garfagnana is a high valley Commune with a very small population. Since these three communes are only a minor contingent of the almost 30 of the studied area, consequently it can be assumed that the total amount of Lucchese migrants recorded as residing in Australia could be approximately 2,000, that is ten times more. These figures would still not take into consideration all the migrants who never cancelled their residence from the local communal registries, and therefore do not appear in the count. Finally, in the mid-1980s, the Italian Ministry of Foreign Affairs estimated in about 9,000 the number of first-generation Tuscan migrants living in Australia, with a net predominance of those who are now settled in the urban areas of Perth, Adelaide and Melbourne.[118]

Unfortunately, there are not precise figures, neither of Australian nor Italian source, on migrants from the Tuscany Region to Australia. Even though there are data of Italian authorities on the number of residents of the Tuscany Region, single Provinces and even Communes, who annually left the country for overseas, the destination was not so certain. Very often, the declaration of intended destination was left to the migrant's mere statement, thus rendering figures and statistics uncertain and not extremely reliable, in particular when migrants moved from one nation of destination to another. Nevertheless, these figures can be used as a touchstone to study specifically circumscribed sub-regional communities in further detail. On the other hand, Australian Census figures do not state any form of more geographically specific area of origin of migrants than the sole country of birth. Hence, study of some migrants' circumscribed areas of origin relies on specific research, as is the case in this work.

CHAPTER 5

TUSCAN MIGRANTS IN WESTERN AUSTRALIA - SOURCES AND METHODS

SOURCES OF INFORMATION

The principal source of quantitative information used for this study has been the Australian Archives of Western Australia. The Australian Archives of W.A. hold a large number of documents related to migration, such as the naturalization files regarding foreign-born residents in Western Australia (mainly from the mid-1920s to the late 1950s), and the Commonwealth Entry forms that prospective migrants had to fill in on their arrival in Western Australia (for the period 1949-1964). Files, ordered by surnames and entry forms, held by separate nationalities, have all been screened, with the aim to find records of those from Tuscany. Collection of information on naturalization files has been performed by querying the computerized database of the Australian Archives of W.A. with the utilization of a large list of about 3,000 different Italian surnames that are commonly spread in the studied area, as revealed by the Italian local phone directories. Information on entry forms has been collected by consulting approximately 24,000 forms related to Italian nationals, and selecting those from the two provinces of Lucca and Massa Carrara. The collection of data about both these different sources has taken a total of about 300 hours spent at the Australian Archives.

Records cover approximately the period from the mid-1920s to the mid-1960s, which was the peak period of arrival of Italian migrants to Australia. Naturalization papers give more information on the earlier period and on Italian and Tuscan migrants who had already settled in Western Australia, early enough to apply for naturalization. Hence, this source offers more information on their occupation and place of settlement during their period of stay. The Commonwealth Entry Forms, on the other hand, provide more information on the social and occupational background of migrants from Tuscany at their arrival in Australia. Nevertheless, the two different types of documents give ample information on several fields of interest for this study, such as age, geographical areas of origin, occupations in Italy and in Australia (only intended, in the case of the Commonwealth Entry forms), year of arrival in Australia, residence and occupation in Western Australia (only intended, in the case of the Commonwealth Entry forms).

Additional information has been collected at other institutions. Due to the presence of Italian migrants in Western Australia, two Italian pensioners' offices are present in Perth and Fremantle (Enasco and Inca-Cgil), with the task of meeting the needs of the ageing Italian population residing in Australia when applying for Italian pensions. Enasco offices hold over 11,000 Italian pensioners' files, while Inca-Cgil has about 8,000. The two offices collect information on migrants who are now at retirement age, between 60 and 90 years old. Each file contains information on the occupational history of applicants, both in Italy and in Australia. As the files are kept during the pension recipients' lifetime, consequently, most of the collected data relate to Italian migrants who were still alive at time of data collection (1997) and therefore generally refer to migrants who came to Western Australia after WWII. In this case, information on migrants from the studied area has been gathered by screening the files by the Italian province of birth. Collection of data from both the two institutions has taken a total of about 150 hours.

Gaining access to the pensioners' offices has allowed the collection of information on a considerable number of migrants from Tuscany, who performed working activities either in Italy, before migration, or in Western Australia, or in both countries. Comparing the data gathered at the pensioners' agencies with those collected at the

Australian Archives has shown that, in a large number of cases, there were records related to the same migrants. Often, migrants whose identity had been recorded through the Commonwealth Entry forms as entering Western Australia, also appeared as recipients of pensions from Italy at the end of their working life. In a few cases, information related to identical data from different sources has been integrated into a single record.

Two more sources have been utilised within the data collection process, merely as data integrators rather than additional sources. Firstly, the Italian Consulate in Perth has allowed informal access to its archive, which holds files on more than 26,000 Italians and Italians who became naturalised Australians, for the period between the early 1930s and the mid-1960s. The collection of data has taken a total of about 100 hours. Files have been screened by provinces of birth, and data have then been compared with records collected at the Australian Archives and the pensioners' offices, in order to integrate a considerable amount of information. Unfortunately, while access to the consular archive was allowed only on an informal basis, the files themselves lack homogeneity, as no particular method or rule was applied in the information gathered by the Consulate. Files often state only the name of Italian migrants, without additional information on their origin, occupation and residence. Many Italians and Italians who became naturalised Australian are not registered by the Italian consular office, as it was not specifically required by the Italian law. Consequently, records have little value and cannot be considered a reliable and complete data source.

An additional source was represented by contacts with the local Tuscany Club of Balcatta, W.A., a cultural association that gathers a considerable number of migrants from Tuscany now residing in the Perth Metropolitan Area. The club has more than 600 members, although the membership is not strictly limited to Tuscans. While information on their social activities and on Tuscan identity in Western Australia will be widely examined further, it is worth stating that a considerable number of members have been helpful in identifying and integrating most of the records collected through the mentioned sources. Contacts with the Tuscan association have been useful to integrate the data, adding information on single migrants, even of the pre-war period, whom most members had known directly. This last source has been considered helpful for an additional qualitative survey, which is part of the present study and whose outcomes will be extensively analysed further ahead. By combining all of these sources, it has been possible to collect detailed information about over 1,200 people of Tuscan origin who arrived in Western Australia between the late 1890s and the mid 1960s, with a large group that arrived mainly between 1924 and the mid 1960s.

Records providing details such as date and place of birth, occupation in Italy, date of entry in Australia, occupation and place of residence in WA, have been computer databased in order to elaborate migratory patterns, occupational status and mobility. Data on the number of migrants from the studied area have been compared with information supplied by other research outcomes. There is no published work showing figures on the precise number of migrants from Tuscany who moved and settled in Western Australia, and this circumstance confirms the originality of the present work. Farnocchia, in her study of migratory patterns from Garfagnana to foreign destinations, provides some figures with respect to the number of those who moved to Australia between 1920 and 1969.[1] The extrapolation of records of migrants from the same area of Garfagnana and for the same period has allowed a comparison of figures from the two sources, as shown in Table 5-1.

Table 5-1 - Number of Migrants from Tuscany to Western Australia and to Australia, 1920-1969

	to W.A.	to Australia
1920-1929	174	171
1930-1939	115	125
1940-1949	100	31
1950-1959	550	286
1960-1969	77	277
TOTAL	1,016	890

Source: Farnocchia, 1996: 42

Except for the period 1950-69, the number of Lucchesi in Western Australia of this study corresponds to that of Australia by Farnocchia. An explanation is that the main focus of pre-war Lucchese migration to this country was in fact directed to Western Australia, whereas migrants from other Tuscan areas are recorded in other states. For the period 1950-59, however, figures on Lucchesi in Western Australia are higher than those in Australia as a whole (550 against 286). This difference is due to the sources utilised in the two studies. Farnocchia has examined archival records in local communities of Garfagnana, whose records on departure of migrants lack completeness, due to the nature of the records themselves. Many prospective migrants, in fact, never cancelled their presence at the local registry office at time of departure, probably because when they left for Australia they still aimed to reside abroad for a short period of time, unlike what happened in reality. Nevertheless, the source of the Australian Archives used for this study unmistakably 'photographs' the presence of migrants in Australia. Hence, the more accurate figures of the latter source.

With respect to the period 1960-69, on the other hand, the smaller figures shown in this study are explained by the unavailability of access to records on migrants after the mid-1960s, since the Australian Archives do not allow public access to documents unless they are at least 30 years old. Farnocchia, instead, in her record of migrants to Australia, could count on the same access to communal archives of Garfagnana, thus showing higher figures. Additional confirmation of the reliability of figures used for this thesis comes from the comparison between the number of migrants from Garfagnana and the mid-valley of River Serchio to Australia, drawn from Farnocchia, and the number of those from the same areas who went to Western Australia, whose records have been collected at the Australian Archives of W.A. (Table 5-2). In this graph, data are split per single commune of origin and for the period 1921-1991. These curves have similar patterns too. The comparison of figures shows only notable differences in the records of few Communes (i.e., Coreglia Antelminelli, Fabbriche Vallico, Giuncugnano and Piazza Serchio), probably due to particular circumstances in the data registration of each commune archive.

Table 5-2 - Number of Migrants from the high and mid-valley of River Serchio to Australia and to Western Australia, 1921-1991

	to Australia, 1921-1991	to WA, 1898-1966
Bagni di Lucca	47	42
Barga	21	18
Borgo Mozzano	51	69
Camporgiano	16	10
Careggine	14	10
Castelnuovo Garfagnana	46	72
Castiglione Garfagnana	0	0
Coreglia Antelminelli	31	89
Fabbriche Vallico	3	31
Fosciandora	30	36
Gallicano	27	34
Giuncugnano	120	64
Minucciano	71	104
Molazzana	6	13
Piazza Serchio	47	109
Pieve Fosciana	9	12
Sillano	17	11
S.Romano Garfagnana	88	52
Vagli Sotto	8	6
Villa Collemandina	11	8
TOTAL	663	790

Source: Farnocchia, 1996: 44

The number of migrants recorded by Farnocchia is lower in some communes (Coreglia Antelminelli, Fabbriche Vallico and Piazza Serchio) and higher in others (Giuncugnano, San Romano Garfagnana), in comparison to the data of the present study. On the whole, the tendency of over-estimation and under-estimation in the figures of a limited number of communes, drawn from the two sources, seems to reduce the risk of errors and ultimately confirm again the reliability of the sources and methods applied in this study.

Furthermore, it is possible to compare the figures drawn from these two studies on a more limited period of time, as in Table 5-3. In this case, the curves related to the number of Lucchesi, who are respectively recorded in Australia and in Western Australia in the 1950s per single Commune of origin, are even more similar.

Table 5-3 - Number of Migrants from the high valley of River Serchio to Australia, compared to the number to Western Australia, 1950s

	to Australia1950s	to WA, 1950s
Camporgiano	10	5
Careggine	18	11
Castelnuovo Garfagnana	38	23
Castiglione Garfagnana	3	0
Fosciandora	30	16
Gallicano	32	14
Giuncugnano	53	40
Minucciano	56	27
Molazzana	7	4
Piazza Serchio	34	22
Pieve Fosciana	3	6
S.Romano Garfagnana	51	60
Sillano	12	4
Vagli Sotto	18	1
Villa Collemandina	6	2
TOTAL	371	235

Source: Farnocchia, 1996: 204-208

The figures shows a prevalence of records by Farnocchia on those of this research. Again, two reasons are possible. First, figures by Farnocchia are related to Australia in general, when, as previously outlined how, during the post-war Italian emigration other Australian states were chosen by Tuscan migrants, unlike the general trend of the 1920s and 1930s, which had seen a major intake of Lucchesi in Western Australia. Secondly, the larger number of records of this study has been drawn from the naturalization files, held by the Australian Archives. This circumstance implies that the wider and more reliable number of records used in this study is related to the period between the 1930s and the early 1950s. In fact, naturalizations of migrants who arrived during the 1950s took place in a later period, more likely from the early to mid-1960s, and their files are not yet available at the Australian Archives.

Whilst some methodological problems are examined in the next section, the discussion demonstrates the reliability of the records collected on migrants from Tuscany in Western Australia. Hence, the usefulness of the sources, which can be consulted for other ethnic-related purposes and in relation to other migrant groups.

METHODOLOGICAL PROBLEMS

The records collected do not give a completely accurate picture of emigration from the Province of Lucca and Massa Carrara to Western Australia, due to the characteristics of each single source. First, the naturalization files of the Australian Archives of W.A. give an account only of Tuscan migrants who applied for naturalization between the mid-1920s and the late 1940s. Although the number of those who became naturalized was considerable during the late 1930s and immediately after WWII, this source does not offer any possibility to count with precision the migrants who arrived in Western Australia from the mid-1920s and chose not to naturalize. Some of the reasons for this choice lie in the fact that Italian migrants either did not want to surrender their Italian nationality, although settling permanently in Australia, or returned to Italy after a period of residence in the host country. It can be argued that the proportion of those who decided to settle permanently in Australia and maintained Italian allegiance is negligible. In addition, aspects of return migration, although important in migration studies for many reasons, have not been considered within this study, although it would deserve a wide and further research.

Second, the use of the Commonwealth Entry forms as a source for the present study does not offer a complete picture of migrants who entered Western Australia. There are cases in which Italian migrants first landed in other Australian ports and then moved to Western Australia to work and settle. Conversely, there may be cases in which they landed in Fremantle (the main port of Western Australia), but then moved interstate. In the first instance, some records of interstate migrants have been retrieved through the files of the pensioners' agencies. In the second instance, extra care has been taken in cross-tabulating the records gathered through the Commonwealth Entry forms with the data collected with the additional sources (pensioners' agencies and Italian Consulate in particular), to ensure that most records of Italian migrants entering Western Australia were retrievable. The outcome of the cross-tabulation confirms that a very large percentage of the migrants from Tuscany who landed in Fremantle settled permanently in Western Australia.

Additional problems arising from the sources chosen are more easily identifiable. Files of migrants held by Italian pensions' agencies in Perth and Fremantle give account only of those who had previous occupational experience in Italy, such to allow them to apply for an Italian pension as residents abroad, either they were Italians or Australian naturalised Italians. Consequently, these data are not useful to identify migrants who came to Western Australia as minors or in schooling age, whereas a relatively small number of other Italians residing in Western Australia might not be aware or interested in the possibility of applying for an Italian pension. Nevertheless, the high correspondence between the number of migrants, whose files are held by the pensioners' offices, with the records collected through the Commonwealth Entry forms (especially for the post-war period), confirms the accuracy of sources and collected data. Finally, information on migrants collected at the Consular archive and the Tuscan Association have integrated the records, rather than adding new ones. Reasons lay in the inaccuracy and incompleteness of the Consular source, whereas contacts with informers and interviewees of the Tuscany Club have been mostly utilised for the qualitative aspect of this study.

The analysis of data presents some weaknesses. First, as Price as noted in his quantitative study on southern Europeans in Australia,[2] some migrants have not always been accurate about the dates in which they moved from one place in Australia to another, when filling in their applications for naturalization.[3] In some cases they did not remember minor moves and places where they settled for short periods of time. Secondly, with respect to occupational patterns in Western Australia, when filling in the Commonwealth entry form at time of disembarking in Fremantle, some migrants may have stated their intended occupation in the country, therefore being inaccurate in what may have later been their real occupation. Nevertheless, records do give some measure of their geographical distribution and occupational patterns, enabling the extent to which places and occupations in Western Australia attracted, and maybe repelled, Tuscan labour.

The most laborious step in the analysis of geographical distribution, mobility and occupational patterns of Tuscan migrants in Western Australia was to construct charts related to these needs. Each record, corresponding to a migrant, contains several information set in fields, such as their identity, date and place of birth, occupation in Italy, year of arrival in Western Australia, occupation in the host country, residence, split by suburbs (for the Perth urban area) and by towns/villages (for rural and remote areas of Western Australia). The geographical distribution of migrants, pivotal for this study, has been classified by post codes, as the subdivision by these areas - by single suburbs in the Perth Metropolitan area and by larger geographical areas in rural and remote Western Australia - has resulted in a graphically acceptable display of their spatial presence.

By linking the Geographical Information System (GIS) data sets available by post codes for the Perth Metropolitan region and Western Australia, with the database gathered on migrants, it has been possible to cross-tabulate fields to answer different questions. The GIS maps drawn from all sort of different queries are the object of the wider analysis of the distribution and mobility of migrants from the provinces of Lucca and Massa Carrara in Western Australia, which form the contents of the following chapter.

Data analysis and map drawing involved at least two technical problems. The first problem was related to the life cycle of each single migrant, as recorded in the database. Files of naturalisation and Commonwealth Entry forms do not give account for the length of life of each migrant, unless information was supplied by additional sources, such as those of the Consular archive and from direct informers. More likely, data were integrated and corrected according to information gathered at the pensioners' offices, as these agencies hold records only of people alive at the time of collection (1997). In the cases where this integration was not possible, a life expectancy of about 75 years for men and 80 for women was established, in order to interrupt the life cycle of the migrants' data when unknown, for the purpose of indicating their residential location without over-representing their distribution for too long a period.

The second technical problem, similar to that noted by Price in his cited work,[4] appeared when some migrants, mainly at time of filling in their naturalization papers, did not indicate any suburb of residence. Where Tuscan settlers simply put 'Perth' without any suburb, there was no alternative but to lump them together in Perth as the central city district. As there were undoubtedly some Italian and Tuscan concentrations in the inner city, and in particular in the inner city suburb of Northbridge, the extent of their agglomeration has been exaggerated, as it results from the thematic maps of their concentration in Perth Metropolitan Area.

As Price also noted in his work on the study of naturalization records of southern Europeans,[5] there are other difficulties about assessing ethnic agglomerations by counting migrant moves. While settlers often indicated suburbs or townships to which they moved when filling in their applications for naturalization, not the same accuracy has been noted for the indication of the occupations performed. Hence, the method used here does not give the exact account of the number of activities performed by migrants in any kind of agglomeration at any one time. In some cases, naturalisation files give information only on a little, and a relatively smaller number of activities carried out. Nevertheless, it is impossible, even at micro demographic levels, to split occupations and moves in more accurate figures. The real imperfection is that the method gives greater weight to 'wanderers' than to those who stayed in the first place of settlement for their whole working cycle. Given these circumstances, the stress on wanderers (or temporary migrants), from Tuscany give more value to the study, for at least two different reasons. First, as the method highlights with more emphasis mobility than 'stability', it will draw more attention to some of the characteristics of the century-long Lucchese migratory pattern, as examined in the previous chapters. Secondly, although migration studies focus on the analysis of migrant settlements and their continuity in time, the migration process itself is a phenomenon of mobility. If mobility is the primary factor affecting migration, as such it should be examined within the host country, where internal migration in different geographical areas and occupational sectors often continues.

One example of this stress on mobility rather than stability is offered by the following report of one of the informers contacted at the Tuscany Club. He reported that he arrived in Fremantle from the Province of Lucca in 1927. On arrival, he joined some relatives in the rural area of Karragullen, near Perth, where he worked as farm hand for a few months. He then went to live in the Northbridge area, and was employed as a kitchen hand and labourer in a restaurant run by some migrants from his same Tuscan community. In the early 1930s, he moved to the remote mining town of Wiluna, where he joined his father who had resided in Australia for over a decade. There he worked as a miner for over ten years, before settling in Yokine, a northern suburb of Perth, where he was a janitor, labourer and later a fish and chip shop-owner, until his retirement in the late 1960s. While this detailed report has been supplied by a direct informer,[6] his naturalization file, held by the Australian Archives of WA, contains a shorter amount of information: periods of residence in all areas are indicated, but there is no evidence of the activities performed in the initial stages of settlement (Karragullen and Northbridge), as the only occupation registered was as a miner in Wiluna.[7] While the records related to the migrant's mobility path contribute for four different units to the total of his geographical settlements (Karragullen, Northbridge, Wiluna, Yokine), his occupational choice contributes for only three (miner, janitor and trader). Conversely, a migrant who settled in Perth and remained in the same area/suburb for all his/her working life would contribute to the mobility's analysis with just one unit.

With respect to occupations performed by Tuscan migrants in Western Australia, it is still possible to delineate occupational patterns from any data, as they often give with accuracy the occupational range within which migrants moved throughout their working cycle. However, the difficulty represented by the contribution of different record units to the analysis of geographical mobility and occupation is apparent. In fact, one of the aims of this study is to analyze the extent of the migratory mobility of Tuscans within Western Australia, in order to assess this factor in the light of historical, economic and social background factors of which Lucchese migrants are carriers. As Price has clearly indicated, "Mobile persons are more important than immobile ones, since it is during movement that a person can most easily shake off ethnic ties; consequently, the strength of ethnic ties becomes clearest during movement".[8]

In sum, the tendencies to errors of overestimation and underestimation of the various kinds of information of mobility and occupational patterns seem to work in opposite directions: mobility of Tuscan migrants has probably been overestimated, whereas occupational preferences are underestimated. This, however, should not carry undue weight, because one of the main purposes of this study is to stress the importance of Tuscan occupational tendencies within circumscribed areas (either townships or metropolitan suburbs) of Western Australia, as a characteristic of Lucchese people. An under-estimation in calculations therefore seems preferable to an over-estimation. In addition, no other statistics are as informative and reliable as these on such a small scale case study, referred to a specific Italian regional group within one Australian state. In particular, Australian Census statistics of birthplace are not split by geographical sub-areas of origin, although there are cultural and social differences between migrants from different areas of the same country. Census statistics present the difficulty of lumping most Italian migrants residing in Australia into the deceptive category of nationality at birth, and of saying nothing about their spatial movements within the host country during the intercensual periods. Consequently, provided due recognition is given to the drawbacks outlined, the method of assessing Tuscan settlements and migrant mobility by moves, as shown on naturalisation records, according to a methodology first used by Price[9] and here adjusted and integrated by additional sources, seems reliable and most informative.

PRELIMINARY CONSIDERATIONS ON FIRST SETTLEMENTS OF TUSCAN MIGRANTS IN WESTERN AUSTRALIA

Ethnic concentrations are a natural consequence of the need to adjust to new environments, often characterised by discrimination and disadvantage that immigrants experience in the labour and housing markets.[10] Thus, migrant groups are not uniformly distributed throughout Australia's economy and society. This has been reflected in the spatial distribution for most overseas-born groups, which differs from that of the Australian-born population, significantly influencing the distribution of population and changes in the labour force.[11]

The spatial distribution of Italians in Australia is of particular interest because, as Price outlined in his classic study of southern Europeans in Australia, patterns of settlement are inextricably bound up with a whole range of social and economic elements influencing their occupations, mobility and social life. Before WWII, one of the highest concentrations of Italians in Australia (over one third of the whole number) was in Queensland, where migrants were mainly employed in the sugar cane industry. The mechanization of this sector in the early 1960s has drastically reduced the farming workforce in the state.[12] At present, less than 7 per cent of Australia's Italian-born population reside in Queensland.[13] In a similar way, the first considerable Italian settlements in Western Australia of the 1920s were in the goldfields, where migrants were employed in the mining and timber industries. Gradually, from the late 1930s, migrants tended to move away from mining and timber cutting, and towards farming. During the 1940s and 1950s, the wheat belt of the eastern and south-western areas of Western Australia saw numerous groups of Italian migrants employed in farming activities.[14]

Shortly after WWII, Western Australia was still the most rural of the Australian states, and 57 per cent of the Italian-born population still lived in rural areas.[15] Nevertheless, from the late 1950s, these communities of migrants moved towards the metropolitan area of Perth, where a large majority of them now live.[16] For Australia as a whole, the proportion of Italian-born people living in cities has been considerably below the average of the total population until the mid-1950s. Since that period, there has been a tendency for the overseas born to concentrate in circumscribed urban districts, as a growing characteristic of migratory movements in industrialized countries.[17] Possible reasons lie in the availability of work opportunities in factories and the tertiary industry in general, the closeness to workplace,[18] as well as lower costs of housing in some inner city suburbs and industrial areas.[19] Many ethnic groups in Australia tend to be more concentrated during the first period of their settlement in the host country, and they disperse in the outer suburbs at a second stage, in order to satisfy housing aspirations associated with life-cycle stage and ability to pay for better housing.[20]

Migrants from Tuscany do not differ markedly from these settlement and occupational patterns, although there are some variations, which can be considered specific for this Italian sub-regional group. As will be examined below, their arrival, mobility, occupational and settlements patterns followed specific paths. Differences can be noted between Italian migrants as a whole, and Tuscans in particular, in the attitude towards the many aspects of the migratory process, such as the choice of initial destinations and occupations, as well as their mobility in relation to job and housing availability. One of the aims of this study is to highlight these differences as originated by a different attitude to migration, which finds its roots in the historical and socio-economic contexts that the Provinces of Lucca and Massa Carrara have experienced during these recent centuries.

Studies on migrants' spatial distribution and mobility have outlined several factors influencing where immigrants settle upon their arrival in Australia. These factors have been summarized in recent work by Hugo as job and housing opportunities, timing and scale of migratory waves, language barriers, marginalisation through social control mechanisms, and location of family members and fellow countrymen in the host country.[21]

Job opportunity is the major factor attracting migrants within certain areas. What has been outlined with respect to the settlement of

Italian migrants in both Queensland and Western Australia at the earlier stage of Italian migration to Australia, also applies to the major urban Italian concentrations in Australia of the post-war period. With respect to migration from Tuscany, the presence of working opportunities within the most important economic areas of Western Australia has attracted workers on temporary and permanent bases at different stages, as will be examined further. The gold mining industry from the late 1890s to the late 1930s, the massive South-West woodcutting from the 1920s and the 1960s, market gardening in the outskirts of Perth and tertiary urban businesses, such as catering and trading, from the late 1920s to the 1960s, have all lured large contingents of migrants from Tuscany.

Housing opportunities is another relevant factor effecting the settlement of ethnic groups in the host society. Especially between the 1920s and the 1960s, the bulk of cheap rental housing in the inner city suburbs of Perth has attracted Italians and Tuscans migrants. With particular reference to the northern suburbs of Perth, large contingents of Tuscans have settled there because of cheaper rental and purchase costs and the proximity to areas where they performed their occupations, like suburban market gardening, factory or small business employment.

In his study on migrant settlement factors, Hugo indicated that timing is an additional element influencing spatial distribution:

> *"When the peak immigration of the waves of particular groups occurs makes a difference. The spatial distribution of particular job and housing opportunities is constantly changing so that the pattern that existed during the peak immigration of one group will not necessarily apply during the peak period of settlement of another group".*[22]

This consideration can be applied to Italians in general and to Tuscans in particular, since the migration patterns from Lucca developed in times slightly different from those from other Italian regional areas. Consequently, their distribution appears to illustrate different characteristics.

The number of Italian and Tuscan migrants arriving in urban or rural areas is therefore significant. A small migratory flow is more likely to be dispersed than a large number, especially in urban areas. When the flow of migrants from a specific area is larger, their settlements will tend to be absorbed within specific urban clusters, either at the fringe of the city, where the main stock of newly constructed housing is concentrated,[23] or where housing is cheaper. Since migrants from Lucca arrived in Western Australia in a more notable number only from the 1930s, their spatial distribution was not visible until that period. Conversely, from the early 1950s, with the mass arrival of migrants from Tuscany, some Perth suburbs reflected these concentrations. Additional factors of the geographical settlement of migrants are their incapacity to master English, thus pushing many of them to congregate for mutual support, and the marginalisation through social control mechanisms, such as those in the housing market, preventing some migrant groups from entering particular market niches.[24]

Finally, the location of family members and fellow countrymen amongst Italian migrants is considered more important than for the Australian-born. The importance of family and community ties in determining the initial location of Italian migrants is indicative of the importance of the role of chain migration. As its definition implies, chain migration can only operate once an immigrant community is in place, and is vital in generating flows of immigrants and determining their location in Australia.[25]

CHAIN MIGRATION

The formation of spatially-defined ethnic settlements is a complex phenomenon that reflects absorption trends within society,[26] as the result of the various factors discussed in the previous section. Migration patterns are crucial elements in residential distribution. Price and Martin classified the migratory patterns towards Australia assisted, free, chain and refugee. In particular:

> *"The great majority of British and Dutch migrants have been Government-assisted, the migrants normally paying only $20 per person for passage to Australia. Unassisted migrants*

> *have had to pay their own way: chain migrants, mainly from southern Europe, have not been assisted by governments so that the cost of passage, often prohibitive, has had to be borne by the migrant of his family. Chain migration too, with its family and kinship networks, has given rise to many strongly clustered settlements which are in reality multiple nuclei, either within major ethnic concentrations or in separate parts of the city".*[27]

A large number of studies on Italian migration to Australia[28] confirm that the majority of Italian migrants have come through a chain migration process. This procedure means that migration began with a pioneer who, after having spent a few years in Australia, was joined by either relatives or people from the same community of origin. Later, migrants were joined by other relatives or friends. Italian migration to Australia became considerable only from the mid-1920s. Like the earlier migration to the United States and Latin American countries, Italian migrants, acting as 'pioneers' in Australia since the 1920s, paid their own fare, thus confirming the social and economic conditions of Lucchesi migrants previously discussed. They were not from the poorest areas of Italy, but from areas where independent peasants and small proprietors predominated, and where economic pressures had not yet reduced living standards to a level which made the cost of emigration to Australia impossible.[29]

Chain migration on a large scale can operate only once an immigrant community is in place. For a community to generate a flow of immigrants proportional to its size, it must also be fairly youthful. In fact, "older communities do not generate significant chain migration as potential sponsors will have parents who are no longer alive and/or brothers and sisters who are established in their home country and who are unlikely to wish to emigrate".[30] As migrants arrive in the host country through a chain process, it is likely that they will initially settle in the same place as their sponsors. Very often, relatives took charge of providing accommodation and contributing to the payment of the ship passage of the prospective immigrants.[31] This assistance from family members and siblings played an important role in the selection of migrants in Italy and their subsequent settlement patterns in Australia.

As Lee has well documented in his case study on Italian migrants in Melbourne,[32] strong migration chains were largely drawn from small areas, rather than on an Italian national basis. This circumstance reflects the fact that family and community loyalties were (and, at some extent, still are) strong amongst Italians and Lucchesi coming from rural areas. In her study on the social network generated within the migration process, Piselli states that kinship implies the observation of mutual obligations that reproduce and confirm the relation. To pass information to a relative means to comply with a past obligation and to create a new one for the future. Relatives help each other in the supply of information on job availability and this help gives a new stimulus to their relationship.[33] These relations, and the social networks generated by them, were so strong as to create a 'comfort zone' and such that "the *paesano* in the Dantesque hell of the new world was not lost to his hometown but was merely sojourning in his hometown's 'colony' abroad".[34]

The geographical space of departure and of arrival becomes less relevant than the strong network of social solidarity from where the migratory process starts. The efficacious social network of the community of migrants is now the focus, and, as such, it eases the migratory flow towards a specific community of arrival, giving ample explanation of spatial concentrations of migrants in some areas rather than in others.

Another explanation why Italians and Lucchesi did not disperse throughout the urban areas of Australia as quickly as other immigrants is found in their migrating goals, as Cinel observed in his study on Italians in San Francisco.[35] Because Italian immigrants did not intend, at least at first, to stay in Australia, most of them secured only temporary, usually seasonal, employment, through well-established compatriots who mediated between the new arrivals and the local Australian working environment. Under these circumstances, they were under no compulsion to move out of their settlements. This is the case of Lucchesi, already observed in other host countries as France.[36]

Furthermore, Lancaster Jones has demonstrated that at the sub-regional and provincial level, a whole series of independent chain migrations amongst Italians took place from different villages.[37] In this respect, the present work examines why, how and where Tuscans and Lucchesi settled in Western Australia for a range of different historical and socio-economic reasons. An additional purpose of analysing their spatial distribution in the Perth Metropolitan area is to show the territorial concentration of migrants, according to the many migratory chains initiated in different townships and communities of origin.

Patterns of chain migration show two essential movements of Italians arriving in Australia since the mid-1920s. First, a series of single males of relatively young working age, as representatives of the pioneering stage of the consistent Italian Australian settlement. First arrivals were followed by a second wave of wives and children. This pattern was unintentionally reinforced by Australian immigration policy: under sponsorship arrangements, Italians already in the country could help their relatives to get visas by providing accommodation and work for them on arrival.[38] In his study on southern Europeans in Australia, Price integrated the sequential arrival of these two waves of males and their families with the development of a third migratory stage, in which the re-joined families of Italian migrants, now geographically settled, and economically more secure, are followed by the arrival of parents and siblings,[39] as other scholars have indicated in the specific case of northern Italians and Tuscans.[40]

Family and interpersonal contacts of migrants have played an important role in channelling migration from distant, often rural and mountain areas of origin to Australia. The whole process has been described by some social geographers:

> *"Typically, one person, a family, or a few families migrate from a small town or rural area to a distant city. Upon finding*

work in that city they write to friends and relatives "back home" indicating that work may be found and perhaps telling about some of the attractions of city life. More individuals then migrate and, in turn, write back to their friends and relatives. Through this process, potential migrants find out more about opportunities in that particular city than they would be likely to find out through media sources. Also, they are attracted by the fact that they already have friends and relatives at their destination who might provide comfort, help in a job search, or perhaps offer them a place to stay initially. Over time a channelized flow develops and becomes entrenched, based upon a social-communications network that short-circuits distance with comparative ease".[41]

Within the third stage, as described by Price, and particularly the arrival of a money remittance or a letter to relatives in Italy, constituted for a long time one of the most convincing motives to expatriate.[42] Migrants' letters telling with enthusiasm about 'America' circulated amongst prospective migrants in the communities of origin since the beginning of Italian mass migration of the late 1880s and 1890s. Accounts of host countries where migrants were settling used to go around the townships and rural areas of origin, following family and community 'paths', and often producing new migratory waves that reflected the intricate network of family and social links.[43]

What actually pushes a person's decision to emigrate is not merely the presence of relatives and friends abroad or the existence of ethnic communities and institutions abroad. Nevertheless, letters from 'America' about the living standards and economic conditions in Australia have certainly had a strong influence in the communities of origin, often overriding other considerations,[44] and becoming a strong pull factor. Consequently, Italian chain migration to Australia has been very sensitive to economic booms and depressions in the host country, as is inevitable when migrants abroad may have to finance their relatives' passages and find them accommodation and employment at their first stage of settlement in Australia.

MIGRATORY CHAINS FROM TUSCANY TO WESTERN AUSTRALIA

Informal interviews conducted between mid-1997 and early 1998 with members of the Tuscan community of Perth have generated data on spatial distribution, occupational choice and social activities of over 30 first generation Lucchesi and Tuscans residing in Western Australia, whose outcomes will be extensively examined further. As part of the interviews, migrants have also been asked to recall previous records of migration of their ancestors. The objective was to draw selected layouts of family trees in order to analyse whether evident patterns of chain migration were present within the Lucchese community of Western Australia, with the further aim to possibly link these chains to their spatial distribution both in Perth and in Western Australia. The methodology of interviewing first generation migrants with the purpose of drawing family trees tracing migratory experiences of their ancestors has been successfully utilised in Australia with respect to another northern Italian sub-regional group.[45]

While over forty interviews were conducted, a smaller number of family trees has been drawn because of the lack of memory of interviewees about identity, occupation and overseas destinations of their ancestors. Nevertheless, it has been possible to collect information on about 35 family trees, the data of which are in the Appendix of this thesis. Family trees show records on all the relatives that the interviewees remembered, often indicating names, dates of birth, and foreign countries where their relatives moved and worked as migrants, both on a temporary or permanent basis. Except for some cases in which the migrant interviewed acted as a 'pioneer' in Western Australia, without being proceeded by relatives, the large majority of family trees show a pattern of migratory chains. For instance, the first member of the family D.S., originally from the Commune of Capannori (in the low valley of the River Serchio), who emigrated to Australia was Edoardo (born in 1846), the grandfather of Ernesto, the interviewee.[46]

The family tree shows that Edoardo had already performed frequent seasonal trips to Corsica in his younger years (between the 1860s and the mid 1880s), according to a pattern of temporary migration. During the mid-1870s, he settled back in the community of origin (possibly with more trips to Corsica during the winter months), and established his family, as is shown by the years of birth of his children, all born between 1874 and 1882. He then departed by himself for Western Australia in the late 1880s, where he resided until 1908, sending money to his family in Capannori. As soon as the two elder sons - Angelo (born in 1877) and Giovanni (born in 1879), the father of Ernesto - reached the working age, they joined their father in Western Australia in 1895. The family tree shows that Giovanni also worked seasonally in Corsica the year before migrating to Australia. Angelo, the eldest son, worked in Western Australia with his father Edoardo until 1910, while his brother Giovanni moved with the youngest brother Tommaso to the United States in 1898, where he resided for about 10 years. It is worth observing that the two daughters of Edoardo never moved from the Commune of Capannori.

Both the father, Edoardo, and the three sons, Giovanni, Angelo and Tommaso, returned to Italy in 1910 and settled permanently there. Giovanni established his own family, whilst there are no records of his brothers and sisters. He left again for Western Australia in 1924, where he was finally joined by his first son Ernesto in 1927, while his other brothers and sisters never moved from Italy. Nevertheless, Giovanni finally returned permanently to Italy in 1935.

The study of the family tree of Ernesto delineates fascinating patterns of chain migration and mobility. The first aspect is the adaptability to move around foreign and geographically distant countries, pursuing occupational opportunities in order to make money to bring back to the community of origin. On the other hand, chain migration is here in its 'embryonic' form. The 'pioneer' Edoardo opened the path to Western Australia to his two sons Angelo and Giovanni, whereas Tommaso, the third male child, went to the United States with Giovanni, who had remained in Western Australia only for a few years. Unfortunately, the interviewee Ernesto did not recall any other older relatives or township folk in the United States who may have facilitated access to this country to

Tommaso and Giovanni, although it is likely that this circumstance took place. After the American experience and the First World War, Giovanni left again for Western Australia, thus facilitating the access to Australia to his son Ernesto. Within this family, Lucchese migration demonstrated a temporary character. While his grandfather, uncle and father returned to Italy and settled permanently back in Capannori, it is only with Ernesto, and, possibly, by his marriage with an Anglo-Australian woman in the mid-1930s in the remote mining town of Wiluna, that the migratory experience took a permanent character.

Furthermore, the family tree of first generation Tuscan-Australian migrant Pietro C. (born in 1928), from the Commune of Casola Lunigiana in the upper valley of Garfagnana and now Province of Massa Carrara, suggests another type of chain migration and settlement patterns.[47] His grandfather Pietro had migrated to France on a temporary basis before the turn of the twentieth century, with intermittent trips home, where his family resided.

There he was joined for temporary work by his children Francesco, Domenico and Annita. On the other hand, the fourth child of Pietro, Cesare, moved with his male cousin Samuele to Western Australia in 1924, both working in the Swan Valley area (not distant from Perth) as vignerons. While there, by the turn of the 1930s, they were joined by Amante, nephew of Samuele, who was also employed in the same area and occupation. It is interesting to observe that both the cousins Cesare and Samuele returned to Italy by the late 1930s, confirming a pattern of temporary migration. None of their brothers and sisters ever joined them while in Western Australia. On the other hand, Amante remained and settled in Western Australia when his uncle Samuele departed for Italy. None of Amante's three brothers ever joined him. As a more interesting pattern of chain migration, it must be added that in the early 1950s, when migration from most Italian regions took off in large numbers again, Amante acted as an Australian sponsor for one of his nephews, Ruggero, and the latter's cousin Pietro, the interviewee. These two migrants joined their sponsor in the Upper Swan and settled permanently in Western Australia.

This second example illustrates a more complex form of chain migration. As the layout of the family tree graphically shows, the kinship links between the two first generation Tuscans at the bottom of each one of the two family branches (Pietro and Ruggero) imply strong family ties, that are certainly reflected in different patterns of spatial distribution. In both cases the geographical destination and, quite often, the occupational pattern of sponsored migrants from small rural and mountain communities of northern Tuscany, coincide with those of their sponsors at the first stage of their settlement in Western Australia.

As a provisional conclusion, it can be stated that the large majority of family trees drawn confirm the importance of family and village links within Italian migration to Western Australia. The layout of family trees displays the tendency of migratory chains to concentrate, on the long period, in cognate economical and geographical areas of destination[48] and to strengthen the formation of kinship links, as already examined in a similar study on migrants from Valtellina (northern Italy) to Australia.[49] This pattern derives from the century-long tradition of seasonal migration of Lucchese and northern Italian people in general. Since the unification of Italy, the trend expanded into a migratory strategy focused on the goal of quick money accumulation to bring back to the community of origin, as has been examined in previous chapters with respect to what has been called the 'Lucca model'. Nevertheless, this pattern has been later modified by a long series of domestic and international reasons of historical and economic nature, such as the rise of Fascism in Italy, the economic Depression of the early 1930s, WWII and mass migration to Australia in the 1950s. These reasons have certainly affected Italian migration to Australia, changing the pattern of temporary migration into a permanent one.

CHAPTER 6

THE SPATIAL DISTRIBUTION OF TUSCAN MIGRANTS IN WESTERN AUSTRALIA

INTRODUCTION

Economic factors have been repeatedly analysed within this study, as reasons to migrate from the country of origin to that of destination. Furthermore, the assumption of this discussion is that Italian migrants concentrate or disperse in their spatial distribution in Australia according to factors such as social and cultural background, the migration patterns they followed, occupational and residential opportunities and the reception/reaction of the host country. The pattern is one of a community consolidation with a relatively low degree of residential dispersion. This pattern is explained within the ethnic context of stages of settlements and adjustments of Italian migrants, which have been part of a wider process of social integration. The possible indices of this are naturalization, intermarriage, occupation and knowledge of English,[1] as will be examined later.

This process of social integration, whether it can be now considered completed by Italian migrants in Australia or not, is certainly not completed with respect to their spatial distribution in urban Australia.[2] The present work has already shown that Lucchesi hold a historical, economical and social background dissimilar from other Italian migrants. Furthermore, previous chapters have examined how the particular socio-economic context in the communities of origin has influenced patterns of chain migration from the Provinces of Lucca and Massa Carrara. It is now worth considering how these historical, social and migration patterns have influenced Lucchese settlements in Perth and Western Australia, in the light of the additional factors of occupational and residential opportunities, and whether the combination of these elements has created a specific Lucchese spatial distribution context in Western Australia or not.

As maps of the geographical presence of Tuscany-born migrants have been drawn, it is worth repeating that all data have been collected at the Australian Archives of W.A. and at the other cited sources. In addition, all boundaries, whether in Perth Metropolitan Area, in the South-West of Western Australia or in Western Australia state as a whole, relate to the Australian post code classification.

THE PIONEERING PERIOD OF TUSCANS TO PERTH, 1890-1918

As previously stated, the number of Tuscany-born migrants who moved to Western Australia is irrelevant until the end of the First World War. It is important to specify that, although the number of records collected about migrants from Tuscany in Western Australia is over 1,200, only records with all completed fields are taken into account, thus reducing the number to about one thousand. The graph shows a higher number of migrants arriving between 1920 and 1964, which, independently from the sources utilized, remains the peak period of Italian migration to Australia.

Australia certainly did not represent an appealing destination for Tuscan migrants until the United States imposed strict entry restrictions in the early 1920s. Nevertheless, if data on Tuscany-born migrants in Western Australia are disaggregated by Perth's suburbs of destination, it is possible to observe how their distribution is concentrated in a very limited number of areas, although the distribution-related maps require a methodological explanation.

Where the number of migrants from Tuscany in each suburb, or shire in rural Western Australia, is very low for each class of values (class one containing just one migrant, class two with two migrants and so forth), the maps will represent the absolute number of migrants in each suburb. On the other hand, where the number of migrants per each suburb is higher, the maps will show their distribution by standard-deviation units.

The northern suburb of Osborne Park had the highest number of Lucchesi, since they were only four, and the number is confirmed by Gentilli, who reports from a previous study by Gava the arrival of four Lucchesi in the two suburbs of Osborne Park and Wanneroo between 1898 and 1914.[3] Scattered migrants are recorded in West Perth and single Tuscans in the northern suburbs of North Perth, Leederville, and along the Upper Swan River, in the suburbs of Bassendean and Guildford. These relatively small figures are partially confirmed by other studies. In his work on Italians in Western Australia, in fact, Gentilli notes the presence of Francesco Guelfi, and his family, from Capannori (Province of Lucca), initially in Leederville as a market gardener in 1901, and later, in 1911, involved in pig raising in the swampy lands around Osborne Park.[4] Furthermore, Price had already noted that Italians in their initial stage of settlement in Australia tended to distribute in the horticultural zones included within the metropolitan boundaries of the major Australian cities concentrating, with respect to Perth, to the "north of Osborne Park"[5] and acting as small-scale farmers.[6]

In addition, Gentilli states that Perth had a few Italian market gardeners by the end of the nineteenth century, and that traditional gardening sites were Osborne Park and Wanneroo (north of Osborne Park). Other areas were the alluvial flats of the Swan River,[7] in particular the suburbs of Bassendean and Guildford, once the most important wine-producing centre in Western Australia.[8] In this latter location there were also quarries and furnaces which would have attracted migrant workers.[9] For many years, market gardening in Australia was usually associated with the Chinese and yet the Italians managed to carve out a niche for themselves in the business, by importing and growing a large variety of vegetables more typical of European tastes and not yet known in Australia.[10]

The number of Tuscany and Lucca-born settlers in Perth was very small for the period 1890-1916, and limited to a maximum of 15-20 people.

THE INTER-WAR PERIOD IN PERTH, 1920-1939

The early 1920s brought many changes of significance for international migration. Again, the introduction of new criteria for the establishment of immigration quotas by the United States pushed many prospective Italian migrants to alternative countries of destination. Australia assumed for many of them the role of a 'new America' to conquer, and a direct shipping service by Italian ships to Australia was initiated.[11] As the number of migrants departing for Australia increased, this period can be identified as the beginning of the grouping of Italians within certain specific areas. In Perth, the larger intake of Italians between 1921 and 1933 was in the main areas of metropolitan development.[12] Inner city areas became the initial zones of more consistently concentrated Italian settlements, probably due to the fact that Italians sought their livelihoods in a narrow range of occupations.[13] Also, in the inner city suburbs (as James Street in the suburb of Northbridge) were located the settlements of the 'pioneers', who were now inviting relatives and friends to join them. On the whole, the pattern of settlement formed by Italian migrants in the Perth Metropolitan area in the 1920s laid the framework of subsequent ethnic concentrations. These locations provided in fact the stepping points from which the immigrants of the post-WWII period have been guided in their choice of residence, as it will be analysed in the next section.

If chain migration played a vital role in the arrival of a large number of migrants from Italy, on the other hand it conditioned the decision to locate in certain areas once they arrived in Perth. In this regard, Gentilli writes:

> *"It may also be held that chain migration, while of great help to the migrants during his move, may become a hindrance, if the ties continue to restrict his movement when it comes to the decision to choose a vocation between, on the one hand,*

the feeling of security given by closeness to familiar persons and a shared but limited environment and, on the other hand, the challenge to build a future among strangers in a new and almost boundless world".[14]

This consideration is here examined with respect to Lucchesi, analysing whether their patterns of chain migration limited their settlement and occupational decisions. The number of Lucchesi who moved to Western Australia increased during the period 1920-39 and their distribution in Perth was more dispersed than in the previous period. The highest concentration of Lucchesi is recorded in the areas which had been previously witnessed the presence of some migrants, as in Perth (which includes the suburb of Northbridge), North Perth and Osborne Park.

A notable number of Tuscan migrants are recorded in the south-east semi-rural suburbs of Kelmscott and Karragullen. Following the end of the First World War, the Discharged Soldier Settlement Act of 1918 initiated a scheme to settle returned soldiers on the land. Some of the areas in Perth to be opened for a scheme were around Kalamunda and Karragullen, as well as in Wanneroo, about twenty kilometres north of the city. Ex soldiers attended special schools to learn the rudiments of horticulture and, as soon as some work was done on the assigned land, the settlers were eligible for loans. While settlers with sufficient finances survived the years it took to clear the land and bring an orchard into production, others had to walk off the land, opening the way for the Italian-born population to move into the area from the mid-1920s. Accustomed to long hours of hard work, many Italians and Tuscans transformed the land into green oases of vegetable gardens or pasture for their dairy cattle.[15]

Rarely could recently-arrived Italian settlers buy land. Many Italian migrants who had been a few years in the country, working long hours in rural and remote areas, as will be examined further in this chapter, had saved enough money to either return home or buy land in the Karragullen and Kalamunda areas.[16] Apart from this main reason, it is worth stating that some Italians from the northern Apennines near the Province of Lucca had already settled at Kalamunda in the last decade of the nineteenth century,[17] although there are no records to prove that there were already some patterns of chain migration.

Several families of Lucchesi, namely the Bovani from Bagni Lucca (mid-valley of River Serchio), the Casotti from Minucciano (upper valley) and the Ghilarducci and Di Marco from Capannori (low valley) had established their residence as market gardeners and orchardists in the Kalamunda/Karragullen areas since the mid-late 1920s.[18] In the light of what has been stated with respect to patterns of chain migration, it is worth stressing that Ugo Bovani left Italy in 1926 to reach his brother-in-law Dante Di Marco in Western Australia, before being joined by his family in 1929. The two families decided to buy a small piece of land, which was cleared and adjusted to market garden, orchard and cow grazing.[19] Giovanni Ghilarducci arrived in Western Australia in 1927 with his son Sebastian, leaving his wife and other children in Italy. According to a pattern followed by many other Lucchesi, before migrating to Western Australia he had already spent a few years in the United States, while his sister had migrated to Argentina.[20] On arrival in Australia, he initially grew vegetables in Balcatta, a suburb located north of Osborne Park. When his family joined him in 1930, they all moved to Roleystone, near Karragullen and, in 1933, they finally bought land in Karragullen and developed orchards. In the early 1930s some of these areas were widely forested, and timber was an important industry around Karragullen. As a consequence, Giovanni decided to set up a timber mill in the nearby suburb of Kelmscott, later sold to another Tuscan, Mr Coli.[21] The mill was so successful that it provided employment for many Italian migrants, mainly from the Lucca area.[22] According to some of the interviews of Tuscan migrants, there are confirmations that, in the late 1930s and early 1950s, the Bovani, Ghilarducci and other families sponsored many migrants from the Province of Lucca to Australia.[23] A considerable number of them moved to the suburbs of Karragullen and Kelmscott, finding employment in orchards and sawmills at the first stage of their settlement in the country.

There was a notable number of Tuscans also in the proximity of Karragullen and Kalamunda, namely the rural districts of Pickering Brooks and Mundaring. Pickering Brooks represented since the 1930s the area where some of the mills and orchards were located, thus attracting many migrants employed as woodcutters and millers. As observed with Bovani and Ghilarducci, in Pickering Brooks the orchard of the Tenardi family, from Giuncugnano (upper valley of River Serchio), offered for a few decades working and accommodation opportunities to many Lucchesi.[24] In some areas of the large Shire of Mundaring, on the other hand, there were more mills and stone quarries for the building needs of Perth, and many Italians, and Tuscans in particular, were employed, among others.[25]

Other areas with a large number of Lucchesi were the city centre of Perth (and its suburb Northbridge), North Perth and, again, Osborne Park, followed by Leederville, Balcatta, Wanneroo, more north of the city, and the suburbs of Bassendean and Guildford along the north-eastern banks of the Swan River. The inner city suburbs were the areas in which the increasing flow of Italians and Tuscans of the 1920s was directed. Migrants tended to congregate in the areas that offered cheap and easy access to the services they needed as migrant workers.

The large majority of Italians arriving in Australia during that period were males, since migration maintained a temporary characteristic that is confirmed also by the data gathered in this study. The percentage of arrivals from Tuscany to Western Australia shows that the number of males is disproportionately higher than females for a long period, such that between 1900 and 1929 the percentage of males oscillated between 80 and 100 per cent. If the number of migrants split by gender is limited to those from the studied area of Garfagnana, the comparison between the intake of males and females in Western Australia with that in Australia as a whole for the period 1921-1970 is even more striking. Figures show that, during the 1920s, the number of males going to Western Australia was exceptionally higher than those to Australia in general.[26]

Except for the few migrants who were joined by their families, a high proportion of Lucchesi in Perth were males, often with wives and children living in Italy. To accommodate the needs of single men, there were boarding houses in William Street, Northbridge[27] and also in East Perth, often managed by other migrants, mainly northern Italians, where guests were able to have meals and accommodation, staying even for long periods of time.[28] According to some interviewees, from the early 1930s a couple of restaurants, managed by Lucchesi, were opened in James Street and William Street, both in Northbridge.[29] These circumstances can partly explain the recording of a high number of Tuscany-born migrants, employed in all sort of activities in Perth city. The presence of Lucchesi in North Perth and Leederville during the 1930s is in proportion to the Italian community as a whole. As stated earlier, these inner city suburbs, approximately along Wanneroo Road, represented, since the mid and late 1920s, the area in which a high number of Italian migrants found cheap rental housing and occupational opportunities in nearby factories.[30]

On the other hand, the number of Lucchesi in Osborne Park, Balcatta and the northern suburb of Wannero, whose presence has been confirmed by other studies,[31] has to do with the specific occupational and spatial pattern of the studied group. According to references,[32] and interviews, the presence of the family from Capannori played the role of catalysing more relatives and friends, who migrated to Western Australia during the period 1924-1939 mainly from the same Commune of origin, such as the Francesconi, Della Santina, Masini, Scatena and others. Most of them arrived as single men, either settling in the same areas or later moving to the goldfields of remote Western Australia in search of faster money accumulation. In any case, either they stayed in that area or moved outside Perth, Osborne Park and the nearby suburb of Balcatta became for many Lucchesi from Capannori the 'comfort zone', the 'home away from home'.[33] The presence of Guelfi members in Western Australia has been vital in facilitating many more prospective migrants, from the same enlarged family or community of origin, to leave for the 'long America', as Australia was perceived in the Lucca area for a long time. Australia appeared less strange and hostile as the local communities were filled by the presence of so many people from the same areas of origin.

Two single male brothers from the Commune of Porcari (low valley of River Serchio), Pietro and Angelo Menchetti, established a farm in the late 1920s in the rural area of Wanneroo, along the Wanneroo Road. They were later joined by more relatives and friends from the same community, who settled in the areas as market gardeners.[34]

Similar patterns of chain migration from rural and mountain areas of Lucca took place in the upper banks of the Swan River (Guildford and Bassendean) and in the semi-industrial suburbs of Cannington, south-east of Perth and Coogee, south of the river and near the port of Fremantle. In the first case, there are archival records of a noticeable concentration of people (namely the families of Giorgi, Grassi and Moscardini) from San Romano Garfagnana (upper valley of the River Serchio) who first moved to the Upper Swan area. In particular, Ferdinando G. arrived in 1926 to work as a farm hand and then moved to Bassendean where he purchased a parcel of land, and was joined by his younger brother Sesto and his family in 1939.[35] In the next section it will be examined how the family established in the 1950s such a consistent flow of migrants from San Romano Garfagnana to Bassendean, to represent one of the most evident models of chain migration expressed by Lucchesi in Western Australia.

With respect to the presence of Tuscan-born migrants in the Cannington and Coogee areas, apparently there are no records showing that they were from a specific community of origin. Since the areas held a few minor industrial activities, such as an abattoir in Coogee attracting many foreign-born workers over a long period of time, as stated by an interviewee,[36] it appears that the presence of migrants was related to the proximity of the working location rather than explainable in terms of migratory chains.

It is of interest that in the distinctive semi-rural suburbs on the outskirts of the Perth Metropolitan area, Karragullen, Osborne Park-Balcatta, Wanneroo and Guildford-Bassendean, the initial presence of a quantitatively small colony of Lucchesi fuelled the arrival of many more from the same geographical communities. From the comments expressed by some interviewees, it seems that each one of these areas was characterized by the existence of a 'Little Lucca', mainly made up of people from Capannori in Osborne Park, from Porcari in Wanneroo, from San Romano Garfagnana in Bassendean and from a selection of the whole Lucca territory in the case of Karragullen.[37]

If the data on the distribution of migrants between 1920 and 1940 are split by their two major occupations (farming and labouring), the maps will show even more clearly their spatial distribution in relation to occupations. Figure 6-1 displays how the Lucchesi engaged in farming activities were almost exclusively located in the same districts previously indicated. In this case, the presence of Lucca-born migrants in the coastal areas is non-existent, and definitely irrelevant in the city of Perth and its nearby suburb of North Perth. On the other hand, Lucchese performing their activities as labourers were mainly confined within the inner city boundaries (Perth) and, in lower numbers, in the slowly growing industrial districts of Cannington, Coogee-Munste, and Osborne Park.

Figure 6-1 - Distribution of Farmers from Tuscany in Perth Metropolitan Area, 1920-1940

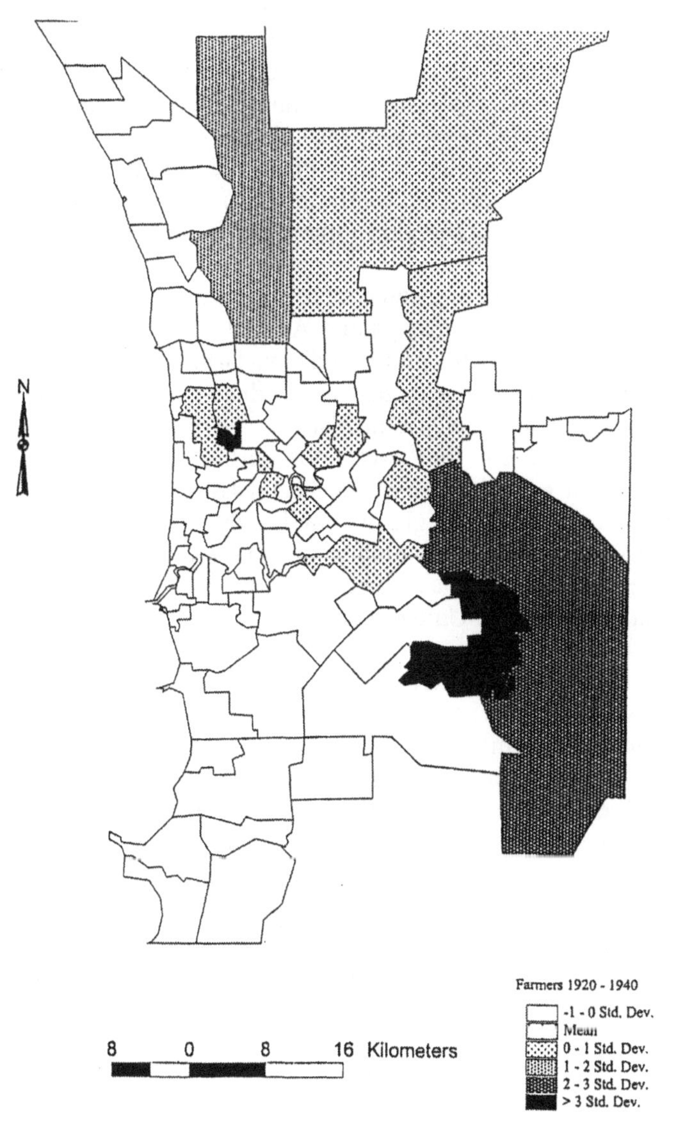

The different spatial distribution of Tuscan-born migrants in the Perth Metropolitan area in relation to their occupations indicates how the location of most of them within the farming activities attracted many more prospective workers from the communities of origin in the same suburbs through a chain migration process. This operation certainly created spatial concentrations that helped their participants to find accommodation and work more easily, within the same 'protected' environment. Therefore, it can be implied that Lucchesi who settled in such protected environments moved outward from their urban concentrations more slowly and reluctantly than those who had occupations other than farming.

Those involved in trading came more frequently into social contact with both other ethnic groups and Australian society as a whole. Lucchese migrants who performed non-farming activities in the Perth Metropolitan area tended to be distributed in fairly small groups, near the inner city to take advantage of the first established ethnic societies, but they were not part of a solid residential concentration, as in the case of Lucchesi performing rural activities. As a consequence, willingly or unwillingly, many of them began the slow process of assimilation to the host society as soon as they found such occupations, as has been observed for some other Italian migrant groups in the United States.[38]

Since the mid-1870s, when mass migration from northern Tuscany to overseas destinations increased dramatically, migrants with previous experience in farming were the large majority. The combined number of workers expatriating from Tuscany with previous farming experience (including woodcutters) has been much higher than the number of those with experience as labourers (including in this category miners, artisans, bricklayers and stonemasons, as from the classification of Italian statistical figures).[39] According to data gathered at the Australian Archives, the highest proportion in the range of activities Tuscan migrants performed in Western Australia, is represented by peasants and farmers, followed by labourers, a category which included factory workers and bricklayers (Table 6-1).

Table 6-1 - Occupational distribution of Migrants from Tuscany in Western Australia (Perth, rural W.A. and mining areas), 1921-1939

	Perth Metro Area	Rural W.A.	Mining Areas
Farmers (incl. Woodcutters)	58	29	2
Labourers (incl. Bricklayers)	30	23	1
Craftsmen	4	0	2
Other Services (incl. Cooks, Waiters. Etc.)	6	0	2
Miners	13	8	29
Entrepreneurs	14	2	2
Traders (incl. Restauranters)	10	1	1
Professionals	1	0	0
House duties	49	8	9
Total	185	71	48

It is interesting to observe the low number of craftsmen involved in the occupational distribution of Tuscan migrants in Western Australia. As Ercole Sori noted in his classic work on Italian migration, historically, the component of artisans within the Italian migratory flow has always been insignificant.[40] Within the international labour market in general, the demand was towards either migrants with homogeneous skills within the production sector (such as bricklayers and stonemasons) or non-skilled people, such as peasants and labourers, for the less qualified tasks, rather than semi or highly skilled artisans. The Australian labour market had similar needs, thus not having any particular interest in the immigration of semi- or highly skilled artisans. Already in 1881, an Italian traveller writes about the more sought after skills of Italian migrants in Australia:

> *"Il contadino, il minatore, il manovale, il terraiolo e le donne di servizio sono i soli che possono essere sicuri della loro sorte, e di fare anche una discreta fortuna".*[41]

> *(Farmers, miners, labourers, farm hands and house maids are the only ones who can be sure of their own future, and hope to make some good money).*

The occupational categories of entrepreneurs and traders were not present in the skills that Tuscan migrants had brought with them from their communities (Table 6-2). Many Tuscan migrants relocated in the Perth urban environment and started an independent activity, often linked to services for the Italian community (fruit and deli shops, restaurants, boarding houses), as previously stated and confirmed by Price.[42] In a number of cases, migrants who began in the market gardening business became, or expanded their business to become grocers and provisioners, as in the case of one interviewee[43] and as a pattern confirmed in other host countries by the literature.[44]

Table 6-2 - Occupational distribution of Migrants from Tuscany in Western Australia, 1921-1939

	in Italy	%	in Australia	%
Farmers (incl. Woodcutters)	187	62	89	29
Labourers (incl. Bricklayers)	31	10	54	18
Craftsmen	19	6	6	2
Other Services (incl. Cooks, Waiters. Etc.)	0	0	8	3
Miners	5	2	50	16
Entrepreneurs	0	0	18	6
Traders (incl. Restauranters)	3	1	12	4
Clerks	1	0	0	0
Professionals	1	0	1	0
Housewives/Minors	57	19	66	22
Total	304	100	304	100

The reason for the gravitation of migrants from the northern Tuscan mountain and rural communities into a restricted range of activities in Australia is linked to the traditional peasant desire for independence, as the occupational background of a large majority of them was peasantry.[45] Cinel, in his work on Italian and Lucchesi migrants in San Francisco, states that, although most immigrants entered jobs totally new to them, it is possible to highlight several links between their work in the host country and that of their fathers in Italy.[46] There are similarities between the occupational paths followed by

Lucchesi in Western Australia and that of their ancestors in Lucca. Nevertheless, once in Australia, most migrants had to adjust to the local job availability and shift into new occupational fields, although their employment often reflected that peasant desire of independence for which they had migrated. Other reasons for their choice within a limited occupational area resulted partly from their sponsorship by relatives who had to guarantee employment, partly from a lack of formal qualifications. Furthermore, language difficulties induced many to work with Italian companies and other Italians in general.[47]

Many could count on a small amount of capital accumulated with a few years of working long hours in heavy manual labour, such as in the woodcutting and mining industry in remote areas of Western Australia, as will be examined in the next sections. The preference was therefore given to new activities that could be run in urban and suburban areas,[48] partly explaining the slow process of Perth-bound migration, which took place in the mid-late 1930s. Again, for this sense of security, market gardening and small family-run businesses were ideally suited. This second sector was often particularly successful by dint of hard work and the combining of family resources.[49] Italians are to be found in greater concentrations in the secondary sector, working in the building industry as self-employed workers (bricklayers, carpenter, tilers), in the tertiary industries (butchers, barbers, bootmakers, tailors) and in commerce, both in Australia[50] and in other communities abroad, as some comparative studies have demonstrated.[51] Some reasons lay also in the nature of these activities, which made it unnecessary for them to participate in the Australian environment, as they generally did not bring the employees into competition with organized labour,[52] unlike what happened in the mining areas that will be detailed further in this study. Consequently, the high number of Lucchesi performing in rural activities and small businesses, combined with patterns of chain migration adopted in Western Australia, are clear indicators of models of their spatial distribution in both the inner city and the semi-rural areas of Perth, and their spatial segregation in a few suburbs.[53] These concentrations certainly helped the Tuscan community to maintain a specific ethnic identity, as has been previously examined and is confirmed by other studies on the Italian rural identity abroad.[54]

Although the history of Lucchesi who settled in the Perth Metropolitan area is linked to the spatial distribution of those who moved in rural and remote Western Australia, it has been considered convenient to keep distinct their geographical patterns of settlement. On the contrary, after WWII, Italian mass migration and the more complex interaction between the economy of Perth and the rest of the state, to which the history of Italian migrant settlements is linked, require an overall analysis of spatial and occupational interaction of Tuscan-born migrants.

LUCCHESI IN RURAL WESTERN AUSTRALIA, 1890-1939

Until the end of the First World War, the arrival of Lucchesi in Western Australia was minimal, as it has been previously outlined. The same low figures of their spatial distribution in the Perth Metropolitan area are replicated at the State scale. Few and small concentrations of Tuscan workers were recorded in Harvey (South-West), where an Italian community had already settled in the previous years.[55] Following the American immigration restrictions of 1924, a higher number of arrivals from Italy to Australia are recorded.

Tuscan migrants in rural districts of Western Australia concentrated in activities linked to the occupational skills they were bringing with them from Italy, as confirmed by Price's work.[56] Consequently, it is not surprising that they never settled within the long-established Italian communities of the Western Australian coastal cities, as in Fremantle, Albany, Bunbury and Geraldton, as the fishing industry has never been a common occupation in the Lucca area. The farming belt and the wood-cutting districts were concentrated in the South West of the State. Migrants from Tuscany moved in notable numbers to the rural districts of Harvey[57] (potatoes and orchard farming and wood-cutting) and Manjimup (tobacco farming and wood-cutting).[58] In this latter shire there are records of Archimede Fontanini, from Giuncugnano (upper valley of the River Serchio), who arrived in the area in 1904, and bought a large orchard.[59]

As other scholars have stressed with respect to the settlement of Italians in general in Western Australia during the inter-war period,[60] Tuscans moved to the South-West of the State, working either as farmers or as labourers in the timber industry. Nevertheless, it seems likely that labourers - in a higher number than farmers - played a valuable economic role in providing timber and wood for the mining industry. This is to say that the figures on occupations performed by Tuscans in these rural areas could slightly hide a more relevant number of workers who were employed in activities linked to the mining industry of the eastern goldfields.

Conversely, the absence of Italian migrants engaged in the sheep and beef-cattle grazing areas of Western Australia requires explanation. By the time they began to enter Australia, most of the good pastoral land was already occupied.[61] Furthermore, grazing properties required much capital to buy and maintain. Italians, and Tuscans in particular, who might have also been shepherds and grazers in the Apennines communities, possibly realized that they were unlikely to obtain their own properties or gain the income that they could get through working long hours in heavy manual activities such as woodcutting and mining. In addition, station life, with its long periods of loneliness, was a far cry from the conditions most of them derived. Market gardening, but also any labouring activity in an urban or semi-rural environment, made possible a way of life much akin to the sort of settlement in which they had grown up.

It can be inferred that Tuscan and Italian migrants liked a more active community and social life, as that in the area of origin. Consequently, it could be assumed that they did not like any activity in other remote areas, as in the mining towns of inland Western Australia. On the contrary, figures show that the presence of Italians was notable in the Western Australian goldfields from the late 1890s.[62] There are records of Angelo Diletti, from Capannori (low-valley of the River Serchio), who arrived in Albany in 1896,[63] together with others from the same community, as confirmed by an interviewee.[64] After searching for gold in the mining town of Kalgoorlie, he moved to work in the timber industry of the South West, before returning to Italy by the mid-1910s. The path of Angelo was later followed by one of his sons, Lino, who migrated to the Western Australian goldfields in 1927, and there he settled.[65] In particular, several Tuscan migrants were in the mining areas in the 1920s and 1930s, where over 60 per cent of them were directly involved in mining activity (Table 6-1).

Migrants' search for immediate economic reward was the main goal. Price noted that between the period 1912-1931, over half the southern European-born population of Australia moved in and out of occupational areas each year, continuously in search of better economic opportunities.[66] It was not the quality (or, in many cases, the safety) of the activity to be taken into consideration, but rather the potential to make money quicker than in other activities. It is vital to understand this concept in order to frame the attitude of 'temporary' migration of Tuscan workers, that comes from a century-long tradition of seasonal movements, as previously examined. Their search for bread abroad was perceived as a resource to accumulate, in the shortest possible time, enough money to return home and settle with more financial comfort than at time of departure. This explains the relatively young age of migrants, the vast majority of non-married males, their clustering among friends belonging to the same community of origin, as well as their adaptability to accept any jobs offered, regardless of their skills.

Records show how, for the period 1931-40, the arrival of Lucchesi in the age group between 26 and 45 years is proportionately the highest of any other decade considered. These figures are an additional confirmation of the relatively younger age of the many Lucchesi who, since the mid-1920s, decided to go to Australia as an alternative to the United States, with the intention to gain, in a limited period of time, enough money to bring back to Italy.

In this regard, it is worth analysing the presence of Lucchesi in the Western Australian mining industry of the 1930s.

LUCCHESI IN THE GOLDFIELDS OF WESTERN AUSTRALIA, 1920-1939

Since the early 1930s, concentrations of Tuscan migrants are recorded in the mining areas of Cue, Leonora, Kalgoorlie and Wiluna, as shown in Figure 6-2, illustrating the distribution of Lucchese miners in Western Australia during the period 1920-1940. While there are records of some of them in Kalgoorlie, a larger number was present in Wiluna. All the gold mining centres had

Figure 6-2 - Distribution of Miners from Tuscany in Western Australia

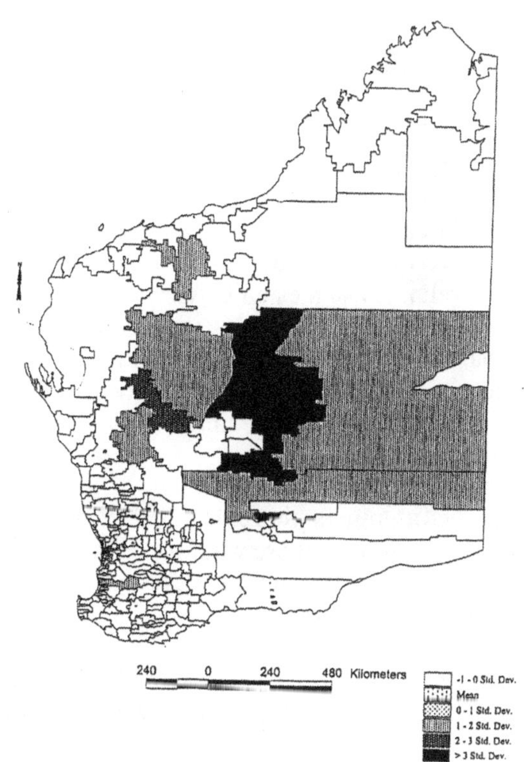

a large percentage of foreign workers who were either singles or whose wives and children lived elsewhere.[67] In fact, looking at the sex ratio amongst Tuscans in mining areas and comparing it to that of Italian migrants in general in the same areas, as from Pascoe and Bertola,[68] it is possible to observe similarities for the four Western Australian mining towns (Table 6-3).

Table 6-3 - Sex Ratio amongst Tuscan and Italian Migrants in some mining areas of Western Australia, 1921-1939

	Tuscan Men	Tuscan Women	Italian Men	Italian Women
Cue	2	1	22	8
Leonora(incl.Gwalia)	6	3	169	24
Kalgoorlie	3	1	61	14
Wiluna	15	3	220	29

Source: Pascoe & Bertola, 1985

Hence, the reliability of the records collected on Tuscan migrants, and the confirmation of a goldfields' population with a large majority of male workers. Their presence, although prolonged for a few years, was still considered temporary and aimed to accumulate quick earnings to re-invest in either their community of origin or in urban areas of Australia. As suggested by Gentilli, a reason for undertaking the long journey from the mountain communities of central Italy to the harsh outback of the Australian mining towns, was that they did not want to expose their wives (if married) and any children to the hardship and uncertainties they expected to meet.[69]

All the migrants employed as miners were either farmers or labourers in Italy. Unlike what happened with those who worked as farmers in Western Australia, miners from Tuscany in Western Australia had a different occupational background.

Migrants chose woodcutting or mining as a way to facilitate fast accumulation of money, and that they accepted a 'temporary' working situation in view of future investment of small capital in occupational areas which were undoubtedly more congenial to them.

Their choice was also compatible with that of the State government, willing to locate Southern Europeans in areas other than urban, in order to both better control them socially and enhance the economy in areas where the Anglo-Australian community was not keen to go. "The mines or the Bush" became the catch-cry of immigrant Italians in the inter-war period.[70]

In the late 1930s, the major component of arrivals in Australia from the studied area is represented by women and children, as confirmed by Price.[71] The change in the migratory pattern was probably due to the external factors already outlined in this study, such as the growing political instability of Fascism in Italy and the stricter entry conditions adopted by the Australian immigration authorities.[72] As a response to the Federal policy, this situation pushed many Tuscan and Italian migrants to sponsor their relatives in order to be joined in Australia and, if possible, to obtain naturalisation. In any case, males would tend to defer naturalisation until they had finally established their homes in Australia, as stated by Borrie[73] and confirmed by some interviewees.[74] With the coming of the families, the group took on more permanent characteristics, becoming the stepping stone of Tuscan post-war mass migration.

Nevertheless, Italians had begun to arrive in the Western Australian Goldfields in significant numbers at the turn of the century, such that there were over 500 working in the Kalgoorlie-Boulder area between 1896 and 1902.[75] During this period, the gold mining industry was passing into a period of consolidation and rationalisation. In order to make new large capital investments, gold companies sought to cut labour costs and increase productivity. Italian migrants, in desperate search for highly paid work, were perfectly suitable for such a new trend. The main assets that this class of immigrants brought to Western Australia were all labour related: more than specific skills, they had the willingness to work harder and for lower wages than the local working class, plus the flexibility to accommodate fluctuations in employers' needs, which is typical of many migrants' taskforces.[76]

Italian workers in the mines not only obtained employment, often through intermediaries, at the expense of local labour, but were also used in the process of cutting costs and employed to break strikes over conditions and piece rates.[77] This was an attitude that the Western Australian Labour Party had pointed out on a few occasions, lodging a petition to the Federal government in 1906, in order to extend the Immigration Restriction Act (then applicable to coloured workers) to Italians. However, this was rejected.[78]

The behaviour of many Italian migrants was to take full advantage of the possibility to make money quicker than everywhere else in the Australian working environment, without indulging in the Anglo-Australian working class lifestyle, as it is described in this excerpt from an Italian traveller's account of the 1930s:

> *"A differenza degli Australiani che contrappongono con una specie di furore a questa vita d'inferno orgie di alcool nei bar notturni di Kalgoorlie e Boulder, i nostri si mantengono parsimoniosi, e anziche' abbandonarsi a giuochi d'azzardo, si limitano a onorate partite di bocce e di scopone. Con le loro economie provvedono a mandare danari in Italia per istruire i figli e mantenere la famiglia".*[79]
>
> *(Unlike Australians, who react to this infernal life with orgies of alcohol in the night pubs of Kalgoorlie and Boulder, our nationals keep sober and, rather than loosing themselves in gambling, simply and honestly play bowlsand cards. They send their savings to Italy in order to educate their children and maintain their families).*

The number of Italians and other southern Europeans in the mines increased through the 1910s, such to represent in 1913 over 20 per cent of the underground workforce.[80] The recession hit the mining industry in the 1920s and the numbers employed in gold mines in Western Australia fell from a pre-war figure of over 13,000 in 1913 to a low of 3,766 in 1928.[81]

By early 1934, Italians and Yugoslavs still made up over 18 per cent of the underground workforce in Kalgoorlie and 41 per cent in the associated mines, as from the Australian historian Bertola.[82] As a consequence, rising unemployment among Anglo-Australians in the early 1930s drew more attention to the presence of Southern Europeans, to calls to restrict their immigration in the local press, as also happened in the woodcutting industry.[83]

Italians, as well as Tuscans, had arrived in Kalgoorlie and Boulder by the early 1910s. Cecilia reports the presence of Giulio Davini, also confirmed by the archival research, who migrated from Minucciano (upper valley of the River Serchio) to New South Wales, and worked in the copper mines of Cobar (New South Wales), about 1,000 kilometres north of Sydney. After a few years he moved to the Richmond River, where he grew sugarcane for seven years. Giving this up, he spent a short time in New Zealand, then returned to New South Wales and embarked on a ship for a visit to Italy, where he remained for one year. On his return, he settled in Western Australia, where he worked on the construction of the Southern Cross-Coolgardie railroad. Finally, he worked for several mining companies until he began to prospect on his own and, in 1899, become a co-owner of the Hidden Cross Mine in Western Australia.[84]

Apart from this successful episode of Tuscan mining in Western Australia, there are Italian government sources and other private reports stating that by 1906, the large majority of the about 25 Italians employed in the catering business of Kalgoorlie were Tuscans.[85] There was even a statuette vendor[86] from the Province of Lucca. In this regard, it is interesting to read what an Italian consular agent wrote in 1906 about the occupational choices of Italian regional groups in Western Australia:

> *"I Valtellinesi si dedicano quasi esclusivamente al lavoro delle miniere, al taglio delle foreste ed alla preparazione del carbone vegetale; i Piemontesi, i Toscani e i Liguri all'agricoltura, orticoltura e viticoltura, ai lavori di sterro e ferroviari a cottimo ed ai mestieri di oste, cuoco e cameriere".*[87]
>
> *(Migrants from Valtellina, Lombardy, perform almost exclusively in mining, timber logging and charcoal burning; Piedmontese, Tuscans and Ligurians work as farmers and*

market gardeners, general labourers on the railway line and as hosts, cooks and waiters).

By the late 1910s, more mines were opened at Leonora-Gwalia, 250 kilometres north of Kalgoorlie, which could easily be called an Italian mine, as the management employed so many of these migrants, almost exclusively from the northern Italian Alpine valleys of the Provinces of Bergamo and Sondrio, Region of Lombardy. Over 150 Italian miners were present there during this period.[88]

From the mid-1920s, they increased in number to the extent to have their own neighbourhood and local stores, hotels and boarding houses.[89] In 1933, there were 133 Italians in Boulder and 132 in Kalgoorlie,[90] although not more than half were employed in the mining industry. About 250 Italians were in Wiluna, thus making up to ten per cent of the total population.[91] A large number of migrant workers were single men. Therefore, the town had several boarding houses which offered meals and accommodation, and some of them were owned and run by Lucchesi, such as the Lamberti, from Borgo Mozzano, and the Moscardini, from San Romano Garfagnana.[92] Two boarding houses in Wiluna were run by Mr Raffaele Masolini, an unusual "adventurer" from the Province of Florence. After committing a few minor crimes in Italy, Mr Masolini had lived in France, Mexico and the United States before arriving in Wiluna. There, he was repeatedly charged for illicit sale of liquor in the early 1930s, according to a report written in 1933 by the Wiluna police officer, and addressed to the Commissioner of Police in Perth.[93]

Nevertheless, the general aim of Italian miners in the goldfields was similar to that already highlighted for Tuscans, namely to make money as quick as possible, as an interviewee, who resided in Wiluna in the 1930s, has confirmed.[94] The higher wages paid in the remote mining areas were therefore perfectly suited to this aim. In addition, the relatively small size of their settlements in the Goldfields worked against the creation of unions or political organizations with a large following. Many migrants had a temporary aptitude for the local working environment and tended never to stop for long at any one place, thus making it difficult for them to take part in social, political or union activities. The economic conditions of most Italians must also be borne in mind; they did not allow for much time to engage in activities other than working long hours.[95] Tuscans were often peasants and labourers: there was no articulate middle class, nor intellectual elite which could express a variety of ideas for a positive political and/or union action. On the whole, Italian and Tuscan workers preferred to congregate with people of the same community of origin, with whom they had a common heritage and culture.

This situation was well established in the late 1910s, before a more notable number of Tuscans arrived, as a report on the "Italian aliens on the Kalgoorlie Goldfields", written by officers of the Intelligence Section in 1919, implies. "The Italians at Kalgoorlie have their own 'National' hotels and retain to a marked degree their national characteristics".[96] The same situation, with a stress on the identity of migrants as coming from Tuscany, has been described by another Tuscan interviewee who lived in Kalgoorlie in the mid-1930s[97] and worked as a cook in a local hotel.

Again, although there are a few records of Fascist[98] and anti-Fascist sympathies[99] amongst Italian and Tuscan migrants,[100] the large majority of them were driven by economic needs and displayed little interest in politics, or in the local Anglo-Australian society. Hence, the evident segregation of southern European migrants within the host mining community, with particular regard to Wiluna, where the presence of Tuscans was higher than average, and where this sense of exclusion was experienced by an interviewee.[101] The spatial segregation of first-generation Tuscans was not the result of any conscious withdrawal from the Australian environment, but rather due to the nature of their economic activity. Already culturally distinct and isolated, as well as relatively powerless and dependent upon their work, Tuscans and Italians in general became the object of growing ill-will.

In addition, the Great Depression of the early 1930s had brought unemployment, hunger and suffering, and had certainly re-awakened the hostility towards migrants. During the Depression, only the Australian mines of the Goldfields supported by American investments continued to operate and grow, because gold was the only marketable resource left. The unemployed poured into the mining areas from every corner of the State, such that Kalgoorlie was swarming with people in search of work.[102] It is within this environment that, in January 1934, the Kalgoorlie riots occurred. An Italian bartender of Tuscan origin hit and accidentally killed a local Anglo-Australian sports hero.[103] This accident sparked the resentment of many Anglo-Australian miners against the Italians residing in Kalgoorlie, and culminated in two days of riots. A raging crowd of miners devastated and burnt many shops and private adobes of Italians and other southern Europeans in Boulder and Kalgoorlie, and pushed hundreds of migrants to shelter in the surrounding countryside.[104]

Notwithstanding the condemnation of the fact in the media, the riots did not modify the attitude and general opinion towards Italians. In the 1930s, the Anglo-Australian community maintained a perception of cultural inferiority of Italians that owed much to longer-term racial conceptions, which were confirmed by the lifestyle of the migrants, "by their apparent willingness to be used in efforts to drive down wages and conditions, and by their inability to transcend the boundaries that separated them from the host culture".[105] In a military intelligence manuscript of 1919, in relation to previous riots, this racial discrimination was already openly admitted even by the authorities. "An expression of the unrest which has occurred at Kalgoorlie has been by way of a desire to get rid of the Italian alien".[106] Anti-Italian feelings were not merely an aspect of the Western Australian mining environment, as this image of the Italian comes from a century-long 'Italophobia' that encouraged stereotypes about race, culture and level of trustworthiness.[107]

Hence, a general antipathy emerged towards Italians, which was partly based on racial and cultural comparisons that inferred inferiority, and was inextricably bound up with questions of Anglo-centrism and with the decade-long relations between capital and labour in the mining community. As some have clearly stressed, "racism enmeshed with what are termed the social relations of production".[108]

Although spatial and social self-segregation from the Anglo-Australian environment took place in Perth as well as in the goldfields, other reasons, particularly the competition with organized labour within the mining industry, have been here indicated as the causes to exasperate forms of social rejection by the host society. Conversely, the previous sections have examined how, in the urban areas of Perth of the 1920s and 1930, Lucchesi could cluster in a few specific suburbs without entering into direct competition and conflict with organized labour, simply because they performed in activities not directly linked to the Anglo-Australian working environments, such as market gardening and tertiary occupation within the Italian community.

POST-WAR MASS MIGRATION OF LUCCHESI IN WESTERN AUSTRALIA, 1946-1970S

This work will not analyse the historical and social consequences of the presence of Tuscan migrants in Western Australia during WWII, because their communities in the country were not big enough to show marked dissimilarities from the general pattern of Italians. Many Italian migrants, especially those who had not become naturalized before the outbreak of WWII, were treated as 'Enemy Aliens', often suffering the confiscation of their properties and internment in remote areas of Australia for most of the length of the war. While some interviewees highlighted this aspect in their long stay in Australia,[109] literature on the internment of Italian workers in Australia is ample,[110] and the topic does not deserve further analysis. On the contrary, this section focuses on the spatial and occupational distribution of Tuscan migrants in the Perth Metropolitan area during the post-war period, when a large number of migrants from Italy and other southern European countries arrived.

Since 1947, immigration to the major state capitals of Australia has been of such volume that it has greatly affected the population composition within the metropolitan areas. The impact on the social and population structure of Australian cities has been distinctive because over 60 percent of post-war migration to Australia was formed by migrants coming from countries other than the United Kingdom and Ireland, which had supplied 90 percent of immigration in the pre-war period.[111] The study of the impact of Italian immigration on the Australian social structure of the cities and of the processes shaping the patterns of their concentration, requires the analysis of the major factors involved. Particular attention must be paid to additional factors that can be ascribed to the specificity of Lucchese migration within the Italian flow between the 1950s and 1960s.

According to the study by Hugo on the demographic and spatial aspects of immigration, general factors appear to be grouped in two main areas, namely the distribution of job and housing opportunities of particular types at the time of arrival, and the timing of the peak immigration of a migrant group, associated with its scale.[112] This work on Tuscan migrants in Western Australia will adjust the above general factors to the presence of Lucchesi in Perth, reinterpreting the analysis in the light of possible variations in their territorial and occupational composition.

This study has already previously shown how the peak of Tuscan immigration to Western Australia is concentrated in the period 1950-59, with figures that have been confirmed by other recent studies.[113] The peak of the arrivals from Tuscany is therefore concentrated in a short period of time, within the flow of Italian migrants in general, although the latter is spread over a few more years, from 1950 to 1970. In the case of Lucchesi in Perth, their peak of arrivals covers one decade and it numbers about 550. It is not a large group, but certainly larger than the number witnessed in the pre-war period. Nevertheless, the previous paragraphs have shown how Lucchesi, particularly if involved in market gardening and farming, remained highly concentrated in a few suburbs.

Figure 6-3 shows the overall distribution of Lucchesi migrants who arrived in Perth between 1946 and 1965. Compared to their distribution during the period 1920-1940, this map illustrates a different geographical distribution, with Tuscans spread over a larger number of suburbs, according to similar consideration made for the Italian community as a whole since the early 1960s.[114] While most Tuscan-born migrants had resided in the 'zone of transition' during the 1920s and 1930s, dispersion into other suburbs of the city took place with both their second generation[115] and the larger intake of the 1950s. While the Perth city centre and North Perth are still areas with a notable concentration of migrants, Osborne Park has lost its primacy in favour of the nearby northern suburbs ofBalcatta, Tuart Hill, Morley and Bassendean, all suburbs located north of the Swan River. The data collected at the Australian Archives confirm and widen similar observations on their geographical distribution, which were made by Gentilli in his pioneering analysis drawn from a survey of telephone subscribers with the most common surnames present in the areas of origin.[116]

Figure 6-3 - Distribution of Migrants from Tuscany in Perth Metropolitan Area, 1946-1965

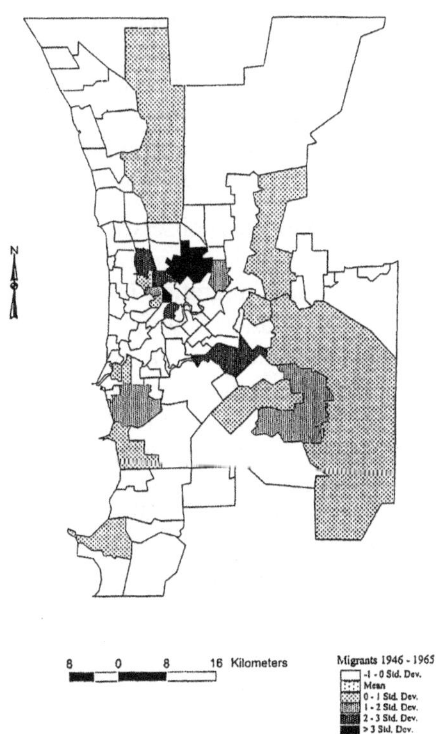

These different spatial concentrations have a few reasons. Since the 1960s, Osborne Park passed from a rural low-density suburb, with many market gardening farms, to a light industrial area, due to its proximity to the city of Perth and its process of industrial expansion. The land of several market gardeners became sought after by developers, who wanted to set up industrial plants.[117] Since the mid-1960s, many Lucchesi who resided in the area decided, or were forced, to move out of Osborne Park, and relocated in the nearby suburbs, in particular Balcatta (north of Osborne Park), Tuart Hill and Yokine (east of Osborne Park), as well as in the fast growing residential areas of Dianella and Morley, where the number of Italians is, at present, still particularly high. A few migrants from Capannori (low valley of the River Serchio) are recorded as residing in Tuart Hill, Yokine and Balcatta, as a few Tuscans stressed in their interviews.[118]

This circumstance suggests that the century-long arrival in Osborne Park of market gardeners from Capannori stimulated a virtually uninterrupted flow of peasants and farmers from the same area, who are still residing in the surrounding suburbs. As a confirmation, the social club of Tuscans in Western Australia, with its large representation of people from Capannori, was founded in Balcatta.

On the other hand, as it has been previously observed, the Perth upper-eastern suburb of Bassendean owes its high presence of Lucchese to a particularly strong pattern of chain migration from the Commune of San Romano Garfagnana. A migration flow from this community began in the late 1930s, and was reinforced during the 1950s, when many single male migrants, later followed by their wives and children, arrived in Western Australia through the *Atto di Richiamo* (the call notice) signed by Mr Ferdinando G., a winemaker and trader from San Romano Garfagnana living in Bassendean, as his son Terziglio has stated in the interview.[119] During the 1950s and 1960s, their house at 17 Ivanhoe Street became the first stepping stone of a large number of community fellows, who could initially work in the wine cellars and find accommodation in the nearby boarding house, owned and managed by the same family. As many have confirmed in the interviews, there was "a genuine sense of community",[120] and the boarding house acted as a "home away from home" for many new migrants.[121]

Several interviewees from San Romano Garfagnana stated that, after an initial period in Bassendean, most of them went to work elsewhere before returning, even after long periods of time, to work and settle in Bassendean. The occupational and residential paths of Mr Duilio R. from San Romano Garfagnana and Mr Gino L. from the nearby Commune of Camporgiano, confirm these patterns. Duilio left Italy in 1951 with some working experience as a market gardener. When he arrived in Western Australia, he was guest of the above mentioned family for a few weeks, before going to work as a labourer in a saw mill in Perth. In 1953, Duilio moved back to Bassendean, where he found work as a labourer in a chemical factory and, later in 1954, as a carpenter in the nearby suburb of Upper Swan. In 1956 he decided to move to Queensland, where he worked as a cane cutter for about five years. Finally, he moved back again to Bassendean, where, in 1961, he started his own carpentry business, that he has kept until retirement. Presently, he lives in Bassendean, a few blocks from where the owner of the boarding house had established his wine cellars in the late 1930s.[122]

Mr Gino L. arrived in Western Australia in 1956, after a few years spent as a bootmaker in his own community town. After a few months spent with the above mentioned family from S.Romano Garfagnana, he moved to the remote area of Bullfinch to work as a miner until 1962. Then, he returned to Midland (in the upper valley of the Swan River, near Bassendean), where he worked for two more years in a brick furnace. In 1963, with savings accumulated while working as a miner, he opened a deli shop in Guildford, a suburb between Midland and Bassendean. Finally, in 1968, he went to work for the wine factory of his community fellows in Bassendean, where he still lives.[123]

The occupational and residential patterns of these two interviewees confirm that, although the number of migrants from a specific sub-regional area is small, it is not always likely that they will disperse throughout the city. Both Mr Dulio R. and Mr Gino L. referred to the 'familiarity' of the boarding house at their first arrival in Western Australia, thus reinforcing the links with the community of origin. Notwithstanding this familiarity, which made them feel less alone, they worked in areas different from their original skills, and, in doing so, they even moved to remote areas in search of good working opportunities. Activities performed in unfamiliar areas and climates did not represent serious obstacles to their goal to make money as quickly as possible and return in urban areas to perform other activities. Their goal, as those of many other Lucchesi who migrated to Australia after WWII, was no longer to return to the community of origin, as it had been for their previous generations. Nevertheless, they established an occupational and residential pattern in which a quick remuneration was still the key to a financially safe settlement. The sense of community was now established overseas, in Bassendean, and the presence of people from the same towns of origin, thus representing a sort of social 'comfort zone'.

These two examples, confirmed by similar statements during other interviews, offer the possibility to 'frame' aspects of chain migration within a wider picture, in which the safe presence in a host country of members of the same family or community produces forms of what can be called 'circular spatial concentration'. Members of a specific community of origin arrive in the country of destination and, before searching for job opportunities that can take them anywhere, they establish a sort of 'second' community within the host country, by initially staying with their relatives or community people. Other studies and some interviews of this work[124] confirm that newly-arrived migrants stayed with relatives who treated them with most comfort, often charging no rent until they could find work and become more familiar with language and housing opportunities.[125] They could always return to this community at the end of their working peregrinations in case of need, and this circumstance rendered the adjustment to a new country socially and psychologically less stressful.

Figure 6-3 shows a notable concentration of Tuscan migrants in the coastal suburbs of Coogee and Spearwood and in the suburb of Cannington (post code 6107), located south of the Swan River. As previously explained, Coogee's abattoir attracted many low skilled migrant labourers during the study period. In addition, in the early

1950s the construction of the refinery in the nearby suburb of Kwinana attracted about 2,500 general and specialized labourers, with Italians representing 25 percent of the whole workforce.[126] Furthermore, Spearwood witnessed the proliferation of market gardening patches[127] (some of which owned and run by Lucchese), due to the suburb's proximity to the fruit and vegetable markets of Perth.[128] In addition, since the 1960s, Cannington began to represent the industrial area of the city, thus attracting more low or medium skilled migrants.

If the data shown in Figure 6-3 are disaggregated by the two major occupations, farming and labouring, the related figures will offer an even clearer representation of the occupational distribution of Lucchesi in the Perth metropolitan area. The inland suburb of Karragullen still counts the highest number of market gardeners and orchardists of Tuscan origin, where their presence in other Perth suburbs is not so marked. Conversely, there is a notable concentration of labourers in the Cannington district and in the northern suburbs of North Perth, Tuart Hill, Balcatta, Morley and Bassendean. These areas still represent the districts with the largest concentrations of Italian immigrants in Perth,[129] and, consequently, a similar high percentage of Lucchesi is not, in this case, of any specific significance for the Tuscan migrants' settlement patterns. The central district of Perth does not show a very high number of labourers, probably due to the fact that here people within this area were employed in other activities, such as catering services and small businesses (importers, dealers, merchants and salesmen), according to patterns already observed by Price in his study on southern Europeans in Australia.[130] On the other hand, the number of labourers residing in other suburbs north of the river - where there are no records of heavy or light industrial activities - allows us to deduce that these areas were merely the residential location of the migrants, working elsewhere in either the growing industrial precincts of Osborne Park, or at the railway centre of Guildford/ Midland.

Tuscan migrants employed in labouring activities were the majority during the 1950s, as shown in Table 6-4, which compares data collected at the Australian Archives with those from other published sources. Tuscan migration to Western Australia during the 1950s witnessed a lower amount of peasants and, conversely, a number of Lucchesi better skilled than those which proceeded them in the inter-war period. The absence of miners implies that Lucchesi were no longer migrating with the intention to accept any jobs. Now they were coming with some more skills and not in such need to make money as their predecessors. Even the few cases of Tuscan miners of the 1960s were then directed to the asbestos mines of Wittenoom, rather than to the Goldfields.

Table 6-4 - Number and Percentage of Migrants from Garfagnana to Australia and Western Australia, 1951-60, split by Occupation

	to Australia	% to Australia	to W.A.	% to W.A.
Farmers	51	18	55	25
Labourers	74	26	78	36
Miners	2	1	4	2
Artisans/Other	57	20	15	7
Professionals	12	4	1	0
House duties	56	20	56	26
Students	33	12	10	5
Total	285	100	219	100

Source: Farnocchia, 1996:92

MIGRANTS' OCCUPATIONAL AND RESIDENTIAL INTERACTION BETWEEN PERTH AND THE REST OF THE STATE, 1946-1970S

The occupational path followed by one of the interviewees, Mr Ottavio P. from San Romano Garfagnana,[131] is fascinating, and offers a notable contribution to the understanding of the Lucchese migratory pattern in search of work. Furthermore, it offers an insight of the economic and social relations between the city of Perth and the rest of Western Australia in the 1950s, at the peak of Italian migration to Australia.

Ottavio arrived in Western Australia in 1951, at the age of 39, from the mountainous slopes of the Commune of San Romano Garfagnana. In Italy, he had worked as peasant and shepherd for a few years, while in Australia he had a cousin working in the South West of W.A. and knew some members of the boarding house family in Bassendean. After a few weeks there, he joined his cousin in the South West, first working as a mill hand in a timber mill, and then as a miner in the local coal mines. In 1954, he moved closer to Perth, and worked in the Coogee's abattoir for a few months, before going to work in the remote mining town of Kalgoorlie as a bricklayer. One year later, Ottavio again moved to the northern coastal town of Geraldton (400 kms north of Perth), and was employed as a farm hand for a few months, and then as a labourer in a small factory. In 1957, he was in Bassendean again, working for a few months in a furnace. Since 1957, Ottavio settled in Perth metropolitan area, where he performed more skilled activities, such as truck driver (1957-1965), owner of a fish and chip shop in North Perth (1965-1977), and as a bartender at the Italian Club of North Perth, from 1977 until retirement in 1980.

As previously stated, since the mid-1950s there has been a slow Perth-bound trend of the Italian-born population of Western Australia. Many Tuscan males, who had arrived in the 1920s, had first gone to work either to the mining towns of Cue, Kalgoorlie and Wiluna or to the 'woodline', serving the mining industry.[132] In a few cirumstances, in fact, northern Italians woodcutters, including Tuscans, were the sole suppliers of timbers to the mines.[133] As a general pattern, in the late 1930s, once they had accumulated enough capital to open a small business, many of them were joined by wives and children in the urban areas of Perth, where they settled more permanently.

In the 1950s, two new trends took place. Firstly, a more consistent wave of semi-skilled Lucchesi arrived in Western Australia. In a few cases, they maintained the intention to return home with a small capital, as drawn from the interviews, but were less keen to face the isolation and discomfort of their predecessors of the 1920s and 1930s. Secondly, the mining industry faced a period of rationalization and mechanization of production, and thus could not attract as many workers as it did in the pre-war period. Many Italians and Tuscans looked towards the woodcutting industry, as an economic sector that could provide alternative income in exchange for hard work. Already at the beginning of this century, there was large scale clearing of forests to create rich farmland.[134] Italians took part in this work, and their numbers increased considerably in the first half of the twentieth century. Woodcutting could be considered the economic sector that stood between farming, with the possibility to cultivate new land (as in the case of the cleared farmlands of the inland Perth suburbs of Karragullen and Pickering Brooks), and mining, since timber was necessary in the mining works. Many migrants, lured by higher economic rewards, shifted from one activity to the other, as referred in some interviews.[135] In the early 1950s, Tuscan woodcutters lived in groups of five to ten, in clusters of mobile tents for several months and until a certain portion of forest was cleared. The areas were located in the South West of the state.[136] In the vicinity there were - and still are - large numbers of timber mills, where more Italians and Lucchesi worked in the 1950s. As stated earlier, it is interesting to observe that in some of these areas, the shire of Manjimup in particular, there are records of other Tuscans performing rural activities.[137]

"*TUTTO IL MONDO È PAESE*" (THE WORLD IS JUST LIKE A VILLAGE)

In the light of this scenario, the occupational path of Ottavio is now less complex, and shows a pattern which is common to many other Lucchesi who arrived in the early 1950s in Western Australia. Many of them spent the first years in the South West of the state, passing from one casual activity within the timber industry to another. They pursued quick money accumulation that could permit them to either return home or, more likely, to settle comfortably in the urban context of Perth. The latter option replicates, under different forms, the pattern of 'temporary' migration that Lucchesi had adopted in Italy since time immemorial. Within the Western Australian context, the community of origin was replaced by the Perth urban environment in which the newly-arrived migrants reached both relatives and friends through a migratory chain. The unbroken relationship between those who emigrated and those who remained (and, in this context, between those who moved to rural/remote Western Australia and those who had settled in Perth) provided channels through which a continuous flow of information reached both the areas of origin and destination, creating a form of 'cosmopolitanism' which we normally do not associate with peasants or rural life.

As it has been noted by the American historian Roland Sarti,[138] this cosmopolitanism permitted the Lucchesi in Australia to feel quite comfortable and secure, first in the Australian urban environment where they joined relatives and friends, and later, even in hostile urban or remote areas of the host country. Since the turn of the century, Lucchese migrants have been saying *Tutto il mondo e' paese* ('The world is just like a village'). This conventional wisdom implies the recognition that "fundamental human similarities ease the crossing of geographical distances".[139] Crises and stagnation within the Australian economic system between the 1920s and 1950s undoubtedly increased the human mobility of migrants in search of occupation. This circumstance caused more hardship for those who were not familiar with the host society, but the Lucchese attitude towards the host country certainly helped to relieve social and mental stress and to perceive the surrounding environment 'just like a village'.

Since the early 1950s, the geographical destinations of the 'temporary' migration of Tuscans were represented either by the mines or the bush, with the further goal to return to the more familiar Lucchese communities of the Perth Metropolitan area in order to undertake financially stable and secure activities. More occupational paths followed by some interviewees can be brought in as additional confirmations.

Mr Leonardo B., from San Romano Garfagnana, arrived in Western Australia in 1955, at the age of 30, with previous experience as a labourer in Italy and as miner in Belgium. First, he joined his brother in Balcatta, and, after a few months, moved to the South West town of Darkan, where he worked in a saw mill for seven years, before returning in 1962 to Perth. Here, with some savings, he opened a restaurant in the Osborne Park area, which he ran until retirement.[140]

Mr Alessandro D. P., from Coreglia Antelminelli, arrived with his brother as assisted migrant in 1952, at the age of 20. He had some previous experience as apprentice carpenter. As he did not have any relatives here, after a few weeks in the migrant centre of Bonegilla, Victoria, he moved to Perth where he had a few friends coming from the same Lucchese community. Alessandro went to work as a miner in the remote area of Gwalia for two years, and three more years as wood machinist in a South West saw timber mill, before returning to Perth in 1957, where he worked as truck driver until 1969. Since then, he set up his own company of concrete transporter, which he ran until 1998.[141]

Some Lucchesi have experienced the whole range of occupations that characterized the migratory flow of the 1950s. Mr Gilberto R., from Piazza Serchio (upper valley of the River Serchio), arrived in Western Australia in 1951, at the age of 18, to join his uncle, who had lived in Australia since 1924. In his own community of origin, Gilberto had worked as a peasant, but in Western Australia he first worked as a bricklayer in Perth, and from 1952 to 1954, as a miner in the remote town of Cue. In 1954, he moved to Kojonup, in the South West of the State, where he was employed as a woodcutter for two more years. In 1956, he settled in the nearby rural town of Korda, where he worked his own farm until the late 1960s. Finally, he moved to the outskirts of Perth, where he has owned and run a large pig farm until retirement in 1996.[142] In this case, the migrant returned to perform his original occupation of peasant/ farmer after living in places and experiencing activities which were quite familiar within the post-war migratory occurrences of Lucchesi.

While these examples show the Perth-bound process that many Lucchesi adopted during the first 5-10 years of their post-war residence in Western Australia, in other cases, the occupational path of Tuscan migrants involved a more complex strategy of interaction between rural areas, Perth and the Tuscan community of origin. In 1952, Mr Pietro C. from Casola Lunigiana (now Province of Massa Carrara, but still Province of Lucca until 1927), arrived in Western Australia, where some relatives had already settled since the late

1920s. In Italy, Pietro had worked as a part-time postman. After a few weeks with his relatives in the Upper Swan, he went to work as a labourer in a saw mill at Kojanup (South West) for two years. In 1954, he decided to return to Italy, and moved to his community of origin where he worked as a labourer in a dairy farm. In 1956, he left again for Western Australia, and worked for another saw mill at Kojonup until, in 1966, he set up his own saw mill in the nearby Manjimup. While maintaining his successful business in Western Australia, Pietro spent one more year in Italy (1968-69) with the intention, then abandoned, to set up a commercial enterprise. He then returned to Manjimup before moving again, in the mid-1970s, to Perth where he established a large wholesale and retail shop of timber and machinery.[143]

In this case, the pattern of 'temporary' migration of Tuscans was still at the centre of Pietro's migratory experience in Western Australia, although 'amalgamated' with the effects of the economic interaction between rural and urban Australia. The working opportunities in rural and remote Western Australia represent the migrants' 'temporary' destination, whereas Perth replaces the community of origin as the 'final' destination of migrants. Again, the migrant accepts Western Australia, and Perth in particular, as the final goal of his peregrinations across different countries, in the same way Lucchesi across the world had returned for centuries to the community of origin, as previously outlined.

The display of the map representing the distribution of all Tuscan migrants, who resided in the South West of the State throughout the whole period considered in this study (Figure 6-4), allows us to conclude that Lucchesi in rural Western Australia moved quite extensively throughout the geographical area. The map, in fact, shows a fairly scattered presence of migrants, mainly in the districts where the timber industry was present. Data confirm the overall propensity of most migrants in rural Western Australia to search for employment in the timber sector rather than in agriculture, thus reinforcing the attitude of Lucchesi for occupations that could lead to quicker money accumulation than agriculture could ever warrant. Gentilli reports that the percentage of the Italian male occupation in Western Australia in agriculture fell from 35 per cent in 1947 to 25 per cent in 1954, while in timber it increased from 4 to 9 per cent.[144]

Figure 6-4 - Distribution of Migrants from Tuscany in rural Western Australia, 1890s-1970s

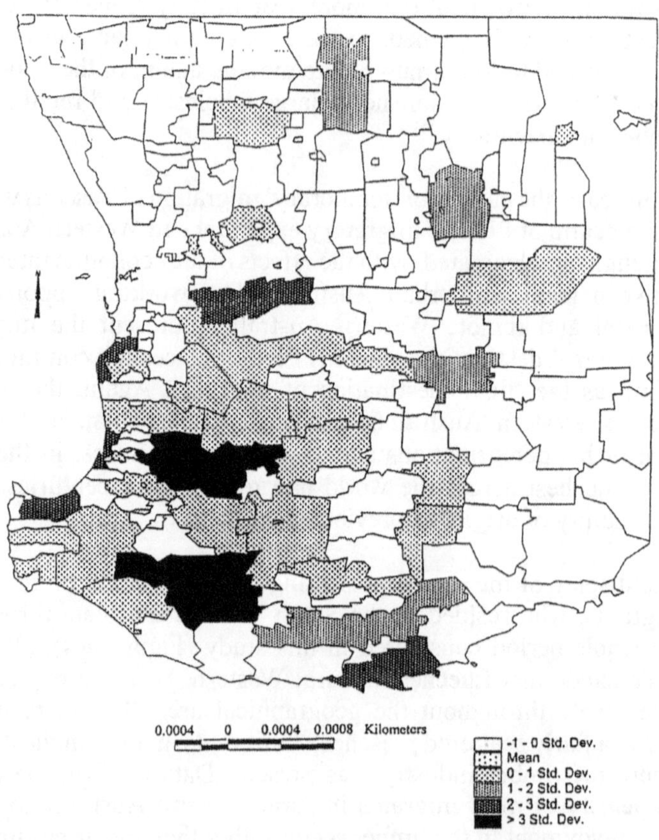

Conversely, on the long period, the highest number of Lucchesi migrants is present in Perth, North Perth, Dianella-Morley (north of the river), as well as Cannington and Karragullen (south of the river), with other notable concentrations in Osborne Park-Balcatta (north of the river) and Coogee-Spearwood (south of the river). Enough has been discussed about the distribution in the above areas, and how patterns of chain migrations and specific occupational areas have generated these spatial concentrations of Lucchesi. It is worth adding two more observations. First, the considerably lower number of Tuscans in the coastal city of Fremantle, unlike the figures of Italian migrants, particularly from the South, who have settled there as fishermen since the 1890s.[145] This can be interpreted as an additional confirmation of the peculiarity of Lucchese migration, which did not always follow the spatial and occupational patterns of Italian migrants as a whole. Secondly, notwithstanding the dispersion of the Tuscan-born population in Perth, there is a very little presence of Lucchesi living in the affluent suburbs of Perth. This circumstance is explainable as a form of spatial segregation (as in the case of the low-medium income residential suburbs of Morley and Dianella), and as an uneven income distribution in the first generation Lucchesi of Western Australia.

The analysis of their distribution in the Perth Metropolitan area suggests that Lucchese tended to concentrate in the suburbs closer to their occupations, and where Italian migrants in general did too. Differences from the Italian national pattern of settlement are represented by the distinctive presence of Lucchesi in the semi-rural suburbs east of the city, where they performed rural activities, and in their absence in the Fremantle coastal area.

CONCLUSIONS

The previous sections have analysed how patterns of chain migration have generated the arrival of the large majority of Lucchesi in Western Australia, as has been the case of Italian migrants in general in urban Australia.[146] Most of the urban and semi-urban concentrations of Tuscans in Perth have been created by the arrival of a consistent number of migrants from the same communities, whose links were mainly of kinship and friendship. Their spatial distribution is in strict relation to the areas of residence of the relatives they went to join in Western Australia. According to their original skills and peasant culture, they performed in a limited range of activities, either within the occupational areas of their relatives or in rural and remote areas where migrants had more chances to accumulate money to later re-invest in other businesses.

This chapter has examined in detail the different stages of the Lucchese settlement within Perth and the rest of the State. The process can be seen as comprising several stages. The first stage saw the arrival of mobile 'pioneers' in search of opportunities, whether they went to the mining goldfields in search of quick fortunes, or they settled as woodcutters in the South West. The inter-war period witnessed a second stage of arrivals of a more substancial group of Tuscan migrants, who took advantage of the informal network of knowledge made by their predecessors. While many moved to work in the timber and the mining industries, others established farming activities in the outskirts of Perth and set more stable businesses in Perth, thus creating the conditions for the consolidation of the Lucchese community. A third stage of Tuscan migration in Western Australia took place with the post-war larger flow from Italy, who adjusted to the Australian environment by re-creating the Lucchese community abroad, as the stepping stone for further 'temporary' migration to rural and remote Western Australia.

Because of the large intake of migrants who have arrived through a process of chain migration, after WWII there has been, in fact, a shifting of identity in the case of those who initially went to work in remote areas. The identity of the 'community of origin' has shifted from that left behind in Italy to the newly-formed Australian communities of migrants coming from the same towns of Garfagnana and the Provinces of Lucca and Massa Carrara. The sense of security that a 'little Lucca' abroad could offer allowed many to 'transplant' the century-long tradition of seasonal and temporary migration of the Tuscan Apennine valleys into the Western Australian working and residential environment. Because of the geographical distance from Italy and the making of a Lucchese environment in many spatial clusters of Perth, since the late 1960s many more migrants decided to reside permanently in Western Australia, and re-create within the Australian State the pattern of temporary migration in search of money.

Many aspects of this 'Lucca model' of temporary migration abroad have been extensively analysed in the previous chapters, as well as the Australia-bound process of Lucchese migration. This chapter has examined how these two major components combined and manifested themselves within the spatial and occupational distribution of Lucchesi in Perth and Western Australia throughout its major stages and until the 1970s, when the availability of the archival sources finishes, more or less at the same time of the end of Italian emigration abroad. Nevertheless, the study of social aspects of the Lucchese community, its identity as Lucchesi and as Italians within the Australian society, will take place in the next chapter, which will draw together the results of the extensive qualitative survey of the interviews with members of the Tuscan community of Western Australia.

CHAPTER 7

THE SOCIAL LIFE OF TUSCANS IN WESTERN AUSTRALIA

INTRODUCTION

Following the analysis of the spatial and occupational distribution of migrants from Tuscany in Western Australia, this chapter will analyse their 'identity' as Tuscans and Italians, and their social aggregation during recent decades, particularly within the Perth Metropolitan area. The study will take into account the distribution of migrants from Lucca and Massa Carrara as one of the major factors affecting their propensity and availability to social aggregation, with particular regard to the Toscany (sic) Club of Balcatta, Western Australia, a social club that caters mainly to Tuscan-born migrants from Tuscany in the Perth suburb of Balcatta, where it was founded in the early 1970s.

As the original sources used for this study are chronologically limited to the mid-1960s, the examination of the social life and aggregation of the Tuscan and Lucchese community of Western Australia is necessary in order to put into context the issue of their presence within the host country, and to verify the many layers of their Tuscan and Italian identity, the adjustment to the host country and their degree of self-realisation within the Australian society, particularly in relation to the social positions achieved.

The main finding is related to the diverse cultural identities (Lucchese, Tuscan and Italian) that emerge among Tuscan migrants in Australia. Very often, these identities (local, regional and national) are perceived as in contrast, and even incompatible with each other. On the contrary, this chapter suggests that these diverse identities are just aspects of the broader national one, which reveals itself properly only when in contact with a foreign identity.

ITALIAN AND TUSCAN (AND LUCCHESE...?) IDENTITY

One of the most common stereotypes of the Italian migrant is that of a dark-skinned peasant from a poverty-stricken rocky mountain village of the southern Italian Apennines, wandering through the enchanting lights of an American metropolis in search of working opportunities, often becoming easy labour-force prey for Italian organized crime within the host country. The reality is rather different. Emigration from Italy has a complex history, such to initially involve the northern and central Italian regions rather than Southern Italy. In fact, the geographical and social differences between the two (or many more) areas of the country are quite striking. The Australian historian Robert Pascoe writes:

> *"It is impossible to speak of 'the Italians': despite the many myths and caricatures surrounding the Italians, the only truth about them is their extreme regional diversity. Almost every region of Italy is cut off from the next by geography and culture. Not only do specific landscapes change from one area of Italy to another, but so do building styles and townscapes, and also the people, their customs, language and family life".*[1]

It can be argued that culture is certainly shaped by the external influences of the physical, economic, political and social environments. A 'distillation' of traditions and customs that we previously indicated as the 'moulders' of the Tuscan and, more specifically, Lucchese culture, later transplanted within the host societies where migrants moved.

If the geography of a place, with its physical conditions, certainly shapes its culture, economy and, consequently, the predisposition of its inhabitants to either prosper or migrate, in many areas of Italy space has contributed to generate the sense of diversity of the many Italian identities present in the country.

> *"Space was the Italian peasant's enemy. When it came to land for cultivation, the* contadino *never had enough; what he had, demanded backbreaking labor for only meager returns. When it came to exchanging goods and services, the cost of traversing lengthy distances condemned the peasant to reliance on exploitative local intermediaries and distant patrons. The need to control space, to understand and create order out of the seeming infinity of space, gave rise to* campanilismo, *a melodious word which literally refers to the sound of the church bell. In a curious symbiosis of space and person, Italian peasants perceived a fundamental distinction between their* paesani, *born within the bell's ring, and "*stranieri*", outsiders".*[2]

This is to say that, although figures tell of Italians as migrants from Italy, each Italian community abroad is not homogeneous at all, and, often, statistics ignore *campanilismo*, meaning those social, economic and psychological dimensions which affect the cultural identity of individuals and small groups, although all come from the same 'Italy'. This phenomenon was probably generated within the village culture of the many small rural centres of Italy by several factors, such as the century-long economic autonomy of the villages and the proud individualism of their inhabitants.[3] The American historian Rudolph Vecoli wrote:

> *"The intense sentiment of* campanilismo *(parochialism) which dictated that the townsmen cluster together in a particular quarter also caused the immigrants to shun Italians from other villages and provinces".*[4]

There are extreme forms of *campanilismo* in virtually every single village of Italy. Cinel, in his contribution on the regional loyalties within the Italian community of San Francisco, reports examples of local frictions, as part of the ancient rivalry between the cities of Florence and Siena, both located in Tuscany, at a little distance from each other. This animosity, due to a military conflict between the two cities in 1260, in which Florence took control over the territory formerly of Siena, was still present in the conversations of the late nineteenth century among Tuscans in San Francisco.[5] With respect to Italian regional and sub-regional *campanilismo* in the United States during the 1920s and 1930s, Vecoli stated further:

> *"The Italian immigrants were also divided by regional hatred and jealousies which hindered any collective efforts for their advancement. The failure of the Italians to rise as a group in power and prestige as rapidly as the Irish or Germans was due in large measure to their lack of unity. The Italians, for example, were singularly unsuccessful in establishing organizations and institutions which would promote the welfare of their ethnic group".*[6]

Cinel reports further about some forms of regional subdivision among Italian migrants in San Francisco in the nineteenth century, which are worth describing briefly as examples of the occupational boundaries of Italian regional and sub-regional groups. He discusses the long monopoly, since the 1860s, of migrants from Genoa (Region of Liguria) in the San Francisco area, both in the fishing and the market gardening businesses. These businesses were only slowly ceded to other numerically emerging regional groups, like the Sicilians with respect to the fishing industry, and the Lucchesi in the case of market gardening.[7] These examples are extremely interesting for the purpose of the present study, as they draw attention on two different factors, such as the regional/sub-regional identity and the occupational patterns of a specific regional group, as is the case of Lucchesi. Therefore their identity, as migrants coming from a relatively homogeneous area, is now analyzed, with the purpose to study their degree of adjustment to the host environment.

'*CAMPANILISMO*' IN AUSTRALIA

As there were and, to some extent, still there are extreme forms of *campanilismo* in Italy and in some Italian communities abroad, so there are also regional - and, very often, sub-regional - loyalties among Italian migrants in Australia, as some have stressed.[8] This different sense of identity, often expressed as a form of pride to belong to a specific rural village or town rather than another, finds historically its origin within the Italian peasant culture, and is replicated in Italian communities abroad. *Campanilismo* is re-created with reference to the specific place of origin in Italy and the areas and time of settlement in the host country, such that it would be even more appropriate to speak of various Italian-Australian communities, rather than of one single community.

As summarized by Rosoli, until a few years ago scholars on Italian migration pursued the idea that many Italian communities abroad had slowly abandoned the *campanilismo* in a step-by-step process of identification into a generic sense of *Italianita*,' of Italian national identity,[9] as part of a socially gradual adjustment to the host community and the contemporary rise of a generic discovery and acknowledgement of one's ethnic roots. To this respect, Vecoli wrote in 1965:

> *"The mass of immigrants from Italy had no sense of a common nationality. Paradoxically, the growth of consciousness of being Italian was a product of their experience in America. The distinction among Abruzzese, Perugians, and Sicilians escaped most Americans who lumped them together as "Eye-talians".*[10]

On the contrary, other works have noted the re-activation of regional and sub-regional *campanilismo*.[11] These processes, which are particularly evident within the Italian Australian community,[12] are due to various factors. First, regional loyalties reflect the intensity of chain migration processes, which brought a significant number of migrants from the same communities to a foreign destination, as has been previously outlined. Secondly, the size and the geographical dispersion of a regional or sub-regional group are important factors in determining the rise of a specific identity, especially in urban contexts. As is evident, when a community from a given area reaches a critical density, sub-regional and, often, parochial *campanilismo* revives or emerges, as Harney has also observed in the case of the Italian community in Toronto.[13] These patterns reinforce the loyalty of the community group, as a little 'cocoon' protecting the migrants from the host environment and from other Italian regional and sub-regional groups, both perceived 'different' and *stranieri* (foreign), as has been diagrammatically presented in Figure 7-1, which shows the shift of *campanilismo* from the community of origin to the community abroad. The process, previously described by Bell, has been recently confirmed by the Australian anthropologist Loretta Baldassar, in her study of the Italian family domain in Australia, perceived in opposition to the 'outside', that is everything beyond the family.[14]

Even in the interviews carried out among Tuscan migrants in Western Australia, which form the core of next chapter, Italian informers recall not social interactions but rather personal qualities and times. As observed by Yans-McLaughlin in her paper on the oral narrative of migrants,[15] family relationships are the recurrent leitmotif of the Italian interviews. Furthermore, Pascoe reports examples of the Italian community of Melbourne, in which the *campanilismo* of regional and sub-regional groups is replicated and expressed by unaware residential choices, so that groups from the same Italian regions and even from the same provinces and villages, gather in specific areas.[16]

As Harney observed,[17] a second reason for the growing regional *campanilismo* among Italian communities overseas, is due to the administrative creation of the Italian regional councils in 1970, in which the Republic of Italy allocated financial and political autonomy to twenty Italian regions. As a consequence, many Italian regional politicians began to look at the Italian communities abroad according to their regional composition, with the aim to gain a political consensus, which has re-activated 'sleeping' Italian *campanilismo* overseas. In fact, as will be examined with respect to the Toscany Club of Balcatta-Perth, although the association was wanted by a large portion of members of the Tuscan community, who self-funded the initiative, a relevant financial contribution was given by the Regional Council of Tuscany in the 1970s.

Figure 7-1 - The shift of* Campanilismo *from within Italy to overseas Italian communities

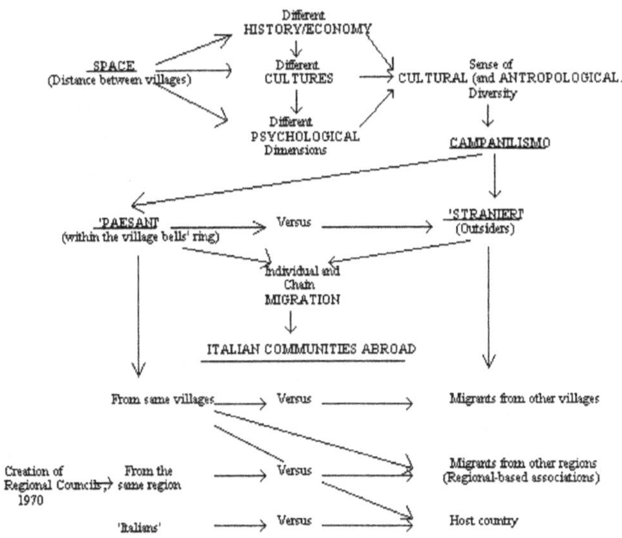

In the light of these factors, it is therefore worth examining in the next two sections the social aggregation of Lucchesi and the reasons for the foundation, in Perth as well as in Adelaide, Melbourne and Sydney, of social clubs catering to a large number of migrants from the same region.

THE SOCIAL AGGREGATION OF LUCCHESI

In his report of the state of Italian Australian studies in the early 1990s, the Australian historian Richard Bosworth observed that very little had yet been written about the cultural attitudes of Italian migrants in Australia with particular reference to their religious beliefs, habits and their cultural associations.[18] A recently published book by Paganoni and O'Connor has finally cast some light on the religious practices of the Italian community of South Australia.[19] In addition, this section and the next one intend to highlight the socially complex formation processes leading to the foundation of many

Italian Australian associations and clubs, with particular reference to the Toscany Club of Western Australia, as a case study.

It has been suggested that, for all non-English-speaking migrants, the possibilities of forming personal social relationships outside the family can be limited, as many migrant groups at the first stage of their settlement are restricted by language difficulties.[20] Single migrants, isolated from their own ethnic groups, can be therefore particularly vulnerable. By definition, migrants move across different cultural and social environments, experiencing situations of risk and uncertainty that can threaten their behavioural models and even their lives. In her study of migrants' social networks, Italian sociologist Piselli writes that none of the cultural and social 'signs' that define the status and the identity of migrants before their departure has a meaningful significance in the context of the host country. Uncertainty is not simply related to personal problems of integration into the new environment, but involves interpersonal relations and the overall society, such to push migrants to deeply re-define their own situation and re-locate themselves in a totally new "symbolic field of behaviour". Nevertheless, at the same time migrants will also tend to defend the boundaries of their distinctive culture, re-affirming their own values and preferences and finding meaning and continuity in their collective identity.[21]

It is within this process of re-definition and re-affirmation of old and new collective identities that migrants associate in the host countries. Migrants who, in Italy, probably never considered the possibility to cooperate and socialize or even to contact co-nationals from other towns and provinces as a result of the previously examined century-long *campanilismo*, found themselves forced to deal with these new issues, especially in Australian urban areas. In rural and sparsely populated areas, in fact, an ethnic community is forced in upon itself, or can maintain a desired isolation, with a view to quick money accumulation to re-invest elsewhere, as it has been observed in the case of Tuscans in remote Western Australia. In urban contexts, on the other hand, contacts of one type or another with the Australian environment are unavoidable, thus requiring the cultural and social adjustments that associations can facilitate.

Some observers may assume that Australian ethnic communities and their institutions reproduce homeland surroundings, maintaining the speech, the ideals, and the manner of life of the rural communities of origin. While this is true to some extent with respect to the many Italian Australian associations[22] and to the Toscany Club of Western Australia, in reality the Italian Australian community represents an important step away from the culture of origin. Neither the community nor its institutions are fully Italian in character; nor are they Australian. As another scholar noted with respect to Italian communities and associations in the United States,[23] these institutions serve as an interim group, the immigrant generation with its traditions as well as, to some extent, the host environment.

As previously explained, many newcomers sought - and still seek - to solve life's complexities by joining benefit groups and cultural clubs, which are not transplanted institutions carried to Australia, but rather newly-conceived associations bridging the gap between the Italian culture of origin and the sense of cultural displacement within the host environment. The presentation of the complex phenomenon of *campanilismo* abroad allows us to understand why in the early years of Italian settlement in Australia, associations and institutions formed typically on the basis of place of origin, either villages, towns or provinces of birth.

While the previous chapter highlighted the importance of parental and kinship links as facilitators for the Italian chain migration patterns to Australia, the growth and development of benefit and cultural associations among Italian migrants add new components to the long process of adjustment to the host environment. It indicates a significant movement away from the rural Italian distrust of anyone outside the family circle. In the new and, often, urban environment, and in the absence of sufficient family members to provide the resources necessary to meet all emergencies, Italian migrants found it necessary to co-operate with *stranieri* (outsiders), although many associations still attract people from the same geographically circumscribed area of Italy. The condition of being overseas shortened the cultural difference and diffidence towards people outside their own village. In other words, Italian migrants in Australia, who would have regarded each other as strangers in Italy, found that in Australia they had in common enough traditions to warrant banding together. As the Italian social historian Maria Corti wrote in her study of Italian regional communities abroad, when migrants are overseas and increase their opportunity to stay in contact with the 'other', they will also acquire the awareness of being migrants, and will re-elaborate a new identity in which the "bell tower" of *campanilismo* will be widened beyond the boundary of the village of origin.[24]

With respect to the direct observation of the activity of the Toscany Club of Western Australia, it is worth adding that local frictions of *campanilismo* - that affected the relations between Tuscan cities like Florence and Siena, as previously noted - are sometimes overcome within the association. As will be outlined in detail in the next section, The Toscany Club, in fact, is formed by a high proportion of people from the Province of Lucca, although there are many from other provinces, such as Massa Carrara. While in the past many cultural frictions at the village level were expressed between people within the same province of Lucca, now these forms of *campanilismo* within the members of the Toscany Club are instead declared towards people coming from other regions of Italy. Not surprisingly, this pattern is expressed by most of the long-established Italian regional and sub-regional communities of Australia: often, in fact, Italian-Australian associations on a regional base attract first-generation migrations from geographically circumscribed areas of Italy, as a "necessarily reasonable communication between individuals, their families and the close community".[25]

REASONS FOR SOCIAL AGGREGATION

As observed in the previous chapter, Lucchese family and village links fulfilled the function of not prolonging traits and patterns of the community of origin, which was rather 're-produced' within the host environment. Instead, they provided important first steps in introducing newcomers to the Australian society. Help, mainly provided by members of enlarged families to the Lucchese newcomers to Australia, was expressed as the provision of room and board at minimal expense or no cost, the granting of services and favours in emergencies, as well as the emotional support. These were all necessary steps for the introduction of settlers to the new host environment. In addition, institutions such as the Toscany Club have played the role of introducing Tuscan migrants directly to living patterns of the host culture, and thus served as an outside force influencing their social adjustment. In this regard, Lee wrote in 1970:

> *"One of the most important non-spatial roles assigned to the ethnic community is that of a buffer between two societies, an area through which filter newly-arrived immigrants so that they might become more easily adjusted to an alien environment. In this light the ethnic community can be conceived as arising from the importation of an ethos into an alien environment".*[26]

After an initial concentration within a few distinctive suburbs, settlers disperse to other suburbs within the city, mainly due to family and occupational reasons. Nevertheless, from time to time, they still need informal (and formal) social interaction and cultural reinforcement with their peers. Gathering in a specific area, as it has been observed with respect to Italian migrants in Australia,[27] or the establishment of a social club remains a symbolic and practical foci for many.

Local communities and migrants' associations certainly accomplish a few functions of social aggregation within the host country.[28] More in detail, the following statement acutely analyses the development of the social aggregation of many migrant groups within a host society, from the 'comfort zone' created by family kinship and community ties at the arrival of newcomers to the creation of associations and clubs at a further stage of settlement:

> *"Individuals are the centres of webs of social bonds that radiate outwards to the people they know intimately, those they know well, those they know casually and then the wider society. Individuals create these networks but build them within constraints which include language, kin obligations, status, community of interest, the workplace, location, or level of maturity".*[29]

This process certainly applies to Lucchesi as well. After the first logistic support to the newcomers within the family ties, once migrants find more permanent occupations and settle within a suburb, their need to socialize pushes them to congregate with people of their own country, possibly of their closer regional or sub-regional area, or even of their community of origin. For example, a generic principle of mutuality, "brotherhood" and sense of Italian national identity is identifiable in the intentions of the Lucchese founders of the association "*Unione e Fratellanza*" (Union and Botherhood), created in Cordoba (Argentina) in 1894, as in the following excerpt of the association's statutory declaration:

> *"Proteggersi reciprocamente in tutti i casi della vita sociale, risultando dal bene comune anche il proprio bene, e fare una continua propaganda onde inculcare questi principi che uniscono e stringono i soci nel pensiero di una patria comune".*[30]
>
> *(It is necessary to mutually protect each other in all circumstances of social life - since the common good will generate also one's own good - and to disseminate these principles that unite and tie the members at the thought of the homeland).*

The founding principles of the Lucchese-Argentinean association suggest a strong sense of community within the host country. They recall a close relation between common and personal interests, and indicate a continuity between the communal values of the subjects of the Republic of Lucca, and the sense of community of Lucchesi migrants abroad. The difference is that now, at the time of foundation of this association, the values are flagged under the common interest of the 'homeland', which is recognizable as Italy, rather than Lucca. This confirms that any Italian regional or sub-regional group abroad, although still 'visible' in its peculiar culture (dialect, values and traditions), will tend to 'widen' its boundaries and smother the *campanilismo.* As a matter of fact, within Italian communities abroad, the *stranieri* are often represented by the host environment, rather than the inhabitants of the neighbouring community.

Nevertheless, since the Italian mass migration of the 1870s and 1880s, associations of Italians abroad tended to have a very high regional or sub-regional composition, acting as a 'buffer' between the family ties and the social environment as a whole. It is a process that has been observed within Italian communities at different stages of their settlement, both in many host countries[31] and in Australia.[32] The Australian geographer Ian Burnley, in his analysis of Italians congregating in clubs, institutions and religious associations in Australia, interprets these aggregations as a way for members to more easily achieve their own goals,[33] since networking with long-established people from the same community of origin can facilitate the contacts with *stranieri* and the host community as a whole. While the outcomes of this research seem to lead towards similar conclusions, on the other hand, sometimes these institutions simply give a sense of lasting identity to displaced migrants, irrespective of their economic or lobbying utility.[34]

While the ethnic community is still small, its institutions represent a generic Italian identity and *campanilismo* is softened, as other more important issues of 'survival' arise in psychological and social terms. In particular:

> *"The ethnic or immigrant enclave can be defended in social terms as a space whose interstitial character protects the psychological integrity of the newcomer. Given the economic costs of psychiatric disorder, this is not an inconsequential consideration".*[35]

As it has been demonstrated with respect to Italians, "longer resident persons felt more identity with their local community than more recent arrivals", although the statement has quite a few exceptions, as the author has stressed.[36] It is the first generation of migrants and the newcomers in particular who need to congregate with people of their own culture, as a social and psychological response to the host environment. Beyond the practical help offered by the settled migrants to relatives and friends arriving from the community of origin, grouping in associations re-creates that sense of community and social cohesion that the migratory experience had interrupted. Once the social and psychological balance of the migrants had been adjusted to the new environment and the sense of belonging (at least partially) to Australian society is reached, the association can certainly play other roles. These additional and optional roles can be identified in the reinforcement of the Italian national identity and in the 'exploitation' of the network in order to pursue economic and social goals. As a confirmation, it is within the first-generation Lucchese migrants of the post-WWII period in Western Australia that the idea to create a social club was born since the late 1960s.

THE TOSCANY CLUB OF WESTERN AUSTRALIA

A considerable number of migrants from Tuscany arrived in Australia since the early 1950s, and their main destinations were Melbourne and Perth. Consequently, the first associations of Tuscans to operate in Australia were opened in these two cities. The Toscana Social Club of Melbourne was inaugurated in 1969[37] and joined an already large number of other Italian-Australian associations, which had flourished during the 1960s, particularly in Melbourne and Sydney.[38] These associations varied greatly in size and significance, including sporting and social clubs, cultural, education groups, and branches of Italian overseas political parties and trade unions. All across Australia, some Italian associations for religious purposes often attract members with the sole goal to celebrate the feast of the patron saint of the migrants' village of origin, as has been noted in Western Australia by Gentilli[39] and recently confirmed by Paganoni and O'Connor on Italian religious festivities in South Australia.[40]

Many Italian-Australian associations operated, and still operate, social activities ranging from solemn celebrations to recreational purposes, with a focus on local festivities and Italian national anniversaries.[41] Hence, they had and, to some extent, they still have widely differing interests and may be in conflict with groups from the same national background, as the Australian political scientist James Jupp noted .[42] This attitude of *campanilismo*, although attenuated by the distance of migrants from Italy, has been a characteristic highlighted in the previous sections and certainly applies to the Tuscan association of Melbourne.

Mr Giuseppe Giusti, the President of the Melbourne association, so described the activity of his club at the third conference of Tuscan migration, held in Pontremoli (Province of Massa Carrara) in 1990:

> *"Noi con l'aiuto dei nostri soci, lavoratori, imprenditori siamo riusciti a creare delle sedi proprie, delle costruzioni addirittura, un lembo di Toscana nella lontana Australia. Ne abbiamo una a Melbourne con capienze non indifferenti, in particolare quella di Perth che mette a tavola 500 persone comodamente ed ha sette campi di bocce al coperto, cinque squadre di bambini di calcio".*[43]
>
> *(With the help of our members, workers and entrepreneurs, we have been able to found real clubs, looking like real, little pieces of Tuscany in the distant Australia. We have one fairly big club in Melbourne and one in Perth, that can easily cater dinner to over 500 members, has seven indoors bowls fields and five young boys' soccer teams).*

The pride in the constitution of an association is even more highlighted by the pride in having re-created "little piece" of Tuscany overseas. This is also the case of the Toscany Club of Balcatta, a northern suburb of Perth, where the association joined a notable number of other clubs already formed on an Italian regional of sub-regional basis.[44] The Toscany Club was founded in 1969, and its first long-term President (as he remained in this position for almost twenty-seven years) was Mr Mario Casotti, a migrant from Minucciano, in the upper valley of the River Serchio. A large majority of the members of the newly-founded club was from the Province of Lucca, and the first social function, a dinner-and-dance night was organised within the premises of the Macedonia Club of North Perth, as the Tuscan association did not have its own premises. The function attracted over 300 first-generation Tuscan migrants.[45] Because this function gained good success, the committee decided to organise another recreational meeting for its members. The party took place in the Perth hills of Karragullen, close to the semi-rural areas where many Tuscan migrants had established their orchards and market gardening activities, as examined in the previous chapter. The one-day country party was organised with social events, typical Tuscan community games and rural cuisine.[46]

After these functions, the President and the committee of the Toscany Club realised that social functions and sporting competitions were among the most appreciated activities by its numerous members and represented a solid reason to keep alive the culture of the many migrants from Tuscany in Western Australia.[47] One more goal was to build its own premises, an objective that few other Italian-Australian associations had been able to reach[48] because of the lack of necessary funds and the scarce number of club members. Since the early 1970s, monthly or fortnightly dinner-dance occasions, hosted within the premises of other ethnic associations, became a regular tradition of the Toscany Club. The financial contribution of the members participating in the social functions helped to raise money for humanitarian causes, both linked to local and Italian activities, such as research on cancer and muscle dystrophy in Western Australia and financial support to the victims of Italian disasters, as the earthquake in the Italian Region of Friuli of 1976 and of southern Italy of 1980.[49]

It is worth specifying that these money-raising activities have never been highlighted by the promoting committee as the main objective of the occasion, since the declared goal has always been the promotion of social interaction among club members.[50] In other words, the intention of the founding members was to keep - or to retrieve - the culture that many Tuscans felt they were losing by migrating to Australia and by living in a different social environment. To this end, regular social functions, together with sporting activities and tournaments were the best 'excuses' to gather people from the same Italian geographical area and culture within the Australian host environment. Other functions drew their reason from natural following of seasons and rural traditions of the communities of origin, such as *la festa delle castagne* (the chestnut feast), characteristic of central Italian Apennines populations, and *la festa della Befana* (the Befana is the witch who traditionally 'sweeps' away all the Christmas celebrations on the 6th of January).

Together with social functions, fund-raising activities have, on the other hand, contributed to render the club more 'visible' with the Western Australian social environment and the *Regione Toscana*, the Regional Council of Tuscany, when the money raised has been allocated for Italian-based initiatives. As previously stated, the Regional Council of Tuscany obtained its political, financial and administrative autonomy from the Italian central government in 1970, as part of a constitutional process of political decentralization, at the same time that the Tuscan associations of Melbourne and Perth were founded. This timely coincidence allowed the clubs to be taken into serious consideration by the Regional Council of Tuscany, as representatives of a Tuscan identity abroad which was going to have a political correspondent identity within Italian politics and society.

This circumstance certainly favoured the financial contribution that the *Regione Toscana* gave to the Western Australian Toscany Club during the 1970s, to help in the construction of its own premises.[51] Other substantial contributions came from the *Associazione Lucchesi nel Mondo*, the Lucca-based association of Lucchesi around the world that has members all over the world, wherever Lucchesi migrated. This association was founded in the late 1960s. The *Associazione* has a monthly bulletin (*Notiziario Lucchesi nel Mondo*), which is distributed all over the world, and, although irregularly, organizes international conferences on Lucchese migration, the last one being held in September 1998 in Lucca. The sections of the association are around the world, reflecting the distribution of migrants from the Province of Lucca, as previously examined. Over fifteen sections are present in Europe, mainly in Belgium (five), Switzerland (three), France, Germany and the United Kingdom (two, respectively), Holland and Australia (one each). The United States have 18 sections of the *Associazione Lucchesi nel Mondo* in most urban centres, while Canada has three, Argentina nine, Brazil seven, and Peru, Venezuela, Uruguay and Colombia one each. Finally, two more sections are present in South Africa and five in Australia (Perth, Adelaide, Hobart, Melbourne and Sydney).[52] To give an idea of the distribution and representation of the association overseas, it is worth adding that very few other organizations on an Italian regional and provincial basis have a similar presence of sections abroad, and none of them is from Tuscany.

The work for the construction of proper premises for the Toscany Club began in 1980 in Balcatta, a semi-rural area of the northern suburbs of Perth that had previously witnessed the presence of a several Lucchesi market gardeners.

As it has been previously studied, the suburb was also in a central position with respect to the geographical distribution of migrants from Tuscany in the Perth Metropolitan area. Except for the Lucchese orchardists of east hills of Karragullen and those within the industrial areas south of the River Swan (Cannington and Manning in particular), a large majority of Tuscan-born migrants in the northern suburbs (Tuart Hill, Yokine, Leederville, Dianella, Morley and Bassandean) and at a relatively short distance from where the premises were going to be built.[53]

THE CLUB'S MEMBERSHIP

Since then, the association has operated within its new premises, hosting regular monthly dinner-dance functions, the annual ball, and catering for Italian local and national politicians visiting Western Australia. In particular, during the past two decades there has been a presence of notable guests. Several representatives of the *Lucchesi nel Mondo* and of its branches overseas have visited the club, during their tours in order to keep close contacts and cultural links with the several communities of Tuscan migrants across the world. Similarly, personalities of the Chamber of Commerce of Lucca have visited the Toscany Club of Perth on a few occasions, as a way to honour the presence of the many Lucchesi abroad.[54]

These circumstances confirm once again how the number of Lucchesi among Tuscan migrants is predominant. This circumstance is reflected in many aspects of the life of the Toscany Club, notwithstanding the label 'Tuscany' could suggest a wider numerical spread of migrants from the other provinces forming the Tuscany Region. The Regional Council of Tuscany has recently established a web site dedicated to the presence of Tuscans around the world,[55] but a more attentive analysis of the several newsletters dedicated to *Toscani nel Mondo* reveals how a high number of news items are exclusively related to migrants from the Province of Lucca. Even the appointed *Consulta Regionale dei Toscani all'Estero* (Regional

Council of Tuscans Abroad), within the administrative Council of the Tuscany Region, is almost exclusively formed by overseas delegates of the *Associazione Lucchesi nel Mondo* of Lucchese origin.

The Italian regional and provincial composition of the members of the Toscany Club of Balcatta confirms the overwhelming presence of Lucchesi under the label 'Tuscan'. Table 7.1 shows that Lucchesi migrants represent over seventy per cent of all the members of the association, according to the latest figures released by the club.[56]

Table 7.1 - Geographical Origin of the Members of the Toscany Club of Balcatta, Perth

		%
Province of Lucca	389	70.60
Province of Massa Carrara	35	6.35
Province of Pisa	3	0.54
Province of Firenze	5	0.91
Sicily	31	5.63
Calabria	28	5.08
Veneto	20	3.63
Abruzzo/Molise	19	3.45
Lombardy	9	1.63
Other regions of Italy	3	0.54
Anglo-Australians	9	1.63
TOTAL	551	100.00

The percentage of members from the Province of Lucca is similar to that of the overall period 1876-1888, when the number of migrants from Lucca and Garfagnana (then part of the Province of Massa Carrara) oscillated between a minimum of 58% to a maximum of 75% of the whole Tuscan overseas migratory flow.

The percentage of members from different Italian regions, instead, reflects the overall composition of the Italian community of Western Australia, with the Regions Sicily, Calabria, Veneto and Abruzzo having supplied the larger number of Italian migrants in this State.[57] Furthermore, the very limited presence of Anglo-Australian members reflects the cultural and social approach of the club towards non-Italian speakers.

This high percentage of Lucchesi among the members of the Toscany Club requires some explanation. As it has been examined, migration from the Province of Lucca has always been relevant in the migratory patterns of Tuscany. Furthermore, the financial support of the *Associazione Lucchesi nel Mondo* at the moment of the foundation of the Perth club, has certainly influenced the composition of the memberships. Most members of the founding committee were from Lucca and its Province. At its beginning, the club aggregated relatives, friends and supporters of the co-founders. Consequently, the family and community ties played a major role in the social cohesion of the Toscany Club. Throughout the years, very few members have been replaced within the committee board. As already stated, the first president, Mr Mario Casotti, has kept this position for almost twenty-seven years, although he has been re-confirmed annually by the general assembly of the members.[58] Other co-founding members have shifted into different roles of the board (Vice-President, Secretary, Treasurer) through the years of the presidency held by Mr Casotti, so that a minimal turn-over of members has taken place within the hierarchical structure of the association. Hence, it has remained firmly in the hands of members originally from the Province of Lucca.

Although the membership is open to all, with no regard to nationality and culture, even the Regional Council of Tuscany has acknowledged the Lucchese 'supremacy' within the 'Tuscan' club. The Tuscan regional administration has, in fact, allowed the Lucca-based *Associazione Lucchesi nel Mondo* to play the role of interface between the Perth-based club and the Tuscany Region institutions. Many social functions related to the visits of representatives of the Lucca-based association, in fact, have been widely acknowledged by the *Regione Toscana*, within its program of promotion of Tuscan communities abroad, as from the newsletter of the regional institution.[59]

DIRECT OBSERVATION OF THE CLUB'S ACTIVITY AND CONCLUSIONS

Notwithstanding the opening of the Club to local issues, the association keeps a strong Italian regional/sub-regional identity that reflects the Italian geographical composition of its members. The previous sections have demonstrated how forms of *campanilismo* are still present within the overall Italian-Australian community. Many members of Italian associations and clubs of Australia keep in fact an attitude of cultural closure towards *gli stranieri*, the outsiders, no matter whether they belong to the Australian society or whether they come from different regions of Italy.

The direct observation of the Club's activity seems to confirm that similar circumstances prevail also within the Toscany Club of Balcatta, Perth. The presence of members of different Italian regional origin up to twenty per cent of the total memberships may be misleading. Often, some first-generation migrants are members of one club for all sort of reasons. These reasons may include the proximity of the club to the residence, as confirmed by the residence of most non-Tuscan members of the Club.[60] Another reason is the fact that family friends belong to the same association, so that many Tuscan families participate in the social functions of the Toscany Club and invite other non-Tuscan friends over. Conversely, they are invited to dinner-dance functions organized by other regional clubs and to which their acquaintances belong. An additional reason is the presence, within the Toscany Club, of good sporting facilities, billiards and *bocce* in particular, not available elsewhere, as the former president confirmed.[61]

Although the monthly social functions are open to all, invitations to other personalities of the Italian-Australian community and Western Australian politicians are sent only on the occasion of the annual ball, although in a limited number. In this case, recent studies confirm the personal observation of the activity of the club during the years 1997 and 1998. The invitations are aimed to *fare bella figura*, to perform and show the organizers, the members and their guests their mutual social prestige and power, as the American sociologist Nardini noted with respect to the performance of other Italian clubs abroad.[62] The committee and the members of the Club confirm to themselves their social achievement by sitting at the same table with the Consul of Italy, other eminent members of the local Italian community, or Western Australian State and local politicians. Furthermore, in the view of the Club's committee members, the guests will be impressed by the considerable number of members present at the function and will interpret this circumstance, respectively, as a sign of social prestige of the club (and, indirectly, of the Italian community), or as a considerable body of votes for the lobbying of ethnic issues.

The direct observation of the activity of the Toscany Club of Balcatta during the years 1997 and 1998, as well as the interaction with its committee members and affiliates confirm most of the outcomes of the analysis presented in these previous sections. The President of the Club and the whole executive committee, as well as most of the members, have given their full availability to have this study conducted. The support offered has been considerable, in terms of access to membership records and to the archive of correspondence held by the Toscany Club. In addition, most of the interviews with members of the Tuscan community of Perth, whose outcomes form the focus of the next chapter, have been possible with the help and introduction of the either the President or the committee members.

Nevertheless, a few considerations must be noted. Firstly, the expectations of some members of the committee were different from the purpose of this research, and for which reason they had been approached, although all of the intentions of the study were tabled and clearly explained to them. At the initial meetings, the Treasurer of the Club expressed enthusiasm for the research carried out, specifying that "the history of Lucchesi in Australia has not been written yet, although its importance is paramount in comparison to that of other Italians (from different regions)".[63] During another informal meeting, the Secretary of the Club declared that "Lucchesi are very special people, who have always worked hard, harder than anyone else".[64] Some of these considerations certainly cast light on the high sense of collective self-esteem of first-generation Lucchesi in Western Australia. The statements reflect a consolidated perception of Lucchese community identity that is rooted within the socio-historical background of Lucca, and mixed with patterns of local *campanilismo.* The value of this identity is then nourished by the necessity to defend it within the Australian host environment, and is certainly reinforced by the (sometimes apologetic) actions of the *Lucchesi nel Mondo* association about the "lives and fortunes" of

access to knowledge, as my academic background involves, sparks once again the enmity between 'peasantry' and 'academia', as representatives of different and clashing socio-cultural values that have been so part of the Tuscan society of these last two hundred years.[67]

These final personal observations can be taken as a conclusion, since they frame the topic within its aims. The objective of this section, as well as of most of this study is, in fact, to demonstrate the tight link between the historical and socio-cultural background of migrants and their spatial, occupational and social patterns in Western Australia, of which belonging to the Toscany Club is a relevant part.

CHAPTER 8

A SURVEY OF FIRST-GENERATION MIGRANTS FROM TUSCANY IN WESTERN AUSTRALIA

SELECTION OF SAMPLE

Having highlighted the patterns of migrants from Tuscany in Western Australia on a quantitative basis as the subject of this study, the next task, for a qualitative survey, is to first establish a suitable method of sample investigation. The choice of a sample for the detailed analysis of the several issues involved with migrants from Tuscany in the Perth area was found to be a major difficulty in the construction of this research. As Wilson has indicated, one of the difficulties in adopting sampling procedures is that of obtaining a reliable listing of the population of immigrants to sample.[1] Furthermore, with respect to research on Italian migrants in Australia, Heiss has stated that there is no fully adequate method of deriving a sample of the Italian-born population of Metropolitan Perth,[2] and Spedicato has expressed the same concern in her paper on migrants from the Italian Region of Abruzzi in Western Australia.[3]

While studies on ethnic concentrations in Australia are usually based on empirical evidence, mainly drawn from population censuses, studies of immigrant motivations - which often confirm the outcomes of quantitative studies - are largely based on purposive samples drawn from the residents of ethnic concentrations.[4] Even with initial controversies over subjective documents by behaviourists, who continue to prefer statistics with few exceptions,[5] the necessity, in the case of some historians, and the method, in the case of ethnographers and other social scientists, explain the continuous acceptance of personal testimony in immigration studies.[6] The American geographers Rachel Silvey and Victoria Lawson have recently written:

> *"Migration studies are beginning to draw on these insights in order to explore new sites and scales of analysis. Specifically, interpreting the voices of migrants themselves as theoretically meaningful allows researchers to open up "development" and critique categorizations of place as undeveloped, backward, and traditional".*[7]

Furthermore, Smolicz and Secombe have identified the need for the study of the intentions, experiences and activities of individuals within the process of sociological analysis as active agents in the context of their cultural situations and roles.[8]

The consultation of informants as a source of primary data was therefore considered indispensable to fulfill the major purposes of this study. The acceptance of the analysis of personal assumptions thus requires the adoption of a methodology that enables individuals to reveal their social and cultural situations through the expression of their own thoughts, feelings, aspirations and assessments. Within demographic and sociological research, at several points the best that may be said for accompanying statistical data is that they do not contradict an interpretation that rests upon interviews.[9]

It is important to note that the present study does not attempt to isolate those sociological and demographic characteristics, which are essential for interpreting migrants' settlement and occupational patterns. Instead, the study attempts to determine some of the relevant factors worthy of more detailed examination. The research identifies the general trends of the quantitative data with the object of locating, within the qualitative data, further confirmations and the variables worth analysing more deeply in order to obtain a better understanding of migration patterns.

The sample has to be representative of Tuscan-born urban immigrants living in Perth. The term 'representative' refers to the ability of the researcher to generalise from the sample about the characteristics of the chosen population, with a high degree of statistical possibility that the generalisations are in fact correct. This means that the sample is a true cross-section of settlement, occupational and other demographic characteristics of the Tuscan population in the Perth Metropolitan area. The sample has to be of sufficient size so that analysis can be conducted allowing some cross-tabulations among important demographic and sociological characteristics.[10] The form of analysis of the present research, due to many aspects of this particular study, consists of an inspection of a number of the questionnaire outcomes, involving the relationship of more variables, with the aim to confirm the patterns emerging from the quantitative data.

In-depth interviews and extensive contacts through participant observation studies, such as those undertaken in Australia by Zubrzycki,[11] Huber[12] and Bottomley,[13] usually represent a much better source than large-scale and detailed interviews, especially in an exploration of migration causes and motivations.

Interviewees had to be first-generation migrants from Tuscany, as birthplace remains the most satisfactory index for the analysis of the major issues involved with the migration process.[14] As will be further examined, most of the migrants interviewed were between 60 and 80 years old, with a few exceptions.

The huge rise in immigration gains during the post-second World War period was especially selective of particular age groups. The dominant element in the Australian immigration program over the two decades beginning in the late 1940s was labour recruitment, with Italians arriving in large numbers since 1952. Hence, in the selection of immigrants, persons in their twenties (and very often in their late teenage years, such as the case of Tuscan migrants and early thirties were deliberately selected).[15] As a result, many of these post-WWII immigrants were people born in the 1920s, and currently are 65-70 years and above, as confirmed by Gentilli in his paper on the age of Italian migrants in Western Australia.[16]

While the first contacts were taken at the Toscany Club of Perth, the other major source adopted was the snowballing technique (that is, the first interviewees provided the researcher with the names of other friends to be interviewed), an approach already used by Rina Huber, in her research on Italian migrants.[17] Wherever possible, relatives, friends or interviewees who offered their assistance were used to obtain favourable introductions with interviewees, so that more co-operative interviews could be achieved. Interviews among first-generation Tuscans residing in Perth were conducted in 1997 and, intermittently, in 1998, and solely by the writer. Personal knowledge and convenience of access determined the choice of the sample for study, according to the interviewee selection process chosen by Grieco in her sociological research among Scottish migrants in the United States.[18] Quite often, the first persons interviewed were those who, within the Toscany Club assisted in securing access to other additional interviewees.

As a first stage, pivotal individuals within the Tuscan community of Perth were located, and information obtained on the outline structure of family and community relations within their group over the last forty years. Thereafter, information was gathered by comparing them to data and records already collected through the quantitative research and, at a second stage, interviewing more selected migrants. The double check seemed important in the light of possible mistakes sometimes occurring in data collection by direct informers. The confirmation of records already gathered through the quantitative study was instrumental to properly proceed towards direct interviews.

Personal knowledge of the Tuscan community of Western Australia and of its migration process helped when prompts were necessary. It is unlikely that such details could have been generated in the context of an initial impersonal contact. To speak Italian was essential, as confirmed by other researchers' methodologies.[19] Conversely, the fact that the interviewer was neither a long-established Tuscan to Australia nor an Anglo-Australian meant that people could speak freely and without 'fear' about the host country and the same Tuscan-Australian community.

The research intention was to snowball through the networks of selected individuals.[20] The assumption was that name and additional information clustering, provided by initial informers were good indicators of the potential social connectedness of migrants, as implied by literature review and quantitative research outcomes. The sample was initially conceived as 40 informers, which represented a meaningful number in consideration of the several hundred members (between 600 and 800) of the Tuscan community currently present in Western Australia, thus representing between 5 and 7.5 per cent of the whole number. The relatively small number was chosen also with a view to run focussed interviews. The depth of the interview was planned in order to achieve also "...the intensity of personal feeling aroused by the questions",[21] with particular regard to issues related the perception of lifestyle in Italy and in Western Australia, as well as the sense of belonging.

The total number of successful interviews was 34, as six informers did not respond to all of the questions indicated in the questionnaire, mainly for matters of privacy, namely when asked to detail their occupational and economic background. Consequently, these six interviews were dropped.

THE INTERVIEW SCHEDULE AND SITUATION

The interview schedule was designed for a personal interviewing situation, which was outlined with the aid of past research works, such as Cronin,[22] Huber[23] and Thompson.[24] Some difficulties were avoided by referring to literature on survey-research methods, and three most valuable works were those by Madge,[25] Moser[26] and Babbie.[27]

In his analysis of survey techniques, Michelson has highlighted the danger that a coding scheme with too few categories will be insensitive, although statistically elegant, while one with too many categories will be too difficult both to code and to analyse.[28] Given the aims and objectives of this study, and to guard against bias being built into the questionnaire, both pre-coded and open-ended questions were used. For example, in order that the respondent was not restricted in his/her response, some key questions were asked twice, firstly in the open-ended form, such as "What made you/your parents/your grandparents decide to come?". The same question would later be asked in a pre-coded form, such as "When you/they made the decision, what were your/your parents' expectations of Australia?", where the respondent would have to select his/her answer from a number of options.

The final item of coding worthy of special mention is probably the most important. A number of open-ended questions dealt with aspects of expectations and judgement of lifestyle. The questions drew answers which were not identical, but which had a great deal of overlap with pre-coded answers. Some answers included considerations of social and behavioural aspects of the family and its lifestyle, to speak in general terms. Other answers needed a self-evaluation of the interviewees' knowledge of English, as in Martin's work on migrant settlements.[29] Each question could have been coded according to an idiosyncratic, finite list of categories, but each list would have been long. Therefore, a master code of interpretation of answers was created, as adopted by Michelson in his study of Toronto's residential choice,[30] using the same set of values dealing with both relevant open-ended and pre-coded answers, so that the statistical analysis would not be too complex.

The questionnaire was carefully checked for ambiguities and vagueness, as suggested by Burnley.[31] The suitability of the codes was chosen for pre-coded questions, and the wording of the open-ended questions, and in order to gain an indication of the approximate time each interview was to take. The reason was to give the respondents a choice of answer as free and clear as possible, whereas the risks of difficulties in translation or in different attitudes, as indicated by Jupp in his analysis of migrants' attitude towards surveys,[32] were avoided by the interviewer being bi-lingual.

As stated, the information was gathered by means of a prepared questionnaire, in order to give more structure to the interview. Nevertheless, the risk was that the questionnaire might have reduced spontaneity in the answers, as noted by Bell in his survey on demographic changes in rural Italy.[33] This danger was avoided by giving the informant a copy of the questionnaire; the interviewer and the interviewee could go through together, as an 'informal chat' framed within the main issues by the questionnaire itself, and thus encouraging the informant to expand more freely on any answer.

The interviewer rarely took notes in the presence of the respondent, except in a few specific cases of direct quotations of relevance to the survey. As adopted by Huber in her comparative study of Italian settlers in New South Wales,[34] on the contrary, the interviewer wrote an account when coming home each evening after the interviews, filling in the questionnaire and making sure that all questions were answered.

The task of interviewing was, in the majority of cases, a rewarding experience. Interviews were conducted in Italian to secure a willing and enthusiastic response from the interviewees, although two of them preferred to answer in English. As experienced by Iraci in his unpublished study of Italian migrants in Perth Metropolitan area,[35] the fact that the interview was conducted in Italian contributed greatly to its success. The experience of seeing the houses of the respondents gave additional understanding of the background from which Lucchese and Tuscan migrants came. In a few cases, a friendly relation was established between the writer and the respondent.

The average interview took from one hour to two hours, and was directed towards the head of the household, usually the male, when the interview took place in the private residence of the respondent. In fact, the decision to migrate among southern Europeans was more often taken by the male.[36] In addition, as has already been shown, in Australia, Italian male migrants overwhelmed females in large numbers until the late 1960s,[37] according to the general Italian tendency for wives to settle in Australia[38] and elsewhere[39] several years after their husbands, as previously examined. Hence, the excess of males among the interviewees is important when assessing reasons for coming to Australia or reactions to working conditions and Australian social environments. However, exceptions to this were families in which the head of the household was busy, elsewhere at the time of interview or in the case of widows.

No pseudonyms were used, and direct quotations are always from interviewees who were informed that their words might be quoted. None of the interviewees hesitated about allowing his/her name to be used, as the writer made clear to the respondent that the original consent to quote was not given out of friendship but as part of university-based research. In any case, the informer, when cited, is indicated with the first name and the sole initial of the family name.

ABOUT TUSCAN MIGRANTS BEFORE MIGRATING

As stated earlier, all the interviewees were Italian-born and, wherever possible, according to the snowball technique adopted for this qualitative survey, they were chosen in proportion to the number of the Tuscan communes they were coming from. In particular, the interviewees were from the following communes of the Provinces of Lucca and Massa-Carrara (Table 8-1):

Table 8-1 - Communes of origin of the Interviewees

S. Romano Garfagnana	7
Capannori	6
Casola Lunigiana	3
Giuncugnano	3
Bagni Lucca	2
Lucca	2
Minucciano	2
Porcari	2
Barga	1
Camporgiano	1
Coreglia	1
Fivizzano	1
Fosciandora	1
Gallicano	1
Piazza Serchio	1
TOTAL	34

Notwithstanding the evident difficulties in making the sample representative, the high number of migrants from specific communes, such as S. Romano Garfagnana in the upper valley of the River

Lucchesi throughout the world, as they are described in its monthly newsletters.

Secondly, some members perceived the study as a unique opportunity to finally cast light on what has been called "*epopea lucchese*", the Lucchese epos.[65] Hence, the confirmation that the 'Lucca model', as a pattern of the peculiar and extraordinary socio-cultural identity 'exported' by migrants to the countries of destination, is still present in Australia, despite the century-long process of growth that it took to be shaped, as it has been examined in the past chapters.

CAMPANILISMO AGAIN

Furthermore, although the relation between the members of the Toscany Club and this writer has always been harmonious and has allowed the field study, additional considerations about unexpressed forms of *campanilismo* must be introduced here. As a first-generation migrant from Florence, the administrative capital of Tuscany, and resident in Western Australia, I would have been inclined to comfortably consider my belonging to the Toscany Club. This has certainly eased the approach with the members of the association in order to conduct the interviews and all other informal meetings held within the premises of the Club. Nevertheless, contacts with the executive committee members have remained semi-formal, without becoming completely friendly, as my identity (Tuscan in Australia), the time spent together and the in-depth discussions held throughout the years should have rather suggested. The analysis of the factors affecting the identity of Lucchesi in Western Australia and their way to aggregate, as examined in this chapter, is now casting more light on this "non-deep" friendship developed between 'me' and 'them', and suggesting a few reasons. My identity, which has allowed me to gain access to the Club and to many of its members, is also my limit, if screened in the light of the Italian *campanilismo* and the values of the 'Lucca model'. I am Tuscan, but I am not from Lucca; even 'worse', I am from the capital of the Tuscany Region, while Lucca has kept its political independence from Florence almost until the Unification of Italy. This is already a reason to develop forms of *campanilismo.* It is worth quoting a consideration on *campanilismo* between Florence and Lucca, excerpted from a cultural geography paper on local identities written by John Agnew:

> *"In the region of Tuscany (Toscana) in central Italy, the Florence team, Fiorentina, has the largest mass following relative to other major football teams, reflecting the prominent position that the city of Florence has occupied historically within the region. However, in the province of Lucca, to the west of Florence between the Apennine mountains and the Tyrrhenian Sea, Juventus of Turin, the arch-enemy of Fiorentina in contemporary Italian football, has thirteen supporters' clubs to the five of Fiorentina, a figure roughly three times greater than any other Tuscan province...[...]...Even when there is no local team capable of challenging that of Florence, many Lucchesi throw in their lot with a successful team in distant Turin rather than convert to support for Fiorentina".*[66]

In addition to this century-long rivalry between Florence and Lucca, I have not been resident of Western Australia too long, and not engaged in the hard-working tasks of the 1950s and 1960s, as many of the Lucchesi did in the early stage of their migration to Australia. Doubtless, this circumstance plays a role in the cultural reinforcement of a 'Lucca model' of hard-working men crossing the boundaries of the little Republic of Lucca in search of better opportunities abroad. Beyond a dissimilarity of geographical identities, finally, a different socio-cultural background has played its role in the interaction with Lucchesi. As has been examined in the previous chapters, migrants from Tuscany in Western Australia have in general a rural background and are little educated, as the outcomes of the survey will confirm in the next chapter. Furthermore, many of them arrived in the host country according to chain migration patterns. Hence, there are still strong links with the rural communities of origin and with members of the same communities here in Australia. Conversely, I am from an urban background and academically educated. As a consequence, the century-long rivalries of *campanilismo* and contrasts between country and city life are even more exacerbated. In addition, the

Serchio, and Capannori, from the plain area of the Province of Lucca, was reflected in the sample chosen for the interviews.

Unlike migration before WWII, migrants who moved to Australia after the war, kept on sending home some of their earnings at the initial stage of their settlement, but their prime concern was for their own future welfare, as Huber pointed out in her study of Italian post-war migration to Australia. She wrote:

> *"They no longer aimed to subsidize the extended household economy but to save so that they could form their own nuclear family. Furthermore, going overseas did not now connote years of separation and hardship. Some who left for Australia utilized the assisted passage scheme, others saved or borrowed the fare in the knowledge that they could easily repay it".*[40]

Table 8-2 - Activity performed by the interviewees' fathers in Italy

Occupation of the father*	
Farmer (Owner)	19
Peasant	1
Sharecropper	6
Miller	2
Carter	2
Bootmaker	1
Carpenter	1
Smith	1
Quarryman	2
Woodcutter	3
Bricklayer	1
Labourer	7
Trader	1
Shop-owner	1
Butcher	1
Clerk	1
TOTAL	50

* (In a few cases, the interviewee stated more than one occupation)

Examination of the occupations performed by interviewees' fathers shows their rural origin (Table 8-2). The sample of interviewees confirms that their level of education was very low, as the majority of them had completed only the equivalent of the Year 5. Consequently, occupations performed in Italy before departing for Australia were mostly related to rural and unskilled labour activities, with a relatively small number of semi-skilled workers (Table 8-3).

Table 8-3 - Occupation performed by Interviewees in Italy before Migration

Farmer	12
Woodcutter	1
Labourer	6
Miner	1
Carpenter	3
Carter	1
Bootmaker	1
Butcher	1
Painter	1
Clerk	2
Tailor	1
N/A	4
TOTAL	34

On a few occasions, the interviewees indicated more than one occupation for their fathers. This circumstance is due to the fact that, since the turn of the century, rural activities in the Province of Lucca and the upper valley communes of the Province of Massa-Carrara might have not been entirely sufficient for the economic management of the family household. Hence, beyond the usual recurrence of temporary migration to nearby Italian regions, Corsica and other countries, many males were pushed to accept other jobs to be run on a part-time basis, as the occupations of labourer, woodcutter, carter and trader seem to confirm.

With respect to the geographic mobility of first-generation migrants from Tuscany before migration, the figure seems to confirm how migration to Australia was not considered a generic destination, especially in the post-WWII period, but rather a once-in-a-lifetime experience. Migrants interviewed confirmed their minimal propensity to mobility before moving to Australia. In fact, a large majority of them (68 per cent) had never moved out of their native village and community at the time of emigration to Australia. Four of them (12 per cent) had moved to live in other communes of the Province of either Lucca or Massa-Carrara, while only three (9 per cent) had experienced migration abroad, namely to other European countries.

Reasons to Migrate and Expectation about Australia

"Il buon successo di alcuni fa da paravento alle disgrazie di molti".[41]

Giovanni Prezzolini

(The success of a few hides the disgraces of the many).

After World War II, there were several reasons for leaving home, in particular the expectation to earn a lot in a short time. Again, the majority of Italian migrants, and those from Tuscany, were from rural and mountain areas, almost always unskilled, single, and in their early twenties. The survey conducted among Tuscan migrants indicates (Table 8-4) how job search was still the main reason for migrating to Australia, with eleven migrants expressing this preference, although representing only 30 per cent of all possible answers.

Table 8-4 - Reasons for migrating to Australia

Job search	11
Family reunion	9
Better lifestyle	4
Parents' or fathers' will	3
Spirit of adventure	5
Avoid Italian military draft	2
TOTAL	34

Nine of them (26 per cent) declared that they moved to Australia for family reunion. This circumstance confirms how the establishment of a pre-war community of Lucchesi in Western Australia may have influenced the arrival of more relatives.

There are several reasons to generate the complex decision-making process for migration, as those analysed by the American geographers Jakle, Brunn and Roseman in their study of human spatial behaviour.[42] More reasons for migrating were highlighted in the field survey. These reasons were the possibility to pursue a better lifestyle, expressed by four migrants, and the opportunity to avoid compulsory Italian military service, indicated by two interviewees, and confirmed as an outcome of the work by Huber on the Italian community of New South Wales.[43] One more reason, expressed by five migrants, is represented by what they called the "spirit of adventure". This number of respondents is markedly higher than that obtained in a previous study on Italian migrants to the Perth Metropolitan area, which showed this answer only in two cases out of 105 interviewees.[44]

Within the 'spirit of adventure', it is possible to catalogue the search for the new, which can be particularly attractive for the younger generations. One interviewee declared that his only intention, when he migrated to Australia in 1952, was to stay enough time, possibly a couple of years, "...to make money sufficient to return to Italy and buy a brand new motorcycle, as those he had seen the American soldiers riding in Italy after the Liberation of the country."[45] Unlike other Tuscan sub-regional groups of migrants, for which the Italian social historian Roberto Niccolai seems to exclude the spirit of adventure,[46] this spirit recalls the already described adaptability to different cultures of Lucchese people travelling across foreign countries and continents. The capacity of Lucchesi to move overseas in search of economic opportunities was certainly rooted in their century-long spirit of enterprise that pushed so many of them to visit foreign countries and bring the fruit of their search back to the community of origin, since the fourteenth century.

Table 8-5 - Expectations about Australia before migrating

Possibility to get a job	7
Quick money earning to take back to Italy	14
Enhancement of lifestyle	6
Open spaces, freedom	6
N/A	1
TOTAL	34

The cross-examination of the results related to another question of the survey, confirms the outcomes shown in Table 8-6. When asked which were their expectations and perception of Australia at time of departure, a large group of the interviewees (14 out of 34) indicated it as the possibility to make money quickly in order to take it back to Italy (Table 8-5).

As examined in the previous chapters, the perception of the country of migration was often generated by real elements of judgement, such as the letters that migrants in the host countries used to send home, but it was also nourished by the inevitable emphasis put in the news, especially if they were from the 'America'. Some state how very little is still known about the origins and reproduction of stereotypes of the host country by immigrants' perceptions.[47] Another study on different Italian regional groups to Western Australia have demonstrated how an overall percentage of migrants had obtained information about Australia through relatives already in the country.[48]

This circumstance can somehow imply that among Italian migrants there was an overall perception that economic welfare in the host country was "automatically guaranteed".[49] The Italian perception of a generic sense of freedom and independence generated by the immense spaces of Australia[50] was already alive among Italian migrants, as well among Italian intellectual circles,[51] since the first migratory flow of Italians in the late nineteenth century.[52]

Two more answers in the questionnaire were related to economic reasons to migrate, such as 'the possibility to find employment' and 'to enhance their lifestyle'. Taken together, these three answers were chosen by 27 interviewees, thus making the economic push the main reason to migrate to Australia, although under slightly different categories. Independently from the 'spirit of adventure', this circumstance, combined with the young age of migrants, their low level of education and skills, confirms how the post-war generation of migrants, over-represented in the survey, was keen to settle in a new land of opportunities, but on a more permanent basis than those who had gone to Australia during the inter-war period.

Unlike the Lucchese migrants who, since the Unification of Italy, had worked in Corsica and France, and then crossed the oceans establishing communities in Argentina, Brazil and the United States with frequent return trips to their Tuscan villages of origin, the post-WWII flow of Italian and Tuscan migrants was now more resolute to settle. Although the intention of many Lucchese perspective migrants to Australia of the 1950s was linked, in many cases, to the possibility of returning to their community of origin with some money, the option to remain in Australia was taken more and more seriously than by those who had arrived in the 1920s and 1930s.

LIFE CONDITIONS AND ACCOMMODATION AT ARRIVAL

While it is impossible to state with exactness the variety of reasons for which migrants move across different countries, many migrants from Tuscany had moved to Australia for economic reasons, namely to find well-paid jobs more easily than in Italy, and to enhance their lifestyle accordingly. Nevertheless, the outcomes of the quantitative research and the results of this qualitative survey confirm how this migratory process could not take place without the previous settlement of some community members in the host country. While economic factors were crucial in the migration to Australia, migrants chose destinations in Australia for social reasons, as among Italians the presence of kinfolk was much more important in residential choice than for the Australian-born.[53]

When asked to indicate which relatives were already present in Australia at their arrival, only four out of 34 interviewees said they had none (Table 8-6). Furthermore, three out of these four migrants, arriving without being expected by any relative or friend in Australia, had come in 1952, under the Assisted Passage Scheme, which allowed the perspective migrants to have a large reduction on his/her ship passage fee, on condition that he/she remain employed for two years in Australia. These conditions would give the prospective migrants a sort of protective 'shell' against the risks that many had to afford if not assisted by relatives or friends at their arrival in Australia.

Table 8-6 - Relatives of Migrants living in Australia at time of their Arrival

Whole family	1
Father	7
Both parents	0
Brother/s	10
Sister/s	1
Uncles/cousins	6
Other relatives	2
Spouse	0
No relatives/Only friends	3
None	4
TOTAL	3

A large group of the other interviewees had one or more brothers waiting for them at their arrival in Australia, seven had their own father, and six had either a cousin or an uncle, thus indirectly confirming what has been stated with respect to male migration. Furthermore, these answers reflect the family composition of many Lucchese migrants. The family links and the support that they could provide to newly-arrived migrants were extremely important for the settlement of the family members in the host country. Other family members, already established in Australia, could provide accommodation and food to the new arrivals, and later direct them to perform working activities, usually in the same working environment occupied by those who were already in Australia.

The high number of those who were expected in the country by both their brothers and fathers reflects the chain migration process that affected the migratory flow from the rural areas of the provinces of Lucca and Massa-Carrara to Western Australia. This circumstance is confirmed by the fact that only one migrant of those interviewed had the whole family here, and another one had only his sister.

The arrival of new migrants from Tuscany was often in strict relation to the presence of other close relatives in Australia. This circumstance implies that the migratory flow of the 1950s followed the same patterns of the mid-late 1920s, when the migration process from Tuscany to Australia was mainly undertaken by relatively young males in search of job opportunities and quick money accumulation. One of the major differences between the inter-war flow and the migration processes of the 1950s was that, in the post-war period, the migratory flow of Tuscans was more determined to pursue an economic enhancement of their lifestyle, even if this goal would imply the permanent settlement in the host country. Conversely, migrants from Tuscany who moved to Australia during the late 1920s and early 1930s mainly aimed to return home as soon as they had accumulated some money overseas, as examined in previous chapters. This difference in the Tuscan migration patterns is confirmed by the overall Italian migratory flow of the same period, which had more permanent residence patterns in the host countries.

OCCUPATIONAL AND SETTLEMENT PATTERNS

Due to combined factors, such as the low level of education (and, consequently, the language problems faced in Australia), and the occupational background of the interviewees, it is not surprising that they accepted the first form of employment that they were able to obtain. The respondents had usually been able to obtain work within a few weeks from their arrival in Australia, often within the same occupational environment of their relatives, who were already in the host country. Close male relatives, generally fathers, brothers and uncles, were in fact able to access many new arrivals to employment. Given the occupational background of the migrants interviewed and their difficulties with the English language, it should come as no surprise that most of the respondents on arrival in Australia were employed as labourers. Judging from literature,[54] as well as from field investigations,[55] the majority of Italian migrants, and Lucchesi among them, were labourers engaged in such occupations as mining, timber-cutting, fruit and vegetable growing and trading.[56]

Table 8-7 shows the occupational and geographical distribution of the Tuscan migrants interviewed.

Table 8-7 - Occupations performed since arrival in Australia

Farmer	14
Woodcutter	10
Miner	7
Labourer	18
Sawmiller	19
Bricklayer	8
Carpenter	2
Trading	5
Catering	4
Building	3
Other businesses	13
Professional	1
TOTAL	104

It presents a total number of 104 combined occupations, performed by the 34 interviewees, thus reinforcing the high occupational mobility of migrants from Tuscany in their search of a better lifestyle. Two of the most prevalent activities performed are those as sawmiller and woodcutter, since many migrants moved to the South-West of Western Australia at their initial stage of settlement, and were employed in the timber cutting industry. A number of them (7) were employed in the mining industries, mainly in the Wiluna goldfields, among the few interviewees who arrived in Australia in the 1930s, and in Wittenoom's blue asbestos mines for those arrived in the mid and late 1950s.

Table 8-8 shows the geographical origin of the colleagues working in the same environment of the interviewee. In this case, the respondents have been asked to indicate the prevailing working environment in which they have performed in their lifetime. It is interesting to note how the large majority (23 out of 34) was mainly formed by workers either from the same community of origin of the interviewee (namely people from the Province of Lucca and Massa-Carrara), or from other Italian regions. In 10 cases, the respondents have primarily worked in an Anglo-Australian environment and in just one case among other nationals (namely, former Yugoslav migrants in the timber industry). These circumstances confirm how Tuscan migrants tended to concentrate among Italian-speaking workers, probably due to two different reasons. Firstly, one cause can be ascribed to the access to work that the interviewees initially found through the help of relatives and other Italian friends, such to maintain a sort of social 'cocoon' that defended them from the Australian cultural and occupational environment as a whole. Secondly, the difficulty in speaking another language, as will be further examined in the next sections, might have pushed many migrants to remain within an Italian-speaking occupational environment for most of their working life.

Table 8-8 - Colleagues in the working environment

Same community (Province Of Lucca, Massa)	3
Other Regions of Italy	20
Anglo-Australians	10
Other nationalities	1
TOTAL	34

According to the general trend of Italian migrants in Western Australia, after a few years of long-houred work, either in the bush or in the mines, and totally finalised to accumulate savings,[57] many of them moved to the Perth Metropolitan area, where they could open small businesses with the money saved in the South-West or in remote areas of the state. This circumstance, already analysed as the general trend of the quantitative aspect of this study, is confirmed by the number of those involved in trading, catering and other entrepreneurial activities, according to the overall trend of many Italian migrants of rural origin, in which the spirit of entrepreneurial independence is recorded as "very strong".[58]

Accommodation and English Language Skills

Together with the possible establishment of an activity to be run independently, the ownership of a home and an additional piece of land was an important aspiration of Italian and Tuscan migrants, and represented a "...symbol both of status and of the emotional and economic security which should ensure the future stability of the family",[59] which draws its origins in the "...culture of land and home ownership among southern European immigrants".[60] This circumstance is confirmed by personal observation of the furniture and the interior design of the homes where I have been invited to conduct some of the interviews. In most cases, the interiors confirmed a strong sense of cultural belonging. Floors were covered with Italian terracotta tiles, while the large dining table of the lounge was covered with framed snapshots of parents, children, and grandchildren, as well as souvenirs from Italy hung on the walls, similarly to what has been experienced by the anthropologist Rima Huber in her field research among Italian migrants in New South Wales.[61]

With respect to the intrinsic value of family houses for Italians and Italian migrants, the Australian geographer Mariastella Pulvirenti has written:

> *"Family houses in Italy, represented sustenance and employment. They embodied family histories and futures, and they symbolised family unity. Within the context of a devastated peasantry and working class in post-war Italy, their significance increased".*[62]

As the city-bound process was completed within a few years after the arrival in Australia, some interviewees have often stated that the establishment of a business in Perth and the purchase of the home have been their "turning point" in making them realise that future life would then take place in Australia.[63]

The spatial mobility of the Tuscans interviewed confirms the general city-bound trend of migrants, as 32 out of 34 are currently living in the Perth Metropolitan area, whereas the other two are living in rural areas not distant from the city. Nevertheless, 23 of the 34 interviewees have past records of settlement in rural areas, and are identified with those who had initially moved in the South-West of the state, whereas an additional 8 of them have lived in remote areas, and match with those who had moved to perform mining activities in remote Western Australia. Consequently, the survey on the spatial mobility of the Tuscan migrants confirms the outcomes of an overall city-bound trend.

Other Lucchesi established market-gardens and orchards on the outskirts of Perth, counting on the need of fresh fruit and vegetables supply to the city, as it is reflected by the number of those (14) who were employed as farmers, where a few more engaged in activities linked to the semi-skilled occupations of rural origin that they brought with them from Tuscany, such as those of bricklayer (8) and carpenter (2).

The general picture which emerges from the field observation related to the occupational and spatial distribution of first-generation Tuscans in Western Australia can be interpreted as one of limited assimilation, because of the unequal spread of migrants over the general occupational range. According to a study based on the Australian Census of 1976, when the presence of Italian migrants in Australia reached its peak, of the ten major occupational categories, Italian-born persons were under-represented in the professional-technical, administrative, clerical and sales groups, whereas they were found in representative numbers among the farmers and service workers, and clearly over-represented among tradesmen and labourers.[64] Only one of the interviewees had entered the white-collar class, namely as a professional. Many of those who succeeded economically - as is confirmed by wealth shown in the households of respondents visited - established themselves in small businesses, and only two of them in large and well acknowledged Australia-wide businesses.

Apart from education, proficiency in the English language must be considered, as has been indicated in the previous section with respect to the concentration of interviewees in occupational areas shared with other Italian-speaking workers. As examined by Ruth Johnston in her study of migrants' adaptation to Western Australia, "...no matter how educated an immigrant is, he/she has no hope of getting any sort of a white-collar job unless his command of written and spoken English is adequate".[65] Nevertheless, a general question on the self-perception of English language knowledge by the interviewees has given an overall sense of normal mastery of the language, as from Table 8-9.

The interviewees were asked to assess their level of spoken and written English, as this factor has been considered important to evaluate the spatial distribution of migrants in a specific area, and a good measurement of family income.[66] Half the sample of respondents (17) have indicated that they have a 'good' knowledge of English, which meant - according to additional information supplied during the interviews - that they were able to speak, read and write English in most daily situations, whereas they needed the help of other members of the family for more complex situations. Mastering English language was slightly lower for eight respondents, who classified their knowledge as 'normal'. In two cases, English language was self-perceived as 'very poor', and, in four cases, 'modest', thus requiring the assistance of others in a few occasions.

Table 8-9 - Self-perception of the level of English known

Very poor	2
Modest	4
Normal	8
Good	17
Excellent	3
TOTAL	34

The examination of other information supplied by these last six respondents has confirmed that their Italian background education was at the lowest level, and also that they were less exposed to the Anglo-Australian speaking environment during their occupational life (Table 8-8). Finally, the three interviewees who stated that their English was 'excellent', corresponded, respectively, to one who had an Italian university degree and to other respondents who had married an Australian partner.

As was observed by Borrie in his study on Italian and German migrants in Australia, strong family ties with the area of origin, have been an important factor preventing rapid assimilation,[67] encouraging, for example, the persistence of the use of the Italian language at home, and the concentration in specific geographical areas.[68] It is worth stating that, according to the figures based on the Australian Census of 1991, the Italian language is still spoken at home by 221,147 Italian-born people living in Australia, who still represent 87.7 per cent of all first-generation Italians in Australia.[69] Hence, the confirmation that the higher level of education, as highlighted by Borrie,[70] Bettoni[71] and Tosi,[72] and the propensity to marry outside the same ethnic group are major factors influencing the ability to speak English and, consequently, to integrate faster within the host culture and society and move in urban areas outside the ethnic concentrations.

INTER-MARRIAGE

The study of the extent of intermarriage among ethnic groups in Australia is seen as important because it is considered to reflect, to quote the Australian geographer Graeme Hugo, "...the extent and nature and adaptation of immigrant populations to Australia".[73] The situation is certainly different from the way it appeared to the Italian Geographical Society, whose members visited Australia in 1888 and so reported:

> *"I soli italiani che restano in Australia sono quelli che si ammogliano con donne del paese. Questi casi pero' non sono troppo frequenti, e certo non costituiscono una media importante nella nostra colonia. In questi casi pero', la famiglia diventa assolutamente inglese, e i figli nulla sanno dell'Italia e della lingua italiana".*[74]
>
> *(Italians who remain permanently in Australia are only those who marry Australian wives. These case are very few and do not constitute relevant figures of our community abroad. Nevertheless, when they take place, families become fully English, and their children do not know anything about Italy or the Italian language).*

Again, in the earliest years of Italian migration to Australia there was a common pattern in which male immigrants led the migratory flow, and husbands and young unmarried men would come and establish a firm economic base before bringing their wives and families or their fiancées.[75]

The relative isolation of the Italian community at its first stage of settlement in Australia was one of the factors which encouraged high rates of marriage, as life outside marriage was probably very lonely for the Italian-born, often cut off from the broader Australian community by language and cultural barriers. With respect to the Italian and Tuscan migratory flow of the 1950s, we must bear in mind that the first stage of the settlement process in Australia was the loneliest one for the migrants. Migrants moved to Australian rural and remote areas to make money faster than in any other possible city-based occupation. The presence of a spouse or partner of Italian origin was clearly a necessity to fight the solitude and barrenness of the bush and of the other remote locations where Italian workers were employed. This circumstance suggests that the imbalance of the sexes among Italians in Australia during the Fifties could have pushed many of them to marry outside their national group, as sustained by Galvin, stating that migrants who have dispersed in rural and remote areas should be inclined to intermarry more widely.[76] On the contrary, one reason for the low level of intermarriage in this period has been indicated by some scholars, again, in the inadequate command of the English language.[77]

As it has been shown, the period between 1947 and 1968 witnessed the highest number of arrivals from Italy in Australia, with over 70 per cent of Italian-born male migrants chosing their spouse within the same ethnic group. For the same period, Italian-born women in Australia chose an Italian partner in over 90 per cent of the cases.[78] Similar proportions are reflected also in this field study. In consideration of the high number of Tuscan migrants who arrived in Australia during the 1950s, and who presumably married during the same decade or the following, the number of those who married an Italian-born spouse is considerably high (Table 8-10).

Table 8-10 - Geographical origin of Interviewees' Partners

Same village	10
Same Province/Tuscany	12
Other Italian region	7
Southern European	1
Australian	2
Other national	1
N/A	1
TOTAL	34

A marked number of the Lucchesi (over 29 per cent) surveyed, married a spouse from the same village or community, thus confirming a century-long Tuscan proverb, which states: "Mogli e buoi dei paesi tuoi" ('Get wives and oxen only from your community villagers'). An additional 35 per cent of respondents sought their partners among people of either the same Province or within Tuscany, and another 20 per cent married a partner from other Italian regions. The number of those who married an Italian-born spouse reaches 85 per cent of all interviewees, thus representing a figure considerably higher than that related to Italian migrants in general. Finally, two respondents married Australian-born partners and two married other nationals residing in Australia.

Apart for the relatively small sample, one possible explanation of the very limited evidence of intermarriage is related to the extreme cohesiveness of the Lucchese community, whose members migrated overseas through very narrow and selective migratory chains. This pattern, present since the late nineteenth century in other Lucchese communities abroad,[79] has kept the Lucchesi linked together, as shown with the analysis of their occupational strategies and of their social aggregation.

SECOND GENERATION AND LANGUAGE INTERACTION WITH FIRST GENERATION TUSCANS

This survey has not deepened specific aspects of the issues related to second or third generation in Australia, such as some of the studies that have been published on the language spoken in the family[80] and in broader social contexts,[81] or the social and occupational mobility[82] of Australian second generation of foreign-born parents. This limitation was due to the vastness of the issues involved and the circumstance that this study aims to 'photograph' the presence of Tuscan-born migrants in Western Australia. The only aspect which has been highlighted is in relation to the language interaction between the first generation and the second.

Although the terminology of migration studies varies widely, in this context the second generation refers to the Australian-born children of Italian-born parents. The issue of the definition of the second generation is a very complex one, as the Australian demographers Helen Ware and Charles Price outline, since the options are between the inclusion in the category only of those who have two Italian-born parents, and of those who have only either Italian-born fathers or mothers,[83] together with other additional measures to better define the ethnic origin of the Australian population.[84] In the specific survey case, this dilemma is almost irrelevant, as 29 interviewees out of 34 (over 85 per cent of the sample) had married an Italian-born spouse, and another one never got married. Furthermore, the second generation includes those people who were born in Italy and emigrated as children, having done most, if not all, of their schooling in Australia.[85]

The outcomes of the question related to the language spoken by the respondents, when interacting with their partners, children and friends, are interesting. A large majority of the interviewees (27) speak Italian with their spouses, thus reflecting figures very close to those related to the origin of the spouses themselves. The slightly lower number of those who speak Italian with their partners in comparison with the number of Italian-born spouse is explainable by two different reasons. Firstly, the definition of Italian-born does not take rigidly into account the period in which, since birth, the spouses could be exposed to Italian language and culture. In two cases, in fact, the Italian-born partners of the respondents were born in Italy, but had moved to Australia with their families in their younger years. In these cases, the 'exposure' of the partner to the English language and Australian culture was a strong reason to push the interviewee to set the family communication in the language of the host country. Secondly, two of the interviewees had married again after, respectively, the death of one spouse and the divorce from another one, and were, at time of interview, sharing their homes with Australian-born partners.

Nevertheless, the most striking outcomes are those related to the language spoken by the respondents with their children, the second generation. In this case, the English language is spoken in 22 families out of 34. This circumstance implies that there is a shifting from Italian into English, when the respondents interact, respectively, with their partners or children. This is due to the environment in which most second generation are grown, with particular regard to the Australian educational and occupational scenes. As other scholars have noted, while the Australian-born children of Tuscan or Italian-born parents have lived in a family environment often dominated by the use of Italian language and culture,[86] their social life outside the family is ruled by the usage of the English language, as in the schools during the earlier years, and in the working environments during their adult life.[87]

Figures, related to the percentage of the Italian-Australian second generation in Western Australia, state that over 58 per cent of them fall in the age range between 20 and 54.[88] The bulk of Italian migrants (and Tuscans, as previously stated) came, in fact, to Australia during the 1950s, in their early twenties, and therefore established their families slightly later. Hence their children are now between 30 and 50 years old, and are fully integrated into the Australian economic system. Although many second-generation Italians of Australia have developed a double cultural competence[89] and have often set up their businesses and services in the communities in which they grew up,[90] nevertheless, they feel a strong sense of belonging to Australian society.

Language is one of the most powerful vehicles for transmitting a culture.[91] Poor or modest linguistic communication by the first generation, therefore, means an impoverished cultural link between generations, and, in fact, the second-generation Italians tend to reject their parents' ethnic identity.[92] The second generation deals effectively with an Australian social, educational and occupational environment dominated by the use of the English language,[93] and its members often act as "mediators" between the Australian society and their Italian-born parents.[94] Conversely, Italian language remains confined to the family context of their parents.

'TRANSNATIONALISM' VERSUS ITALIAN IDENTITY

A close look at the third pair of columns of Figure 8-1 shows how the highest number of friends of the respondents (26 out of 34) fall into the category of the Italian-born people. As an additional confirmation, 25 interviewees (74 per cent of all respondents) are members of the Toscany Club, 14 (41 per cent) belong to other Italian-based associations in Perth, and only 12 (35 per cent) are also members of Australian-based organisations. Figures are aggregated because a majority of the interviewees hold more than one membership, with the Perth-based Tuscan association having the highest number of affiliates.

A strong majority of Tuscan migrants in Western Australia belong to and actively participate in ethnic organisations. Conversely, there is a limited participation in host society clubs and associations, as is confirmed by the limited literature available.[95] The presence of friends from native Tuscan communities, with whom to talk Italian, and the participation in ethnic clubs, are just two of the several factors that allow an evaluation of the many issues related to ethnic communities. In particular, it is relevant to this study to evaluate the sense of Italian (and Tuscan) identity, the 'Italianity', as well as the conservation of links with Italy and Tuscany, which first-generation migrants have kept with the country of origin. These, and other related factors, may suggest an incomplete integration into the host society.[96] With respect to the integration of Italian migrants in the American society, Vecoli wrote in 1965:

> *"The initial stage of acculturation for the immigrants was not from Italian to American but from Tuscan, 'Neapolitan', or Calabrian to Italian-American. Excluded from the larger American community as 'undesiderable', some immigrants developed a hyphenate mentality compounded of a chauvinistic attachment to the Old Country and a burning desire to be accepted as Americans. This new ethnic identity was most readily accepted by the young immigrants and the second generation, while those who had emigrated as adults tended to remain more parochial in their loyalties".*[97]

In the course of the past decades, migration scholars have increasingly noted that immigrants live their lives across borders and maintain ties to both their country of origin and the host country. To describe this new attitude among migrants, some social scientists have begun to use the term "transnational" to emphasize the emergence of a social process in which migrants establish social fields that cross geographic, cultural, and political borders, as "they develop and maintain multiple relations - familial, economic, social organizational, religious, and political - that span borders".[98] In this sense, transnationalism implies the recognition that the world is currently bound together by a global capitalistic system and, within this perspective, migrants respond with their strategies of cultural practices and identities.[99] The key to the interpretation of migrants' identity, offered by transnationalism, allows to better frame the multiple sense of identities that Italian (and Tuscan, in the specific case of this study) migrants perceive in Australia. While some Italian migrants identify more with one society than the other, in recent years the majority of them seem to maintain several identities linking them, simultaneously, to more than one country, as roots and sense of place are not static, but they sometimes change in relation to the "space-bound action" of migrating.[100]

The outcomes of another survey among Italian migrants in the Perth Metropolitan area showed that many respondents missed Italy rather strongly, and their satisfaction was based primarily upon their economic success. Furthermore, many interviewees declared they wanted to spend the rest of their lives in Australia and that they would want to return to Italy if they could live as well there.[101] Similar tendencies were registered among recently-arrived Italian migrants in Montreal,[102] and are justified by the initial sense of displacement occurring among migrants in host countries.

With particular regard to Italian migrants, in his study of Italian politics and society at the turn of the twentieth century, the Australian historian Richard Bosworth identifies the birth of this sense of strong attachment of Italian migrants to their homeland in an overall sense of national identity that Italian authorities enforced among migrants during the highest peaks of emigration, as a possible defence against the high migratory rates of those years and for the conservation of the national identity abroad.[103]

Somehow, a model of strong attachment to the land and community of origin is manifested also by the Tuscan migrants interviewed, even though a set of other concurrent factors may generate this behaviour. As used in previous studies on Italian migrants in Western Australia, travelling back to the country of origin has been chosen as one of the indices to evaluate this attachment.[104] When Tuscan respondents were asked how often they return to Italy from Australia, a number of answers (12 out of 34) was represented by those who declared they return every 2 to 5 years, followed by those who return to Italy every 16 or more years (11 respondents) and, again, by those who visit Italy and Tuscany every 6 to 15 years (8). Lastly, two interviewees can afford to go every single year of their residence in Western Australia, and one has never returned (Table 8-11).

Table 8-11 - Frequency of trips to Italy

Every year	2
Every 2-5 years	12
Every 6-15 years	8
Once every 16 or more years	11
Never returned	1
TOTAL	34

Previous chapters have shown how the first stage of the Lucchese migratory pattern was temporary, thus presenting a high number of frequent trips back to the community of origin by male migrants in working age, where, for generations, the rest of their families were kept in Italy. This pattern explains the intermittent residences of some fathers and grandfathers of the interviewees in countries such as Corsica, France, the United States and Australia.

Nevertheless, this study has confirmed how the migratory pattern has become permanent, so that the frequent trips to Italy, operated by a consistent number of the Lucchesi interviewed, has to be interpreted in the light of a continuity of links with the country of origin, without interrupting the link established by the migrants with the host country. The case of the two respondents who stated that they return to Italy and Lucca on a yearly basis is not surprising, and similar circumstances are recorded by Bosi, who reports on a Lucchese-

Australian migrant who, since 1964, has returned to Italy 40 times.[105] In our specific cases, one of the two respondents has established an import-export business between Italy and Australia, which is based in the Province of Lucca and operated by a relative, thus allowing him to travel regularly to Italy, whereas the other interviewee is wealthy and can afford to return to the Lucchese community of origin every single year to spend his vacation.

The relatively high number of trips to Italy afforded by many respondents is interpreted as the necessity to maintain a link with the country of origin and, as such, it is confirmed further in the light of the answers supplied to another question related to the contacts kept with relatives in Italy. A large majority of respondents stated that they "sometimes" keep these contacts with their relatives in Italy, where this term was further explained as the usual greetings for Christmas and not much more, while five stated that they keep 'close' links.

When asked to indicate their sense of belonging, 22 of them (representing 65 per cent of the total) stated that they felt Italians, and the other 12 (35 per cent) that they felt more Australians. Reasons and factors affecting interviewees' self-assessments vary and are related to their occupational track record (whether occupations took place in Italian or English speaking environments), the marriage with Italian or Australian-born spouses, and the spatial patterns of residence (and whether they lived in geographical areas with predominant Italian or other ethnic groups).

With respect to the geographical distribution of the migrants at the time of the interview, shows how 25 of them (representing over 73 per cent) live in the suburbs of Perth north of the Swan River, in the same areas where the quantitative study had highlighted the main presence of Tuscan migrants, thus confirming a high degree of spatial concentration in suburbs characterised by the marked presence of Italian-born residents.

Furthermore, the outcomes of another question related to the nationality of the respondents' neighbours confirm how the interviewees tend to concentrate in areas where the foreign-born population is relatively high, according to methods used in other studies for the same purposes.[106] Migrants were asked to indicate the nationalities of the two adjacent houses on either side or across the street, with a maximum of two, thus the total number of 68 neighbours, while 24 (35 per cent) were the neighbours of Italian descent, with an additional 9 (13 per cent) of other Southern European-born, whereas 18 (26 per cent) were the neighbours of nationalities other than Italian or southern European. Finally, only 17 (25 per cent) were the Australian-born neighbours, thus indicating once again the relatively high self-segregation of the Tuscan migrants interviewed.

As indicated in the previous paragraphs, the marked percentage of respondents who declared their sense of belonging to the Italian culture, and speak Italian at home, confirms the importance of the family in many aspects of Italian-Australian culture. As others have suggested, the family remains the domain defined "...in opposition to the 'outside', that is everything beyond the family, apart from Italian clubs and associations, and that is considered not to be 'Italian'".[107] The close domain of the family and the Italian associations seems to imply a declaration, even though in a passive form, of one's own cultural identity and "autonomy" of life experience.[108]

On the other hand, the phenomenon of transnationalism, with its capacity to keep and live across two different worlds, such as the community of origin and the host country, can be found when we further analyse the links that Tuscan migrants have established with Australia, well beyond the long-term residence in the host country and the permanent establishment of their families.

PERCEPTION OF QUALITY OF LIFE IN AUSTRALIA AND CONCLUSIONS

"...I been working in Italy not so hard as I been working in this country. I could live free there just as well. Work in the same condition, but not so hard, about seven or eight hours a day, better

food. I mean genuine. Of course, over here is good food, because it is bigger country, to any those who got money to spend, not for working and laboring class, and in Italy is more opportunity to laborer to eat vegetable, more fresh..."[109]

Nicola Sacco, at his trial's deposition, late 1920s.

The last part of the survey aimed to probe the level of satisfaction of Tuscan migrants in Western Australia. As other studies have confirmed, the period of residence is likely to be connected with satisfaction and identification of respondents with their adopted country.[110] Migrants who were most likely to be in the high or medium group of satisfaction tended to be those married to Australian-born spouses, in highly-paid occupations, and living in relatively low ethnic density areas, such as the Perth suburbs of the eastern hills and some concentrations south the Swan River. Previous graphs have shown how each one of the mentioned groups (inter-marriage, high-skilled occupations, geographical distribution in areas other than the northern suburbs) was relatively small. Conversely, the number of respondents who, respectively, married an Italian-born partner, performed relatively low-skilled activities, and lived in the suburbs north of the Swan River, where the Italian-born population had concentrated since the 1950s together with other southern European migrants, was the majority in the survey.

Within this large group of respondents, and outside the frame of the questionnaire, I have collected the largest number of comments regarding their perception of Australia, with an emphasis on the hardships of settling in Australia, and the initial loss of an Italian identity, as other scholars have stressed in their works.[111] The process of migrants' adjustment to the host country is a hard and complex one, and, with respect to the rural composition of Italian migration, some scholars of migration maintain that it can be completed to a great extent only after three generations.[112] Several migrants interviewed declared that life was harder in the Tuscan villages of origin than in Australia, as the outcomes of other surveys have confirmed.[113] This circumstance certainly acted as a 'push factor', having a negative influence on the quality indicators of life, while the possibility of economic enhancement in Australia acted as a 'pull factor',[114] drawing prospective migrants to Australia.

When asked what interviewees liked about Australia, both multiple choice and open-ended answers appeared to go towards different directions, according to the different perception that Tuscan migrants hold about the host country. Seven out of 34 answered that they enjoyed the privacy, five more liked the freedom, and two enjoyed the sense of democracy in Australia. These are factors that, apparently, could not be fully enjoyed in the Lucchese rural villages of origin, thus confirming very similar outcomes of the field work by Huber. In her study of the Veneto community of Sydney of the mid-1970s, the Australian anthropologist asked the interviewees to compare Australia with Italy, stressing the advantages and disadvantages of both the societies of origin and destination. It is surprising that in Huber's survey many migrants declared that "...in Australia there was more freedom, less gossip and greater independence".[115]

Unlike the job search and the economic success that seemed to dominate the expectations of Lucchesi before their departure for Australia, the 'financial security', as a quality to appreciate in Australia, was chosen by only six respondents, while 14 more of them declared that they mainly enjoy the open spaces of Australia and the climate of Western Australia. It is worth noting that those who chose the 'open spaces' and 'climate' options are also those who have achieved a higher degree of economic independence and social detachment from the Lucchese community of Western Australia, as if their adjustment to the Australian society allowed them to 'concentrate' on issues not strictly related to the family and wider Lucchese community environments. This circumstance may lead to the conclusion that the family and extended kinship networks, which were pivotal at the early stages of settlement of Lucchesi in Western Australia for the provision of accommodation and occupation and of a social network to keep alive an Italian and Tuscan identity, have often broken down because of different work practices and lifestyle of the Lucchese community members.

Even though many first-generation Lucchesi and Italians have not, as a rule, developed close relations with Anglo-Australians or other migrant groups,[116] nevertheless, they have found other venues to adjust and integrate into the host society, such as marriage, economic success in their occupations (and the related up-ward social mobility that this process implies), and the spatial removal from suburbs with a highly concentrated Italian-born population. The shifting of identity - from Lucchese to Australian - has rendered useless the tight family links and the social networks created by the members of the same villages or communities of origin.

This circumstance does not necessarily mean that one component of first-generation Lucchesi of Western Australia has cut its roots with Lucca or the Lucchese community, as it is likely that they are the members of the Tuscan community who can financially afford to return to Italy more often and keep contacts with the country of origin. On the contrary, their 'release' from the community of origin, and the clubs and associations that the Lucchese community generated in Western Australia to 'protect' its identity abroad, has allowed them to become members of the transnational process previously explained. As the Italian historian of migratory processes Gianfausto Rosoli stated a few years ago, many first-generation Italians, and many Tuscans in the current case study, can now fully bridge two different cultures and societies.[117] These Tuscan/Italian and Australian groups are in search of a 'transnational' identity, which would allow them to take advantage of both the worlds. After all, again, "*tutto il mondo è paese*" ('The world is just like a village'). It is a process, enriched by different traditions and cultures, that requires the negotiation and the development of new needs and identities, and that would deserve further study.

CONCLUSIONS

To the geographer, the basic impacts of migration are transformations in certain spatial patterns brought about by population movement. Migration is a purposive move in response to perceived spatial diversity, and therefore the basis for an explanation of the spatial patterns of movements lie in those patterns of 'diversity' that gave rise to it. Accordingly, in the first part of this study, it was proposed that the features of migrants' settlements are fundamentally related to the historical and socio-economic background of the area of origin. In the second part of this study, the spatial, occupational and social patterns of migrants from Tuscany in Western Australia were presented as a case study, to demonstrate their distinctive features and to show the extent to which these features were derived from migrants' history and culture.

Three main actions were undertaken to meet the aims of this research:

- The integration of migration study and history through geography.
- The analysis of the patterns of Tuscan migrants as a case of potential interest to geography of population.
- The identification of the constraints and opportunities to study migrants in Australia for the knowledge and management of ethnic groups which are created by historical and social legacies.

Integration was achieved through using an interdisciplinary

approach in the research process, and in the description and analysis of the reasons affecting migration from Tuscany to Australia. Further integration was made by documenting the links and connections between historical, economical, social events and the patterning of migrants in the host country.

The second aim, to make a contribution to Australian geography of population, has also been fulfilled, as the spatial, occupational and social patterns and adjustments of migrants from Tuscany have been examined as a unique and distinctive history of social, economic and cultural events within the host country. By documenting the geographical distribution and occupational choices of migrants in Western Australia throughout a considerable period of time; and later explaining their social and personal adjustment to the surrounding, analyses were undertaken of the processes involved in this migration process.

The last aim, the identification of the constraints and opportunities to study migrants in Australia in order to enhance the knowledge and management of ethnic groups, is met, as a conclusion, in this brief chapter. The potential applications of this work are then presented as a possible new outcome within social sciences and migration studies in particular. Finally, as some of the findings appear worthy of further examination, suggestions are made for further research.

MAIN FINDINGS

The following three findings of the study are considered to have some relevance to the geography of population and migration studies. The significance of the findings is in the originality of their source documentation and, consequently, the introduction of small-scale cases to the discourse of these disciplines. The findings reinforce the view that, as migrants' patterning in the host country is a social issue, the search for understanding them should of necessity consider the historical and cultural background together, and hence the justification for an integrated and multidisciplinary approach.

· Factors affecting migration from Lucca and Tuscany were of historical and socio-economic order, although additional factors were identified as part of a "Lucca model".
· Spatial, occupational and social patterns of migrants in Western Australia, although 'moulded' by the peculiarity of the host country, reflected that model.
· The understanding of migrants' settlement patterns is linked to the full interdisciplinary knowledge of the historical and cultural heritage that they carry with them from the country of origin.

The first significant finding is related to the highlighting of the historical, economic and social factors that have affected migration from the Province of Lucca. While historical and economic motivations of migration have been a key continuity in understanding mobility, additional reasons have been identified within the migratory processes of Lucchesi. The study has revealed their "overall attitude to temporary migration",[1] which is rooted in a century-long tradition in which many factors (neither merely economic nor historical) merge. The study has shown how the return to Lucca component applied quite well until the 1950s, whereafter it reverted to a more "normal" model of push and pull theory without the return to Lucca component. Both the analysis of primary and secondary sources, as well as the outcomes of the survey showed how the Lucchese 'spirit of adventure' and the restless sense of new enterprises across the world have determined the migratory flow. As an accredited confirmation of the thesis' finding, the Australian demographer Charles Price so wrote in 1963:

> *"The founding migrants' reasons for coming are almost as numerous as the founders themselves, and anyone wishing to understand the history of any immigrant group or chain must be prepared to trace the story back to the original pioneer and his particular reasons for coming to Australia".*[2]

Studies that focus on the complex ways in which migrants' identities shape their mobility patterns have also expanded conceptualisations of place, breaking down boundaries between public and private, and interrogating the ways migrants shape (and are shaped by) places in the host countries. This statement leads us to the second major finding of the study, the geographical and occupational patterns of migrants as a reflection of their specific culture of origin. The spatial distribution and the occupational choices of Tuscan migrants in Western Australia had similarities with the Italian migration process in Australia as a whole (i.e., being explainable in terms of phenomena of chain migration[3]), as well as differences, which are distinctive effects of the 'Lucca model'. These distinctive elements of patterning confirm the necessity of an in-depth analysis of the historical and cultural background of migrant groups, as a key to the interpretation of migrant and ethnic groups in Australia. While this writer is aware that chain migration is an important part of the social process of migration, nevertheless it does not account for the totality of the spatial expression of the migratory processes, as they have often been thought of in terms of dispersion, enclaves (voluntary concentrations) and ghettoes (forced concentrations).

The third significant finding of the study, the understanding of migrants' settlement patterns as linked to the knowledge of their historical and cultural heritage, was through the experience of conducting the research as an exercise in interdisciplinary integration. The study proved to be effective in locating and integrating a variety of sources to reveal relationships and connections between individuals, social groups and migrants' societies of origin and destination. The links between migrants (and their culture) and the country of origin and destination were also identified and documented. In so doing, a contribution was made to the broad field of Australian migration studies. The study was integrative of concepts drawn from different disciplines and of a variety of research methods, so that multiple sources of evidence enabled the case study to be constructed more fully.

Although the disciplines of history, sociology and anthropology were bridged, rather than fully integrated, it is hoped that the findings render a potential contribution to discourse in those disciplines, as well as creating a bridge between them. Likewise, migrants themselves 'bridge' two or more different cultures, rather than either fully remaining in the old one or integrating into the new one.

NOTES

GLOSSARY

1. Gentilli, 1982
2. Gentilli, 1982: 2

INTRODUCTION

1. Lucassen, J. & L., 1997: 10
2. Gentileschi, 1983: 11-13
3. White & Woods, 1980: 7
4. Lucassen J.& L., 1997
5. Massey *et al.*, 1993: 432
6. Reported by Grigg, 1977
7. Clark, 1986: 83
8. Todaro, 1969 and 1976
9. Massey *et al.,* 1993: 434
10. Portes & Borocz, 1996: 157
11. Portes & Borocz, 1996: 161-162
12. Lee, 1966
13. Massey et al., 1993: 436
14. Moon, 1995: 514
15. Silvey & Lawson, 1999: 122
16. Silvey & Lawson, 1999: 123
17. Ragionieri, 1962; De Felice, 1964
18. Sori, 1979: 5
19. Ciuffoletti & Degl'Innocenti, 1978
20. Sori, 1979
21. Rosoli, 1978
22. Franzina, 1992
23. Pizzorusso and Sanfilippo, 1990; Sanfilippo, 1990; Reginato et al., 1999
24. Pozzetta & Ramirez, 1992

25. Foerster, 1924
26. Barton, 1975
27. Briggs, 1978
28. Baily, 1969
29. Vecoli, 1965; Barton, 1975; Cinel, 1987; Zucchi, 1988
30. Nelli, 1970; Tomasi, 1972; Iorizzo, 1980; Harney & Scarpaci, 1981; Harney, 1981
31. Gabaccia, 1994; and 1997 (a)
32. Rosoli, 1992: 5
33. Sarti, 1985; Audenino, 1986; Angelini, 1992; Sensi-Isolani, 1993
34. Pacini, 1994: xix
35. Sori, 1979: 6
36. Dada', 1993 (a): 489
37. Franzina, 1976 and 1991
38. Franzina, 1988
39. Franzina, 1988: 19
40. Corti, 1990; Rovai, 1993; Piselli, 1997
41. Rapetti, 1986; Pomponi, 1988; Devoto, 1991; Boncompagni, 1998 (a); Dibueno, 1999
42. Trento, 1984; Franzina, 1991; Dada', 1994 (a); Douki, 1994; Templeton, 1995; Jannon, 1996; Martellini, 1999
43. Corti, 1995
44. Corti, 1990: 17
45. Dada', 1993 (a): 490
46. Lukomskyj & Richards, 1986
47. Hugo, 1996 (b): 51
48. Borrie, 1954
49. Price, 1963 (a)
50. Ware, 1981
51. Hempel, 1959
52. Douglass, 1995
53. Martinuzzi O'Brien, 1982
54. Pascoe, 1987
55. D'Aprano, 1995
56. Gentilli, 1983
57. Cheda, 1979
58. Bosworth, 1993
59. O'Connor, 1996
60. Cresciani, 1980
61. Cresciani, 1983
62. Rando, 1992
63. Thompson, 1980
64. Vasta, 1993; and 1994

65. Cronin, 1970
66. Huber, 1977
67. Baldassar, 1994
68. Baldassar, 1999
69. Gamba, 1949; and 1952
70. Gava, 1978
71. Iraci, 1979; and 1986
72. Wigley, 1973
73. Bertola, 1993; Longton, 1997
74. Jones Lancaster, 1964; Zubrzycki, 1964; Burnley, 1975; 1985; and 1996; Galvin, 1985; Hugo, 1994; and 1996 (b); Forrest & Johnston, 1999
75. Zubrzycki, 1960
76. Corti, 1990
77. Bottomley, 1992: 62-63
78. Burnley, 1993: 22 and 27
79. Wooden et al., 1994: 23
80. Hugo, 1994: 37
81. Hugo, 1994: 52

CHAPTER 1

1. Gramsci, 1975 (I): 385
2. Commissariato Generale Emigrazione, 1926
3. Foerster, 1924: 152
4. Romano, 1994:1
5. Rosoli, 1978
6. Rosoli, 1994 (a): 309
7. Lopez & Temime, 1990
8. Bosworth, 1996:114
9. Rosoli, 1978
10. Packer, 1947:12
11. Bosworth, 1996:115
12. Rosoli, 1994:4
13. Cerabolini et al., 1996:238
14. Pizzorusso, 1990
15. Cecilia, 1987:45
16. Franzina, 1991:47
17. Massey et al., 1993:432
18. Foerster, 1924:48
19. Massey et al., 1993:434
20. Price, 1963:122
21. Sartl, 1985: 99
22. Gabaccia, 1997 (b):22
23. Corsini, 1969

24. Audenino, 1986: 780 and Foerster, 1924: 532-533
25. Sori, 1979: 12
26. Murphy, 1993: 64
27. Gabaccia, 1997: 181
28. Sori, 1979: 15
29. Franzina, 1992: 16
30. Cerabolini, 1996: 238
31. Corsini, 1969
32. Ramella, 1991: 262
33. Iorizzo, 1980: 70
34. Ciuffoletti, 1978: 142
35. Sori, 1979: 255-256
36. Sori, 1983: 25
37. Sori, 1979: 258-260
38. Rosoli, 1984: 15
39. Ciuffoletti, 1978(I):257
40. Ciuffoletti, 1978(I):276
41. Ciuffoletti, 1978(II):80
42. Nobile, 1974:1325
43. Ciuffoletti, 1978(II):107
44. Ciuffoletti, 1978(II):139
45. Rosoli, 1990
46. Murphy, 1993:71
47. Ciuffoletti, 1978(II):140
48. Bosworth, 1996:122
49. Migliazza, 1983:254
50. Mammarella, 1966:12-124
51. Lampugnani, 1987: 204
52. Ciuffoletti, 1978(II): 230
53. Moch, 1997: 51
54. Murphy, 1993: 73
55. Mammarella, 1996
56. Ciuffoletti, 1978(II): 282
57. Rosoli, 1994: 3
58. Savona & Straniero, 1976: 81
59. Sori, 1979: 16
60. Huber, 1977: 28
61. Piselli, 1997: 6
62. Zucchi, 1988: 30
63. Pugi, 1994: 16
64. Pizzorusso & Sanfilippo, 1990
65. Ramella, 1991: 271
66. Ramella, 1991: 272

67. Cinel, 1982: 36
68. Rosoli, 1978
69. Ruberti, 1993: 13
70. All figures supplied by Camera di Commercio, 1993: 147
71. Favero & Tassello, 1978: 27
72. Castles & Vasta, 1992: 99
73. Ruberti, 1993: 26
74. Rovai, 1993: 122
75. Sori, 1979: 28
76. Straniero, 1978: 116-117
77. Dottori, 1988: 168
78. Commissariato Generale dell'Emigrazione, 1926: 1538
79. Dubost, 1997
80. Brenna, 1918: 91
81. Foerster, 1924: 129
82. Foerster, 1924: 151
83. Wlocevski, 1934: 31
84. Paris, 1975: 528
85. Paris, 1975: 533
86. Bacchetta & Cagiano de Azevedo, 1990: 92
87. Foerster, 1924: 203
88. Foerster, 1924: 203
89. Sponza, 1988: 2
90. Ministero degli Affari Esteri, 1893: 621
91. Ministero degli Affari Esteri, 1893: 7
92. Bacchetta & Cagiano de Azevedo, 1990: 144
93. Cabrini, 1911: 219
94. Paris, 1975: 575
95. Foschi, 1988: 15
96. Paris, 1975: 576
97. Sori, 1979: 44
98. Sori, 1079: 44
99. Commissariato Generale dell'Emigrazione, 1926: 430
100. Trento, 1984: 23
101. Commissariato Generale dell'Emigrazione, 1926: 1540
102. Paris, 1975: 592
103. Rosoli, 1993: 6
104. Rosoli, 1993: 7
105. Savona & Straniero, 1976: 48
106. Paris, 1975: 593
107. Romano, 1994: 4
108. Iorizzo, 1908: 10
109. Foerster, 1924: 323

110. Massara, 1976
111. Pizzorusso, 1992: 25
112. Foerster, 1925: 323
113. Iorizzo, 1980: 30
114. Iorizzo, 1980: 42
115. Vecoli, 1965: 217 and Cinel, 1982: 21
116. Vecoli, 1965: 219
117. Gabaccia, 1997: 184
118. Ciuffoletti, 1978(I): 239
119. Cinel, 1982: 104 and 106
120. Commissariato Generale dell'Emigrazione, 1926: 1539
121. Rosoli, 1994: 4
122. Ministero degli Affari Esteri, 1988: 52
123. Farnocchia, 1981: 544
124. Farnocchia, 1981: 547
125. Vaccari Italian Historical Trust, 1987: 229
126. Farnocchia, 1981: 548
127. Zucchi, 1988: 44
128. Borrie, 1954: 51
129. Castles, 1992: 42
130. Templeton, 1995: 393
131. Ware, 1981: 27
132. Castles, 1992: 43
133. Castles, 1992: 47

CHAPTER 2

1. Pomponi, 1988: 213
2. Distretto Scolastico Garfagnana, 1984(I): 28
3. Repetti, 1835 (II): 407
4. Caciagli, 1992: 19
5. Comunita' Montana Lunigiana, 1990(a): 51
6. Comunita' Montana Lunigiana, 1990(b): 14
7. Regione Toscana, 1985: 169
8. Istituto Nazionale Economia Agraria, 1938: 11
9. Distretto Scolastico Garfagnana, 1984(I): 28
10. Bertacchi, 1973: 32
11. Pacchi, 1967: 178
12. Pasquali, 1922: 40
13. Mori, 1910: 12
14. Frediani, 1978: 287
15. Dada', 1994 (a): 6
16. Wickham, 1988: 5
17. Regione Toscana, 1985: 171

18. Wickham, 1988: 17
19. Regione Toscana, 1985: 171
20. Lombardi-Lotti, 1979: 17
21. Meek, 1994: 62
22. Ciano, 1960: 14
23. Blomquist, 1971: 159
24. Blomquist, 1971: 161
25. Mola', 1994: 21
26. Lombardi-Lotti, 1979: 18
27. Mola', 1994: 21 and Vola, 1990: 111-113
28. Blomquist, 1971: 163
29. Mola', 1994: 30
30. Pascal, 1935: 297
31. Lombardi-Lotti, 1979: 18
32. Berengo, 1974: 280
33. Manselli, 1986: 88
34. Manselli, 1986: 94
35. Le Roy Ladurie, 1974: 160
36. Rovai, 1993: 14
37. Manselli, 1986: 99
38. Berengo, 1974: 400
39. Regione Toscana, 1985: 172
40. Ciano, 1960: 14
41. Manselli, 1986: 109
42. Bertacchi, 1973: 42
43. Bertacchi, 1973: 215
44. Manselli, 1986: 111
45. Distretto Scolastico Garfagnana, 1984: 83
46. Berengo, 1974: 348
47. Fabbri, 1975: 27
48. Manselli, 1986: 118
49. Manselli, 1986: 121
50. Camaiani, 1979: 31
51. Camaiani, 1979: 25
52. Camaiani, 1979: xvii
53. Sardi, 1912: 119
54. Berengo, 1974: 341
55. Camaiani, 1979: 105
56. McDonald, 1956: 452
57. Regione Toscana, 1985: 169
58. Regione Toscana, 1985: 172
59. Comunita' Montana Lunigiana, 1990(a): 45
60. Comunita' Montana Lunigiana, 1990(a): 46

61. Caciagli, 1992: 267
62. Piovene, 1993: 417-418
63. Fabbri, 1975: 28-29
64. Mola', 1994: 262
65. Pugi, 1994: 118
66. Raffaelli, 1879: 232
67. Fabbri, 1975: 28
68. De Stefani, 1977: 243
69. Distretto Scolastico Garfagnana, 1984, pp. 66 and 105
70. Caciagli, 1992: 268
71. Raffaelli, 1879: xiv
72. Pacchi, 1785: 178-179
73. Raffaelli, 1879: 189
74. Pasolini, 1976: 5
75. Ciano, 1960: 16
76. Distretto Scolastico Garfagnana, 1984: 151
77. Caciagli, 1992: 290
78. Caciagli, 1992: 300
79. Distretto Scolastico Garfagnana, 1984: 47
80. Ciano, 1960: 16
81. Distretto Scolastico Garfagnana, 1984: 61
82. Bertacchi, 1973: 33
83. Raffaelli, 1879: 73
84. Distretto Scolastico Garfagnana, 1984: 63
85. Raffaelli, 1879: 75
86. Sardi, 1912: 129
87. Sardi, 1912: 129
88. Busu, 1886: 1 and Cecilia, 1987: 83
89. Sarti, 1985: 58
90. Distretto Scolastico Garfagnana, 1984: 74
91. Pugi, 1994: 119
92. Distretto Scolastico Garfagnana, 1984: 74
93. D'Aprano, 1995: 13
94. Gestri, 1976: 5
95. Gestri, 1976: 33
96. Gestri, 1976, pp. 47 and 61
97. Raffaelli, 1879: 151
98. Raffaelli, 1879: 386
99. Raffaelli, 1879: 529
100. Raffaelli, 1879: 530
101. Bertacchi, 1973: 188
102. Raffaelli, 1879: 327
103. Distretto Scolastico Garfagnana, 1984: 65 and Lera, 1986: 6

104. Ciano, 1960: 22
105. Pascoli, 1980: 301-302
106. Camaiani, 1979: 121
107. Moch, 1997: 47
108. Douki, 1993: 33 and Pugi, 1994: 81
109. Sereni, 1980: 19
110. Douki, 1993: 34
111. Pugi, 1994: 56
112. Jan Lucassen, 1987: 110
113. Foerster, 1924: 533
114. Sarti, 1985: 85
115. Leo Lucassen, 1987: 117
116. Baroni, 1990: 13
117. Camaiani, 1979: 205
118. Istituto Nazionale Economia Agraria, 1938: 19
119. Distretto Scolastico Garfagnana, 1984: 120
120. Cianferoni, Ciuffoletti & Clemente, 1991: 196
121. Kertzer, 1984: 18
122. Sanminiatelli, 1912: 222
123. Pecout, 1990: 729
124. Pugi, 1994: 121
125. Istituto Nazionale Economia Agraria, 1938: 30
126. Camaiani, 1979: 207
127. Cinel, 1982: 80
128. Pugi, 1994: 121
129. Camaiani, 1979: 209
130. Sarti, 1985: 101
131. Sarti, 1985: 106
132. Cinel, 1982: 25
133. Camaiani, 1979: 211
134. Livi-Bacci, 1977:26
135. Lera, 1986: 7
136. Livi-Bacci, 1977: 140
137. Camera Commercio Lucca, 1993: 139
138. Distretto Scolastico Garfagnana, 1984: 121
139. Farnocchia, 1995: 14
140. Pasquali, 1922: 43
141. Sturino, 1990: 55
142. Pascoe, 1987: 243
143. Rapetti, 1986: 20
144. Distretto Scolastico Garfagnana, 1984: 137
145. Distretto Scolastico Garfagnana, 1984: 139
146. Rombai, 1988: 17

147. Istituto Nazionale Economia Agraria, 1938: 15
148. Telleschi, 1996: 129 and Pecout, 1990: 725
149. Cianferoni, Ciuffoletti & Clemente, 1991: 203
150. Pugi, 1994: 48
151. Pasquali, 1922: 53
152. Camera di Commercio, 1993: 149
153. Sardi, 1912: 129
154. Cinel, 1982: 23
155. Monterisi, 1993: 142
156. Monterisi, 1993: 143
157. Pugi, 1994: 107
158. Sanminiatelli, 1912: 225; Distretto Scolastico Garfagnana, 1984 (I): 152
159. Distretto Scolastico Garfagnana, 1984(II): 68
160. Istituto Nazionale Economia Agraria, 1938: 13
161. Corti, 1990: 45
162. Niccolai & Beneforti, 1998: 44
163. Sarti, 1985: 107
164. Dada', 1993: 111
165. Corti, 1990, 38-41
166. Pugi, 1994: 54
167. Losacco, 1931: 12
168. Pugi, 1994: 122
169. Istituto Nazionale Economia Agraria, 1938: 21
170. Cabrini, 1911: 255 and Losacco, 1931: 13
171. Rovai, 1993: 83
172. Sanminiatelli, 1912: 225
173. Toscano, 1976: 14
174. Cianferoni, Ciuffoletti & Clemente, 1990: 221
175. Rovai, 1998 (a): 8
176. Toscano, 1976: 14
177. Sanminiatelli, 1912: 224

CHAPTER 3

1. Reported by Savona & Straniero, 1976: 183
2. Farnocchia, 1995: 11
3. Mori, 1910: 12
4. Accademia Georgofili, 1908, *Memorie* No.2:1
5. Trapani, 1993: 138
6. Moch, 1997: 44
7. Ottolenghi, 1894: 7
8. Dada', 1993 (a): 495 and Paradisi, 1993: 302
9. Lee, 1966
10. Camaiani, 1979: 217

11. Camaiani, 1979: 216
12. Losacco, 1931: 13
13. Romano, 1994: 2
14. Lera, 1986: 7
15. Lera, 1986: 8
16. Briganti, 1993: 199
17. Pugi, 1994: 43
18. Sarti, 1985: 84
19. Audenino, 1986: 779
20. Angelini, 1992: 311
21. Sponza, 1988: 75
22. AAVV, 1987(II):21-22
23. Franchi, 1998; Pierattini, 1998
24. Dada', 1994: 11
25. Sponza, 1988: 76
26. Tognetti, 1993: 225
27. Rovai, 1993: 22
28. Rovai, 1993: 61
29. Lera, 1986: 8 and Rovai, 1993: 22
30. Rovai, 1993: 23
31. Rovai, 1993: 23
32. Farnocchia, 1995: 47
33. Paradisi, 1993: 305
34. Bargellini, 1927
35. Mori, 1910: 3
36. Pomponi, 1988: 201
37. Leo Lucassen, 1997: 225
38. Mori, 1910: 19
39. Jan Lucassen, 1987: pp. 119 and 249
40. Rovai, 1993: 19
41. Dada', 1994 (a): 8
42. Dada', 1994 (a): 25
43. Dada', 1993 (a): 499
44. Tognetti, 1993: 223
45. Cherubini, 1977: 44
46. Foerster, 1924: 133
47. Pomponi, 1988: 202
48. Telleschi, 1996: 128
49. Commissariato Generale Emigrazione, 1926: 546-48
50. Lazzareschi, 1934
51. Pugi, 1994: 66
52. Pugi, 1994: 66
53. Tognetti, 1993: 233

54. Douki, 1993 (b): 42-44
55. Paradisi, 1993: 313
56. Tognetti, 1993: 236
57. Bell, 1979: 8
58. Pugi, 1994: 45
59. Lopez & Temime, 1990:73 and Paradisi, 1993: 323
60. Lopez & Temime, 1990: 75
61. Farnocchia, 1995: 39
62. Sarti, 1985: 119 and Pugi, 1994: 46
63. Dada', 1993 (b): 115
64. Rovai, 1993: 116
65. Farnocchia, 1995: 53
66. Sponza, 1988
67. Farnocchia, 1995: 39
68. Rosoli, 1990
69. Cinel, 1982: 68
70. Rovai, 1993: 20
71. Hoerder, 1997: 83
72. Dada', 1994 (a): 38
73. Sturino, 1990: 69
74. Tognetti, 1993: 244-245
75. Istituto Nazionale Economia Agraria, 1938: 22
76. Sarti, 1985: 88
77. Accademia Georgofili, 1908, *Memorie* No.4:31-32
78. Apollinaire, 1972: 19
79. Nascimbene, 1987: 78
80. Rosoli, 1978
81. Briganti, 1993: 161
82. Briganti, 1993: 163
83. Briganti, 1993: 164
84. Pugi, 1994: 68
85. Briganti, 1993
86. Martellini, 1999, pp. 165-229
87. Briganti, 1993: 168
88. Briganti, 1993
89. Commissariato Generale Emigrazione, 1926: 151
90. Rovai, 1998 (a): 13
91. Briganti, 1993: 192
92. Trento, 1984: 56
93. Briganti, 1993: 195
94. Farnocchia, 1995: 42
95. Ministero Affari Esteri, 1988: 21
96. Paris, 1975: 593

97. Ungaretti, 1975: 76
98. Rovai, 1993: 26
99. Farnocchia, 1995: 55
100. Rovai, 1993: 27
101. Rovai, 1993: 91
102. Farnocchia, 1995: 76
103. Rovai, 1998: 18
104. Farnocchia, 1995: 99
105. Losacco, 1931: 13
106. Accademia Georgofili, 1908: 7-8
107. Vecoli, 1965: 175
108. Farnocchia, 1995: 40
109. Mirola, 1974: 62
110. Cinel, 1982: 32
111. Cinel, 1987: 348
112. Cinel, 1987: 348
113. Paoli Gumina, 1978: 102
114. Paoli Gumina, 1978: 101-102
115. Vecoli, 1964
116. Harney, 1984 and Zucchi, 1988: 53
117. Price, 1963
118. Boncompagni, 1998 (a); 401
119. Price, 1963
120. Farnocchia, 1995: 72
121. Sensi-Isolani, 1987: 63
122. Sensi-Isolani, 1987: 59
123. Sensi-Isolani, 1987: 60-61
124. Farnocchia, 1995: 55
125. Sensi-Isolani, 1987: 63

CHAPTER 4

1. Cresci, 1986: 78
2. Rando, 1992: 51
3. Martellini, 2000
4. Rando, 1992: 51-52
5. D'Aprano, 1995: 9
6. Messina, 1976: 112-113
7. Cresciani, 1983: 309
8. Pyke, 1948: 100
9. Pyke, 1948: 101
10. Societa' Geografica, 1890: 101-102
11. Costanza, 1995: 49
12. Pesman, 1984: 156

13. Cresciani, 1983: 314-315
14. Michieli, 1935: 6
15. Lyng, 1927: 99
16. Gentilli, 1982: 10
17. Rando, 1992: 53
18. Lyng, 1927: 99
19. Rando, 1992: 53-54
20. Pyke, 1948: 102
21. Rando, 1992: 53
22. Pyke, 1948: 102
23. Corte, 1898: 232
24. Pyke, 1948: 103
25. Pyke, 1946: 36
26. O'Connor, 1996: 62
27. Societa' Geografica Italiana, 1890: 180
28. Capra. 1909: 11
29. Sori, 1979: 282
30. Cresciani, 1980: 3
31. Pyke, 1948: 104-105
32. Murphy, 1993: 28
33. Iacovino, 1983: 2-3
34. Murphy, 1993: 32
35. Melia, 1991
36. Cresciani, 1983: 316
37. MacDonald et al., 1970: 250
38. Bosworth, 1996: 123
39. Porter, 1966: 68-74
40. Douglass, 1995: 156
41. O'Connor, 1994: 4
42. Cresciani, 1983: 334
43. MacDonald, 1970: 254
44. Gentilli, 1982: 23
45. Cresciani, 1982: 293
46. Marchi, 1988
47. O'Connor, 1994: 153
48. Cresciani, 1980: 23; Cresciani 1982 and Missori, 1982: 319
49. Cresciani, 1980: 82
50. Iacovino, 1983: 7
51. Cresciani, 1983: 339
52. Lampugnani, 1987: 198
53. Zubrzycki, 1960:42
54. Stiassi, 1979: 39
55. Zubrzycki, 1960: 114

56. Pyke, 1948: 108
57. Borrie, 1954: 123
58. Cresciani, 1983: 340
59. Fitzgerald, 1981: 1
60. Stiassi, 1979: 82
61. Stiassi, 1979: 82
62. Borrie, 1954: 141
63. Murphy, 1993: 77
64. Borrie, 1954: 226
65. MacDonald, 1970: 255
66. Borrie, 1954: 229
67. MacDonald, 1970: 256
68. Cox, 1975: 37
69. Bosworth, 1990: 2
70. Cox, 1975: 39 and Bosworth, 1990: 2
71. Pascoe, 1987: 244
72. Favero and Tassello, 1983: 59
73. Hugo, 1996: 59
74. Rando, 1992: 60
75. Hempel, 1959: 44
76. Ware, 1981: 15
77. Hugo, 1993: 42
78. Burnley, 1975: 329
79. Capra, 1911: 11
80. Capra, 1911: 16
81. Alcorso, 1992: 13
82. Bosi, 1997: 19
83. Gentilli, 1984: 230
84. Ministero Affari Esteri, 1906: 518
85. Martellini, 2000
86. Alcorso, 1992: 13
87. Cecilia, 1987: 341
88. Cecilia, 1987: 341
89. Corte, 1898: 229
90. D'Aprano, 1995: 127
91. Martinuzzi O'Brien, 1989: 31
92. D'Aprano, 1995: 128
93. Alcorso, 1992: 27
94. Cecilia, 1987: 336-337
95. Bosi, 1997: 73
96. Alcorso, 1992: 13
97. Cecilia, 1987: 64
98. Commissariato Generale Emigrazione, 1926: pp. 1719,1721 and 1723

99. Messina, 1976
100. Boncompagni, 1996
101. Douglass, 1995: 25
102. Lucchesi, 1988: 227-228
103. Marletta, 1996: 176-177
104. Bosi, 1997: 94 and 111
105. Ministero Affari Esteri, 1906: 522
106. Ministero Affari Esteri, 1906: 522 and Capra, 1909: 14
107. Templeton, 1995: 414
108. Boncompagni, 1998 (a): 396
109. MacDonald, 1970: 261
110. Lancaster Jones, 1964: 250
111. Price, 1963: 18-19
112. Mirola, 1974: 64
113. Boncompagni, 1998 (a): 399
114. Bosi, 1997: 142
115. Hempel, 1959: 2
116. Bertelli, 1988: 78
117. Bertelli, 1987: 42
118. Ministero Affari Esteri, 1987: 384

CHAPTER 5

1. Farnocchia, 1996
2. Price, 1963: 1-2
3. Price, 1963: 16
4. Price, 1963: 21
5. Price, 1963: 22
6. Interview with Mr Ernesto D.S., Yokine WA, 30 April 1998
7. Australian Archives of WA, Series PP 302/1, Item WA 8953
8. Price, 1963: 23
9. Price, 1963
10. Zang & Hassan, 1996: 567
11. Hugo, 1994: 89
12. Tomasi et al., 1994: 348
13. Castle & Vasta, 1992: 108
14. Cecilia, 1987: 237
15. Borrie, 1954: 61
16. Castles & Vasta, 1992: 108
17. Zubrzycki, 1960: 69
18. Inglis, 1975: 338
19. Zang & Hassan, 1996: 567
20. Burnley, 1996: 88
21. Hugo, 1996: 59-60

22. Hugo, 1996: 59
23. Hugo, 1996: 60
24. Hugo, 1996: 60
25. Dawkins, 1991: 14
26. Price & Martin, 1976: A142
27. Price & Martin, 1976: A142-A143
28. Price, 1963; Lee, 1970; Huber, 1977 and Burnley, 1988.
29. Borrie, 1954: 80
30. Dawkins et al., 1991:14
31. J.&L.Macdonald, 1970: 249
32. Lee, 1970: 60-61
33. Piselli, 1997: 8
34. Zucchi, 1988: 33
35. Cinel, 1982: 114
36. Dottori, 1988: 170
37. Lancaster Jones, 1964: 262
38. Tomasi et al., 1994: 347
39. Price, 1963
40. Stefanoni, 1990: 258
41. Jackle et al., 1976: 171
42. Sori, 1979: 159
43. Franzina, 1992: 68 and Dada', 1994 (a): 16
44. Price, 1963: 120
45. Stefanoni, 1990
46. Interview with Mr Ernesto D.S., Yokine WA, 30 April 1998
47. Interview with Mr Pietro C., Dianella WA, 25 August 1997
48. Price & Martin, 1976: A143
49. Stefanoni, 1990

CHAPTER 6

1. Galvin, 1985: 224-227
2. Hugo, 1996
3. Gentilli, 1983: 109
4. Gentilli, 1983: 55
5. Price, 1963: 157
6. Ministero Affari Esteri, 1906: 553
7. Gentilli, 1983: 64
8. Cecilia, 1987: 267
9. Wigley, 1973: 14
10. Cecilia, 1987: 267
11. Gentilli, 1983: 76
12. Wigley, 1973: 15
13. Borrie, 1954

14. Gentilli, 1983: 80
15. Cecilia, 1987: 264-265
16. Gentilli, 1983 and Keast, 1987:31
17. Cecilia, 1987: 263
18. Karragullen Primary School & Pagotto, 1988
19. Karragullen Primary School & Pagotto, 1988: 41-41
20. Keast, 1987: 74
21. Keast, 1987: 34
22. Karragullen Primary School & Pagotto, 1988: 72-73
23. Interviews with Mr Costantino G., Highgate WA, 12 May 1998, Mr Mario S., Tuart Hill WA, 5 July 1997 and Mr Rino M., Yokine, 14 August 1998
24. Keast, 1987: 40
25. Ministero Affari Esteri, 1906: 554; Keast, 1987: 46
26. Farnocchia, 1996: 64, 67, 85, 89 and 109
27. Gentilli, 1983: 100
28. Keast, 1987: 13
29. Interview with Mr Mario C., Morley WA, 17 September 1997 and Mr Pietro O., South Perth WA, 25 November 1997
30. Hugo, 1996 (a)
31. Gentilli, 1983: 109 and Pascoe & Bertola, 1985: 31
32. Bosi, 1997: 215
33. Interview with Mr Richard G., Yokine WA, 22 April 1998
34. Bosi, 1997: 92
35. Interview with Mr Terziglio G., Bassendean WA, 25 August 1997
36. Interview with Mr Ottavio P., Morley WA, 2 December 1997
37. Interviews with Mr Angelo M., Wanneroo WA, 16 July 1997, Mr Ernesto D.S., Yokine WA, 30 April 1998 and Mr Gino L., Bassendean WA, 27 November 1997
38. Nelli, 1970: 100
39. Commissariato Generale Emigrazione, 1926: 255-56
40. Sori, 1979: 92
41. Gagliardi, 1881: 6
42. Price, 1963: 149
43. Interview with Mrs Matilde P.P., Leederville WA, 21 August 1997
44. Harney, 1981: 49; Cinel, 1982
45. Panucci et al., 1992: 161
46. Cinel, 1982: 138
47. Lindsay Thompson, 1983: 36
48. Boncompagni, 1998 (a): 401
49. Walters et al., (no date): 67
50. Ware, 1981: 50; Bertelli, 1987: 45
51. Tomasi et al., 1994: 146

52. Price, 1963
53. Rother, 1989: 406-407
54. Nelli, 1970: 86, Rother, 1989: 411 and Pascoe, 1992: 181
55. Borrie, 1954: 61, Ministero Affari Esteri, 1906: 550-551 and Cecilia, 1987: 265
56. Price, 1963: 143
57. Gentilli, 1983: 99
58. Price, 1963: 150; Gentilli, 1983: 100
59. Bosi, 1997: 214
60. Packer, 1947: 72, and Gillgren, 1997: 74
61. Price, 1963: 147
62. Ministero Affari Esteri, 1906: 551
63. Bosi, 1997: 216
64. Interview with Mr Mario Scatena, Tuart Hill WA, 5 July 1997
65. Bosi, 1997: 217
66. Price, 1963: 173
67. Longon, 1997: 128
68. Pascoe & Bertola, 1985: 30
69. Gentilli, 1983: 77
70. Pascoe & Bertola, 1985: 13
71. Price, 1963
72. Macdonald, 1970: 272
73. Borrie, 1954: 123
74. Interview with Mr Ernesto D.S., Yokine WA, 30 April 1998, Mr Costantino G., Highgate WA, 12 May 1998 and Mr Angelo M., Wanneroo WA, 16 July 1997
75. Cecilia, 1987: 251
76. Portes & Boeroecz, 1996: 166
77. Bertola, 1993: 7
78. Cresciani, 1983: 320-321
79. Miserocchi, 1937: 200
80. Bertola, 1993: 8
81. Bertola, 1998: 14
82. Bertola, 1998: 14-15
83. Gillgren, 1997: 75 and 76
84. Cecilia, 1987: 251
85. Ministero Affari Esteri, 1906: 556; Capra, 1909: 16
86. Cecilia, 1987: 252
87. Ministero Affari Esteri, 1906: 522
88. Cecilia, 1987: 253
89. Pascoe & Bertola, 1985: 22
90. Packer, 1947: 40-41
91. Longton, 1997: 127

92. Longton, 1997: 128
93. The Australian Archives of WA, Series PP302/1, Item WA 9386
94. Interview with Mr Ernesto D.S., Yokine WA, 30 April 1998
95. Cresciani, 1980: 3
96. Sector of Military Intelligence, The Italian Aliens on the Kalgoorlie Goldfields, 18 November 1919, Australian Archives of WA, Series PP14/1, Item 16/1/290, p.1
97. Interview with Mr Armando R., Balcatta WA, 14 April 1999
98. Fabiano, 1983: 234 and Gentilli, 1983: 91
99. Cresciani, 1979: 151, Missori, 1982: 319 and Pascoe & Bertola, 1985: 34
100. O'Connor, 1996: pp. 147 and 153
101. Interview with Mr Ernesto D.S., Yokine WA, 30 April 1998
102. Cecilia, 1987: 240
103. Bosi, 1997: 85
104. Cresciani, 1983: 339
105. Bertola, 1993: 8-9
106. Sector of Military Intelligence, The Italian Aliens on the Kalgoorlie Goldfields, 18 November 1919, Australian Archives of WA, Series PP14/1, Item 16/1/290, p.1
107. Harney, 1985: 9
108. Bertola, 1998: 21
109. Interviews with Mr Angelo M., Wanneroo WA, 16 July 1997, Mr Ernesto D.S., Yokine WA, 30 April 1998 and Mr Costantino G., Highgate WA, 12 May 1998
110. Cresciani, 1979 and Cresciani, 1980
111. Burnely, 1975: 320
112. Hugo, 1994: 96-97
113. Farnocchia, 1996
114. Gentilli, 1983: 201
115. Burnley, 1996: 83
116. Gentilli, 1983: 146-147
117. Gentilli, 1983: 99
118. Interviews with Mr Rino M., Yokine WA, 14 August 1997, Mrs Velia P., Tuart Hill WA, 5 July 1997, Mr Armando R., Balcatta WA, 15 April 1999, and Mr Mario S., Tuart Hill WA, 5 July 1997
119. Interview with Mt Terziglio G., Bassendean WA, 25 August 1997
120. Interviews with Mr Gino L., Bassandean WA, 27 November 1997, Mr Ottavio P., Morley WA, 2 December 1997, and Mr Giuseppe T., Balcatta WA, 21 December 1997
121. Interview with Mr Duilio R., Bassendean WA, 27 November 1997
122. Interview with Mr Duilio R., Bassendean WA, 27 November 1997
123. Interview with Mr Gino L., Bassendean WA, 27 November 1997
124. Interviews with Mr Luigi B., Dianella WA, 1 December 1997, Mr

Domenico B., Balcatta WA, 13 August 1997 and Mr Mario C., Morley WA, 17 September 1997

125. Iraci, 1986: 87-89
126. Gentilli, 1983: 123
127. Price, 1963: 157; Rother, 1989: 407
128. Gentilli, 1983: 99
129. Iraci, 1986: 121-123 and Hugo, 1996: xxvi
130. Price, 1963: 155
131. Interview with Mr Ottavio P., Morley WA, 2 December 1997
132. Borrie, 1954: 146
133. Cecilia, 1987: 256-257
134. Cecilia, 1987: 256
135. Interviews with Mr Gilberto R., Dianella WA, 26 November 1997, Mr Alessandro D.P., Subiaco WA, 22 July 1997 and Mr Domenico B., Balcatta WA, 13 August 1997
136. Cecilia, 1987: 256
137. Bosi, 1997: 213
138. Sarti, 1985
139. Sarti, 1985: 115
140. Interview with Mr Leonardo B., Balcatta WA, 13 August 1997
141. Interview with Mr Alessandro D.P., Subiaco WA, 22 July 1997
142. Interview with Mr Gilberto R., Dianella WA, 26 November 1997
143. Interview with Mr Pietro C., Dianella WA, 25 August 1997
144. Gentilli, 1983: 122
145. Gentilli, 1984
146. Burnley, 1988: 276

CHAPTER 7

1. Pascoe, 1987: 19
2. Bell, 1979: 151
3. Corti, 1990: 25
4. Vecoli, 1965: 224
5. Cinel, 1987: 333
6. Vecoli, 1965: 225
7. Cinel, 1987: 343-351
8. Bertelli, 1994: 25
9. Rosoli, 1992: 15
10. Vecoli, 1965: 236
11. Harney, 1991; Franzina, 1991
12. Boncompagni, 1999 (b)
13. Harney, 1981: 44-45
14. Baldassar, 1999: 6
15. Yans-McLaughlin, 1990: 275
16. Pascoe, 1992: 183

17. Harney, 1991
18. Bosworth, 1990: 6
19. Paganoni & O'Connor, 1999
20. Walters et al., (no date): 86
21. Piselli, 1997: 13
22. Boncompagni, 1999 (b)
23. Nelli, 1970:87-97
24. Corti, 1990: 21
25. Tosi, 1991: 166
26. Lee, 1970: 56-57
27. Price & Martin, 1976: A141
28. Warren, 1972
29. Burnley, 1985: 167
30. Monterisi, 1993: 151
31. Farnocchia, 1981: 566-567; Franzina, 1992: 100-101; Nardini, 1999.
32. Huber, 1977; Martinuzzi O'Brien, 1982: 82-84; Cecilia, 1987: 138; Ministero Affari Esteri, 1988; 222-223; Gardini, 1993: 146; Walters et al. (n.d.): 65-65.
33. Burnley, 1988: 263-264
34. Pascoe, 1992: 185
35. Pascoe, 1993: 159
36. Burnley, 1985: 167 and 194
37. Bosi, 1996: 281
38. Huber, 1977: 104
39. Gentilli, 1993: 22
40. Paganoni & O'Connor, 1999
41. Franzina, 1992: 108
42. Jupp, 1993: 209
43. Regione Toscana, 1991: 116
44. Gentilli, 1993: 22
45. Interview with Mr Mario C., Morley WA, 17 September 1997
46. Bosi, 1996: 283
47. Interview with Mr Mario C., Morley WA, 17 September 1997
48. Gentilli, 1993: 22
49. Bosi, 1996: 283
50. Interview with Mr Angelo S., Balcatta WA, 22 May 1999
51. Interview with Mr Mario C., Morley WA, 17 September 1997
52. Newsletter of Lucchesi nel Mondo, several monthly issues, 1998 and 1999
53. Toscany Association Members list, 12 February 1997 (typed)
54. Interview with Mr Mario C., Morley WA, 17 September 1997
55. http://www.regione.toscana.it/ita/uff/polcom/sottoind.htm
56. Toscany Association Members list, 12 February 1997 (typed)
57. Gentilli, 1983

58. Interview with Mr Mario C., Morley WA, 17 September 1997
59. Issues of Toscani nel Mondo, 1998 and 1999
60. Toscany Association Members list, 12 February 1997 (typed)
61. Interview with Mr Mario C., Morley WA, 17 September 1997
62. Nardini, 1999
63. Interview with Mr Alessandro D.P., Subiaco WA, 22 July 1997
64. Interview with Mr Oliviero B., Balcatta WA, 5 July 1997
65. Interview with Mr Mario C., Morley WA, 17 September 1997
66. Agnew, 1992: 52
67. Mori, 1986: 125-143

CHAPTER 8

1. Wilson, 1973: 152
2. Heiss, 1966:165-171
3. Spedicato, 1988
4. Jupp, 1966; Burnley, 1985; Galvin, 1985
5. Michelson, 1977
6. Yans-McLaughlin, 1990: 255-256
7. Silvey & Lawson, 1999: 123
8. Smolicz & Secombe, 1985
9. Bell, 1979
10. Wilson, 1973
11. Zubrzycki, 1964
12. Huber, 1977
13. Bottomley, 1979
14. Borrie, 1954
15. Hugo, 1994: 54
16. Gentilli, 1993: 12-13
17. Huber, 1977
18. Grieco, 1987: 183
19. Huber, 1977: 215; Bell, 1979
20. Huber, 1977; Grieco, 1985.
21. Madge, 1965
22. Cronin, 1970
23. Huber, 1977
24. Thompson, 1980
25. Madge, 1965
26. Moser, 1985
27. Babbie, 1990
28. Michelson, 1977
29. Martin, 1976
30. Michelson, 1977
31. Burnley, 1993: 24-26

32. Jupp, 1966: 126
33. Bell, 1979: 224
34. Huber, 1977: 216
35. Iraci, 1979
36. Jupp, 1966: 127
37. Favero & Tassello, 1983: 62
38. Borrie, 1954: 89-90
39. Cinel, 1987: 127
40. Huber, 1977: 143
41. Prezzolini, 1963
42. Jacke et al., 1976: 150
43. Huber, 1977:143
44. Iraci, 1979: 98
45. Interview with Mr Loris P., Balcatta (WA), 13 August 1997
46. Niccolai & Beneforti, 1998: 118-119
47. Wooden et al., 1994: 217
48. Iraci, 1979: 87
49. Franzina, 1992: 68-70
50. Ugolini, 1988: 10
51. Pesman Cooper, 1993: 173
52. Gentilli, 1973: 191
53. Burnley, 1985: 169
54. Ware, 1981
55. Huber, 1977
56. Borrie, 1954: 142
57. Spedicato, 1988: 214
58. Gentilli, 1993: 19
59. Walters et al., (no date): 68
60. Webber, 1992: 176
61. Huber, 1977: 149-150
62. Pulvirenti, 1997: 36
63. Interviews with: Mr Mario S., Tuart Hill WA 5 July 1997; Mr Gino L., Bassandean WA, 27 November 1997; Mr Giuseppe T., Balcatta WA, 21 December 1997; Mr Duilio R., Bassendean
64. WA, 27 November 1997.
65. Ware, 1981: 48
66. Johnston, 1979: 83
67. Burnley, 1985
68. Borrie, 1954: 86
69. Burnley, 1985
70. Bertelli, 1994: 32
71. Borrie, 1954: 88
72. Bettoni, 1983: 103-104

73. Tosi, 1991: 165-166
74. Hugo, 1994: 79
75. Societa' Geografica Italiana, 1890: 253
76. Borrie, 1954: 53
77. Galvin, 1985: 225
78. Vasta, 1993
79. Favero & Tassello, 1983: 68
80. Cinel, 1987: 169
81. Inglis, 1975
82. Bettoni, 1988; Smolicz, 1983 and 1993
83. Guicciardo, 1987; Vasta 1993 and 1994
84. Ware, 1981: 24
85. Price, 1963(a); Price, 1985: 51-57; Price, 1996
86. Guicciardo, 1987: 1
87. Inglis, 1975
88. Borrie, 1954: 99-100; Vasta, 1994: 415
89. Bertelli, 1994: 30
90. Castles & Vasta, 1992: 112-113
91. Vasta, 1994: 413
92. Smolicz, 1993
93. Bernardi, 1982: 7
94. Bettoni, 1988: 201
95. Vasta, 1992: 294
96. Burnley, 1985: 189
97. Burnley, 1985: 177
98. Vecoli, 1965: 238
99. Schiller et al., 1992: ix
100. Schiller et al., 1992: 8
101. Sarup, 1994: 96
102. Heiss, 1964: 69
103. Farnocchia, 1981: 568-569
104. Bosworth, 1979: 421-422, and Franzina, 1992
105. Iraci, 1979 and 1986; Baldassar, 1994
106. Bosi, 1997: 210
107. Burnley, 1985: 177-181
108. Baldassar, 1999: 6
109. Cresciani, 1987: 199
110. Reported by Bell, 1979: 178
111. Wilson, 1973: 83
112. Cerase, 1970; Cresciani, 1983
113. Lucassen, J. & L., 1977: 23
114. Thompson, 1980; and 1983
115. Bogue, 1969; Moon, 1995

116. Huber, 1977: 185
117. Rando, 1992: 61
118. Rosoli, 1992

CONCLUSIONS

1. Dada', 1994 (a): 10
2. Price, 1963: 126
3. Jones Lancaster, 1964: 262

BIBLIOGRAPHY

ARCHIVAL SOURCES

Australian Archives (WA) (Series and File)

A 7919/1	100040.
K 258/10	477/26/163.
K 273/57	1958/98/54.
K 1171/1	4345, 6543, 6571, 7354, 3649, 8720, 1504, 8521, 8812, 9865, 6291, 339, 8510.
K 1174/1	(PW) 161206, 149390, 121316, "Lamberti Biagio", 48147, 59837, 62272,
	"Giannini", 67374, 48147, 59893, 61546, 63364, 61586, 61591, 67348, 59337, 67454, 62688, 62693.
PP 6/1	1950/H/5170.
PP 9/1	51/63/12096 'Lakewood'.
PP 9/4	'Baldisseri', 'Barbetti', 'Canestrini', 'Carmignani', 'Cassettai, 'Consolini', 'Corrieri', 'Costa', 'Donati', 'Fiori', 'Giannasi', 'Giorgi', 'Giovannoni', 'Grassi', 'Lamberti', 'Lucchesi', 'Lunardi', 'Malatesta', 'Mannolini', 'Mariotti', 'Nicoli'.
PP 14/1	'Italian Aliens on the Kalgoorlie Goldfields'.
PP 302/1	29042, 1264, 13324, 14315, 15485, 16080, 18901, 11362, 19560, 7258, 13260, 2974, 13992, 1210, 6715, 4931, 20274, 6611, 6795, 1311, 8953, 4704, 9819, 19451,13896, 21773, 4141, 8445, 12396, 20558, 11206, 29201, 13108,9016, 6209, 20926, 3392, 28483, 12696, 6655, 12188, 3913, 4683, 7005, 13853, 19245, 6390, 11824, 14816, 18309, 28789, 8340,8780, 9654,

10317, 11872, 13215, 19558, 1184, 6183, 10267, 11523, 15923, 19208, 6408, 29496, 29784, 7040, 12145, 19396, 21942, 10616, 3654, 20107, 3879, 17426, 2845, 6126, 11206, 29201, 13108, 6209,20926, 9016, 3392, 28483, 12696, 8942, 16295, 36652, 9386, 18029, 14718, 1314, 2874, 6437, 29470, 7881, 16595, 19605, 20858, 21240, 5518, 6037, 4996, 6159, 28442, 12627, 12924, 16509, 19310, 10992, 3135, 29285, 11080, 15938, 7395, 11172, 11210, 18540, 18885, 29118, 6610, 20951, 3454, 7419, 20183, 5382, 6585, 15394, 13263, 18149, 6390, 1813, 16531, 5130, 6248,6586, 5130, 14493, 13152, 1575, 2500, 4029, 4030, 12486, 15947, 13915, 19364, 21972, 9595, 17981, 10254, 14314, 18861, 21770, 2992, 19651, 21254, 8048, 9120, 16026, 8270, 8271, 28507, 7955, 11125, 36415, 16019, 1586, 3172, 11214, 11231, 19223, 18311, 5139, 8261, 12590,11258, 21675, 8285, 10002, 8366, 7844, 11275, 9547, 11213, 7258, 20603.

PP 513/7 — 'Alien registration Entry Forms/ Italian (23 Boxes, from B32 to B54)

PT 143/1 — 1298 Cons.

GENERAL TEXTS, ARTICLES, NEWSPAPERS AND CIRCULARS

AA.VV., 1987, *La Toscana - Paese per Paese*, Firenze, Bonechi, 2 Vol.

Agnew, John, 1992, "Place and Politics in post-war Italy: a cultural geography of local identity in the Provinces of Lucca and Pistoia" in Anderson, Kay and Gale, Fay (Eds.), 1992, *Inventing Places - Studies in Cultural Geography*, Longman Cheshire, Melbourne, pp. 52-71.

Alcorso, Caroline, 1992, "La prima immigrazione italiana e la costruzione dell'Australia europea, 1788-1939", in Castles, Steven - Alcorso, Caroline - Rando, Gaetano & Vasta, Ellie (Eds), *Italo-australiani - Le popolazioni di origine italiana in Australia*, Torino, Fondazione Agnelli, pp. 11-31.

Angelini, Massimo, 1992, "Suonatori ambulanti all'estero nel XIX secolo: considerazioni sul caso della Val Graveglia", *Studi Emigrazione/Études Migrations*, XXIX (106): 309-319.

Apollinaire, Guillaume, 1972, *Zone*, Dublin, The Dolmen Press.

Audenino, Patrizia, 1986, "The Paths of the Trade: Italian Stonemasons in the United States" *International Migration Review*, XX(4), Winter 1986, pp. 779-795.

Bacchetta, Piero & Cagiano de Azavedo, R, 1990, *Le comunità italiane all'estero*, Torino, Giappichelli.

Baily, Samuel L., 1969, "The Italian and the Development of Organized Labor in Argentina, Brazil and the United States, 1880-1914", *Journal of Social History*, 1969 (3), pp. 123-134.

Baldassar, Loretta, 1999, "Marias and marriage: ethnicity, gender and sexuality among Italo-Australian youth in Perth", *Journal of Sociology*, Vol. 35 (1), March 1999, pp. 1-22.

Bargellini, Piero, 1927, "Lucchesi in Corsica", *Illustrazione Italiana*, October 1927.

Baroni, Fabio, 1990, "Per la storia di chi non ha storia", in Comunità Montana della Lunigiana, 1990(b), *Per terre assai lontane*, Sarzana, Comunita' Montana della Lunigiana, pp. 11-14.

Barton, John, 1975, *Peasants and Strangers: Italians, Romenians and Slovaks in an American City 1890-1950*, Cambridge, Harvard University Press.

Bell, Rudolph M, 1979, *Fate and Honor, Family and Village. Demographic and Cultural Change in Rural Italy since 1800*, Chicago and London, The University of Chicago Press.

Berengo, Marino, 1974(2), *Nobili e mercanti nella Lucca del Cinquecento*, Torino, Einaudi.

Bernardi, Savino, 1982, *Second Generation Italians in Australia: an ambivalent Generation*, North Fitzroy, Catholic Intercultural Resource Centre.

Bertacchi, Sigismondo, 1973, *Descrizione Istorica della provincia di Garfagnana*, Lucca, Cassa di Risparmio di Lucca-Centro di Studio Carfaniana Antiqua.

Bertelli, Lidio, 1987, "Profilo Socio-Culturale della Collettivita' Italiana in Australia", *Il Veltro*, XXXI(1-2), pp. 31-53.

Bertelli, Lidio, 1988, "Profilo della Comunita' Italo-Australiana", *Il Veltro*, XXXII(1-2), pp. 61-73.

Bertelli, Lidio, 1988, "La Comunità Italiana nell'Australia Multiculturale", *Il Veltro,* XXXII(1-2), pp. 75-82.

Bertelli, Lidio, 1994, "The Italo-Australian Community: the Challenges to the Year 2001 and after" in Bivona, Antonina (Ed.), *Italian Towards 2000 International Conference, 22-24 Sept 1994,* Melbourne, Victoria University of Technology, pp. 25-34.

Bertola, Patrick, 1993, "Italian Migration to Western Australia before WWI: some observations on ethnicity and conflict", *Italian Historical Society Journal,* I(2), Dec. 1993, pp. 5-10.

Bertola, Patrick, 1998, "Racially Exclusive Provisions in Western Australian Mining Legislation", *Paper presented to the Australian Historical Association Conference, Sydney, July 1998*, pp. 1-27.

Bettoni, Camilla, 1983, "Italian in Australia: Language Change or Language Shift ?" in Cresciani, Gianfranco (Ed.), 1983, *L'Australia, gli Australiani e la Migrazione Italiana*, Milano, Angeli.

Blomquist, Thomas , 1971, "Commercial Association in Thirteenth Century Lucca", *Business History Review,* XLV, Vol.I (2) Summer 1971, pp. 157-170.

Bogue, D, 1969, *Principles of Demography,* New York, Wiley.

Boncompagni, Adriano, 1996, "Italiani a Jacksons Bay, Nuova Zelanda (1875-78) tra scelte governative e presenza dell'Altro", *Altre Italie,* Jan.-June 1996, No. 14.

Boncompagni, Adriano, 1998 (a), "Migrants from Tuscany in Western Australia", *Studi Emigrazione - Journal of International Migration Studies*, XXXV, No. 131 (September 1998), pp. 390-406.

Boncompagni, Adriano, 1998 (b), "Distribuzione geografica e scelte occupazionali dell'emigrazione lucchese in Australia Occidentale", *Rivista Geografica Italiana*, 105 (1998), pp. 257-275.

Boncompagni, Adriano, 1999 (a), "From the Apennine to the Bush: 'temporary' migrants from Tuscan communities to Western Australia, 1921-1939", in Hood, Robert and Markey, Ray (eds.), *Proceedings of the Sixth National Conference of the Australian Society for the Study of Labour History, Wollongong, NSW 2-3 October, 1999,* Wollongong, The Australian Society for the Study of Labour History, Illawarra Branch, 1999, pp. 26-31.

Boncompagni, Adriano, 1999 (b), "Il senso di identita' nazionale della comunita' italiana d'Australia, tra patriottismi e pulsioni particolaristiche", in Bartocci, Enzo and Cotesta, Vittorio (eds.), *L'identita' italiana: emigrazione, immigrazione, conflitti etnici*, Roma, Edizioni Lavoro, 1999, pp. 257-266.

Borrie, W.D., 1954, *Italians and Germans in Australia*, Melbourne, Australian National University.

Bosworth, Richard, 1979, *Italy, the Least of the Great Powers: Italian Foreign Policy before the First World War*, Cambridge, Cambridge University Press.

Bosworth, Richard, 1990, "Storia dell'Emigrazione e Storia Nazionale: Australia", in *Altre Italie*, 1990, 4: pp. 24-34; pp. 35-42.

Bosworth, Richard & Melia, Margot, 1991, "The Italian Feste of Western Australia and the Myth of the Universal Church", in Bosworth, Richard and Melia, Margot (Eds.), *Aspects of Ethnicity. Studies in Western Australian History*, XII, April 1991: pp. 71-84.

Bosworth, Richard & Michal, 1993, *Fremantle's Italy*, Rome, Gruppo Editoriale Internazionale.

Bosworth, Richard, 1996, *Italy and the wider world 1860-1960*, London and New York, Routledge.

Bottomley, Gillian, 1992, *From Another Place. Migration and the politics of culture*, Cambridge, Cambridge University Press.

Brenna, Paolo, 1918, *L'emigrazione italiana nel periodo ante bellico*, Firenze, Bemporad.

Briganti, Lucilla, 1993, "La Lucchesia e il Brasile: storia di emigranti, genti e autorità", *Documenti e Studi*, 14/15, 1993, pp. 161-229.

Briggs, John W., 1978, *An Italian Passage. Immigrants to Three American Cities, 1890-1930*, New Haven, Yale University Press.

Burnley, Ian H,.1975, "Immigrant Absorption in the Australian City 1947-1971", *International Migration Review*, IX(3), Fall 1975, pp. 319-332.

Burnley, Ian H., 1985, "Neighbourhood, communal structure and acculturation in ethnic concentrations in Sydney, 1978", in Burnley, Ian H. - S.Encel & Grant McCall (Eds.), *Immigration and Ethnicity in the 1980s*,' Melbourne, Longman Cheshire, pp. 167-197.

Burnley, Ian H., 1988, "L'insediamento italiano in Sydney, 1920-1978", in Lucchesi, Flavio (Ed.), 1988, *Orizzonte Australia. Percezione e realtà di un continente*, Milano, Unicopli, pp. 261-280.

Burnley, Ian H., 1993, "Migration and Mobility Issues in Australia and New Zealand", *New Zealand Population Review*, Vol. 19 (1&2), May/Nov. 1993, pp. 15-31.

Burnley, Ian H., 1996, "Relocation of Overseas-Born Populations in Sydney" in Newton, P.W. and Bell, M. (Eds.), *Population Shift. Mobility and Change in Australia*, Canberra, Australian Government Publication Service.

Busu, Luigi, 1886, "L'Emigrazione Italiana specialmente nelle nostre Province" *Il Telefono*, VI, No. 329, 28 November 1886.

Cabrini, Angelo, 1911, *Emigrazione ed emigranti*, Bologna, Zanichelli.

Caciagli, Giuseppe, 1992, *Storia della Lunigiana*, Pontedera, Arneva Edizioni.

Camaiani, Piergiorgio, 1979, *Dallo stato cittadino alla Citta' Bianca. La "Societa' Cristiana" Lucchese e la rivoluzione Toscana*, Firenze, La Nuova Italia.

Camera di Commercio, Industria, Artigianato e Agricoltura di Lucca (Ed.), 1993, *Ai Lucchesi che hanno onorato l'Italia nel Mondo. Speciale America*, Supplemento a *Lucca Economia,* April-May-June 1993, Lucca, S.Marco Litotipo.

Capra, Giuseppe, 1909, *Emigrati Italiani in Australasia,* Milano, Tipografia Salesiana.

Capra, Giuseppe, 1911, *L'Australia Occidentale. Studio illustrativo per gli italiani*, Milano, Salesiana.

Carpi, Leone, 1874, *Delle colonie e dell'emigrazione d'Italiani all'estero sotto l'aspetto dell'industria, commercio, agricoltura e con trattazione d'importanti questioni sociali*, 4 Vol., Milano, Tipografia Editoriale Lombarda.

Castles, Stephen, 1992, "The Australian Model of Immigration and Multiculturalism: is it Applicable to Europe ?", *International Migration Review*, XXVI (2), pp. 549-567.

Castles, Stephen & Vasta, Ellie, 1992, "L'emigrazione italiana in Australia", in Castles, Steven - Alcorso, Caroline - Rando, Gaetano & Vasta, Ellie (Eds), *Italo-australiani - Le popolazioni di origine italiana in Australia*, Torino, Fondazione Agnelli, pp. 97-120.

Cecilia, Tito, 1987, *We didn't arrive yesterday*, Red Cliffs, Scalabrinians.

Cerabolini, Fabio & Lucarno, Guido, 1996, "Indici di emigratorieta' dalle province d'Italia (1876-1915)" in Ceretti, Claudio (Ed.), *Genova, Colombo , il mare e l'Emigrazione Italiana nelle Americhe - Atti del XXVI Congresso Geografico Italiano, Genova, 4-9 Maggio 1992*, Roma, Istituto della Enciclopedia Italiana, pp. 238-252.

Cerase, Francesco, 1970, "Nostalgia or Disenchantment: Considerations on return Migration", in Tomasi, Silvano M. & Engel, Madeline H. (eds.), *The Italian Experience in the United States*, New York, Centre for Migration Studies, Inc., pp.217-239.

Cheda, Giorgio, 1979, *L'emigrazione ticinese in Australia*, Vol. II, Locarno, Dado'.

Cherubini, Bruno & Marcello (Eds.), 1977, *Bagni di Lucca fra cronaca e Storia,* Lucca, Maria Pacini Fazzi.

Cianferoni, Reginaldo - Ciuffoletti, Zeffiro & Clemente, Pietro, 1991, "Crisi della Mezzadria e Lotte contadine" in Ballini P. *et alii* (Eds.), 1991, *La Toscana nel secondo dopoguerra*, Milano, Angeli, pp. 195-231.

Ciano, Cesare, 1960, *Aspetti dell'organizzazione mercantile lucchese nell'Ottocento*, Lucca, Camera di Commercio, Industria ed Agricoltura.

Cinel, Dino, 1982, "Apprendistato per le migrazioni internazionali: le migrazioni interne in Italia nel secolo XIX", *Comunità*, No. 184, October 1982.

Cinel, Dino, 1987, *From Italy to San Francisco. The Immigration Experience*, Stanford, Stanford University Press.

Ciuffoletti, Zeffiro & Degli Innocenti, Maurizio (Eds.), 1978, *L'emigrazione nella storia d'Italia 1868/1975*, Firenze, Vallecchi (2 vol).

Clark, W.A.V., 1986, *Human Migration*, Beverly Hills, Sage Publications.

Comunità Montana della Lunigiana, 1990(a), *Lunigiana,* Aulla (Italy), Prisma.

Comunità Montana della Lunigiana, 1990(b), *Per terre assai lontane*, Sarzana, Comunita' Montana della Lunigiana.

Corsini, Carlo A., 1969, "Le migrazioni stagionali di lavoratori nei dipartimenti italiani del periodo Napoleonico (1810-12)", *Saggi di Demografia Storia*, Firenze, Dipartimento Statistico-Matematico, Universita' di Firenze, Serie Ricerche Empiriche No. 2, pp. 90-157.

Corte, P., 1898, *Il Continente Nuovissimo ossia l'Australasia Britannica*, Torino, Roux Frassati & co.

Corti, Paola, 1990, *Paesi d'emigranti: mestieri, itinerari, identità collettive*, Milano, Angeli.

Costanza, Salvatore, 1995, *Socialismo Emigrazione e Nazionalita' tra Italia e Australia,* Roma, Corrao Ed.

Cox, David - Martin, Jean J., 1978, *Welfare of Migrants*, Canberra, Australian Government Publishing Service.

Cresci, Paolo, 1986, *Il pane delle sette croste. Cento anni di emigrazione*, Lucca, Banca del Monte di Lucca.

Cresciani, Gianfranco, 1979, "Italian Anti-Fascism in Australia 1922-1945"in De Felice, Renzo (Ed*),* 1979*, Cenni storici sull'emigrazione italiana nelle Americhe e in Australia*, Milano, Angeli, pp. 143-163.

Cresciani, Gianfranco, 1980, *Fascism, Anti-Fascism and Italians in Australia 1922-1945*, Canberra, Australian National University.

Cresciani, Gianfranco, 1982, "I socialisti italiani in Australia" in Taddei, Francesca (Ed.), 1982, *L'Emigrazione socialista nella lotta contro il fascismo 1926-1939*, Firenze, Sansoni, pp. 293-303.

Cresciani, Gianfranco (Ed.), 1983, *Australia, the Australians and the Italian Migration*, Milano, Angeli.

Cresciani, Gianfranco, 1987, "Appunti per una Storia degli Italiani in Australia", *Il Veltro*, XXXI(1-2), Jan-April 1987, pp. 191-201.

Cronin, Constance, 1970, *The Sting of Change. Sicilians in Sicily and Australia*, Chicago and London, The University of Chicago Press.

Dada', Adriana, 1993 (a), "Emigrazione e Storiografia. Primi risultati di una ricerca sulla Toscana", *Italia Contemporanea*, n. 192, September 1993, pp. 486-502.

Dada', Adriana, 1993 (b), "Dalla Lunigiana alla 'Barsana'. Il processo di trasformazione da lavoratori agricoli stagionali in venditori ambulanti specializzati", *Sides - Bollettino di Demografia Storica*, No. 10, pp. 111-133.

Dada', Adriana, 1994, "Lavoratori dell'Appennino Toscano in Corsica nel secolo XIX" in *Altre Italie*, n.12, pp. 6-38.

D'Aprano, Charles, 1995, *From Goldrush to Federation. Italian Pioneers in Victoria: 1850-1900*, Pascoe Vale South (Vic), International Press.

Dawkins, Peter - Lewis, Philip *et alii*, 1991, *Flows of Immigrants to South Australia, Tasmania and Western Australia*, Canberra, Australian Government Publishing Service.

De Felice, Renzo, 1964, "L'emigrazione e gli emigranti nell'ultimo secolo", *Terzo Programma*, 1964 (3), pp. 152-198.

De Stefani, Carlo, 1977, "Proprietà comuni nell'Appennino della Garfagnana" in Guidetti, Massimo & Stahl, P.H. (Eds.), 1977, *Un'Italia sconosciuta. Comunità di villaggio e comunità familiari nell'Italia dell' 800,* Milano, Jaca Books, pp. 239-255.

Devoto, Fernando, 1991, *Estudios sobre le emigracion italiana en la Argentina*, Buenos Aires, Biblos.

Dibueno, Caterina, 1999*, Sulle tracce dei toscani in Uruguay. Tras las huellas de los Toscanos en Uruguay,* Aulla (Italy), Comunita' Montana della Lunigiana - centro di Documentazione dell'Emigrazione Lunigianese.

Distretto Scolastico della Garfagnana - Regione Toscana - Amministrazione Provinciale di Lucca - Comune di Pieve Fosciana - Comunità Montana della Garfagnana, 1984, *La Garfagnana 1883-1983. Aspetti economici, agricoli, urbanistici e socio-culturali,* Vol. 2, Castelnuovo Garfagnana (Italy), Ed. Ciapetti.

Dottori, Marcel, 1988, "L'emigration Toscane a Marseille dans la premièr moitié du XX siècle", in Temine, E. and Vertone, T. (Eds.), *Gli Italiani nella Francia del Sud e in Corsica (1860-1980),* Milano, Franco Angeli, pp. 168-178.

Douglass, William A., 1995, *From Italy to Ingham*, St.Lucia, University of Queensland Press.

Douki, Caroline, 1993, "Gli Italiani in Francia, 1938-1946 - Convegno", *Altre Italie*, No. 10. July-December 1993, pp. 89-91.

Douki, Caroline, 1993 (b), 'L'emigration toscane de 1806 à 1914: rythmes et flux', *Studi Emigrazione/Ètudes Migrations*, XXX(109), pp. 29-47.

Douki, Caroline, 1994, "Les maires de l'Italie liberale à l'epreuve de l'emigration: le cas des campagnes lucquoises", *Mélanges de l'Ecole Française de Rome* - MEFRIM, Tome 106 - 1 (1994), pp. 333-364.

Dubost, Jean-François, 1997, *La France italienne. XVIe-XVII siècle*, (no place of publication, France), Aubier.

Fabbri, Giulio, 1975, "Ricerche sul movimento eremitico in Italia. L'eremitismo irregolare in Garfagnana nel secolo XVIII", in *Rivista di Storia della Chiesa in Italia*, XXIX, 1975, pp. 12-49.

Fabiano, Domenico, 1983, "I Fasci italiani all'estero", in Bezza, B. (Ed.), 1983, *Gli Italiani fuori d'Italia : gli emigrati italiani nei movimenti operai dei paesi d'adozione 1880-1940*, Milano, Franco Angeli.

Farnocchia, Franca, 1981, "Italiani in Canada: il caso di Montreal", *Bollettino della Societa' Geografica Italiana*, CXIV, 1981, pp. 543-573.

Farnocchia Petri, Franca, 1995, *Risorse e Popolazione. Settant'Anni di Emigrazione dalla Garfagnana e Media Valle del Serchio: 1921-1991*, Lucca, Accademia Lucchese di Scienze, Lettere ed Arti.

Favero, Luigi & Tassello, Graziano, 1983, "Caratteristiche demografiche e sociali della Comunità Italiana in Australia e della seconda generazione", in *Studi Emigrazione/Ètudes Migrations*, XX(69), 1983, pp. 58-80.

Fitzgerald, Alan, 1981, *The Italian farming soldiers. Prisoners of War in Australia 1941-47*, Carlton (Vic), Melbourne University Press.

Foerster, Robert F., 1924, *The Italian Emigration of Our Times*, Cambridge, Cambridge University Press.

Forrest, James and Johnston, Ron, 1999, "Disadvantage, Discrimination and the Occupational Differentiation of Migrants Groups in Australia", *International Journal of Population Geography*, 5, (1999), pp. 277-296.

Foschi, Franco, 1988, *Cento anni fa, l'emigrazione italiana*, Roma, Bulzoni Editore.

Franzina, Emilio, 1976, *La grande emigrazione. L'esodo dei rurali dal Veneto durante il secolo* XIX, Venezia, Marsilio.

Franzina, Emilio, 1988, "Emigrazione transoceanica e ricerca storica in Italia: gli ultimi dieci anni (1978-1988)", *Altreitalie*, 1, pp. 5-56 (*now on http://www.fga.it/altreitalie/1_saggi1a.htm*).

Franzina, Emilio, 1991, *Storia dell'emigrazione veneta. Dall'Unita' al Fascismo*, Verona, Cierre Edizioni.

Franzina, Emilio, 1992, *L'immaginario degli Emigranti. Miti e raffigurazioni dell'esperienza italiana all'estero tra i due secoli*, Paese (Italy), Pegus Edizioni.

Frediani, Giuseppe, 1978, "Aspetti e caratteristiche agricolo-bancarie dell'emigrazione tosco-lucchese-ligure in America", in Assante, Franca, (Ed.*), Il movimento migratorio italiano dall'unita' nazionale ai giorni nostri*, Génevè, Libraire Droz, pp. 287-289.

Gabaccia, Donna, 1994, "Worker internationalism and Italian labor migration", 1870-1914", *International Labor and Working-Class History*, 45 (Spring), pp. 63-79.

Gabaccia, Donna, 1997 (a), "The 'Yellow Peril' and the 'Chinese of Europe'. Global Perspectives on Race and Labor, 1815-1930", in Lucassen, Jean & Luc (Eds.), *Migration, Migration History and History. Old Paradigms and New Perspectives*, Bern, Peter Lang, pp. 177-196.

Gabaccia, Donna, 1997 (b), "Per una storia dell'emigrazione", *Altreitalie*, No.16 (July-December 1997) (on http://www.italians-world.org/altreitalie/16_saggi1a.htm).

Gagliardi, Ferdinando, 1881, *Australia. Lettere alla Gazzetta d'Italia*, Firenze, Tipografia Editrice della Gazzetta d'Italia.

Galvin, J., 1985, "The residential mobility and integration of the Lettesi Italian community in Newcastle, New South Wales", in Burnley, Ian H. - S.Encel & Grant McCall (Eds.), *Immigration and Ethnicity in the 1980s*,' Melbourne, Longman Cheshire, pp. 211-230.

Gamba, Charles, 1952, *The Italian Fishermen of Fremantle*, Nedlands, UWA Text Book Board.

Gardini, A., 1993, "Reclaiming the Town", in *The First Conference on the impact of Italians in South Australia*, 16-17 July 1993, Adelaide, Flinders Univesity of South Australia, pp. 135-151.

Gentileschi, Mario L. - Simoncelli, R. (Eds.), 1983, *Rientro degli Emigrati e Territorio,* Napoli, Istituto Grafico Italiano.

Gentilli, Joseph, 1982, "Italian Migration to Western Australia 1829-1946", *Geowest*, No. 19, December 1982, pp. 9-35.

Gentilli, Joseph, 1983, *Italian Roots in Australian Soil*, Marangaroo, Italo-Australian Welfare and Cultural Centre.

Gentilli, Joseph, 1984, 'I Pescatori Italiani nell'Australia Occidentale: mito e realtà', *Studi Emigrazione/Ètudes Migrations*, XXI (74), 1984, pp. 219-240.

Gentilli, Joseph, 1993, 'Gli Italiani nell'Australia Occidentale: una comunità isolata in fase di invecchiamento, *Studi Emigrazione/ Ètudes Migrations*, XXX (109), 1993, pp. 2-27.

Gestri, Lorenzo, 1976, *Capitalismo e classe operaia in provincia di Massa Carrara*, Firenze, Leo Olschki Editore.

Gillgren, Christina., 1997, "Boundaries of Exclusion: a Study of Italian and Croatian Immigrants in the Western Australian Timber Industry 1920-1940", in *Limina*, 3, pp. 71-82.

Gramsci, Antonio, 1975, *Quaderni del carcere* (4 vol.), Torino, Giulio Einaudi Editore.

Grieco, Margaret, 1987, *Keeping it in the Family. Social Networks and Employment chance*, London, Tavistock Publications.

Grigg, D.B., 1977, "E.G.Ravenstein and the 'Laws of migration'", *Journal of Historical Geography*, 3, 1(1997), pp. 41-54.

Gucciardo, Tonina & Bertelli, Lidio, 1987, *The best of both worlds. A study of second generation Italo-Australians*, North Fitzroy, Catholic Intercultural Resource Centre Papers.

Harney, Robert F. & Scarpaci, J.Vincenza (Eds.), 1981, *Little Italies in North America,* Toronto, Multicultural Historical Society of Ontario.

Harney, Robert F., 1981, "Toronto's Little Italy, 1885-1945", in Harney, Robert F. & Scarpaci, J.Vincenza (Eds.), 1981, *Little Italies in North America,* Toronto, Multicultural Historical Society of Ontario, pp. 41-62.

Harney, Robert F., 1985, "Italophobia: English speaking malady", in *Studi Emigrazione/Etudes Migrations*, XXII (77), March 1985, pp. 6-43.

Harney, Robert, 1991, "Undoing the Risorgimento: emigrants from Italy and the politics of regionalism", *Annali Accademici Canadesi*, II, 1991, pp. 49-72.

Heiss, J., 1964, 'The Italians of Perth', *Westerly*, 1, March 1964, pp. 67-69.

Heiss, J., 1966, 'Residential Segregation and the Assimilation of Italians in an Australian City', *International Migration*, Vol. IV (4), 1966, pp. 165-171.

Hempel, J.A., 1959, *Italians in Queensland*, Canberra, Australian National University- Department of Demography.

Hoerder Dick, 1991, "Segmented Macrosystems and Networking Individuals: the balancing Functions of Migration Processes", in Lucassen, Jean & Luc (Eds.), *Migration, Migration History and History. Old Paradigms and New Perspectives*, Bern, Peter Lang, pp. 73-84.

Huber, Rina, 1977, *From Pasta to Pavlova*, St.Lucia, University of Queensland Press.

Hugo, Graeme, 1994, "Demographic and spatial aspects of immigration", in Wooden, Mark - Holton, Robert - Hugo, Graeme & Sloan, Judith (Eds.*), Australian Immigration. A Survey of the Issues*, Canberra, Australian Government Publication Service, pp. 30-110.

Hugo, Graeme, 1996 (a), *Atlas of the Australian People. 1991 Census. Western Australia*, Canberra, Australian Government Publishing Service.

Hugo, Graeme, 1996 (b), "Diversity Down Under: The Changing Ethnic Mosaic of Sydney and Melbourne", in Roseman, Curtis J. – Laux, Hans Dieter & Thieme, Guenther (Eds.), 1996, *EthniCity. Geographic Perspectives on Ethnic Change in Modern Cities*, London, Rowman & Littlefield Publishers, Inc., pag. 51-76.

Iacovino, Livia, 1983, *Legislative and Administrative Requirements in relation to Italian Migration to Australia during the Inter-War Years*, Carlton (Vic.), Italian Historical Society.

Inglis, Christine, 1975, "Some recent Australian writing on Immigration and Assimilation", in *International Migration Review,* IX, No. 3 (Fall), 1975, pp. 335-344.

Iorizzo, Luciano, 1980, *Italian Immigration and the Impact of the Padrone System*, New York, Arno Press.

Istituto Nazionale di Economia Agraria, 1938, *Monografie di famiglie agricole. Contadini della Montagna Toscana (Garfagnana, Pistoiese, Romagna Toscana),* Roma, Osservatorio di Economia Agraria per la Toscana.

Jakle, John A., Brunn, Stanley and Roseman, Curtis C., 1976, *Human Spatial Behavior. A Social Geography*, North Scituate (USA), Duxbury Press.

Jannon, Giorgio, 1996, *Oltre gli Oceani. Storia dell'emigrazione piemontese in Australia*, Torino, Paravia.

Johnston, Ruth (Ed.), 1979, *Immigrants in Western Australia*, Nedlands, University of Western Australia Press.

Jones Lancaster, F., 1964, 'The Territorial composition of Italian emigration to Australia 1876 to 1962', *International Migration*, Vol. II, 1964, pp. 247-265.

Jupp, James, 1966, *Arrivals and Departures*, Melbourne, Lawnsdone Press Pty.

Jupp, James, 1991, *Immigration*, Sydney, Sydney University Press.

Jupp, James, 1993, "The ethnic lobby and immigration policy", in Jupp, James and Kabala, Mria (Eds.), *The Politics of Australian Immigration*, Canberra, Australian Government Publication Service, pp. 204-221.

Karragullen Primary School & Pagotto, Barbara (Eds.), 1988, *Over new Bridges. The Story of the Italian Migration to Karragullen,* Karragullen (W.A.), Karragullen Primary School.

Keast, Jenny, 1987, *Valleys of Solitude - Italian Settlers of the Kalamunda District 1890-1945*, Kalamunda (W.A.), Kalamunda & Districts School Society.

Kertzer, David I., 1984, *Family Life in Central Italy, 1880-1910. Sharecropping, Wage Labor, and Coresidence*, New Brunswick (USA), Rutgers University Press.

Lampugnani, Rosario, 1987, "Postwar Migration Policies with Particular Reference to Italian Migration to Australia", in *The Australian Journal of Politics and History*, Vol. 33 (3), 1987, pp. 197-208.

Lazzareschi, Emilio, 1934, "I figurinai della Lucchesia", *La Nazione*, 22 August 1934.

Le Roy Ladurie, Emmanuel, 1974, *The Peasants of Languedoc*, Chicago, University of Illinois Press.

Lee, E., 1966, "A Theory of Migration", *Demography*, III, 1966, pp. 47-67.

Lee, Trevor R., 1970, "The Role of the Ethnic Community as a Reception Area for Italian Immigrants in Melbourne Australia", *International Migration*, VIII (1/2), 1970, pp. 50-63.

Lera, Maria, 1986, *Gipskatter.Gatti di gesso*, Lucca, Maria Pacini Fazzi Editore.

Livi-Bacci, Massimo, 1977, *A History of Italian Fertility during the last Two Centuries*, Princeton (NJ), Princeton University Press.

Lombardi-Lotti, Mansueto, 1979, *Fatti e figure di storia lucchese*, Lucca, Maria Pacini Fazzi Editore.

Longton, Adelma, 1997, "Wiluna in the Thirties: the Italian presence. A case study", *Studi Emigrazione/Ètudes Migrations*, XXXIV (125), pp. 123-137.

Lopez, Renee & Temime, Emile, 1990, *L'expansion marseillaise et "l'invasion italienne (1830-1918)",* Aix-en-Provence, Edisud.

Losacco, Michele, 1931, *La Garfagnana ne' suoi aspetti generali ed in rapporto all'emigrazione*, Gubbio, Scuola Tipografica Oderisi.

Lucassen, Jan, 1987, *Migrant Labour in Europe 1600-1900*, London, Croom Helm.

Lucassen, Leo, 1997, "Eternal Vagrants? State Formation, Migration and Travelling Groups in Western Europe, 1350-1914", in Lucassen, Jean & Luc (Eds.), *Migration, Migration History and History. Old Paradigms and New Perspectives*, Bern, Peter Lang, pp. 225-251.

Lucassen, Jean and Luc, 1997, "Migration, Migration History, History: Old Paradigms and New Perspectives" in Lucassen, Jean & Luc (Eds.), *Migration, Migration History and History. Old Paradigms and New Perspectives*, Bern, Peter Lang, pp. 9-38.

Lucchesi, Flavio, 1988, "La scoperta del mondo socio-politico australiano: le riviste geografiche italiane (1861-1914)", in Lucchesi, Flavio (Ed.), *Orizzonte Australia. Percezione e realtà di un continente*, Milano, Unicopli, pp. 189-260.

Lukomskyi, Oleh & Richard, Peter, 1986, "Return Migration from Australia. A Case Study", in *International Migration*, XXIV (3), September 1986, pp. 603-629.

Lyng, Jens, 1927, *Non-Britishers in Australia. Influence on Population and Progress,* Melbourne, Macmillan & Co.

Macdonald, J.S., 1956, "Italy's rural social Structure and Emigration", *Occidente*, XII, No. 5, September-October 1956, pp. 437-456.

Macdonald, J.S. and Leatrice, 1970, "Migration from Italy to Australia: Conflict between Manifest Functions of Bureaucracy Versus Latent Functions of Informal Networks", in *Journal of Social History*, III (3), Spring 1970, pp. 249-276.

Madge, John, 1965, *The Tools of Social Science. An Analytical Description of Social Science Techniques*, Garden City (NY), Doubleday & Co.

Mammarella, G., 1966, *Italy after Fascism 1943-1965,* Notre Dame (Indiana), University of Notre Dame Press.

Manselli, Raul, 1986, *La Repubblica di Lucca*, Torino, Utet.

Marletta, Cesare, 1996, "Pionieri Italiani. Presenza italiana nel Queensland dell' 800", *Affari Sociali Internazionali*, XXIV (2), 1996, pp. 165-190.

Martellini, Amoreno, 1999, *Fra Sunny Side e la Nueva Marca. Materiali e modelli per una storia dell'emigrazione marchigiana fino alla grande guerra*, Milano (Italy), Franco Angeli.

Martellini, Amoreno, 2000, *I candidati al milione. Circoli affaristici ed emigrazione d'élite in America Latina alla fine del XIX secolo*, Roma, Edizioni Lavoro.

Martin, Jean, 1976, *A Decade of Migrant Settlement*, Canberra, Australian Government Publishing Service.

Martinuzzi O'Brien, Irma, 1982, *Australia's Italians*, Carlton (Vic), The Italian Historical Society & The State Library of Victoria.

Massara, Giuseppe, 1976, *Viaggiatori italiani in America (1860-1970)*, Roma, Edizioni di Storia e Letteratura.

Massey, Douglass - Arango, Joaquin - Hugo, Graeme - Kovaouci, Ali - Pellegrino, Adela and Taylor, J.Edward (Eds.), 1993, "Theories of International Migration: a Review and Appraisal" *International Migration Review*, 19(3), September 1993, pp. 431-466.

Meek, Christine, 1994, "Public Policy and Private Profit: Tax Farming in Fourteenth Century Lucca" in Blomquist, Thomas W. & Mazzaoui, Maureen F. (Eds.), 1994, *The Other Tuscany. Essays in the History of Lucca, Pisa and Siena during the Thirteenth, Fourteenth and Fifteenth Century*, Medieval Institute Publications, Western Michigan University, pp. 41-69.

Messina, Nunzia, 1976, "L'emigrazione italiana in Australasia (1876-79)", *Studi Emigrazione/Ètudes Migrations*, XII (41), March 1976, pp. 102-118.

Michelson, William, 1977, *Environmental Choice, Human Behaviour and Residential Satisfaction*, New York, Oxford University Press.

Michieli, Adriano Augusto, 1935, "Un tragico episodio della nostra emigrazione. La spedizione del Marchese De Rays", *Rassegna Italiana* (Estratto), Gennaio 1935, Roma, Edizione della Rassegna Italiana.

Migliazza, Alessandro, 1983, "Il Problema dell'Emigrazione e la Legislazione Italiana sino alla seconda guerra mondiale" in Bezza, B., 1983, *Gli Italiani fuori d'Italia : gli emigrati italiani nei movimenti operai dei paesi d'adozione 1880-1940*, Milano, Franco Angeli.

Mirola, Gian, 1974, "L'emigrazione in Garfagnana", *La Provincia di Lucca- Periodico di informazione e attualita' edito dall'Amministrazione Provinciale*- Supplemento 1974.

Miserocchi, Mario, 1937, *Australia continente minorenne,* Milano, Garzanti.

Missori, Mario, 1973, "Le condizioni degli emigranti alla fine del XIX secolo in alcuni documenti delle autorità marittime", in *Affari Sociali Internazionali,* No. 3, 1973, pp. 93-133.

Moch-Page, Leslie, 1997, "Dividing Time: An Analytical Framework for Migration History Periodization", in Lucassen, Jean and Luc (Eds.), *Migration, Migration History and History. Old Paradigms and New Perspectives*, Bern, Peter Lang, pp. 41-56.

Mola', Luca, 1994, *La Comunita' dei Lucchesi a Venezia. Immigrazione e industria della seta nel Tardo medioevo*, Venezia, Istituto Veneto di Scienze, Lettere ed Arti.

Monterisi, Maria Teresa, 1993, Migracion internacional y expansion comercial: el caso de los emigrados 'lucchesi' en Cordoba 1880-1914, *Revista de Economia*, XLIV, 69 (Abril-Junio), pp. 135-173.

Moon, Bruce, 1995, "Paradigms in migration research: exploring 'moorings' as a scheme", *Progress in Human Geography*, 19(4), 1995, pp. 504-524.

Mori, Attilio, 1910, "L'emigrazione toscana dalla Toscana e particolarmente dal Casentino", in *Bollettino Emigrazione,* IX (12), 1910, pp. 3-80.

Mori, Giorgio (Ed), 1986, *La Toscana*, Torino, Einaudi.

Moser, Claus Adolf, 1985 (2nd Edition), *Survey Methods in Social Investigation*, London, Haldershots and Hands.

Murphy, Brian, 1993, *The Other Australia. Experiences of Migration*, Cambridge, Cambridge University Press.

Nardini, Gloria, 1999, *Che Bella Figura! The Power of Performance in an Italian Ladies's Club in Chicago*, Albany (USA), State University of New York Press.

Nascimbene, Mario C., 1987, "Origini e destinazioni degli italiani in Argentina (1835-1970)", in Korn, Francis (ed.), *La popolazione di origine italiana in Argentina*, Vol. II, Torino, Edizioni della Fondazione Giovanni Agnelli, pp. 69-91.

Nelli, Humbert S., 1970, "Italians in Urban America", in Tomasi, Silvano M. & Engel, Madeline H. (eds.), *The Italian Experience in the United States*, New York, Centre for Migration Studies, Inc., pp. 77-107.

Niccolai, Roberto & Beneforti, Barbara, 1998, *E tutti va in Francia, in Francia per lavorare*, Campi Bisenzio, Nuova Toscana Editrice.

Nobile, Annunziata, 1974, "Politica migratoria e vicende dell'emigrazione durante il fascismo", *Il Ponte*, XXX, No. 11-12, Nov-Dec. 1974, pp. 1322-1341.

O'Connor, Desmond, 1994, "A Change of Image: the Impact of Italy on Young Second-Generation Italians in South Australia" in *Studi Emigrazione/Ètudes Migrations*, XXXI (114), June 1994, pp. 269-283.

O'Connor, Desmond., 1996, *No need to be afraid - Italian settlers in South Australia between 1839 and the Second World War,* Kent Town, S.A.

Ottolenghi, Costantino, 1894, *L'emigrazione agricola italiana dal 1884 al 1892*, Torino, Carlo Clausen.

Pacchi, Domenico, 1967, *Ricerche storiche sulla Provincia della Garfagnana*, Bologna, Forni Editore.

Packer, D.R.G., 1947, *Italian Immigration into Australia*, Melbourne, University of Melbourne, MA Thesis (unpublished).

Paganoni, Antonio & O'Connor, Desmond, 1999, *Se la processione va bene...Religiosita' popolare italiana nel Sud Australia*, Roma, Centro Studi Emigrazione.

Panucci, Frank - Kelly, Bernadette and Castles, Stephen (Eds.), 1992, "Il contributo italiano alla costruzione dell'Australia", Castles, Steven - Alcorso, Caroline - Rando, Gaetano & Vasta, Ellie (Eds), *Italo-australiani - Le popolazioni di origine italiana in Australia*, Torino, Fondazione Agnelli, pp. 153-172.

Paoli Gumina, Deanna, 1978, *The Italians of San Francisco 1850-1930,* New York, Centre for Migration Studies.

Paradisi, Maria Virginia, 1993, "Emigrazione e assistenza: la Pia Casa di beneficienza di Lucca in aiuto ai minori divenuti orfani o abbandonati a causa dell'emigrazione negli ultimi 20 anni dell'Ottocento", in *Documenti e Studi,* No. 14/15, 1993, pp. 293-334.

Paris, Renzo, 1975, "L'Italia fuori d'Italia", in *Storia d'Italia*, vol. IV/1, Torino, Einaudi, pp. 507-818.

Pascal, Arturo, 1935, "Da Lucca Ginevra", *Rivista Storica Italiana*, Vol. 52 (4), 1935, pp. 253-316.

Pascoe, Robert, 1987, *Buongiorno Italia. Our Italian Heritage*, Richmond (Vic), Greenhouse Publications.

Pascoe, Robert, 1992, "Luogo e comunita': la costruzione di uno spazio italo-australiano", in Castles, Steven - Alcorso, Caroline - Rando, Gaetano & Vasta, Ellie (Eds), *Italo-australiani - Le popolazioni di origine italiana in Australia*, Torino, Fondazione Agnelli, pp. 173-187.

Pascoe, Robert, 1993, "The Immigrant Sense of Place", in Rando, Gaetano & Arrighi, Michael (Eds.), 1993, *Italians in Australia. Historical and Social Perspectives*, Wollongong, University of Wollongong, pp. 155-159.

Pascoe, Robert & Bertola, Patrick, 1985, "Italian Miners and the Second Generation Britishers at Kalgoorlie, Australia", in *Social History*, Vol. 10, 1985, pp. 9-35.

Pascoli, Giovanni, 1960, *Lettere agli amici lucchesi,* Firenze, Le Monnier.

Pasolini, Pier Paolo, 1976, *Le Poesie*, Milano, Garzanti.

Pasquali, A., 1922, *Cenni sull'emigrazione rurale in Italia con particolare riferimento alla Toscana,* Pisa, Esperienze e ricerche della Regia Università di Pisa.

Pecout, Gilles, 1990, "Dalla Toscana alla Provenza: emigrazione e politicizzazione nelle campagne (1880-1910)", *Studi Storici*, Vol. 3 (July-September 1990), pp. 723-738.

Pesman, Roslyn, 1984, "I visitatori australiani in Italia nel XIX secolo", in Cresciani, Gianfranco (Ed.), 1984, *L'Australia, gli Australiani e le migrazioni Italiane*, Milano, Angeli, pp. 141-158.

Pesman Cooper, Roslyn, 1993, "Italian Views of Australia in the First Half of the Twentieth century", in Rando, Gaetano - Arrighi, Michael (Eds.), 1993, *Italians in Australia. Historical and Social Perspectives*, Wollongong, University of Wollongong.

Piovene, Guido, 1993, *Viaggio in Italia*, Milano, Baldini & Castoldi.

Piselli, Fortunata, 1997, "Il network sociale nell'analisi dei movimenti migratori", *Studi Emigrazione/Ètudes Migrations*, XXXIV (125), Marzo 1997, pp. 2-16.

Pizzorusso, Giovanni, 1990, "I fenomeni migratori a lungo raggio in Italia dal XV al XVIII secolo: un percorso storiografico", *Bollettino di Demografia Storica*, N. 12 (1990), pp. 45-54.

Pizzorusso, Giovanni, 1992, "Dal viaggiatore all'emigrante: mestieri italiani nelle Americhe 1492-1876", in *Il Veltro*, XXXVI (1-2), 1992, pp. 9-34.

Pizzorusso, Giovanni and Sanfilippo, Matteo, 1990, "Rassegna storiografica sui fenomeni migratori a lungo raggio in Italia dal basso medioevo al secondo dopoguerra", *Bollettino di Demografia Storica*, N. 13 (1990), pp. 9-181.

Pomponi, François, 1988, "Le Lucchesi en Corse" in Temine, E. - Vertone, T. (Eds.), *Gli Italiani nella Francia del Sud e in Corsica 1860-1980*, Milano, Angeli.

Porter, John, 1965, *The Vertical Mosaic. An Analysis of Social Class and Power in Canada*, Toronto, University of Toronto Press.

Portes, Alejandro & Borocz, Jozsef, "Contemporary Immigration: Theoretical Perspectives on Its Determinants and Models of Incorporation", *International Migration Review*, XXIII (3), pp. 606-630.

Pozzetta, George E. & Ramirez, Bruno. (Eds), 1992, *The Italian Diaspora. Migration Accross the Globe*, Toronto, Multicultural Historical Society of Ontario.

Prezzolini, Giovanni, 1963, *I trapiantati*, Milano, Longanesi.

Price, Charles A., 1963 (a), *Southern Europeans in Australia*, Melbourne, Oxford University Press.

Price, Charles A. & Martin, Jean J., 1976, *Australian Immigration. A Bibliography and Digest*, 2 Vol., Canberra, Department of Demography, Australian National University.

Pulvirenti, Mariastella, 1997, "Unwrapping the Parcel: an Examination of Culture Through Italian Australian Home Ownership", in *Australian Geographical Studies*, 35 (11), April 1997, pp. 32-39.

Pyke, N.O., 1948, An Outline History of Italian Migration into Australia", *The Australian Quarterly*, XX, (3), 1948, pp. 99-109.

Raffaelli, Raffaello, 1977, *Descrizione geografica storica economica della Garfagnana*, Milano, Insubria.

Ragionieri, Ernesto, 1962, "Italiani all'estero ed emigrazione di lavoratori italiani. Un tema di storia del movimento operaio", *Belfagor*, 2, XVII, 1962, pp. 639-669.

Ramella, Franco, 1991, "Emigration from an Area of Intense Industrial Development: the case of Northwestern Italy", in Vecoli,

Rudolph & Sinke, Suzanne M. (Eds.*), A Century of European Migration, 1830-1930*, Champaign, University of Illinois Press, pp. 261-274.

Rando, Gaetano, 1992, "Italians in Australia: Assimilation, Integration, Multiculturalism", in Pozzetta, George E. & Ramirez, D. (Eds), 1992, *The Italian Diaspora. Migration Across the Globe*, Toronto, Multicultural Historical Society of Ontario, pp. 51-68.

Rapetti, Caterina, 1986, *Archivi familiari. Storie, volti e documenti dell'emigrazione lunigianese*, Firenze, Nuova Grafica Fiorentina.

Regione Toscana, 1985, *La Toscana e i suoi comuni*, Firenze, Edizioni La Mandragora.

Repetti, Emanuele, 1835, *Dizionario Geografico fisico storico della Toscana* (6 vol.), Firenze, Presso l'Autore e Editore.

Romano, Ruggiero, "The Long Journey of Italian Emigration", in Tomasi, Lydio F. - Gastaldo, Piero & Row, Thomas (Eds.), 1994, *The Columbus People. Perspective in Italian Immigration to the Americas and Australia*, New York, Center for Migration Studies - Fondazione Giovanni Agnelli, pp. 1-14.

Rombai, Leonardo, 1988, "Paesaggio e territorio nella Toscana moderna e contemporanea: una traccia di storia dell'organizzazione territoriale", in Corsini, C.A.(Ed.), 1988, *Vita, morte e miracoli di gente comune: appunti per una storia della popolazione della Toscana fra XIV e XX secolo*, Firenze, Usher, pp. 15-36.

Rosoli, Gianfranco (Ed.), 1978, *Un secolo di emigrazione italiana: 1876-1976*, Roma, Centro Studi Emigrazione.

Rosoli, Gianfranco, 1984, "Il cattolicesimo e la questione dell'emigrazione", in Cresciani, Gianfranco (Ed.), 1984, *L'Australia, gli Australiani e le migrazioni Italiane*, Milano, Angeli.

Rosoli, Gianfranco, 1990, "L'immaginario dell'America nell'emigrazione italiana di massa", *Bollettino di Demografia Storica*, N. 12 (1990), pp. 189-208.

Rosoli, Gianfranco, 1992, "Un quadro globale della diaspora italiana nelle Americhe", *Altreitalie*, 10, July-December 1992 (now on http://www.fga.it/altreitalie/8_saggi.htm), pp. 1-16.

Rosoli, Gianfausto, 1993, "L'emigrazione italiana nel Rio Grande do Sul, Brasile meridionale", *Altreitalie*, 10, July-December 1993, pp. 5-24.

Rosoli, Gianfausto, 1994, "Il cattolicesimo e la questione dell'emigrazione", in Cresciani, Gianfranco (Ed.), *L'Australia, gli Australiani e le migrazioni Italiane*, Milano, Angeli.

Rother, Klaus, 1989, "Gli Italiani del Murray (Australia*)", Bollettino della Societa' Geografica Italiana*, CXXII(6), 1989, pp. 401-422.

Rovai, Davide, 1993, *Lucchesia, terra di emigrazione. Tracce per una storia dell'emigrazione lucchese attraverso i secoli*, Lucca, Mara Pacini Fazzi.

Rovai, Davide, 1998*, Profilo dell'emigrazione lucchese. Memorie, Diari, Lettere di Emigrati un secolo fa*, Lucca, Arte della Stampa.

Ruberti, Alessandra, 1993, "Le tipologie dell'Italiano all'estero", *Affari Sociali Internazionali*, XXI (4), 1993, pp. 5-33.

Samminiatelli, Donato, 1912, *Sull'emigrazione rurale specialmente nella Toscana*, Firenze, Atti della Reale Accademia dei Georgofili, Quinta Serie, Vol. IX, pp.216-269.

Sardi, Cesare, 1912, *Lucca e il suo Ducato dal 1814 al 1859*, Bologna, Forni.

Sarti, Roland, 1985, *'Long Live the Strong' : A History of Rural Society in the Apennine Mountains*, Amherst (USA), University of Massachusetts.

Sarup, Madan, 1994, "Home and identity", in Robertson, George et al. (Eds*), Travellers' Tales. Narratives of home and displacement*, London & New York, Routledge, pp.93-104.

Savona, Alberto V. & Straniero, Michele, 1976, *Canti dell'emigrazione*, Milano, Garzanti.

Schiller, Nina Glick – Basch, Linda & Balnc-Szanton, 1992, "Toward a Definition of Transnationalism. Introductory remarks and Research Questions", and "Transnationalism: A New Analytic Framework for Understanding Migration", in Schiller, Nina Glick – Basch, Linda & Balnc-Szanton (Eds.), *Towards a Transnational Perspective on Migration. Race, Class, Ethnicity, and Nationalism Reconsidered*, New York, The New York Academy of Sciences, (respectively), pp. ix-xv; pp. 1-24.

Sensi-Isolani, Paola A., 1993, "Tradition and Transition in a California Paese", in Sensi-Isolani, Paola A. & Cancilla Martinelli, Phylis (eds.*), Struggle and Success. An Anthology of the Italian Immigrant Experience in California*, New York, Center for migration Studies, pp. 58-75.

Sereni, Bruno, 1980, *Pagine di Storia Fornacina*, Barga, Edizioni Il Giornale di Barga.

Silvey, Rachel and Lawson, Victoria, 1999, "Placing the Migrant", *Annals of the Associations of American Geographers*, 89(1), 1999, pp. 121-132.

Smolicz, Jerzy J., 1983, "Modification and maintenance of Italian Culture among Italian-Australian Youth", *Studi Emigrazione/ Ètudes Migrations*, XX (69), pp. 81-104.

Smolicz, Jerzy J., 1993, "Is Italian language a core value of Italian culture in Australia? A Study of second generation Italian-Australians", *Studi Emigrazione/Ètudes Migrations*, XXX(110), pp. 311-342.

Smolicz, Jerzy J. & Secombe, M.J., 1985, "The Australian school through Polish eyes: a sociological study of student attitudes from their own memoirs", in Burnley, Ian H., S.Encel and Grant McCall (Eds.), *Immigration and Ethnicity in the 1980s'*, Melbourne, Longman Cheshire, pp. 119-142.

Societa' Geografica Italiana, 1890, *Indagini sull'emigrazione italiana all'estero (1888-1889)*, Roma, Societa' Geografica Italiana.

Sori, Ercole, 1979, *L'emigrazione italiana dall'Unità alla Seconda guerra mondiale*, Bologna, Il Mulino.

Sori, Ercole, 1983, "Il dibattito politico sull'emigrazione italiana dall'Unità alla crisi dello stato liberale", in Bezza, B., 1983, *Gli Italiani fuori d'Italia : gli emigrati italiani nei movimenti operai dei paesi d'adozione 1880-1940*, Milano, Franco Angeli, pp. 19-43.

Spedicato, Elide, 1988, "Internati al bosco. Autobiografia di emigranti abruzzesi in Australia", in Schino, Francesco (Ed.), 1988, *Cultura nazionale, cultura regionale, comunità italiana all'estero*, Roma, Istituto dell'Enciclopedia Italiana, pp. 209-218.

Sponza, Lucio, 1988, *Italian Immigrants in Nineteenth Century Britain: realities and Images*, Avon (UK), Leicester University Press.

Stefanoni, Silvia, 1990, "Catene migratorie e strutture familiari. Un caso italo-australiano", *Studi Emigrazione*, XXVII (98), 1990, pp. 255-275.

Stiassi, Angelo R., 1979, *Gli Italiani e l'Australia*, Bologna, Patron.

Straniero, Michele (ed.), *Canzoni di Francesco Guccini*, Milano, La Voce del Padrone.

Sturino, Frank, 1990, *Forging the Chain. A case study of Italian Migration to North America, 1880-1930,* Toronto, Multicultural History Society of Ontario.

Telleschi, Aldo, 1996, "Aspetti dell'emigrazione dalla Toscana nel cinquantennio 1876-1925", in Ceretti, Claudio (Ed.), *Genova, Colombo , il mare e l'Emigrazione Italiana nelle Americhe - Atti del XXVI Congresso Geografico Italiano, Genova, 4-9 Maggio 1992*, Roma, Istituto della Enciclopedia Italiana, pp. 127-134.

Templeton, Jacqueline, 1995, "The Swiss Connection: the Origins of the Valtellina-Australia migrations", *Australian Historical Studies*, Vol. 26, No. 104 (April 1995), pp. 393-414.

Thompson, Stephanie Lindsay, 1980, *Australia Through Italian Eyes - A study of settlers returning from Australia to Italy*, Melbourne, Oxford University Press.

Thompson, Stephanie Lindsay, 1983, "Italian Migrant Experiences of Australian Culture (1945-1970), in Cresciani, Gianfranco (Ed.), 1983, *Australia, the Australians and the Italian Migration*, Milano, Angeli, pp. 27-47.

Tognetti, Annarita, 1993, "Un secolo di emigrazione dal Comune di Pescaglia", *Documenti e Studi*, 14/15, pp. 221-256.

Tomasi, Lydio, 1972, *The Italians in America: The Progressive View 1891-1914*, New York, Center for Migration Studies.

Tomasi, Lydio F. - Gastaldo, Piero & Row, Thomas (Eds.), 1994, *The Columbus People. Perspective in Italian Immigration to the Americas and Australia*, New York, Center for Migration Studies - Fondazione Giovanni Agnelli.

Toscani nel Mondo (magazine), 1997 and 1998, published by the Giunta Regional Toscana, Firenze.

Toscano, Mario A., 1976, *Industrializzazione e classe operaia. Il caso della Garfagnana*, Pisa, Feltrinelli Libreria Pisana.

Tosi, Arturo, 1991, *L'Italiano d'Oltremare. la Lingua della Comunità Italiana nei paesi anglofoni*, Firenze, Giunti.

Trapani, Maria, 1993, "L'emigrazione lucchese nella seconda meta' del sec. XIX riflessa nei documenti d'archivio", Supplement of *Lucca Economia*, n.2, April-May-June 1993.

Trento, A., 1984, *Là dov'è la raccolta del caffè. L'emigrazione italiana in Brasile, 1879-1940*, Padova, Anthenore Edizioni.

Ugolini, Romano (Ed.), 1991, *Italia-Australia 1788-1988, Atti del Convegno di Studio,* Roma, Edizioni Ateneo.

Ungaretti, Giuseppe, 1975, *Vita d'un uomo. 106 Poesie (1914-1960)*, Milano, Mondadori.

Vaccari Italian Historical Trust, 1987, *Italians in Australia. Conference Proceedings 1985 - Australia's Italian Heritage. Conference Proceedings 19 June 1987*, Brunswick (Vic.), Vaccari Italian Historical Trust.

Vasta, Ellie, 1993, "Cultural and social Change: Italo-Australian Women and the second generation", in *Altre Italie*, 9, January-June 1993, pp. 84-101.

Vasta, Ellie, 1994, "Cultural and social Change: Italo-Australian Women and the second generation", in Tomasi, Lydio F. - Gastaldo, Piero & Row, Thomas (Eds.), 1994, *The Columbus People. Perspective in Italian Immigration to the Americas and Australia*, New York, Center for Migration Studies - Fondazione Giovanni Agnelli, pp. 406-425.

Vecoli, Rudolph, 1964, "*Contadini* in Chicago: A Critique of *The Uprooted", Journal of American History*, Vol. LI, No. 51 (December 1964), pp. 404-417.

Vecoli, Rudolph, 1965, *The People of New Jersey*, New York, D.Van Nostrand Co. Inc.

Vola, Giorgio, 1993, "I Lucchesi a Londra nel XVII secolo: appunti per una ricerca", Actum Luce - Rivista di Studi Lucchesi, XXII (1-2), Aprile-Ottobre 1993, pp. 111-129.

Walters, J. - Mellor, K.B. - Cox, D.R. - Taylor, J. McD. & Tierney, L.J., (no date), *Culture in Contexy. A Study of Three Ethnic groups and their Welfare needs in Australia, Melbourne*, Victorian Council of Social Studies.

Ware, Helen, 1981, *A profile of the Italian community in Australia*, Melbourne, Australian Institute of Multicultural Affairs.

Warren, R.L., 1972, *The Community in America*, Chicago, Rand McNally.

Webber, Michael, J., 1992, "Settlement characteristics of immigrants in Australia", in Freeman, Gary P. -& Jupp, James (Eds.), *Nations of Immigrants. Australia, United States and International Migration*, Melbourne, Oxford University Press, pp. 165-181.

White, Paul & Woods, Robert (Eds.), 1980, *The geographical impact of migration*, London, Longman.

Wickham, C.J., 1988, *The Mountains and the City. The Tuscan Apennines in the Early Middle Ages*, Oxford, Clarendon Press.

Wilson, Paul R., 1973, *Immigrants and Politics,* Canberra, Australian National University Press.

Wlocevski, Stephane, 1934, *L'installation des Italiens en France*, Paris, Librarie Felix Alcon.

Wooden, Mark - Holton, Robert - Hugo, Graeme & Sloan, Judith (Eds.), 1994, *Australian Immigration. A Survey of the Issues*, Canberra, Australian Government Publication Service.

Yans-McLaughlin, Virginia, 1990, "Metaphors of Self in History: Subjectivity, Oral Narrative and Immigration Studies", in Yans-McLaughlin, Virginia (Ed.), 1990, *Immigration reconsidered. History, Sociology, and Politics,* New York, Oxford University Press, pp. 254-290.

Zang, Xiaowei & Hassan, Riaz, 1996, "Residential Choices of Immigrants in Australia", *International Migration*, XXIV (4), 1996, pp. 567-581.

Zubrzycki, Jerzy (assisted by Kuskie, Nancy), 1960, *Immigrants in Australia: a Demographic Survey based upon the 1954 Census*, Canberra, Department of Demography - Australian National University.

Zubrzycki, Jerzy, 1964, *Settlers in the La Trobe Valley*, Canberra, Australian National University Press.

Zucchi, John E., 1988, *Italians in Toronto. Development of a National Identity, 1875-1935*, Kingston & Montreal, McGill-Queen's University Press.

OFFICIAL PUBLICATIONS AND OTHER DOCUMENTS

Commissariato Generale dell'Emigrazione, 1926, *Annuario Statistico dell'Emigrazione Italiana dal 1876 al 1924 con notizia sull'emigrazione negli anni 1869-1875*, Roma, Commissariato Generale dell'Emigrazione.

Commissariato Generale dell'Emigrazione, 1926, *L'Emigrazione Italiana dal 1910 al 1923*, Roma, Edizioni del Commissariato Generale dell'Emigrazione.

Department of Immigration, Local Government and Ethnic Affairs, 1982, *Australia's Immigration: Consolidated Statistics,* Canberra, Australian Government Publishing Service.

Ministero degli Affari Esteri, 1893, *Emigrazione e Colonie. Rapporti di RR. Agenti Diplomatici e Consolari*, Roma, Tipografia Nazionale G. Bertero.

Ministero degli Affari Esteri - Commissariato dell'Emigrazione, 1901, *Legge 31 gennaio 1901, n.23 Sull'emigrazione e Regio decreto 10 luglio 1901*, Roma, Tipografia del Ministero degli Affari Esteri.

Ministero degli Affari Esteri - Direzione Generale Emigrazione e Affari Sociali, 1988 (a), *Comunita' Italiane nel Mondo 1985-1987*, Roma, Ministero degli Affari Esteri.

Ministero degli Affari Esteri - Consiglio Nazionale dell'Economia, 1988 (b), *Raccolta delle leggi usuali sull'emigrazione e le Comunità Italiane all'Estero*, Roma, Fratelli Palombi.

Ministero degli Affari Esteri - Consiglio Nazionale dell'Economia e del Lavoro, 1988 (c), *Profilo Statistico dell'Emigrazione italiana nell'ultimo Quarantennio*, Roma, Fratelli Palombi.

Ministero dell'Agricoltura, Industria e Commercio - Direzione Generale della Statistica, 1883, *Censimenti della popolazione del Regno d'Italia al 31/12/1881, Vol. I, part 1 (Popolazione dei Comuni e dei mandamenti),* Roma.

Ministero dell'Agricoltura, Industria e Commercio - Direzione Generale della Statistica, 1899, *Statistica dell'emigrazione italiana all'estero nel 1897*, Roma, Tip.G.Bertero.

Ministero dell'Agricoltura, Industria e Commercio - Direzione Generale della Statistica, 1913, *Censimenti della popolazione del Regno d'Italia al 10/6/1911, Vol. I. Popolazione presente, popolazione temporaneamente assente, popolazione residente*, Roma.

UNPUBLISHED MATERIAL – MANUSCRIPT SOURCES

Accademia Economico-Agraria dei Georgofili di Firenze, 1908, *Bando in data 5 luglio 1908 sul tema: 'Studiare le cause che hanno determinato il sensibile aumento della emigrazione in molte zone della Toscana; determinare le conseguenze buone e cattive di tale fatto specie nei riguardi dell'agricoltura e del sistema di mezzadria e ricercare quali provvedimenti potrebbero porre riparo agli effetti dannosi che ne fossero ricavati'*, Archivio Storico, Busta 122.136.1908.

Baldassar, Loretta, 1994, *Visit to the shrine: a study of migration as transnational interaction between the San Fiorese in Western Australia and Northern Italy*, Ph.D. Thesis (unpublished), Nedlands, University of Western Australia – Department of Anthropology.

Bosi, Pino, 1997, *I Toscani d'Australia. I personaggi principali e le loro opere (1676-1996)*, Sydney (Draft - Typed).

Gamba, Charles, 1949, *The Italian Immigration to Western Australia*, MA thesis (unpublished), Nedlands, University of Western Australia – Department of Geography.

Gava, Dino M, 1978., *The History of Italian migrants in Osborne-Wanneroo 1900-1950*, MA thesis (unpublished), Nedlands, University of Western Australia - Department of Geography.

Iraci, Charles, 1979, *Italian Immigration to the Perth Metropolitan Area of Western Australia,* BA (Honors) thesis (unpublished), Nedlands, University of Western Australia - Department of Geography.

Iraci, Charles, 1986, *Return migration of North Eastern Sicilians from Fremantle*, MA thesis (unpublished), Nedlands, University of Western Australia - Department of Geography.

Pugi, Catia, 1994, *Emigrazione e territorio in Lucchesia : il caso di Crasciana*, (unpublished thesis), Firenze, Universita' di Firenze-Facolta' di Magistero.

Wigley, G.E.C., 1973, *The Residential Decision of naturalized Italians in North Perth and Balcatta*, BA thesis (unpublished), Nedlands, University of Western Australia - Department of Geography.

PERSONAL COMMUNICATIONS AND INTERVIEWS

About 40 in-depth interviews with first-generation migrants from Tuscany have been conducted by the Author in the Perth Metropolitan area, mainly between July 1997 and February 1998. While the outcomes of the qualitative study generated by the interviews are presented in Chapter 8, throughout the book the interviews are referred in the footnotes, when some communications were relevant to the research.

Index

Index of Names

Agnew, John 262, 325, 330
Alcorso, Caroline 163, 317, 330, 334, 346-347
Angelini, Massimo 304, 313, 331
Apollinaire 314, 331
Arango, Joaquin 344
Argenti 153
Arrighi, Michael 347
Audenino, Patrizia 304, 306, 313, 331
Babbie 269, 325
Bacchetta, Piero 307, 331
Baily, Samuel xv, 25, 304, 331
Baldassar, Loretta 29, 244, 305, 323, 327, 331, 356
Ballini, P. 335
Balnc-Szanton 350
Baracchi 162
Bargellini, Piero 313, 331
Baroni, Fabio 311, 331
Barton, John 25, 304, 331
Basch, Linda 350
Bell, Rudolph 241, 244, 248, 270, 314, 323, 325-327, 331, 334
Beneforti, Barbara 312, 326, 346
Berengo, Marino 309, 331
Bernardi, Savino 327, 331
Bertacchi, Sigismondo 308-310, 331
Bertelli, Lidio 166, 318, 320, 323, 326-327, 331-332, 340
Bertola, Patrick xiii, 29, 214, 216, 305, 320-322, 332, 347
Bettoni, Camilla 326-327, 332
Bezza 338, 345, 351
Bivona 332
Blomquist, Thomas 309, 332, 344
Bogue 327, 332
Boncompagni, Adriano 1, xiv-xvi, 304, 315, 318, 320, 323-324, 332-333
Borocz, Jozsef 21, 303, 348
Borrie, W.D. 28, 155, 285-286, 304, 308, 317-319, 321, 323, 325-327, 333
Bosi, Pino 162, 166, 293, 317-318, 320-324, 327, 356
Bosworth, Richard 28-29, 47, 245, 292, 304-306, 316-317, 324, 327, 333
Bottom 98, 103, 150, 193
Bottomley, Gillian 31, 267, 305, 325, 333
Bourbons 79
Bovani 200-201
Brenna, Paolo 307, 333
Briganti, Lucilla 77, 129-131, 313-314, 333
Briggs, John xv, 304, 333
Brunn, Stanley 275, 341
Burnley, Ian 32, 159, 251, 270, 305, 317-319, 322-327, 333-334, 339, 351
Busu, Luigi 310, 334
Cabrini, Angelo 307, 312, 334
Caciagli, Giuseppe 308, 310, 334

Cagiano, De Azevedo 307, 331
Camaiani, Piergiorgio 91, 95, 112, 309, 311-313, 334
Camera di Commercio 307, 311-312 , 334-335
Capra, Giuseppe 147, 160, 316-318, 321, 334
Carl the Fifth 76
Carpi, Leone 118, 121-122, 334
Casotti 200, 253, 258
Castles, Stephen 307-308, 318, 327, 330, 334, 346-347
Castracani, Castruccio 72
Catani 162
Cavour, Camillo Benso 44
Cecchi 162
Cecilia, Tito 162, 217, 305, 310, 317-324, 335
Cerabolini, Fabio 305-306, 335
Cerase, Francesco 327, 335
Ceretti, Claudio 335, 352
Cheda, Giorgio 28, 304, 335
Cherubini, Bruno 313, 335
Cianferoni, Reginaldo 93-94, 99, 311-312, 335
Ciano, Cesare 309-311, 335
Cinel, Dino xv, 95, 97, 100, 125, 134-135, 187, 208, 241-242, 304, 307-308, 311-312, 314-315, 319-320, 323, 326-327, 335
Ciuffoletti, Zeffiro xiii, 24, 303, 306, 308, 311-312, 335
Clark, W.A. 303, 335
Coli 200
Commissariato Generale Emigrazione 165, 305, 307-308, 313-314, 317, 320, 355
Comunità Montana Lunigiana 308-309, 331, 335, 337
Corsini, Carlo xiii, 305-306, 335, 349
Corte, Paolo 145, 316-317, 336
Corti, Paola 248, 304-305, 312, 323-324, 336
Costanza, Salvatore 315, 336
Cox, David 317, 336, 353
Cresci, Paolo 315, 336
Cresciani, Gianfranco 28, 147, 304, 315-317, 321-322, 327, 332, 336, 347, 349-350, 352
Cronin, Constance 28, 269, 305, 325, 336
D'Aprano, Charles 142, 304, 310, 315, 317, 337
Dada', Adriana 101, 112, 119, 125, 304, 308, 312-314, 319, 328, 336
Dawkins, Peter 319, 337
De Felice, Renzo 303, 336-337
De Stefani, Carlo 310, 337
Della Santina, Ernesto 202
Devoto, Fernando 304, 337
Dibueno, Caterina 304, 337
Distretto Scolastico Garfagnana 96, 98, 308-312, 337
Dottori, Marcel 307, 319, 337
Douglass, William 151, 304, 316, 318, 337, 344
Douki, Caroline 91, 304, 311, 314, 337
Dubost, Jean Francois 307, 338
Emperor 72, 76-77
Fabbri, Giulio 309-310, 338
Fabiano, Domenico 322, 338

Farnocchia Petri, Franca 109, 172-175, 228, 308, 311-315, 318, 320, 322, 324, 327, 338
Favero, Luigi 307, 317, 326-327, 338
Fitzgerald, Alan 317, 338
Foerster, Robert 25, 37, 40, 55, 92, 121, 304-308, 311, 313, 338
Fontanini, Achimede 210
Forrest, James 305, 338
Foschi, Franco 307, 338
Francesconi 202
Franchi 313
Franzina, Emilio 24, 26, 303-306, 319, 323-324, 326-327, 338-339
Frediani, Giuseppe 308, 339
Freeman 354
Gabaccia, Donna xv, 42, 304-306, 308, 339
Gagliardi, Ferdinando 320, 339
Galvin, J. 287, 305, 319, 325, 327, 339
Gamba, Charles 29, 305, 339, 356
Garden 200, 343
Gardini, A. 324, 339
Gastaldo, Piero 349, 352-353
Gava, Dino 29, 197, 305, 356
Gentileschi, Mario 303, 339
Gentilli, Joseph xiii, 28-29, 197-198, 214, 223, 233, 267, 303-304, 316-317, 319-326, 339-340
Georgofili 312, 314-315, 350, 356
Gestri, Lorenzo 88, 310, 340
Ghilarducci 200-201
Gillgren, Christina 321, 340
Giusti 253
Glyn, John 163
Gramsci, Antonio 37, 305, 340
Grassi, Ferdinando 2, 203, 329
Grassi 2, 203, 329
Green 199
Grieco, Margaret 268, 325, 340
Grigg, D.B. 303, 340
Guccini, Francesco 54, 352
Guelfi, Richard 197, 202
Guicciardo, Tonina 327
Guidetti, Massimo 337
Harney, Robert 243-244, 304, 315, 320, 322-324, 340
Hassan 318, 354
Heiss, J. 265, 325, 327, 340
Hempel, J.A. 159, 166, 304, 317-318, 340
Hoerder, Dick 126, 314, 341
Holton, Robert 341, 354
Huber, Rina 29, 268, 271, 273, 276, 283, 297, 305-306, 319, 324-326, 328, 341
Hugo, Graeme 32-33, 158, 183-184, 222, 286, 304-305, 317-320, 322-323, 325, 327, 341, 344, 354
Iacovino, Livia 316, 341
Inglis, Christine 318, 327, 341
Iorizzo, Luciano 304, 306-308, 341
Iraci, Charles 29, 271, 305, 323, 326-327, 356
Jakle, John A. 275, 341
Jannon, Giorgio 304, 341
Johnston, Ruth 284, 305, 326, 338, 342
Jones Lancaster, F. 188, 305, 318-319, 328, 342

Jupp, James 252, 270, 324-326, 342, 354
Keast, Jenny 320, 342
Kelly, Nernadette 346
Kertzer, David I. 311, 342
Kirchner, Samuel 164
Kovaouci, Ali 344
Lampugnani, Rosario 154, 306, 316, 342
Laux 341
Lawson 23, 266, 303, 325, 351
Lazzareschi, Emilio 313, 342
Le Roy Ladurie, Emmanuel 76, 309, 342
Lee, E. 22, 187, 249, 303, 312, 319, 324, 342
Leoni xiii
Lera, Maria 115-116, 310-311, 313, 342
Livi-Bacci, Massimo 97, 311, 342
Lombardi-Lotti, Mansueto 309, 343
Longton, Adelma 29, 305, 321, 343
Lopez, Renee 124, 305, 314, 343
Losacco, Michele 312-313, 315, 343
Lucassen, Luc 19, 23, 303, 311, 313, 327, 339, 341, 343, 345
Lucchesi v, 71, 74, 81, 100, 103, 105, 113, 116-118, 122, 124, 128-129, 131-132, 134-135, 137-139, 161, 165-166, 173-175, 186-188, 190, 195, 197, 199-204, 206, 208-210, 212-213, 218, 221-222, 224, 226-235, 237, 242, 245, 250, 255-258, 260-262, 275-276, 280, 283, 288, 293, 297-298, 301, 318, 324, 329, 331, 334, 343, 345, 347-348, 353
Lukomskyi, Oleh 343
Lyng, Jens 143, 316, 343
Macdonald 150, 156-157, 166, 316-319, 321, 343
Madge, John 269, 325, 343
Malaspina 81
Mammarella, G. 306, 344
Manselli, Raul 103, 309, 344
Marletta, Cesare 318, 344
Marquis de Ray's 143
Martellini, Amoreno 304, 314-315, 317, 344
Martin, Jean 185, 270, 319, 324-325, 336, 344, 348
Martinelli, Phylis 351
Martinuzzi O'Brien, Ilma 28, 304, 317, 324, 344
Masini 202
Masolini 218
Massara, Giuseppe 308, 344
Massey, Douglass 303, 305, 344
Mazzaoui, Maureen 344
McCall 333, 339, 351
Meek, Christine 309, 344
Melia 316, 333
Mellor, K.B. 353
Menchetti, Pietro 203
Messina, Nunzia 315, 318, 344
Michelson, William 269-270, 325, 344
Michieli. Adriano Augusto 316, 344
Migliazza, Alessandro 306,

345
Ministero Affari Esteri 307-308, 314, 317-321, 324, 355
Ministero Agricoltura 355
Mirola, Gian 315, 318, 345
Miserocchi, Mario 321, 345
Missori, Mario 316, 322, 345
Moch-Page, Leslie 345
Mola', Lucia 309-310, 345
Monterisi, Maria Teresa 312, 324, 345
Moon, Bruce 22, 303, 327, 345
Mori 109, 308, 312-313, 325, 345
Moscardini 203, 218
Moser, Claus Adolf 325, 345
Murphy, Brian 306, 316-317, 345
Nardini, Gloria xiii, 259, 324-325, 345
Nascimbene, Mario C. 314, 346
Nelli, Humbert 304, 320-321, 324, 346
Nerli 162
Newton 334
Niccolai, Roberto 276, 312, 326, 346
Nobile, Annunziata 306, 346
O'Connor, Desmond 28, 146, 151, 153, 245, 252, 304, 316, 322, 324, 346
Ottolenghi, Costantino 112, 312, 346
Pacchi, Domenico 308, 310, 346
Pacini, Marcello 304, 335, 342-343, 350
Packer, D. 305, 321, 346
Paganoni, Antonio 245, 252, 324, 346
Pagotto, Barbara 320, 342
Panucci, Frank 320, 346
Paoli Gumina, Deanna 315, 346
Paradisi, Maria Virginia 312-314, 347
Paris, Renzo 38, 45, 74, 116, 307, 314, 347, 354
Pascal, Arturo 74, 309, 347
Pascoe, Robert 214, 240, 244, 304, 311, 317, 320-324, 337, 347
Pascoli, Giovanni 91, 311, 347
Pasquali, A. 98, 100, 111, 123, 308, 311-312, 347
Pecout, Gilles 311-312, 347
Pellegrino, Adela 344
Pesman, Roslyn 143, 315, 326, 347
Pierattini, Maria Giovanna 313
Piselli, Fortunata 187, 246, 304, 306, 319, 324, 348
Pizzorusso, Giovanni 303, 305-306, 308, 348
Pomponi, Francois 304, 308, 313, 348
Pope Pius X 45
Porter, John 151, 316, 348
Portes, Alejandro 21, 303, 321, 348
Pozzetta, George 303, 348-349
Price, Charles 28, 101, 131, 137, 158-159, 166, 177, 179, 181-182, 185, 188-189, 197, 208, 210, 212, 215, 227, 289, 301, 304-305, 315, 318-321, 323-324, 327-328, 348
Pugi, Catia 100, 123, 306,

310-314, 356
Pulvirenti, Mariastella 283, 326, 348
Pyke, N.O. 145, 315-317, 348
Raffaelli, Raffaello 310, 349
Ragionieri, Ernesto 303, 349
Ramella, Franco 306, 349
Ramirez, Bruno 303, 348-349
Rando, Gaetano 28, 142, 144, 304, 315-317, 328, 330, 334, 346-347, 349
Rapetti, Caterina 304, 311, 349
Ravenstein 21-22, 340
Regione Toscana 254-255, 258, 308-309, 324, 337, 349
Regione Toscana 254-255, 258, 308-309, 324, 337, 349
Repetti, Emanuele 69, 308, 349
Romano, Ruggiero 2, 70, 89, 96, 98, 104, 138, 140, 167, 174-175, 203-204, 218, 224-225, 228-229, 231, 272, 305, 307, 313, 349, 353
Rombai, Leonardo xiii, 311, 349
Roseman, Curtis 275, 341
Rosoli, Gianfranco 24, 39, 243, 298, 303-308, 314, 323, 328, 349-350
Rother, Klaus 321, 323, 350
Rovai, Davide 103, 116, 125, 132, 304, 307, 309, 312-315, 350
Row 349, 352-353
Ruberti, Alessandra 307, 350
Sacco, Nicola 296
Samminiatelli, Donato 350
Sanfilippo, Matteo 303, 306, 348
Sardi, Cesare 78, 86, 309-310, 312, 350
Sarti, Roland xv-xvi, 41, 114, 127, 231, 304-305, 310-314, 323, 350
Sarup, Madan 327, 350
Savona, Alberto 306-307, 312, 350
Scalabrini 45
Scarpaci, J.Vincenza 304, 340
Scatena, Mario 202, 321
Schiller, Nina 327, 350
Schino 351
Secombe. M.J. 266, 325, 351
Sensi-Isolani, Paola 137, 304, 315, 351
Sereni, Bruno 311, 351
Sforzas 81
Silvey, Rachel 23, 266, 303, 325, 351
Sinke, Suzanne 349
Sloan 341, 354
Smolicz, Jerzy 266, 325, 327, 351
Societa Geografica Italiana 146, 316, 327, 338, 350-351
Sori, Ercole 24, 207, 303-304, 306-307, 316, 319-320, 351
Spadaccini 162
Spedicato, Elide 265, 325-326, 351
Sponza, Lucio 115, 307, 313-314, 351
Stahl 337
Stefanoni, Silvia 319, 352
Stiassi, Angelo 316-317, 352
Stombuco, Ingegnere 162
Straniero, Michele 306-307, 312,

350, 352
Strano 100
Sturino, Frank 99, 126, 311, 314, 352
Tassello, Graziano 307, 317, 326-327, 338
Taylor 344, 353
Telleschi, Aldo 99, 121, 312-313, 352
Temime 124, 305, 314, 343
Templeton, Jacqueline 165, 304, 308, 318, 352
Tenardi 201
Thieme, Guenther 341
Thompson, Linda 28, 269, 304, 320, 325, 327, 352
Tierney, L.J. 353
Tognetti, Annarita 120, 124, 313-314, 352
Tomasi, Lydio 304, 318-320, 335, 346, 349, 352-353
Toscano, Mario 164, 312, 336, 352
Toscany Club v, viii, 239, 244, 246-249, 252-261, 263, 268, 291
Tosi, Arturo 286, 324, 327, 353
Trapani, Maria 312, 353
Trento, Angelo 304, 307, 314, 353
Ugolini, Romano 326, 353
Vaccari, Foundation 308, 353
Vasta, Ellie 28, 304, 307, 318, 327, 330, 334, 346-347, 353
Vecoli, Rudolph xiii, 134, 241-243, 291, 304, 308, 315, 323, 327, 349, 353
Vertone, T. 337, 348
Vola, Giorgio 309, 353
Walters, J. 320, 324, 326, 353
Ware, Helen 28, 289, 304, 308, 317, 320, 326-327, 353
Warren, R.L. 324, 354
Webber, Michael 326, 354
White, Paul 144, 148, 153, 303, 354
Wickham, C.J. 71, 308-309, 354
Wigley, G.E.C. 29, 305, 319, 356
Wilson, Paul 265, 325, 327, 354
Woods, Robert 303, 354
Yans-McLaughlin, Virginia 244, 323, 325, 354
York 117, 332-333, 335, 341, 344, 346, 349-354
Zang, Ziaowei 318, 354
Zubrzycki, Jerzy 267, 305, 316, 318, 325, 354
Zucchi, John 50, 304, 306, 308, 315, 319, 354
Zunini, Marchese 149

Index of Places

Abruzzo 63, 257
Adelaide 153, 159-160, 167, 245, 255, 339
Africa 255
Albany 210-211, 345
Altopascio 71, 104
America iv, 38, 49, 51, 57, 59, 116, 123-126, 132-134, 165, 189, 198, 202, 243, 277, 334, 339-340, 344, 346, 349, 352, 354
Antwerp 38, 74
Apennines 63, 65, 69-70, 72, 77, 80, 83, 90, 98, 101, 105, 110, 114, 117, 119, 142, 199, 211, 240, 254
Apuan Alps 69-70, 88
Argentina iii-iv, 38-39, 51-52, 56-58, 118, 123, 126, 128-130, 132, 134, 138, 140, 200, 250, 255, 278, 331, 337, 346
Arno 66, 72, 77, 84, 341
Bagni Lucca 70, 103-104, 115, 138, 140, 167, 174, 200, 272, 335
Balcatta viii, 171, 200-202, 223-224, 227, 231, 239, 253, 255, 257, 259-260, 322-326, 356
Baltimore 91
Barga 70, 103-104, 113, 125, 174, 272, 351
Bassendean 197, 201, 203-204, 223-227, 229, 320, 322, 326
Belgium 53, 140, 231, 255
Bologna 334, 346, 350-352
Borgo Mozzano 70, 104, 115, 131, 174, 218
Boulder 154, 216-218, 220
Brazil iii-iv, 38-39, 47, 51, 56-59, 117-118, 123, 126, 128-132, 138, 140, 165, 255, 278, 331
Brisbane 159, 164
Bruges 103
Brunswick 160, 342, 353
Buenos Aires 56, 128, 337
Bunbury 210
Calabria 63, 151, 257
Camporgiano 70, 96, 98, 104, 174-175, 225, 272
Canada iii-iv, vii, 38-39, 47, 49, 52, 61-62, 116, 132, 136, 138, 140, 149, 151, 255, 338, 348
Canberra 334, 336-337, 340-342, 344, 348, 354-355
Cannington 203-204, 226-227, 234, 256
Capannori 71, 103-104, 115, 138, 140, 167, 190-192, 197, 200, 202, 204, 211, 224, 272-273
Capoliveri 153
Caracas 117
Careggine 70, 96, 98, 104, 174-175
Casola Lunigiana 70, 80, 85, 192, 232, 272
Cassia 71
Castelnuovo Garfagnana 70, 98, 104, 174-175, 337
Castiglione 70, 96, 98, 104, 174-175
Champagne 73
Chicago xiii, 91, 117, 126, 137, 331,

336, 342, 345, 353-354
Colombia 140, 255
Coogee 203, 226, 229
Coolgardie 160
Cordoba 250, 345
Coreglia 70, 115-116, 173-174, 232, 272
Corsica iv, vii, 92, 114, 118-126, 129, 190-191, 274, 277, 293, 331, 337, 348
Cue 160, 213-214, 229, 232
Day Down 160
Dianella 224, 235, 256, 319, 322-323
Dusseldorf 116
East Perth 202
Elba 90, 114, 153, 164, 166
Emilia 66, 93, 142
Fabbriche Vallico 70, 104, 115, 173-174
Ferrara 80-81
Fivizzano 70, 80, 85, 88, 272
Florence 71, 79-81, 109, 113, 121, 132, 162, 218, 241, 248, 261-262
Fosciandora 70, 83, 96, 98, 104, 133, 174-175, 272
France iii-iv, 38-39, 49, 52, 54-55, 71-72, 76, 101-102, 106, 114, 116, 118, 122, 124-125, 129, 140, 143, 165, 188, 192, 218, 255, 277, 293, 338, 354
Fremantle xiv, 28-29, 161, 170, 176-177, 180, 203, 210, 235, 333, 339, 356
Friuli 63, 254
Gallicano 70, 96, 98, 104, 115, 174-175, 272
Garfagnana 2, iv, vii-ix, 66, 68-71, 77, 79-90, 92, 96-99, 101-104, 109-110, 113-114, 118, 122-123, 125-128, 130, 132-134, 138-139, 165-167, 172-175, 192, 201, 203-204, 218, 224-225, 228-229, 231, 236, 257, 272, 308-312, 331, 337-338, 341, 343, 345-346, 349, 352
Genoa 43, 74, 119, 142, 242
Genova 335, 352
Geraldton 210, 229
Germany 39, 49, 53, 56, 116, 140, 143, 157, 255
Giuncugnano 70, 96, 98, 104, 173-175, 201, 210, 272
Great Britain iii-iv, 39, 49, 55-56, 115, 124-125
Gwalia 160, 214, 232
Hamburg 141, 164
Harvey 210
Highgate 320-322
Hobart 255
Holland 140, 157, 255
James Street 198, 202
Kalamunda 199-201, 342
Kalgoorlie 146, 154, 211, 213-214, 216-220, 229, 322, 329, 347
Karragullen 180, 199-201, 203-204, 227, 230, 234, 253, 256, 320, 342
Karrawong 160
Kelmscott 199-200
Kojanup 233
Kojonup 232 233
La Spezia 69, 85

Lakeside 160
Latin America 38, 57, 126, 134
Lazio 66
Le Havre 129
Leederville 197, 201-202, 256, 320
Leghorn 163-164
Leichhardt 159-160
Leonora 213-214
Liguria 40, 43, 54, 66, 69, 85, 124, 135, 142, 242
Livorno 91, 118, 122
Lombardy 43, 54, 63, 87-88, 97, 114, 142, 151, 165, 217-218, 257
London 38, 103, 115-116, 331, 333, 336, 340-341, 343, 345, 350, 354
Low Countries 72
Lunigiana iv, 66, 69-70, 72, 80-82, 84-86, 88-89, 91-92, 99, 102, 105, 110, 114, 126, 192, 232, 272, 308-309, 331, 334-337
Magra 66, 69-70, 80
Manjimup 210, 230, 233
Manning 256
Marseille 124, 129, 337
Massa Carrara xv, 88, 115, 118, 122, 129, 163, 166, 169, 176, 178, 183, 192, 196, 232, 236, 239, 248, 253, 257, 340
Massa-Carrara iv, 66, 69-71, 79-81, 84, 89, 118, 272, 274-275, 279, 281
Melbourne xiv, 142, 145, 158-160, 162, 167, 187, 244-245, 252-253, 255, 330, 332-333, 338-339, 341-343, 346, 348, 351-354
Mexico 218
Milan 59
Milano 59, 81, 332, 334-338, 343-345, 347-353
Minucciano 70, 96, 98, 101, 104, 174-175, 200, 217, 253, 272
Modena 80
Molazzana 70, 96, 98, 104, 174-175
Montecarlo 71, 104
Montreal 116, 292, 338, 354
Morley 223-224, 227, 235, 256, 320, 322-325
Mundaring 201
Naples 59, 142
Nedlands 339, 342, 356
New South Wales xiv, 142, 160, 162, 217, 271, 276, 283, 339
New York 117, 332-333, 335, 341, 344, 346, 349-354
New Zealand xiv, 117, 162-164, 217, 334
North Perth Northbridge 199, 201
Nova Milano 59
Nova Padova 59
Nova Venezia 59
Osborne Park 197, 199-202, 204, 223-224, 227, 231
Panama 134
Paris 38, 45, 74, 116, 307, 314, 347, 354
Pernambuco 117, 129
Perù 255
Pescaglia vii, 70, 104, 115, 120, 123-124, 352

Philadelphia 137
Piazza Serchio 70, 96, 98, 104, 173-175, 232, 272
Pickering Brooks 201, 230
Piedmont 40, 43, 59, 63, 142, 151
Pieve Fosciana 70, 98, 104, 174-175, 337
Pisa 91, 115, 118, 121-122, 162, 164, 257, 344, 347, 352
Pistoia 79, 119, 162, 330
Po 65, 69, 80, 82, 92-95, 133, 141
Pontremoli 253
Porcari 71, 103-104, 203-204, 272
Queensland 28, 63, 142, 144-146, 149, 151, 155, 159-160, 162, 164, 182, 184, 225, 337, 340-341, 344
Ragusa 160
Rhone 39
Riviera 92
Rome xiv, 71-72, 116, 333, 337
Russia 116
S. Romano 89, 96, 104, 140, 174-175, 225, 272
San Francisco xiv, 95, 134-135, 137-138, 187, 208, 241-242, 335, 346
San Romano 2, 70, 98, 138, 167, 174, 203-204, 218, 224-225, 228-229, 231
Sao Paulo 58-59
Sardinia 92, 125
Serchio viii-ix, 66, 68, 70-71, 79-80, 84-85, 87, 90, 93, 95-96, 98-99, 103-104, 106, 113-114, 116-117, 120-121, 125, 132, 138, 173-175, 190, 200-201, 203, 210-211, 217, 224, 232, 253, 272-273, 338
Sicily 28, 43, 59, 63, 74, 151, 160, 257, 336
Siena 118, 122, 162, 241-242, 248, 344
Sillano 70, 96, 98, 104, 174-175
South Africa 255
South America 51, 125
South Australia 28, 133, 143, 153, 155, 245, 252, 337, 339, 346
St.Kilda 162
Suez 142
Swan River 197, 201, 203, 223, 225-226, 256, 294, 296
Swan Valley 192
Switzerland 38-39, 49, 52, 56, 140, 255
Sydney 29, 142-143, 158-159, 162, 217, 245, 252, 255, 297, 332-334, 341-342, 356
Toronto 62, 137, 243, 270, 340, 348-349, 352, 354
Tuart Hill 223-224, 227, 256, 320-322, 326
Tyrrhenean Sea 66, 69-70
U.S. xiv
U.S.A. xiv
Umbria 66, 93
United Kingdom 140, 144, 222, 255
United States iii-iv, vii, 38, 47, 49, 51-52, 59-62, 99, 118, 123, 126, 132, 134, 136-140, 142, 146, 149-150, 152-153, 165, 186, 191, 196, 198, 200, 206, 212, 218, 242, 247, 255, 268, 278, 293, 331, 335,

346, 354
Upper Swan River 197
Uruguay 51, 56-57, 255, 337
Vagli Sotto 70, 98, 104, 174-175
Valtellina 165, 193, 217
Veneto 26, 29, 59, 63, 151, 257, 297, 338, 345
Venezia 59, 338, 345
Venezuela 117, 255
Venice 74
Vergemoli 70, 96, 98, 104
Victoria xiii-xiv, 23, 28, 142, 160, 162, 232, 266, 332, 337, 344, 351
Victoria Park xiii
Villa Basilica 70
Villa Comandina 89, 96
Vizzini 160
Wanneroo 197, 199, 201-204, 320-322
West Germany 53, 157
West Perth 197
Wiluna 180, 192, 213-214, 218-219, 229, 281, 343
Wittenoom 89, 228, 281
Yokine 180, 224, 256, 318-322

Finito di stampare nell'aprile 2001 presso le officine della
Montelupo Digital di Montelupo Fiorentino (FI)

www.ingramcontent.com/pod-product-compliance
Lightning Source LLC
Chambersburg PA
CBHW020654270326
41928CB00005B/115

* 9 7 8 8 8 8 3 9 8 0 0 9 1 *